YUCATAN

A World Apart

Alfredo Tzum, Ticul potter, working in ceramics. (Photo by Eugene Wilson, 1969)

YUCATAN

A World Apart

edited by

Edward H. Moseley

and

Edward D. Terry

THE UNIVERSITY OF ALABAMA PRESS
University, Alabama

Copyright © 1980 by
The University of Alabama Press
All rights reserved
Manufactured in the United States of America

Library of Congress Cataloging in Publication Data

Main entry under title:

Yucatan, a world apart.

  Bibliography: p.
  Includes index.
  1. Yucatan—Addresses, essays, lectures.
I. Moseley, Edward H., 1931–   II. Terry, Edward
Davis.
F1376.Y984   972'.6   79-26492
ISBN 0-8173-0025-2

CONTRIBUTORS

Marvin Alisky is Professor of Political Science at Arizona State University.

Eric N. Baklanoff is Board of Visitors Research Professor of Economics at The University of Alabama.

Alfredo Barrera Vásquez is Head of the Department of Philology and Linguistics of the Southeast Regional Center, Instituto Nacional de Antropología e Historia, Mérida, Yucatán. He is also Research Associate in Anthropology at The University of Alabama.

Asael T. Hansen is Professor Emeritus of Anthropology at The University of Alabama.

Gilbert M. Joseph is Assistant Professor of History at The University of North Carolina at Chapel Hill.

Richard A. Krause is Associate Professor and Chairman, Department of Anthropology at The University of Alabama.

Edward H. Moseley is Coordinator of International Studies and Programs, Director of Latin American Studies, and Professor of History at The University of Alabama.

Paul H. Nesbitt is Professor Emeritus of Anthropology at The University of Alabama.

Edward Davis Terry is Professor of Romance Languages at The University of Alabama.

Irving L. Webber is Coordinator, Office of Health-Policy Research and Professor of Sociology at The University of Alabama.

Eugene M. Wilson is Professor of Geography at the University of South Alabama, Mobile.

CONTENTS

PREFACE

Yucatan may be viewed as a cultural and social laboratory, a microcosm of Latin American and Mexican society that lends itself to a sectional analysis. No other part of Mexico represents better the strong elements of regionalism and separatism. The very term "Yucatan" is subject to changing definitions—geographically the peninsula includes parts of Belize and Guatemala, whereas culturally Yucatan is linked to the more extensive region of Mesoamerica with its Mayan heritage. More recently the name has been applied to the political unit that is today a state within the Mexican republic. As a part of the larger mosaic of Amerindian and Hispanic culture, Yucatan is made up of complex ingredients shared by most Spanish American countries.

Within recent years there has emerged a renewed emphasis upon regional or local studies. The objective is to examine the *patria chica* as it fits within the broader national or international scope. Provincial cities are often more representative of a nation than is the more sophisticated and cosmopolitan capital. Such investigations have also illustrated the complexity and breadth of such nations as Brazil and Mexico and have helped to dispel many traditional clichés. This volume is not a comprehensive study, for there are obvious gaps in both topical and chronological treatment, but it may be viewed as an interdisciplinary experiment in the study of a complex and significant region.

The origin of *Yucatan: A World Apart* was in a Latin American Studies seminar conducted at The University of Alabama in the spring of 1970 in which several of the contributors lectured. A number of other activities relating to Yucatan have been sponsored by The University of Alabama. Between 1965 and 1969, David L. DeJarnette supervised an archaeological project at X-Kukicán. At the same time, valuable Yucatecan materials from the Instituto Yucateco de Antropología e Historia were microfilmed with the assistance of its director, Alfredo Barrera Vásquez. The collection of 119 rolls has been made available to researchers in The University of Alabama Library, and a guide prepared under the supervision of W. Stanley Hoole was published in 1970 by The University of Alabama Press. In that same year, Paul Nesbitt and C. Earle Smith conducted a graduate seminar in anthropology at Ticul that resulted in several publications relating to the marketing system of southern Yucatan. Each year since 1973 the University's Latin American Studies Program has sponsored an interdisciplinary course, "Yucatan Past and Present." Over two hundred students and faculty members have participated in this class, thus strengthening relationships with Yucatan and its people. Faculty research done in these field programs has contributed greatly to the present publication.

It is impossible to mention all of the individuals who have assisted in the preparation of this collection. Alfredo Barrera Vásquez, a contributor to the volume and research associate on the faculty of The University of Alabama, has given valuable advice and assistance to most of the authors, and especially to the editors. Other *yucatecos* who have given important aid include Rodolfo Ruz Menéndez, Oscar Palacios, Roldán Peniche Barrera, Manuel Mier y Terán, the Caracashian family, and Juan Ramón Bastarrachea. Special thanks is given to Governor Francisco Luna Kan, who has graciously allowed the reproduction of the Fernando Castro Pacheco murals, outstanding works of art in the state government building. Many faculty and staff members of The University of Alabama have assisted in the preparation of the volume. Laura Stapp, Cynthia Ruiz-Fornells, Susan Patterson Whitmire, Frank Huttlinger, Laila Liddy, Mary Ann Faucett, and Larry Clayton made valuable contributions. Joel Whitman, director of educational media, is responsible for many of the photographs included and assisted in the preparation of visual materials. David DeJarnette shared with the editors material relating to the X-Kukicán archaeological project of which he was co-director. Eugene Wilson of the University of South Alabama not only contributed the chapter on geography but also prepared the maps and many other illustrations. Jeff Brannon of the University of North Alabama, Allen Wells of the State University of New York at Stony Brook, and Thomas Sanders of the American Universities Field Staff all offered valuable advice and guidance at many stages of the project. Special thanks go to Betty John and Mary Jo Cagle, who prepared the index assisted by Linda Dennis, Donna Hawkins, Bobby Liner, Anita Peret, and Cynthia Rodríguez.

The editors would like to express their gratitude to Marvin E. Butterfield, Professor Emeritus of Romance Languages at The University of Alabama. His biography of *Jerónimo de Aguilar, Conquistador,* published in 1955 by The University of Alabama Press, is an important contribution to the field of Yucatecan studies. Furthermore, he was a professor and colleague of several contributors to this volume and as such gave a lasting sense of value for scholarship and integrity. It is to this outstanding teacher and friend that we dedicate this work.

YUCATAN
A World Apart

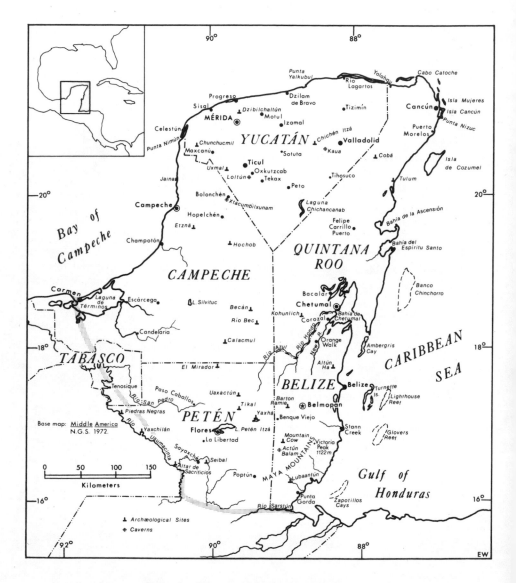

Peninsula of Yucatan. (Map by Eugene Wilson)

INTRODUCTION

Like a giant thumb, the Yucatan Peninsula juts out from Central America, dividing the Caribbean Sea from the Gulf of Mexico. A vast limestone plain almost lacking topsoil and covered with dense, thorny, scrub vegetation, it is a forbidding region. Yet Yucatan has served as a stage for a panorama of dramatic historic events over thousands of years. Cut off from the rest of Mexico by sea, great distance, and harsh terrain, the peninsula has been a virtual "island" during most of its history. This isolation has given the people a sense of cultural and psychological separatism. They consider their land to be "un otro mundo"—a world apart.

The elaborate monuments of Uxmal, Chichén Itzá, and hundreds of other sites stand as fitting tribute to the skills and organizational abilities of the ancient Maya. Their impressive achievements in technology and mathematics are reflected in the splendor of their architecture. Their civilization was a part of a much broader Mesoamerican culture and closely linked with that of the other Mayan people of the Petén and highland regions of Guatemala and Chiapas. Invasions and migrations from central Mexico involved important cultural interchanges and doubtless altered the patterns of life. Despite these external influences, the Yucatecan Maya remained a unique variation on the Mesoamerican theme. Archaeologists still work to unravel the mysteries of that complex and fascinating civilization. It is significant to note, however, that there is a direct and living link between those ancient inhabitants and the modern society of the region. Modern literature is strongly influenced by ancient themes from the *Books of Chilam Balam* and the *Popol Vuh*, and the murals of Fernando Castro Pacheco reflect the psychological impact of the past.[1] The basic diet is spiced with exotic dishes, including *pollo pibil, venado,* and *papadzules*. Thatch huts carved in the façade of the "nunnery" at Uxmal are similar to those scattered throughout the countryside today. Possibly the most significant cultural link is found in the Mayan language, which continues to be spoken throughout the towns and villages and even in the capital city of Mérida. Yet the pervasive nature of Mayan influences and the splendor of ancient monuments tend at times to distort the whole of Yucatecan reality by obscuring other significant ingredients.

Spanish conquistadores introduced patterns of European Renaissance society. Mérida became a center of Hispanic forms; though the Mayan tongue continued to be spoken, Castilian became the language of authority and control. Landholding patterns and labor organization were altered greatly, and a white ruling elite came to dominate the peninsula. Possibly the most powerful single institution transferred from the Old World was the Roman Catholic church. The Franciscan order was especially important in extending the faith to every corner of the peninsula. Bishop Diego de Landa and other friars compiled dictionaries and captured valuable historical and cultural information relating to the Maya, though at the same time attempting to root out the vestiges of the ancient religion. New symbols and new life-styles were injected, and three centuries of Spanish rule left an indelible impression on the region and its culture.

Yucatan, however, was never brought completely under Spanish dominance, and the Europeans themselves were influenced and shaped by the native inhabitants. Moreover, the fusion of races and blending of cultures produced the Yucatecan mestizo, who came to occupy a prominent and eventually a dominant role in the society. The class structure that emerged during the colonial period was partly dictated by the Spanish legal code and was under the daily direction of the Franciscan priests. A special costume prescribed for the natives symbolized the dual class structure that persisted beyond independence. Though eroded in more recent years, the regional dress has continued to serve as a unique aspect of Yucatecan culture.

Declaring its independence from Spain, Yucatan joined the newly formed Mexican nation but found the partnership to be an uneasy and even painful one. From the very beginning, the state demanded its privileges within a federal system and exhibited an intense regional pride. Linked with federalists in other regions of Mexico, and with special ties to the Republic of Texas, Yucatecan political leaders threatened to secede from the nation on several occasions. In 1847, the peninsular elite faced a rebellion from the Mayan forces in a struggle that came to be known as the Caste War. Faced with the destruction of the entire fabric of the Hispanic society, the government sought to join the United States but was rejected. As the Indian forces withdrew from the outskirts of Mérida, having almost achieved victory, state leadership became more dependent upon the Mexican central government. Once again the landed elite began to prosper.

In 1876, Porfirio Díaz gained control over national affairs, initiating three decades of stability and progress based upon the ideals of positivism and the international economy. It was an age of railroads, increasing foreign investments, and growing exports of basic products. Henequen production expanded, giving Yucatan a monopoly in a burgeoning world market. Ownership and control of the "factories in the field" were in the hands of local entrepreneurs, but these enterprises were linked to major North American interests, especially International Harvester. Yucatan became the richest state in Mexico, and the prosperity was reflected in palatial homes that lined the Paseo de Montejo. The late nineteenth century was an opulent era of romantic regional pride, but the area was securely linked to the Porfiriato and to the international sisal market. With the rise of henequen monoculture, local entrepreneurs enforced a classical form of peonage; the traditional class structure, still represented by the dress code, seemed secure.

The Mexican Revolution, which erupted in 1910 and inundated much of the nation in blood throughout the following decade, was slow in coming to Yucatan. Henequen prices continued to rise during World War I, and the ruling class remained firmly entrenched in power. In 1915, however, General Salvador Alvarado led federal troops into the state, initiating basic changes in the structure of rural labor. This was followed by the consolidation of a truly Socialist party under the leadership of Felipe Carrillo Puerto, thus making Yucatan the center for one of the most radical phases of the Revolution. Though this movement was cut short by the execution of Carrillo in January of 1924, Yucatan was later singled out by President Lázaro Cárdenas as a principal target of agrarian reform. In 1937, haciendas were broken up and a system of collective ejidos established under federal supervision. Production fell rapidly as the once efficiently operated plantations suffered disruption and mismanagement. The problems were not entirely due to the ill-fated agrarian reform; increased competition from new sisal-producing regions and general world conditions also contributed to Yucatan's decline. Nevertheless, the once proud and wealthy state entered an era of severe economic depression and became dependent to a great extent upon subsidy from the national government.

Yucatan still has an essentially traditional social system and lacks the basic resources necessary for full-scale modernization. Yet there are growing pressures within every segment of the population to acquire the advantages of the developed world. Traditional cultural values have been eroded in many ways, including emphasis upon the regional costume. Medical care, education, and other social services have been expanded, but never rapidly enough to meet the increasing demand. The situation is further compounded by an alarming population growth rate that shows no signs of being reduced by any substantial degree. These social and economic problems have helped to renew the sense of regionalism that had been so strong in the early days of independence. In the election of 1970, the opposition Partido de Acción Nacional (PAN) party defeated the ruling Partido Revolucionario Institucional (PRI), thus illustrating the extent of alienation within the state. Yet a break with the national system is impossible; not only has centralism triumphed in Mexico, but Yucatan has become more and more dependent upon federal subsidies for the ailing henequen industry and for many public services. In the last quarter of the twentieth century it is clear that Yucatan is one of the problem areas of the nation. The ejidos can no longer provide employment for the growing number of rural inhabitants. Regional planners have attempted to find solutions to the internal dependency, chronic economic depression, and unemployment, encouraging diversification in agriculture and the development of new industries. One of the brightest possibilities for increased income seems to be in the further growth of tourist-related activities.

As is the case with all traditional societies, modernization brings the destruction or alteration of traditional values and social patterns. With expanding industry and the invasion of tourists—both foreign and Mexican—the unique quality of Yucatan will undoubtedly suffer further change. Yet the people have a stoic pride in their region and in their cultural heritage. Although now a part of a rapidly changing age, Yucatan remains *a world apart*.

NOTES

1. One of the best examples in the field of painting can be seen in the murals of Fernando Castro Pacheco in the central stairs of the state capitol building in Mérida. See Alfredo Barrera Vásquez, *Los Murales de Fernando Castro Pacheco en el Palacio del Poder Ejecutivo de Mérida, Yucatán, México* (Mérida, 1971).

CHAPTER I

PHYSICAL GEOGRAPHY OF THE YUCATAN PENINSULA

Eugene M. Wilson

The Yucatan Peninsula is geographically distinctive by its shape, size, and location, which have helped to give it a history much different from that of areas to the south and west. Northern Yucatan is the best-known part of the peninsula because most of its human population has been concentrated there for the past thousand years. From this part of the peninsula comes the most familiar image: large sinkholes that have provided domestic water, sparse soil cover, dense second-growth vegetation, low rainfall and winter drought, and particularly the rocky surface that made a strong impression upon the Spaniards. Diego de Landa observed that "Yucatan is the country with least earth that I have ever seen, since all of it is one living rock."[1] The impressions of the northwest, however, do not apply to all of the peninsula, for it is a region of considerable diversity. It is still true that Yucatan is one of the least explored land areas in North America.[2] The dense vegetation and the poor road system have until very recently kept most of the peninsula *terra incognita*.

Still, there has been considerable interest regarding the region in modern times. The books written by John L. Stephens in the mid-nineteenth century and the fine drawings by his colleague Frederick Catherwood stimulated a great deal of popular interest in the Maya and their homeland.[3] Research in Yucatan was renewed toward the end of the nineteenth century and has continued since. Outstanding are the publications by Angelo Heilprin, Karl Sapper, Franz Termer, and by the Carnegie Institution of Washington; these and a volume edited by Robert C. West are the main sources of geographical information on the Yucatan Peninsula.[4]

A sign of the academic interest in Yucatan by geographers is reflected in the number of theses and dissertations produced during the past fifteen years.[5] In addition, recent studies in ecology, hydrology, soils, and meteorology are of great value and point to a number of possible research topics.[6] The following discussion summarizes material from various publications concerning the physical geography of Yucatan and includes my personal observations of the region.

The Peninsula

The Yucatan Peninsula projects northward from eastern Mexico and northern Central America with the eastern or Caribbean side extending about 290 kilometers farther south than the western side on the Gulf of Mexico. In this discussion, the peninsula is considered to extend northward from the southwestern corner of the Gulf of Honduras (Bahía de Amatique), its southern boundary following the Río Sarstún, then west and northwest to the Río Salinas (Chixoy), northwestward along the Salinas–Usumacinta Valley, along the east side of the Sierra del Lacandón to the Río San Pedro Mártir, then northwestward to the Laguna de Términos west of Isla del Carmen to the Gulf of Mexico. The total area is approximately 222,000 square kilometers.

In an earlier study, Hakon Wadell placed the southern limit of the peninsula at a line across the eastern part of Petén, along the north shore of Lago Petén Itzá into Belize, and across the northern part of the Maya Mountains.[7] This boundary does not, however, follow a clear separation in the age or type of rocks or of landforms. A more distinct boundary, one used in this discussion, is located farther south at the zone of folded sedimentary rocks that extends across the Mexican states of Tabasco and Chiapas and the departments of Alta Verapaz and Izabal in Guatemala.

Geology and Physiography

The most detailed geologic map of the Yucatan Peninsula is that of F. Bonet and J. Butterlin with additions by E. López Ramos.[8] This and the geologic map of Guatemala and Belize are more complete than the national geologic map of Mexico.[9] These maps show limestone and dolomite of Eocene age (50 million years ago) and younger to be dominant over the peninsula from the north coast southward into Petén. Older rocks of Cretaceous age (65–136 million years ago) are exposed on the Libertad Arch, a broad uplift extending east-west across central Petén. At the southeast in the Cockscomb or Maya Mountains uplift, very old Paleozoic rocks (225–570 million years ago) form hills and low mountains in southern Belize.

Yucatan has considerably more variety in its geology than is suggested by most descriptions. The rocks range from unconsolidated calcareous beach sands to igneous and metamorphic rocks in the Maya Mountains. Sandstones have been reported from Petén, and deposits of quartz sand and gravel eroded from the Maya Mountains cover portions of southern Belize.[10] Extensive alluvial deposits from the Usumacinta River drainage basin cover the southwestern portion of the peninsula. In some localities, chert, a primary tool stone of the ancient Maya, occurs within limestone beds. Some unusual clay minerals long used in Maya pottery are found in the northwest.[11] Older limestones are often hard, crystalline, and marblelike in texture. Colors range from pure white to yellow and red and the strata from laminar to massive. The processes of chemical and physical change such as solution and recrystallization have served to destroy fossil forms in most older surface rocks.[12] Crustal movements and warping caused by solution have changed the original horizontal attitude of the strata, and gentle folds together with broken and offset layers are fairly common in the interior.

One of the primary geological facts about the peninsula is the extensive and deep cover of limestone and dolomite. Layers of these rocks total hundreds of feet in thickness, extending far below present sea level. The chief mineral in limestone is calcite, or calcium carbonate, and dolomite is calcium-magnesium carbonate. Both are derived largely from the calcareous remains of marine organisms, such as molluscs and corals, deposited on the ocean floor. When limestones and dolomite are exposed to rainwater or ground water, a chemical reaction occurs in which a small portion of the calcium is made soluble and then is carried off by surface or ground water. Since the rocks are nearly pure, very little residue remains after solution. Following many years of this solution process, hollows, openings, depressions, and even caverns are produced. These landforms, both small and large, are found throughout the peninsula.

Physiographic Subdivisions

The portion of the Yucatan Platform now above sea level is a well-defined physiographic *section,* or major subdivision of the Atlantic–Gulf Coastal Plain physiographic province. Smaller units of the section may be designated as *districts.* The Yucatan Peninsula has at least fourteen districts within the northward-projecting landmass from the Chiapas-Guatemala highlands, briefly described as follows: (1) The *Coastal Zone* (a) on the west contains beach ridges in the Laguna de Términos area, a cliffed and rocky coast farther north around the city of Campeche, and a low, partly flooded coast with short streams to Punta Nimún; (b) on the north and northeast are barrier beaches, beach ridges, lagoons, barrier islands, elevated Pleistocene shorelines, and low cliffs; and (c) on the east includes low cliffs, large and small embayments, and swamps. (2) The *Caribbean Reef* district includes all barrier and fringing reefs, coral heads, and atoll forms on the eastern side of the peninsula from Isla Cancún to Zapotillos Cays. (3) The *Mérida* district, in the northwest portion of the northern karst plain, has low relief, small hills, and mostly small depressions, but includes large circular depressions in the south and west. (4) The *Chichén Itzá* district, in the center of the northern karst plain, has relief to about 25 meters and contains large water-filled depressions (*aguadas* and *cenotes*) and numerous dry depressions (*hoyas*). (5) The *Cobá* district in the northeast portion of the karst plain has an abundance of small depressions and hills, several large lakes, and linear depressions. (6) The *Puuc* or *Sierrita de Ticul* is a northwest-to-southeast trending linear ridge with local relief reaching approximately 100 meters. (7) The *Bolonchén* district is an arcuate area of broad, cone-shaped hills and ridges of relatively high relief; it is not a part of the Puuc or Sierrita. (8) The *Río Candelaria-Río San Pedro* district is an area of low relief, meandering streams, shallow lakes, and alluvial deposits. (9) The *Río Bec* district includes the large central area of broad, conical hills and high linear ridges with elevations to 275 meters, with many intermittent lakes. It has poorly developed drainage patterns, although three large streams originate there: the Río Hondo–Río Azul, the Río Candelaria, and the Río Cham-

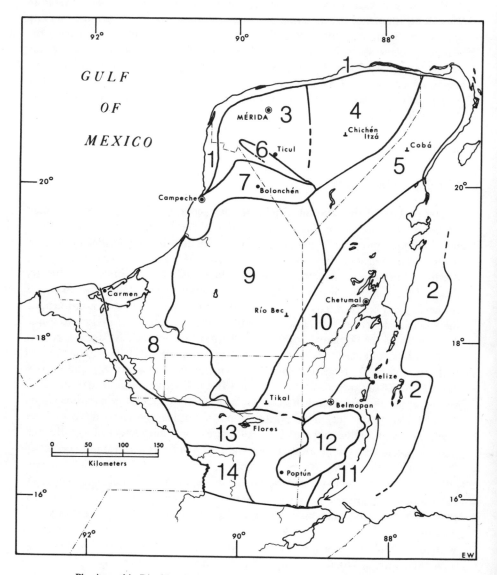

Physiographic Districts of the Yucatan Peninsula. (Map by Eugene Wilson)

potón. (10) The *Río Hondo* district is characterized by low relief, a number of northeast-to-southwest-trending linear fault depressions in which are located streams, lakes, and lake beds, and includes adjacent offshore islands of fault origin. (11) The *Southern Belize coastal plain* is an area of low relief composed mainly of alluvial deposits derived from the Maya Mountains uplift. (12) The *Maya Mountains* are part of a dissected uplift, with elevations to 1,122 meters, in which Paleozoic igneous and metamorphic rocks are exposed. (13) The *Flores* district is an area of dissected limestone ridges and escarpments and includes savanna-covered plains and steep, conical hills. Several lakes fill large depressions, notably Lago Petén Itzá and Yaxhá. (14) The *Pasión* district is a plain mostly of low relief and gentle slopes enclosed by the Río de la Pasión on the east and north and by the Río Salinas on the west.

Until recently, description of much of Yucatan was rather broadly generalized because of the lack of large-scale maps, the poorly developed road systems, the dense vegetation cover, and only partial coverage by aerial photography. Recent satellite imagery (LANDSAT) has greatly aided study of remote places such as Yucatan, but this system is somewhat limited in its ability to define small features. Because of the concentration of population in the northwestern part of Mexican Yucatan and because it also has the best road system, most descriptions have emphasized Yucatan state.

Coastal Landforms

On the southwestern side of the peninsula is the Laguna de Términos, formed behind Isla del Carmen and Isla de la Aguada, barriers partly in the form of beach ridges. The Laguna de Términos is a relatively protected, mangrove-fringed water body approximately 25 by 65 kilometers in size and is the largest lagoon on the peninsula. To the west of Ciudad del Carmen is the margin of the Grijalva-Usumacinta delta, which is primarily of noncalcareous sediments and is geologically different from most of the Yucatan Peninsula. Northward to the vicinity of Champotón the coast remains low with occasional exposures of hardened surface limestone.

On the Gulf Coast between Champotón and Campeche City, long northwest-to-southeast-trending ridges reach to the sea, and erosion has produced a cliffed coast with elevations to approximately 75 meters. These are perhaps the greatest heights to be found on the coast of the Gulf of Mexico. From Campeche City north to Punta Nimún, just south of Celestún, the coast is mangrove-fringed and is marked by numerous short, meandering streams. These drain a nearly flat surface that is covered with shallow water during the wet summer season.

Twelve kilometers south of Celestún is the mouth of a lagoon known as La Ciénaga, El Río, or Río Lagartos that extends intermittently across the north coast to near Yalahau. This narrow, shallow water body is formed between the mainland and a series of beach ridges. The area is particularly noted for its variety and abundance of birdlife, especially migratory waterfowl. Salt col-

Beach ridges and salt basins just north of Celestún, important for bird life and as a source of salt, collected as the water evaporates from basins. (Photo by Eugene Wilson)

lecting was one of the primary activities on the coast during pre-Hispanic times, and the salt deposits are still a significant resource. Some of the most important locations for this mineral include Celestún, San Crisano, Porvenir, Santa Clara, Mina de Oro, and Las Coloradas.[13] Sea water apparently enters the beach ridge swales through seepage and comes into the lagoon at several entrances. The lowest water level in the lagoon occurs during summer, according to Clinton Edwards.[14] *Ojos de agua,* freshwater submarine springs, are present at several localities along the north coast.[15] Circular coral reefs are located on the continental shelf off northern and western Yucatan, the largest being Arrecife Alacrán, 125 kilometers north of Progreso. Barrier beaches a short distance from the mainland extend around the northeast end of the peninsula. The southernmost of these, Isla Cancún, on the Caribbean, is the site of a major luxury tourist complex being developed by the Mexican government. Isla Cancún marks the northern end of the longest barrier reef in the Western Hemisphere, which extends along the coast and offshore discontinuously to Zapotillos Cays in the Gulf of Honduras. Numerous coral heads, shoals, and small islands occur along and behind the reef, particularly off Belize. Very large reefs enclosing lagoons are located off southeastern Quintana Roo and Belize. These include Banco Chinchorro, Turneffe Islands, Lighthouse Reef, and Glovers Reef. Parts of coastal Quintana Roo are rocky and cliffed, notably in the area of Tulum; elevated beach ridges are prominent features of the northeast coast. Cozumel Island and possibly other islands off the east coast have their origin in the faulting (crustal displacement) that occurred along the eastern side of the peninsula. Faulting is probably the cause of the large embayments along the east coast as well as the sharp drop in depth offshore. Less than 5 kilometers from Puerto Morelos, depths reach 600 feet in contrast to the very gentle slope of the Gulf of Mexico, where deep water is found 200 to 270 kilometers offshore. Much of the southeastern coast, particularly in Belize, is low and poorly drained. South of the city of Belize, sediment derived from the Maya Mountains forms coastal barriers enclosing two large lagoons. A short distance inland the alluvium has covered the surface, isolating unusually steep residual limestone towers.[16]

Hardened Surface Limestone

A hard surface limestone is widespread over the peninsula and gives the earthbound traveler perhaps his most enduring impression of Yucatan, particularly in the northern plain. This rock is formed by solution and precipitation of calcium carbonate near the ground surface and cements the loose grains and shell fragments into a hard layer. This is eventually broken up by growing plant roots, and the ground surface is often littered with chunks of rock. The Maya clear these obstacles from house lots and fields in the building of rock fences, one of the characteristic cultural features of northern Yucatan.[17]

Sascab

Below the hard surface layer, the weathering front, a zone of chemical change, has altered the original character of the rock and created in the process a softer, usually friable, nearly pure calcium carbonate material known in Yucatan as *sascab* or *sahcab*. It is unevenly distributed and varies in depth, but in some localities it reaches several meters. Cavities and quarries, or *sascaberas,* are frequently seen in house lots and along modern road cuts where sascab has been removed for domestic use and road building. Its use is ancient, and sascaberas have been identified at archaeological sites. There, sascab was used in the construction of buildings, plazas, and for the *sacbeob* (ancient Maya roads), connecting intersite building groups and associated outlying centers.[18]

Solution Features

Very little has been published on solution landforms in Yucatan other than cenotes, and even recent books on limestone regions contain only brief references to the peninsula.[19] William A. Finch, Jr., first described the abundant microsolution forms, which are small, circular, pitlike depressions a few millimeters to several centimeters in diameter that occur only on exposed rock

A sascab pit (*Sascabera*) near Ticul. Sascab is friable calcium carbonate that is widely used in construction. (Photo by Eugene Wilson)

surfaces.[20] Where soil has covered the rock, the surface is smooth. Furrowlike rills are not usual except on the coasts, but small solution-widened fractures are widespread. Small solution features are common along the coasts, where splash has produced small hollows and rills on steep slopes. Solution pipes several centimeters in diameter and sometimes one or two meters or more in depth also occur on exposed surfaces as do larger depressions with steep or gently sloping sides. These large bowllike features, termed *sartenejas*, vary in diameter from less than one meter to several meters.

Sinkholes

The rounded, steep-walled collapse sinkholes exposing ground water, called *cenotes*, are the best known and perhaps the most interesting landform of Yucatan. Cenotes and associated *aguadas*, or shallow ponds, are more commonly grouped or aligned rather than scattered randomly over the surface. Large cenotes are particularly abundant in the area around the Maya center of Chichén Itzá, extending east from Libre Unión to Valladolid and from just north of Peto to the northern coast. This outstanding cenote area was first described by John L. Stephens in 1843:

The world's most famous sinkhole, the "Sacred Cenote" at Chichén Itzá, is approximately sixty meters in diameter and twenty meters from the rim to the water level. (Aerial photo by Eugene Wilson)

On our journey from Peto . . . we had entered a region where the sources of the supply of water formed a new and distinctive feature in the face of the country, wilder, and, at first sight, perhaps creating a stronger feeling of admiration and wonder than even the extraordinary cuevas, aguadas, and senotes we had formerly encountered. These too, are called senotes, but they differ materially from those before presented, being immense circular holes, from sixty to two hundred feet in diameter, with broken, rocky, perpendicular sides from fifty to one hundred feet deep, and having at the bottom a great body of water, of an unknown depth, always about the same level, supposed to be supplied by subterranean rivers.[21]

In the same area described by Stephens are many *aguadas,* but by far the most numerous depressions are large, dry sinks, or *hoyas.* The relief is noticeably greater in this area, reaching approximately 25 meters.

At least two other areas of cenotes are present in the Mérida district in the northern plain. To the west, about midway between Bella Flor and Celestún, is a belt of deep, water-filled sinks aligned roughly north-south. A second alignment of cenotes and *aguadas* is located approximately 10 kilometers north of the Sierrita de Ticul and trends in the same direction as the Sierrita. This belt of sinkholes is about two kilometers wide and extends from near the village of San

Aguadas and lakes in the vicinity of Cobá, Quintana Roo. (Photo by Andy Dees)

Fernando, northwest of Maxcanú, eastward beyond Sacalum, more than 50 kilometers. Smaller sinks also occur in abundance in relatively small areas, such as those at the Postclassic site of Mayapán. However, the concentration of openings to ground water there seems to be unusual.[22] Sinkholes do exist in other parts of the peninsula, in parts of Belize, and near Flores, Petén, for example; but high-density sinkhole areas are located primarily in the northern plain of Yucatan state and northern Quintana Roo.

A distinction between types of sinkholes should be made in order to clarify the use of the term "cenote." In northern Yucatan, the word is used locally to denote a variety of sinkhole forms that contain water. As a landform term, however, cenote is usually applied specifically to steep-sided, rock-walled, circular collapse sinks in limestone and dolomite in which ground water is exposed. The term cenote is Spanish, derived from the Maya *dzonote,* and occurs in place names in Yucatan state almost exclusively between Peto and the north coast, which coincides with the area of larger sinkholes described by Stephens and later by Ralph L. Roys.[23] The term cenote is not used in Ticul,[24] farther southwest, nor is it used in place names south of the Sierrita de Ticul. The Maya word *chen* is a more widely used term for various kinds of subterranean cavities, including sinkholes, and it also appears in many place names. Large, usually gently sloping depressions having soil-mantled slopes containing a shallow pond with a clay bottom are called *aguadas.* The term *bajo* is used in the southern portion of the peninsula for similar features. *Aguadas* are not favored as sources of domestic water in the north, but they are used as livestock ponds. The distinction between cenote and *cueva,* or cave, sometimes becomes confusing in local use. For example, the "cenote" at Maní has a gently sloping entrance and passage giving access to a pool of water in a domed chamber. The chamber roof has been cut through so that water can be raised to the surface by buckets. Other "cenotes" such as Zací in Valladolid, are also distinctly cavelike.

Caves

Together with the large cenotes, caves are the most spectacular features of Yucatan. Earlier cave descriptions and research were concentrated in the Sierrita de Ticul, where a large number of caves are located,[25] although it is now clear that extensive systems also exist in the Chichén Itzá, Bolonchén, and Río Bec districts as well. Actún Kaua near Chichén Itzá, for example, is reported to have over twenty thousand feet of passages on one level, and certainly other cave systems exist that have never been studied or reported.[26] Speleological research is important to the understanding of Yucatan landforms and hydrology. Because of their accessibility, Loltún Cave near Oxkutzcab, Balankanché near Chichén Itzá, and Xtacumbilxunam near Bolonchén are perhaps the best-known large caves to visitors in Yucatan, where caverns in general constitute a largely undeveloped resource for tourism.

Xtacumbilxunam cavern near Bolonchén, northern Campeche state. (Photo by Eugene Wilson)

To the pre-Hispanic Maya, caves were of great importance as sources of pure water, *zuhuy ha,* used in ceremonies for the petition of rain. The abundance of potsherds found in many caves resulted from the periodic breaking of ceramic vessels in water ceremonies, according to J. E. S. Thompson.[27] The Gruta de Chac near the road to Sayil appears to be one such example, and it is unique in that the water jug fragments are polychrome.[28] The rock carvings of Loltún indicate that it had special significance as a ceremonial cave. The more recently discovered Balancanché Cave near Chichén Itzá is especially noted for ceramic offerings discovered there. In times of stress, caves have provided refuge and have served as sources of domestic water supplies.

Ground Water

Depth to ground water in the northern plain is not more than 27 meters and, near the coast, water in cenotes may be only one meter or less below ground level. At some places along the north coast fresh water flows out of solution channels producing springs termed *ojos de agua* that occur at or below sea level. Some of these are located just west of Progreso, at the mouth of the Río Lagartos, at Conil, Sisal, Dzilam, Yalahau, and Chiquilá.[29] South of the Sierrita de Ticul the ground-water level is considerably deeper than on the northern plain, and wells range in depth from 42 meters at Rancho San José south of Oxkutzcab to approximately 135 meters farther south in the Bolonchén district, although at some places perched water tables exist and wells are shallow. The application of the term "cenote" by Stephens and David Casares to deep caves containing water in this region probably has caused some confusion as to cenote distribution and appears inconsistent with the concept of the cenote held by the Maya in the northern plain.[30] Part of the central region is known by archaeologists as the *Chenes* zone. According to H. E. D. Pollock, it is a name derived "from the numerous shallow wells found there."[31] These natural water sources are, in fact, rare when the size of the Chenes area is considered; it appears that the name best applies not for the abundance of wells there but rather for their existence in a water-scarce region.

According to a recent paper by Donald O. Doehring and Joseph H. Butler, the highly permeable rocks of northern Yucatan provide a single system in which a layer of fresh water overlies saline water.[32] An earlier study noted at least two layers or aquifers of fresh water in Mérida, one at about 8 meters and another at 36 meters.[33] The hydrologic model in the Doehring and Butler paper is essentially the same as that suggested by L. J. Cole in 1910, that is, that interior areas of heavier rainfall produce hydrostatic pressure causing the subsurface water to flow outward from the interior toward the coast.[34] Subsurface water movement is concentrated along systems of rock fracture and does not flow in "underground rivers," as in surface streams. Collection of ground-water data is needed to understand better the hydrologic system. Such data would also be an aid for the location of domestic wells, an important consideration for health.

In the northern districts of the peninsula no large permanent surface streams exist. Only on the northwest coast between Campeche City and Celestún do surface streams occur, and these are short, meandering creeks that drain a nearly flat surface that is flooded during the rainy summer season. The interior of the peninsula, however, is the source of three major drainage systems: the Río Hondo–Río Azul, the Río Candelaria, and the Río Champotón. Other surface drainage patterns also are developed in the interior but evidently drain into the subsurface.

Water and Settlement

It has often been noted that pre-Hispanic and colonial settlements were located near cenotes in the northern plain. Except for the northwest coast, the plain lacked surface streams, and the technology of the pre-Hispanic Maya was insufficient for digging deep wells through the limestone. In the interior of the peninsula south of the northern plain, however, with the exception of scattered springs

One of many small streams draining the northwest coastal area between Campeche and Celestún. Surface streams are found only in this district of northern Yucatan. (Photo by Eugene Wilson)

or water caves, no access to ground water was possible. Maya centers in the Puuc and Chenes areas were self-sufficient in water supplies through the use of cisterns during the Late Classic occupation. Farther south, natural ponds and artificial basins or reservoirs were used. The construction of cisterns, or *chultunes,* cut into the bedrock by the Maya was a solution to the problem of lack of surface water, one that was also employed in limestone areas in other parts of the world. E. H. Thompson described the underground water cisterns at the site of Labná, where possibly as many as sixty of these jug-shaped *chultunes* were used, each having a capacity of approximately seventy-five hundred gallons. When filled, these could have supplied three thousand persons through the dry season on water collected from runoff surfaces during the rainy season.[35] George W. Brainerd further pointed out that "the only known source of water in the Puuc area during the dry season is from cisterns or chultunes which profusely dot the sites. Nearly all the buildings of the Puuc ruins face upon leveled plazas which were paved with carefully laid lime-mortar floors, and seldom if ever does such a plaza floor in a Puuc ruin not drain into the mouth of one or several cisterns."[36]

Caretakers at the sites of Sayil and Xlapak still use cleaned and repaired Classic period *chultunes* for domestic water. With the arrival of the Spanish in the sixteenth century, ranches and towns in the interior were supplied with water from deep wells dug with metal tools and probably with the help of gunpowder. The central portion of the peninsula has, until recently, contained few people, possibly because the Maya population had moved to the north during the Post-classic period.[37]

Linear Physiographic Features

The major landform in southern Yucatan state is a long ridge known as the Sierrita de Ticul, or the *Puuc*. It has recently been interpreted as a landform resulting from faulting, or crustal displacement.[38] For about one-third of its length in the north it is composed of two parallel ridges, the northernmost being lower. The northeast facing slope is approximately 25 degrees; the southwest slope is more gentle and declines into an open, gently rolling lowland. The Sierrita trends roughly southeast for a distance of about 140 kilometers, from just south of Maxcanú to beyond Tzucacab. It is crossed by a number of east-west trending low ridges and valleys, particularly in the central portion of the Sierrita near Ticul. The maximum local relief, or height, of the Sierrita is about 100 meters.

Another prominent feature that may be of fault origin is a ridge that extends from Champotón along the west coast northward to ten kilometers south of the city of Campeche, where a distinct offset in the coastline occurs and the trend changes to approximately northeast. This feature is broken into a series of low ridges and a chain of knoblike hills and, with a break at Hecelchakán, it continues to Dzitbalché, where it forms an elbow and then trends eastward and merges with the Sierrita de Ticul about ten kilometers west of Tzucacab. Between Dzitbalché and the northwest end of the Sierrita near Maxcanú no ridge exists, contrary to what is shown on physiographic maps now in long use, and there is no direct connection between the two except at the southeast end of the Sierrita.[39] These two features would appear to have been formed at different times, the Sierrita being the more recent, having a different trend, and being much less eroded.

In eastern Yucatan, Quintana Roo, and the Cobá and Río Hondo districts are several large northeast-to-southwest trending linear depressions related to geologic events in the Río Hondo fault zone. Some of these depressions are occupied by swamps, wet savannas, and large lakes, including Laguna Chichancanab, Laguna Nohbec, and Laguna Bacalar, and by rivers, particularly the Río Hondo and New River in Belize. The coastal configuration also appears to be affected by faulting, notably at Bahía Ascensión, Bahía Espíritu Santo, and Chetumal Bay. Smaller depressions, savannas, and half-hidden lakes extend to the northeastern corner of the peninsula at Laguna Yalahau.

In Petén, two prominent geologic trends are present. In the south are arcuate east-west folds and faults, associated with the belt of folded rocks in eastern

Chiapas and Alta Verapaz. East-west faults also cut central Petén in the Flores district, where a trench is formed, partly occupied by Lago Petén Itzá, Laguna Yaxhá, and several smaller lakes.[40] Landforms produced by faulting and by differences in rock type are in most instances marked by lines of conical hills, both in Petén and farther north in Yucatan and Campeche.

Limestone Hills

Limestone hills are the most widespread of the large landforms in the peninsula and are physiographically as important as the more famous cenotes. The peninsula presents an interesting case study region for solution landforms, or *karst,* in the tropics since there is considerable range in rainfall, from approximately 472 millimeters at Progreso in the northwest, to above 2,000 millimeters in Petén, as well as variation in age and type of rocks. The limestone hills are termed *cone karst* or *kegelkarst* and form a surface dominated by projecting residual forms instead of closed depressions.[41] These features have been studied in detail in Java, New Guinea, Cuba, Puerto Rico, and Jamaica.

Southern Yucatan contains several areas of steep, cone-shaped hills. Marjorie M. Sweeting makes reference to cone karst in southern Belize, and Termer noted "kegelkarst" of 60 to 150 meters high in southern Campeche.[42] Limestone hills are developed in the northern plain to some degree, but they are not so striking as the depressions. Broad cone karst is developed, however, south of the Sierrita de Ticul and along and behind the escarpment that extends northeastward from the city of Campeche and eastward from Dzitbalché. It forms the northern limit of the Bolonchén district, which contains hundreds of broad, cone-shaped hills that have relief for the most part probably less than 80 meters. Casares termed these hills *Uitzes,* and Sapper referred to the area as the *Sierra de Bolonchén,* from which the district name is taken in this chapter.[43] To the south in the Río Bec district, these conical hills merge with linear ridges of eastern Campeche and western Quintana Roo. Farther northeast, the hills fade out about 20 kilometers west of Laguna Chichancanab, except a small area a short distance east of the lake.

One of the largest cone karst regions in Middle America is to be found in northern Alta Verapaz, in southern Belize, and in the Flores district of Guatemala. It has, in some places, great similarity to Jamaican cockpit karst although the relief is not so great. Cone karst is developed along prominent east-west escarpments in central Petén on either side of the Libertad Arch.[44] The northernmost escarpment in Petén is the termination of the "Sierra de Yucatán" of earlier physiographic discussions, which is the south end of the Río Bec district and has an elevation of about 300 meters. This escarpment, which is clearly visible from Tikal, is broken into irregular hills of conical form with relief of approximately 100 meters.[45] Another area of cone karst with 80 to 120 meters of relief is located about 2 kilometers south of the town of Flores and extends southward for 25 kilometers.[46] In southeast Petén and southwestern Belize another area of prominent cone karst is located along the western flank of the Maya Mountains in the vicinity of the town of Poptún and extends south to the Río Sarstún.

Weather and Climate

The broad weather and climate patterns for the peninsula are known; however, the most reliable data are from a small number of stations, most of which are located in Yucatan state. Although new weather stations have been established in the last decade, it will be years before they can be useful for climate study. Short-term weather records do not indicate the possible cycles of rain and drought. Further, a single storm or hurricane can produce an unusual amount of rainfall, raising the average and giving an incorrect picture of the rainfall distribution, both annually and geographically. Reliability is much improved where the records have been maintained for two decades or longer.

One of the primary climate controls in the peninsula is the presence of high atmospheric pressure over the Atlantic. The southwestward shift of this high pressure during winter produces descending air aloft that diminishes the buildup of clouds through evaporation of the cloud moisture resulting in the dry season. The effects of this evaporation are greatest along the northwestern coastal zone.

Along the northern coast a daily land and sea breeze is established. During the morning, prevailing winds are from the east. As the land heats during the day, air rises from the land surface, and by midday the wind changes direction, blowing landward from the sea to replace air moving upward. Thus, a daily reversal of wind direction occurs. These are relatively strong winds and, combined with the dry air aloft, produce great surface evaporation along the northern coast.

The northern coastal zone receives some rainfall from thunderstorms that originate farther to the east through strong sea breeze convergence. This is caused by the location of Yucatan directly in the path of the trade winds and by the shape of the northeastern corner of the peninsula. Winds from the north coast and from the east coast converge over northern Quintana Roo. This produces vertical or convectional uplifting and the formation of thunderstorms that then drift to the west.[47] A high rainfall anomaly is thus produced over the northern portion of Quintana Roo and eastern Yucatan state, although the effects are also felt farther westward.

Originating in the Atlantic and Caribbean, tropical low pressure troughs known as "easterly waves" are carried by the trade winds into the peninsula. Easterly waves may be identified by masses of thunderstorm clouds moving into the western Caribbean once or twice a week during summer. Their arrival brings heavy rainfall, lightning, and strong winds to the Caribbean coast. In early and late summer, hurricanes may originate from easterly waves in the Caribbean.

Because of its location, Yucatan is affected by most hurricanes in the western Caribbean. For example, the distance from the Río Sarstún on the southeast to Cabo Catoche on the northeast is approximately 660 kilometers. The diameter of

Hurricane "Carmen," 8:50 A.M. CST, 7 Sept. 1974, over the Gulf of Mexico after crossing Yucatan. On 1 Sept. this storm severely damaged Chetumal, Quintana Roo. Synchronous meteorological satellite (SMS-1).

large hurricanes is about the same distance so that any such storm moving in the western Caribbean will be felt along much of the eastern coast of the peninsula. Further, Yucatan lies in one of the main hurricane paths and will be hit frequently by a hurricane or the slightly less powerful tropical storm.

The hurricane develops from a low pressure area (cyclone) over the tropical ocean surface in which rapidly rising moist air gradually develops a spiraling flow (counterclockwise in the Northern Hemisphere) as bands of thunderstorm clouds are drawn into the circulation. Four stages of hurricane development are recognized, although only the more intense tropical storm and hurricane stages are normally recorded on storm charts. The tropical storm has winds from 63 to 118 kilometers per hour, and the hurricane has winds above 118 kilometers per hour. When a hurricane hits land, damage occurs from storm winds, high wind-generated waves along the right front of the storm center, high water level or "storm surge," extremely heavy rainfall, and tornadoes along the advancing storm front.

The time that most hurricanes and tropical storms strike the Yucatan Peninsula is in late summer and early autumn, from August through October, with September having the highest frequency. From 1886 through 1975, an average of one hurricane or tropical storm each year directly hit the Yucatan Peninsula.[48] This does not include many storms that passed near the coast or through the Yucatan Channel into the Gulf of Mexico. The most storm-prone area of the peninsula is from Bahía de la Ascensión northward to Cabo Catoche, which has been hit by forty-nine storms (1886–1975), twenty-three of these being hurricanes and twenty-six being tropical storms. Isla Cancún, the site of a new luxury tourist resort on the northeast coast of Quintana Roo, has been directly hit by fourteen storms, eight hurricanes and six tropical storms (1886–1975). Cozumel Island has been crossed by twelve storms, but it has been much affected by others passing just to the north and to the south. Cozumel has been directly affected by forty to fifty storms during the period of record, one each two or three years on the average. Particularly severe hurricane damage occurred at Belize City in 1931 and 1961. Chetumal was almost completely destroyed in 1955; on September 1, 1974, hurricane "Carmen" caused great damage to Chetumal and then crossed the peninsula and hit the Gulf Coast of the United States. During the fifteen-year period from 1931 to 1946, thirty storms, twelve of them hurricanes, hit the Caribbean coast of the Yucatan Peninsula—twice as many as the average. The most storm-free period was from 1899 to 1930, when only six hurricanes and twelve tropical storms were recorded. Only three consecutive years since 1886 have passed completely storm-free.

Nortes or cold fronts are common weather features during Northern Hemisphere winter—the dry season in Yucatan. Occasional outbreaks of cooler air from the United States then move southward over Yucatan, producing overcast skies, lower temperatures, and even thundershowers. The *nortes* also produce high waves in the Gulf of Mexico that cause local changes in the beaches and islands of the northern and western coasts.

Increase in rainfall from north to south is due in part to the location of the peninsula within the trade wind belt, the southern part of Yucatan being closer to the intertropical convergence. The Intertropical Convergence Zone (ITZ) is a broad area where the northeast and southeast trade winds meet and rise. Heavier rainfall in the south also is caused by the shape of the Caribbean coastline and the highlands in the southeast. The nearly right-angle shape of the coastline in the Gulf of Honduras and the location of the Maya Mountains direct the moisture-laden winds into southern Belize and Petén. The heights of southern Belize and of eastern and central Guatemala channel the winds westward into a narrow entrance at the mouth of the Sarstún River where lifting produces over 4,000 millimeters of rainfall annually. Heavy rainfall is also concentrated in southern Petén, southern Belize, northern Alta Verapaz, and eastern Chiapas, as winds are forced over the high land surfaces.

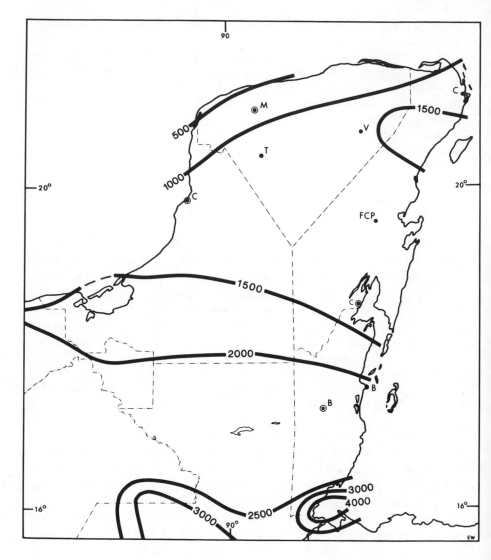

Mean Annual Rainfall Distribution in Millimeters. (Map by Eugene Wilson)

One primary aspect of the rainfall pattern throughout the peninsula is a dry season, or low rainfall period from November through April, as the high pressure aloft over the Atlantic Ocean shifts southwestward. April is the month of lowest rainfall in the southern part of the peninsula, whereas March is the lowest in the north. Two high rainfall periods normally occur in the wet season.[49] In northern Yucatan most stations record the first high rainfall peak during June; some localities in the south record July as the first high rainfall month. The second and highest rainfall peak occurs during September or October for most stations in the peninsula. Another important characteristic is that the amount of annual rainfall may vary as much as 30 percent from the *long-term average* throughout the peninsula. Variation of rainfall from one year to the next is also common and appears to have been manifested by the importance of Chac, the rain god, particularly in northern Yucatan.

The dry season in winter and the wet season during the summer growing period have encouraged the traditional agricultural cycle of one maize crop per year. Today two or three crops a year are possible with ditch and sprinkler irrigation systems now used in several places in the states of Campeche, Quintana Roo, and Yucatan. In Classic Maya times, water may have been applied by hand from ground-water sources to small fields and gardens.

Climate Types

Climate classification is based upon accumulated weather records, preferably two decades or longer in order that any departures from the long-term mean may be included. Mérida has the longest weather record in Yucatan, dating back to at least 1894. Progreso, Maxcanú, Valladolid, and several other places have records for fifty years or longer. The climates of the peninsula are tropical, all stations recording high mean annual temperatures with the coldest month having at least 18°C. Under the Köppen climate classification system, the southern part of the peninsula, where the rainfall is heaviest and the winter drought is least severe, is designated as Tropical Rainy (Af), the driest month having at least 60 millimeters of rainfall. Northward is the Tropical Monsoon (Am) climate that has only one month averaging below 60 millimeters of rain and very heavy rainfall in summer. This type extends across Petén and Belize with Belize City being an example of a Trade Wind Littoral climate, an Am variety. The Am northern boundary in Yucatan is vaguely determined because of the lack of sufficient data. Very likely it extends across southern Campeche and Quintana Roo. Most of the remainder of the peninsula has a Tropical Savanna (Aw) or Tropical Wet-and-Dry climate, for which the driest month has less than 60 millimeters of rainfall. This region has a well-developed dry season that is not compensated for by the rainfall during the wet season. Annual rainfall for Aw locations ranges from 1,000 to 2,500 millimeters and is concentrated in summer. Some rain will be recorded in the winter months, but typically two or three months will have no appreciable rainfall. The extreme northwest coast has a Semi-Arid climate type, Köppen's BS, for which the rainfall is less than 500 millimeters annually and evaporation is quite high.

Vegetation

The abundance and density of plant life in Yucatan is striking, particularly in the northwest where soil is shallow and the surface is very rocky. Plants grow

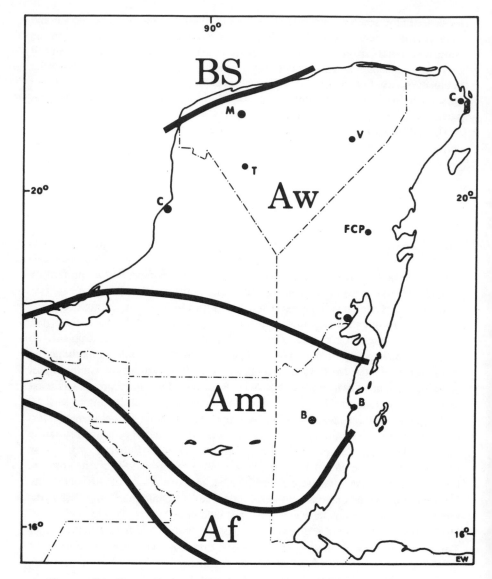

Climates of the Yucatan Peninsula, Köppen System. (Map by Eugene Wilson)
Af - Tropical Rainy, Am - Tropical Monsoon, Aw - Tropical Savanna, BS - Semi-Arid

from every small crevice in amazing profusion. One might expect less vegetation density in a region having a distinct dry season and thin soil cover. Farther south, the great diversity of vegetation has aroused considerable interest on the part of botanists.[50]

Annual precipitation, wet and dry seasons, drainage, and human land use are the principal variables in the distribution of vegetation in the peninsula. Variation in annual precipitation from above 2,000 millimeters to less than 500 millimeters produces natural changes in major vegetation patterns, but land use has caused such large-scale changes that it is difficult to judge exactly what the structure and composition of the natural vegetation would be in the northwest. There, clearing for cultivation has been going on for over two thousand years, resulting in a never-ending cycle of plant succession. In the slash-and-burn or shifting-agricultural cycle, land is periodically rotated and cleared about every four to twenty years. Thus, only in the most isolated places is there likely to be any "natural" vegetation, that is, plant communities disturbed only by nonhuman phenomena, such as storms, floods, or drought. The effects of human activity, according to C. L. Lundell, can still be recognized in mature forests of Petén after ten centuries.[51] In that region, breadnut and sapodilla are closely associated with Mayan sites. These trees, some of which are a thousand years old, may have been planted by the Late Classic Mayan inhabitants. Other plants whose distribution may have been affected by the ancient Maya include guayo, avocado, mamey, and possibly the cohune palm, copal, tropical cedar, and mahogany.[52] J. C. Bequaert also listed a number of plants associated with Mayan ruins in Yucatan state.[53]

In the past twenty-five years a number of ejidos have been established in Quintana Roo, eastern Yucatan, and Campeche, resulting in large areas of cleared land. In Quintana Roo, mahogany, tropical cedar, ramón, guanacaste, and chaca are cut for lumber.[54] Lumbering operations have been in progress for some years around the village of Colonia Yucatán in northeastern Yucatan state and in several places in southern Quintana Roo. Forest exploitation in western Campeche and in Belize has continued since the colonial period, and more recently cutting of tropical wood has become important in Petén since the completion of new roads in the early 1970s. Much of Petén probably will follow the succession of tropical forest to agriculture and grazing land that is taking place elsewhere in the peninsula so that considerable forest depletion can be expected during the next several decades.

In Quintana Roo, livestock grazing is one of the bases for the modern agrarian economy, and an estimated 40 percent of the state can be converted to pasture.[55] At Nuevo Xcán in northern Quintana Roo, approximately 800 hectares (2,000 acres) of forest are being converted to guinea grassland for cattle.[56] Large areas of northern Yucatan state have also been cleared for pasture since 1970. These pastures often have remnants of the forest, such as palms and ceiba trees, and should not be confused with natural savannas. Natural grass-covered areas are found where the ground surface is permanently or seasonally wet or where there has been periodic burning, as along the western side of Lake Chichancanab. Other lakes and many areas in northwestern Petén along the Río San Pedro Mártir drainage are partly or wholly grass covered. Dry savannas, the origins of which are not clearly established, also occur in central Petén.

Forest Classification

Because of the declining rainfall from south to north in the peninsula, the forest composition and structure shows a gradation similar to that described by J. S. Beard for other parts of Middle America.[57] Beard's general sequence of forest types here applied to Yucatan, from south to north, includes Rain Forest, Evergreen Seasonal Forest, Semi-Evergreen Seasonal Forest, and Deciduous Seasonal Forest. In the extreme northwest and north, a category termed Scrub Forest has been added.

Although the average annual rainfall in most of Petén is 2,000 to 3,000 millimeters, the vegetation has been termed "quasi-rainforest" because of the irregular rainfall from year to year, which produces deciduousness in some species.[58] This forest is dominated by evergreen broadleaf trees of which an association of mahogany, sapodilla, and other species may comprise 75 percent of the forest.[59] Rain Forest is structured in three tree layers, or stories, and two lower plant stories. Mahogany (*caoba*) is one of the upper, or A story, dominants that reach 30 to 40 meters and have flattened crowns forming a discontinuous layer of foliage. The B story includes ramón, breadnut, sapodilla, and other species reaching to about 20 meters; these trees have tapering crowns that form a more continuous layer with few openings.[60] The lower, or C story, is made up mostly of young trees of the A and B stories, commonly with tapering crowns, and has the greatest density of foliage and branches that form a continuous layer with a height of about 5 to 15 meters. Many trees of the A and B stories are buttressed, that is, they have vertically enlarged roots spreading out from the base of the trunk. The D story may be poorly defined but includes various saplings, small palms, tall herbs, and large ferns. The E story, or ground layer, is composed largely of seedlings and herbaceous plants.

Mixed into these various stories are climbers or lianes, stranglers, epiphytes, parasites, and saprophytes. Most species of climbing plants are to be found in the tropics, and they are one of the most characteristic plant types of the tropical rain forest. Climbers are more abundant in openings and in young secondary forest, and most do not exceed about 70 meters in length.[61] Some epiphytes are climbers, and certain shrubs and the stranglers are intermediate between lianes and completely independent plants. Epiphytes, or air plants, are only attached to other plants and live on atmospheric moisture. They create interesting microenvironments by trapping humus and moisture and thus provide a home for frogs and insects. Epiphytes are widespread in the peninsula, even in the drier parts of northern Yucatan, particularly around cenotes and cave entrances where the humidity is high. The parasites include fungi, bacteria, and more or less woody, evergreen, shrublike, epiphytic semiparasites that occur in the A and B stories.

Evergreen Seasonal Forest is developed in areas having three months of lower rainfall, 50 to 100 millimeters each, but where the average annual total is over 1,800 millimeters, as in parts of Petén, southern Campeche, and southern Quintana Roo. The main differences between this type and Rain Forest are: (1) the tree stories are lower (at 30, 12 to 27, and 3 to 9 meters); (2) the A story is more discontinuous, and trees that are 3 meters in diameter or larger are uncommon; (3) large trees have lower branches; and (4) some dominants are deciduous or semideciduous in the A story. Buttresses are present on some trees of the A story, and lianes and epiphytes are common. The differences are slight, and this could be regarded as a "subformation" of the Rain Forest.

Semi-Evergreen Seasonal Forest is developed where the average annual rainfall is 800 to 1,300 millimeters and five months have only 25 to 100 millimeters of rain each. This would include parts of the southern and central portion of the peninsula and northern Quintana Roo and is roughly equivalent to the "monsoon forest" of South Asia. It has two tree stories, one at 20 to 26 meters with a fairly closed canopy and a lower story at 6 to 14 meters. Most mature trees average about one-half meter in diameter, branching is relatively low, crowns are umbrella-shaped, and in the upper story about 20 to 30 percent of the individuals are deciduous. The lower story is composed mostly of evergreen species, and lianes are common; some trees have buttresses, and some with thorny trunks are present.

Deciduous Seasonal Forest occurs where the average annual rainfall ranges from 800 to 1,300 millimeters but with two months each below 25 millimeters and a total of five months each below 100 millimeters. This type covers much of the central and northern portion of the peninsula. The forest is composed of two low tree stories, one reaching to 20 meters and the other from 3 to 10 meters. Branching is low; trunk diameters of mature trees are about one-half meter. Every dry season more than two-thirds of the upper-story trees shed their leaves, but the lower story is almost entirely evergreen and small-leaved. Buttressed trees are absent, some trees have thorny trunks, and lianes and epiphytes are scarce. In northern Yucatan, little mature Deciduous Seasonal Forest remains in the agricultural areas. In northeastern Yucatan state, most of the Deciduous Seasonal Forest is rapidly being converted to pastureland for cattle.

Scrub Forest is found in the areas having less than 800 millimeters of average annual rainfall and where four or five months each have less than 25 millimeters of rainfall. Scrub Forest extends inland a short distance from the northern and northwestern coasts where low rainfall is characteristic. Trees in the Scrub Forest reach a maximum of about seven or eight meters, and a dense undergrowth of evergreen and deciduous shrubs is typical.

Special Forest Types

Differences in soil parent material, moisture, and elevation have resulted in natural vegetation patterns that do not fit the preceding classification. These include the coastal mangrove forests, the vegetation of wet depressions, and the forests associated with the Maya Mountains.

Deciduous Seasonal Forest, near Tzucacab, southern Yucatan state. (Photo by Eugene Wilson)

Mangrove forest along the margin of the lagoon, La Ciénaga, grading into savannas with scattered tree islands (*petenes*), east of Celestún. (Photo by Eugene Wilson)

Scrub forest near Río Lagartos, northern Yucatan state. (Photo by Eugene Wilson)

Fringing parts of the coast from Laguna de Términos to the Gulf of Honduras is a dense growth of tropical evergreen species termed "mangrove" that has, in part, been described by Jonathan Sauer, R. C. West, N. P. Psuty, and B. G. Thom.[62] Mangrove refers to individual species and to communities composed of trees and shrubs that occupy coastal areas permanently or periodically covered with water, the main physiological trait being the ability of the plants to grow in variable salinity. Along the northwestern coast between Campeche City and Sisal is a seasonally flooded, low mangrove forest that extends inland several kilometers. Scattered in this forest are many "tree islands," or *petenes,* composed of taller trees that include both mangrove and dry forest species such as chicle.[63] These *petenes* exist on soil moisture derived from springs or from partially filled sinkholes, some of which are only shallow pools of water. Most of the wet season flooding is caused by fresh water spreading over the surface from the sinks, evidently as a result of the heavy rainfall farther inland. Little rain falls in this coastal zone because the sea breeze is usually strong enough to push the rain clouds inland. Along the northern coast of Yucatan and Quintana Roo states are other, more narrow zones of mangrove that include tree islands. These unusual vegetation features result from ground water and are thus indirectly the result of precipitation, which along this coast is only sufficient to support semiarid scrub forest.

Scattered through the interior of the peninsula are many depressions, some of which are more or less water-filled. These *bajos* and *aguadas* sometimes have open shallow water, and others are completely closed with dense vegetation that is different from the surrounding dry forest. Savannas also exist in what are possibly old channels of streams in western Petén and in several large depressions occupied in part by lakes.

A dry forest composed largely of pines is found in the Maya Mountains and extends into the coastal lowlands as well as into the limestone areas to the west and south in Petén. Pines have also been observed in large *bajos,* or depressions, in Petén.[64] The fire-tolerant sandpaper tree (*Curatella*) and the nance or pickle tree (*Byrsonima*) are scattered with oaks, composing a transitional broadleaf forest in parts of the Maya Mountains.[65]

Soils and Agriculture

Soil is a product of parent rock, climate, vegetation, slope and drainage, time, and human management. The nature of the parent rock will initially determine the mineralogy of the decomposed and disintegrated products that comprise the inorganic portion of the soil. Because most of the peninsula is composed of rocks with high calcium content, the inorganic soil minerals are primarily small amounts of insoluble residue remaining after the calcium and other soluble minerals have been removed. The residual material in most of Yucatan lies directly on the parent rock with little if any transition zone.

Small depressions have formed where solution has been locally more active at the surface. As a result, soil has accumulated in hollows and depressions, particularly where the land has been used for agriculture for many years. In this way soil erosion, even on gentle slopes, has occurred, leaving many bedrock exposures in fields. This is especially noticeable in the henequen region around Mérida, where in some places soil covers as little as 50 percent of the surface. The accumulation of soil materials derived from limestone weathering is even more pronounced in the cone karst areas of the peninsula, enriching the basins at the expense of the steep hill slopes. In the northern part of Yucatan, however, maize is cultivated even on the steepest slopes where soil has accumulated in small crevices and solution hollows.

Soil thickness in the north is not great, and rainfall, required for the breakdown of the surface rock, is lower there than in any other part of the peninsula. In spite of thin soil, low rainfall, and centuries of clearing and cultivation, the northwestern part of the peninsula is densely covered with plants that spring up in old fields and go through a succession leading to low forest. The question as to the fertility of these soils as related to the Mayan agricultural system will not be answered until precise measurements are systematically made before and after cultivation in a number of sample plots. Although the fertility of tropical soils in general is low, particularly if weathering is far advanced, the competition of weeds with planted crops plays an important role in determining how long a field will be used in a shifting agricultural system.

One study of northern Yucatan soils noted deficiencies of phosphorus, manganese, and potassium, although the soils were generally so rich that little, if any, fertilizer was required.[66] The soils of most of northern Yucatan are dominated by the mineral kaolinite.[67] Kaolinitic soils occur in places of low to moderate rainfall that are relatively well drained. In areas of heavy rainfall or where the drainage is poor, such as in basins, soils develop that have an abundance of the mineral montmorillonite. The latter soils are very sticky when wet because water can be taken into the mineral structure. When dry, montmorillonitic soils shrink and surface cracks are formed.

The common red color of well-drained soils is caused by the presence of small amounts of iron. Dark red soils usually have greater organic content, but when these are heated, they attain a brighter red color as the organic material is oxidized. Organic material is removed by burning in the Mayan agricultural cycle and through oxidation by exposure in cleared fields.

Palygorskite-sepiolite and mixed layer kaolinite-montmorillonite clays are also present in small amounts in northern Yucatan, where they occur both as thin beds in the Puuc and as massive lenses in several other localities, including Sacalum, Becal, and Hacienda Yo Kat near Ticul.

The palygorskite and mixed-layer clays have long been used in Mayan ceramics. Palygorskite (attapulgite) can be identified in fired pottery because it changes to enstatite, cristobalite, and frequently sillimanite, above 800°C. A greater variety of high-temperature minerals form when montmorillonite clays are heated, the composition depending upon the original minerals in the clay.[68]

Soil Classification

In a useful summary of the soils of the Yucatan Peninsula, Rayfred L. Stephens incorporated studies from Belize, Guatemala, and Mexico.[69] The many soil variations, as Stephens suggests, must be identified and mapped on a large scale throughout the peninsula if Mayan settlement history and ecology are to be well understood. General details of the Petén soils are available in the Guatemalan National Atlas, but most of the peninsula remains literally *terra incognita*. R. Ortiz Monasterio adopted some Mayan names for soils of northern Yucatan, most of which were noted earlier by Roys, as descriptive terms for common soils.[70] *Sahcab* (also *sascab*) is a "white earth"—a soft weathered limestone; *Kancab*, "yellow earth," is a name for a red loamy soil (in spite of the name); *Ek Lum* is a rich black soil, and *Tzekel* is a very stony soil. Ortiz used the combination *Kancab Kat* for a red clay soil overlying yellow clay and *Chichancanab* for a black topsoil overlying a yellowish loam, such as that found in old lake deposits of Laguna Chichancanab.

Under the new soil classification now used in the United States, soils of the peninsula fall into several categories, or soil orders.[71] Without a detailed study of their physical and chemical characteristics, however, it is not possible to classify the Yucatan soils accurately; this may never be done using the United States system since the countries in the peninsula could use their own, or an international system. In the United States classification, older terminology including "laterite," "rendzina," and "terra rosa" is no longer used.

The United States soil orders that would apply to soils of Yucatan include *Entisols, Histosols, Mollisols, Oxisols, Spodosols, Ultisols,* and *Vertisols.*[72] The *Entisols,* recent soils that have little or no horizon (horizontal layer) development, formerly were called "azonal" soils. In Yucatan, these include many residual soils from limestone weathering and recent alluvium. *Histosols,* or bog soils, are represented in swamps and contain organic materials in various stages of decomposition. *Mollisols* formerly were called rendzina, prairie, and chernozem. These have a surface horizon that is dark, strong in structure, and may be high in calcium and montmorillonite. *Oxisols* were formerly known as laterites and latosols. They are kaolinite-rich, have accumulated amorphous iron and aluminum oxides, have very little remaining weatherable material, and are low in bases. *Spodosols* were formerly known as podzol, ground water podzol, and brown podzolic. These soils have a leached topsoil depleted of bases and a subsoil in which clay, iron, and aluminum have accumulated. *Ultisols* were formerly called red and yellow podzolic, red-brown lateritic, and included some half-bog and planosols. These develop mainly under a humid subtropical climate and are characterized by a subsoil enriched with clay. Micas, feldspar, and some illite or montmorillonitic clay is present. *Vertisols,* formerly known as rendzina and grumusols, are associated with semiarid and subhumid climates. They develop from basic rocks, including basalt, limestone, and marl (limey clay). They are rich in montmorillonite and expand when wet and shrink when dry. The surface horizon is very dark, and below this is a zone of calcium accumulation. *Ultisols,* possibly *Spodosols* and *Oxisols,* would be more characteristic of areas in and around the Maya Mountains because of the type of parent materials and the relatively high elevations in that region. *Entisols, Vertisols,* and *Mollisols* would appear to comprise the greatest area in the peninsula.

In summary, it is clear that the Yucatan Peninsula has certain distinctive geographic features. Two physical characteristics are outstanding: the dominance of limestone and the tropical climate with a low rainfall period in winter. These affected the life style of the Maya from the time of his most ancient settlements in the area. Slash-and-burn agriculture was, as elsewhere in the Mayan lowlands, used in northern Yucatan, although the traditional clearing and burning of vegetation decreased both the soil moisture and its organic content. Chac, the rain god, became an important deity to the people in the northern part of the peninsula, a land of undependable rainfall. There was little from this harsh land for the Indians to trade in commercial activities except salt from coastal deposits and honey. The Maya built their great centers near cenotes or constructed underground rainwater storage cisterns in order to have a water supply. Over the centuries man, both ancient and modern, developed in this unusual environment a way of life with characteristics different from those of other regions of Middle America.

Yucatan lacks spectacular physical scenery; karst hills evoke little aesthetic wonder, and the large sinkholes and caverns, although interesting, are clearly not the attractions for the large number of visitors to the peninsula. More important are the dry, warm winters, fine beaches, clear, deep tropical waters, and major archaeological sites complemented by comfortable tourist facilities. Additional industries, possibly including sustained-yield forestry, improved commercial fishing, and more extensive irrigation agriculture, might be used to supplement regional income from tourism. Although the peninsula has modest resources, its further economic development may be decided more by the effort, imagination, and organization of its people than by environmental limitations.

NOTES

1. Diego de Landa, cited in Rayfred L. Stephens, "The Soils of Middle America and Their Relation to Indian Peoples and Cultures," *Handbook of Middle American Indians,* Vol. 1 (Austin: University of Texas Press, 1964), p. 304.

2. Peter Furley, "The University of Edinburgh British Honduras–Yucatan Expedition," *Geographical Journal* 134 (1968): 38.

3. John L. Stephens, *Incidents of Travel in Central America, Chiapas, and Yucatan,* 2 vols. (New York, 1841; London, 1854); *Incidents of Travel in Yucatan* (New York, 1843; reprint, New York: Dover Publications, 1963).

4. Angelo Heilprin, "Geological Researches in Yucatán," *Proceedings, Academy of Natural Science* (Philadelphia) 43 (1891): 136–58; Karl Sapper, "Sobre la Geografía Física y la Geología de la Península de Yucatán," *Instituto Geológico de México,* Boletín No. 3 (1896); Henry C. Mercer, *The Hill Caves of Yucatan* (Philadelphia: J. B. Lippincott Co., 1896; reprint Teaneck, N.J.: Zephyrus Press, 1975); David Casares, "A Notice of Yucatan with Some Remarks on Its Water Supply," *Proceedings, American Antiquarian Society,* n.s., 17 (1907): 207–30; Leon J. Cole, "The Caverns and People of Northern Yucatan," *Bulletin, American Geographical Society* 42 (1910): 321–36; Ramiro Robles Ramos, "Apuntes Sobre la Morfología de Yucatán," *Boletín, Sociedad Mexicana de Geografía y Estadística* 69 (1950): 27–106; Gabriel De Mendiolea, "Geografía de Yucatán," *Boletín, Sociedad Mexicana de Geografía y Estadística* 74 (1952): 161–238; Franz Termer, "Die Halbinsel Yucatan," *Petermanns Geographischer Mitteilungen,* Erganzungshefte 253 (1954); Sylvanus G. Morley, "The Inscriptions of Petén," *Carnegie Institution of Washington,* Publication 437, 5 vols. (1937–38); A. S. Pearse, Edwin P. Creaser, and F. G. Hall, "The Cenotes of Yucatan, A Zoological and Hydrographic Survey," *Carnegie Institution of Washington,* Publication 457 (1936); Ralph L. Roys, "The Political Geography of the Yucatan Maya," *Carnegie Institution of Washington,* Publication 613 (1957); Ralph L. Roys, "The Titles of Ebtún," *Carnegie Institution of Washington,* Publication 505 (1939); George C. Shattuck et al., "The Peninsula of Yucatan, Medical, Biological, Meteorological and Sociological Studies," *Carnegie Institution of Washington,* Publication 431 (1933); Robert C. West, ed., *Natural Environment and Early Cultures: Handbook of Middle American Indians,* Vol. 1 (Austin: University of Texas Press, 1964).

5. Charles F. Calkins, "Beekeeping in Yucatan: A Study in Historical-Cultural Zoogeography" (Dissertation, University of Nebraska, 1974); Roland E. P. Chardon, "Some Aspects of Plantation Agriculture in Yucatan" (Dissertation, University of Minnesota, 1961); Charles M. Croner, "Population Growth and Economic Development in Quintana Roo Territory, Mexico" (Master's thesis, Michigan State University, 1969); Raymond M. Curtis, "The Impact of Land Reform in the Monocrop Region of Yucatan, Mexico" (Dissertation, Brandeis University, 1971); William V. Davidson, "A Study of Settlement Patterns, Cozumel Island, Quintana Roo, Mexico" (Master's thesis, Memphis State University, 1967); Jack Dickerson, "A Comparative Morphology of Selected Towns in the State of Yucatan, Mexico" (Master's thesis, University of Alabama, 1969); J. C. Everitt, "Terra Incognita: An Analysis of a Geographical Anachronism and an Historical Accident, or Aspects of the Cultural Geography of British Honduras" (Master's thesis, Simon Fraser University, 1969); William A. Finch, Jr., "The Karst Landscape of Yucatan" (Dissertation, University of Illinois, 1964); Rodney C. Kirk, "San Antonio, Yucatan: From Henequen Hacienda to Plantation Ejido" (Dissertation, Michigan State University, 1975); R. Langemann, "The Development of a Model for the Life Cycle of a Closed Agricultural Colony: The Mennonite Colonies of South America. The Mennonite Colony of Spanish Lookout, British Honduras" (Master's thesis, Simon Fraser University, 1971); Douglas C. Odaffer, "The Three Capitals of British Honduras" (Master's thesis, California State University, San Francisco, 1970); Michael A. Romanov, "Yucatec Roads and the Orientation of the Maya World" (Dissertation, University of Oregon, 1973); B. L. Turner, II, "Prehistoric Intensive Agriculture in the Mayan Lowlands: New Evidence from the Río Bec Region" (Dissertation, University of Wisconsin, 1974); R. and Victor M. Urrutia, "Corn Production and Soil Fertility Changes under

Shifting Cultivation in Uaxactún, Guatemala'' (Master's thesis, University of Florida, 1967).

6. Alan P. Covich, "Stability of Molluscan Communities: A Paleolomnologic Study of Environmental Disturbance in the Yucatan Peninsula'' (Dissertation, Yale University, 1970); Donald O. Doehring and Joseph H. Butler, "Hydrogeologic Constraints on Yucatan's Development,'' *Science* 186 (1974): 591–95; W. C. Isphording, "The Physical Geology of Yucatan,'' *Transactions, Gulf Coast Association of Geological Societies* 25 (1975): 231–62; A. E. Weidie, ed., *Field Seminar on Water and Carbonate Rocks of the Yucatan Peninsula, Mexico* (New Orleans: New Orleans Geological Society, 1974); A. E. Weidie and W. C. Ward, eds., *Carbonate Rocks and Hydrogeology of the Yucatan Peninsula, Mexico* (New Orleans: New Orleans Geological Society, 1976); Dennis E. Puleston, "*Brosimum alicastrum* as a Subsistence Alternative for the Classic Maya of the Central Southern Lowlands'' (Master's thesis, University of Pennsylvania, 1968); Aaron Williams, Jr., "The Interpretation of Rainfall Patterns in Northern Yucatan Utilizing Meteorological Satellite Imagery,'' *Proceedings, Association American Geographers* 8 (1976): 15–19.

7. Hakon Wadell, "Physical-Geological Features of Petén, Guatemala,'' in Morley, "The Inscriptions of Petén,'' Vol. 4, p. 337.

8. F. Bonet and J. Butterlin, "Stratigraphy of the Northern Part of the Yucatan Peninsula,'' *Guidebook, Field Trip to Peninsula of Yucatan* (New Orleans: New Orleans Geological Society, 1962). An updated geologic map based on Bonet and Butterlin is E. López Ramos, "Península de Yucatán Geología Superficial,'' 1973, in Weidie and Ward, eds., *Carbonate Rocks,* p. 3.

9. Carta Geológica de la República Mexicana, 1:2,000,000 México, D. F. (1968). Instituto Geográfico Nacional, *Atlas Nacional de Guatemala* (Guatemala City, 1972).

10. W. C. Isphording, personal communication, 1975.

11. W. C. Isphording and E. M. Wilson, "The Relationship of 'Volcanic Ash', Sak Luum, and Palygorskite in Northern Yucatan Maya Ceramics,'' *American Antiquity* 39 (1974): 485.

12. A. E. Weidie, "Note on the Regional Geology of Yucatan Peninsula,'' in Weidie, ed., *Field Seminar on Yucatan,* pp. 2–6.

13. Clinton Edwards, "Geographical Reconnaissance in the Yucatan Peninsula'' (Department of Geography, University of California, Berkeley, 1954), p. 4.

14. Ibid., p. 8.

15. Casares, "A Notice of Yucatan,'' p. 219; Termer, "Die Halbinsel Yucatan,'' p. 9.

16. Furley, "British Honduras–Yucatan Expedition,'' pp. 48–50.

17. W. C. Isphording and E. M. Wilson, "Weathering Processes and Physical Subdivisions of Northern Yucatan,'' *Proceedings, Association American Geographers* 5 (1973): 119.

18. William J. Folan, personal communication, September 1975.

19. M. Herak and V. T. Stringfield, *Karst: Important Karst Regions of the Northern Hemisphere* (New York: Elsevier Publishing Company, 1972); J. N. Jennings, *Karst* (Cambridge, Mass.: M.I.T. Press, 1971); M. M. Sweeting, *Karst Landforms* (New York: Columbia University Press, 1973).

20. Finch, "Karst Landscape of Yucatan,'' p. 21.

21. Stephens, *Incidents of Travel in Yucatan,* p. 185.

22. H. E. D. Pollock, et al., "Mayapán, Yucatan, Mexico," *Carnegie Institution of Washington*, Publication 619 (1962), p. 2.

23. Roys, "Titles of Ebtún," pp. 5, 10-14.

24. Dean E. Arnold, "Ethnomineralogy of Ticul, Yucatan Potters: Etics and Emics," *American Antiquity* 36 (1971): 27.

25. Mercer, *Hill Caves of Yucatan;* R. T. Hatt et al., "Faunal and Archaeological Researches in Yucatan Caves," *Cranbrook Institute of Science, Bulletin 33* (Bloomfield Hills, Mich., 1953).

26. James Reddell, personal correspondence, February 1975 and December 1975.

27. J. E. S. Thompson, "The Role of Caves in Maya Culture," in *Mitteilungen aus dem Museum fur Volkerkunde und Vorgeschichte in Hamburg* 25 (1959); Festband Franz Termer, p. 125; J. E. S. Thompson, "Introduction to the Reprint Edition," in Mercer, *Hill Caves of Yucatan,* pp. vii-xliv.

28. E. Wyllys Andrews, IV, "Exploration in the Gruta de Chac, Yucatan, Mexico," *Middle American Research Institute,* Publication 31 (New Orleans: Tulane University, 1965), p. 12.

29. Fresh water from sinkholes and smaller springs is common close to sea level on the west and north coasts. Submarine springs also occur just offshore. See note 15.

30. Stephens, *Incidents of Travel in Yucatan,* p. 185; Casares, "A Notice of Yucatan," pp. 220-23.

31. H. E. D. Pollock, "Architectural Notes on Some Chenes Ruins," in W. R. Bullard, Jr., ed., Monographs and Papers in Maya Archaeology, *Peabody Museum, Harvard University, Papers* 61 (1970): 7.

32. Doehring and Butler, "Hydrogeologic Constraints," p. 591.

33. Shattuck et al., "The Peninsula of Yucatan," p. 462.

34. L. J. Cole, "The Caverns and People of Northern Yucatan," *Bulletin, American Geographical Society* 42 (1910): 328-34.

35. E. H. Thompson, "The Chultunes of Labná," *Memoirs, Peabody Museum, Harvard University,* Vol. I, no. 3 (1897).

36. George W. Brainerd, "The Archaeological Ceramics of Yucatan," *Anthropological Records, University of California Publications,* Vol. 19 (1958), p. 30.

37. Ibid., p. 95.

38. Isphording, "Geology of Yucatan," p. 251.

39. In Shattuck et al., "The Peninsula of Yucatan," Map I, the true extent of the Sierrita de Ticul is in error, and the Sierrita and Bolonchén districts are incorrectly shown as one hill area. This was also incorrectly shown by E. Raisz, *Landforms of Mexico* (1964).

40. Wadell, "Physical-Geological Features," p. 339; Instituto Geográfico Nacional, *Atlas,* "Mapa Geológico," p. 3.6.

41. Jennings, *Karst,* p. 187.

42. Termer, "Die Halbinsel Yucatan," p. 62.

43. Casares, "A Notice of Yucatan," p. 210; Karl Sapper, "Geología de la Península de Yucatán," *Enciclopedia Yucatanense,* Vol. 1 (México, 1944-47), p. 18.

44. Instituto Geográfico Nacional, *Atlas,* "Mapa Geológico," p. 3.6.

45. Wadell, "Physical-Geographic Features," p. 337.

46. See map sheet 2266 IV, *Flores,* 1/50,000, Instituto Geográfico Nacional, Guatemala, C.A., 1969, and adjacent sheets for cone karst south of Flores.

47. Williams, "Rainfall Patterns in Northern Yucatan," pp. 15–19.

48. Storm data 1886–1958 are taken from United States Department of Commerce, "North Atlantic Tropical Cyclones," *Technical Paper No. 36* (Washington, D.C.: U.S. Government Printing Office, 1959); 1959–75 data are from *Weatherwise,* Vols. 13–29 (1960–76).

49. Shattuck et al., "The Peninsula of Yucatan," p. 418; R. C. West, N. P. Psuty, and B. G. Thom, *The Tabasco Lowlands of Southeastern Mexico,* Coastal Studies Series, No. 27 (Baton Rouge: Louisiana State University Press, 1969), p. 8.

50. Furley, "British Honduras–Yucatan Expedition," p. 38.

51. C. L. Lundell, "The Vegetation of the Petén," *Carnegie Institution of Washington,* Publication 478 (1937), cited in Philip L. Wagner, "Natural Vegetation of Middle America," *Handbook of Middle American Indians* (Austin: University of Texas Press, 1964) Vol. 1, pp. 230–32.

52. Ibid.

53. J. C. Bequaert, "Botanical Notes from Yucatan," in Shattuck et al., "The Peninsula of Yucatan," pp. 509–13.

54. Charles M. Croner, "Population Growth," p. 64.

55. Ibid., p. 69.

56. Ibid., p. 72.

57. J. S. Beard, "Climax Vegetation in Tropical America," *Ecology* 25 (1944): 125–58; "The Classification of Tropical American Vegetation Types," *Ecology* 36 (1955): 89–100, cited in Wagner, "Natural Vegetation of Middle America," p. 218. A modified classification used here is taken from P. W. Richards, *The Tropical Rain Forest* (Cambridge: Cambridge University Press, 1964), pp. 317–21.

58. Wagner, "Natural Vegetation of Middle America," p. 228.

59. Ibid.

60. Ibid.

61. Richards, *Tropical Rain Forest,* p. 102.

62. Jonathan Sauer, *Geographic Reconnaissance of Seashore Vegetation along the Mexican Gulf Coast,* Coastal Studies Series, No. 21 (Baton Rouge: Louisiana State University Press, 1967); West, Psuty, and Thom, *Tabasco Lowlands;* B. G. Thom, "Mangrove Ecology and Deltaic Geomorphology," *Journal of Ecology* 55 (1967): 301–43.

63. Edwards observed these tree islands and thought that they might be undisturbed remnants of the northern Yucatan dry forest ("Geographical Reconnaissance in the Yucatan Peninsula," p. 6).

64. B. L. Turner, personal correspondence, 1977.

65. Wagner, "Natural Vegetation of Middle America," p. 259; Furley, "British Honduras–Yucatan Expedition," p. 42.

66. Stephens, "Soils of Middle America," p. 303.

67. This summary of soil·mineralogy is taken from Wayne C. Isphording, "Weathering of Yucatan Limestones: The Genesis of Terra Rosas," in Weidie, ed., *Field Seminar on Yucatan,* pp. 78–93.

68. Wayne C. Isphording, "Combined Thermal and X-Ray Diffraction Technique for Identification of Ceramic Temper and Paste Minerals," *American Antiquity* 39 (1974): 477–83.

69. Stephens, "Soils of Middle America," pp. 265–315.

70. R. Ortiz Monasterio, "Reconocimiento Agrológico Regional del Estado de Yucatán," *Boletín, Sociedad Mexicana de Geografía y Estadística* 69 (1950): 245–324, cited in Stephens, "Soils of Middle America," p. 303; Roys, "Titles of Ebtún," pp. 55–56.

71. U.S. Department of Agriculture, *Soil Classification: A Comprehensive System, Seventh Approximation* (Washington, D.C.: U.S. Government Printing Office, 1960).

72. Summary statements of these soil orders are taken from R. L. Donahue, et al., *Soils: An Introduction to Soils and Plant Growth* (Englewood Cliffs, N.J.: Prentice-Hall, Inc., 1971), pp. 104–29.

CHAPTER II

THE MAYA OF YUCATAN

Paul H. Nesbitt

The Yucatecan Maya are a warm, friendly, and handsome people who deeply believe in moderation and cooperation, but are not always practical. Today they barely subsist in a land that is flat, arid, streamless, and covered with scrub growth. Most have no vehicles or even draft animals. They carry on their backs what they need to survive—wood for their fires, palm leaves for their thatched huts. Old men trudge along the sides of the highway, backs bent under the weight of their bundles of sticks. These old men, these human beasts of burden, are the direct descendants of a great and proud people, who built a rich civilization upon a land that is harsh and often forbidding.

Our knowledge of the people and their culture before the Spanish Conquest stems from many different sources: preconquest native manuscripts or codices, native historical records, and anthropological sources—archaeology, ethnology, and linguistics. The native codices include the Codex Dresdensis, the Codex Peresianus, and the Codex Tro-Cortesianus. These manuscripts chronicle the history and the traditions of the period just before the arrival of the Europeans. Native historical documents such as the *Books of Chilam Balam* and *Popul-Vuh* provide valuable information as do the hieroglyphics found on stelae and monuments. Eyewitness accounts of the sixteenth century, among them Bishop Diego de Landa's description of the northern Maya, provide vivid firsthand glimpses of the Yucatecan people in the final hours of their independence.

For more than a hundred years, archaeologists have unearthed artifacts, stelae, temples, and other monuments that can be dated and placed in time sequence. Comparison is made with remains from other areas to deduce early patterns of trade and influence. Art historians study and define the main stages in the development of art styles. Linguists infer prehistoric tribal movements and language relationships by comparing modern Indian languages and their distribution with known earlier patterns. Finally, the study of the modern-day Mayan people and their culture by ethnologists furnishes clues valuable in reconstructing the social and economic organization of their preconquest ancestors. As anthropological research continues, knowledge of Yucatan's past is considerably modified and refined. So far, it has revealed more than two thousand years of complex human interrelationships and events that culminated in the splendor that so awed the Spanish conquistadores.

Physically, the Maya can be classified as members of the Mongoloid racial stock, the original members of which migrated to the New World sometime around 20,000 B.C. Both archaeological evidence and human skeletal remains testifying to great antiquity have been uncovered in the northern and southern parts of the United States and in Mexico. In general, the early migrants were characterized by short to medium stature, narrow nose, and head shape ranging from mesocephalic to brachycephalic. At Tepexpan, Mexico, a fossilized human skeleton was found in the ten-thousand-year-old lake sediment of Pleistocene age, and at nearby Santa Isabel, Iztapan stone artifacts of human manufacture were found associated with the bones of the now extinct mammoth (Heizer and Cook, 1959). A study of these and other skeletal remains reveals no evidence of a physical type that is not Homo sapiens—all are modern man of the Mongoloid stock.

One of the best documented sources of information of the prehistoric Mayan physical type is from excavations at Zaculeu, the ancient capital of the Mam-speaking Maya of Huehuetenango, Guatemala (Stewart, 1953). The remains of more than three hundred individuals were recovered. Most of the crania were artificially deformed—either conspicuously (fronto-vertico-occipital) or inconspicuously (psuedo-circular). All were brachycephalic and high-headed. A high percentage of the crania had ear exostoses, an abnormal spur or bony outgrowth. Several long bones, particularly the tibia, showed a pathological condition known as periositis, inflammation of the periosteum membrane. The resulting lesions may represent bone syphilis. There is also evidence of arthritis—tough, fibrous connective tissue covering many bones except at the joints. Around 5 percent showed dental mutilations of many different styles.

How do these Zaculeu observations relate to the physical anthropology of the present-day Maya? In 1948, Charles Weer Goff conducted a program of anthropometric measurements, indexes, and morphological and medical observations on sixty-one adult Mayan Indians. This study (Goff, 1948) revealed that they were primarily mesocephalic, but there was little artificial cranial deformation. Based on the average length of the extremities or long bones and their relation to overall height, the Zaculeu skeletons exceeded the body height of the modern Maya by two or three inches. In general, however, the Maya of Yucatan today are physically similar to those ancient wanderers who arrived in Mesoamerica some ten thousand years ago.

Although the Maya are essentially homogeneous physically, there is marked linguistic diversity. In the sixteenth century throughout most of Yucatan, Chiapas, western Honduras, and Guatemala there was a belt of closely related Mayan languages. According to J. Eric Thompson, there are fifteen Mayan languages or major dialects still spoken and two more that are now extinct. In the northern peninsula today only Yucatec (often called Maya) is spoken. As one travels southward in the lowlands there is a gradual and uniform transition from Yucatec to Tzotzil. In the highlands of Guatemala the principal Mayan languages are Quiché, Cakchiquel, Mam, Kekchí, and Pokomán. The transition is so gradual that it is impossible to say where one language stops and another begins. The Mayan dialects are not closely related to any other languages of Mexico or Central America (Thompson, 1966).

The early period of migration was a hunting and food-gathering phase, comparable in some ways to the late paleolithic era of Europe. Man preyed upon the mammoth and other large animals that roamed the cool, moist landscape of central Mexico. Around 7000 B.C., a warmer, dryer climate doomed the mammoth to extinction. The means of livelihood of the hunter and his life-style underwent marked change. Man progressed gradually from a hunting economy to the gathering of wild food plants and to the beginnings of agriculture. Shortly after 6000 B.C., maize, beans, chili, and squash made their appearance, being independently domesticated in widely separated areas of Middle America.

The Preclassic Period

The Formative or Preclassic period began around 2000 B.C. The criteria of its inception are pottery and settled village life based on farming. We do not know as yet where this successful life-style was first achieved, but it seems likely, based on geographical distribution, that this was an achievement of southern Mesoamerica. All Mesoamerican cultures shared certain characteristics during the period of their formation. The maize-beans-squash-chili food complex appears to have been basic to all regional cultures, as do pottery, chipped stone tools, and ground stone tools that are found in all regional areas. In addition to similarities in subsistence, technology, and artifacts, there were other shared traits such as platform mounds, ceremonial structures built atop the mounds, and the arrangement of mounds around plazas. Further indications of common bond are seen in the 260-day sacred calendar, calendrical hieroglyphics, and the representations of deities or mythological figures in the form of serpents and jaguars.

About 1000 B.C., in the region of present-day Vera Cruz, the Olmecs built the first large-scale religious centers. The Olmec culture is best represented at the archaeological sites of San Lorenzo and La Venta. The earliest occupation was at San Lorenzo about 1500 B.C., but it is not until the Chicharras phase (1250–1150 B.C.) that the Olmec culture can first be recognized. During this period, there were introduced a distinctive pottery, figurines, monuments, and monumental stone carvings. Later (1150–900 B.C.), a great variety of new raw materials including obsidian, serpentine, and jade were imported and made into artifacts that were widely traded and carried throughout Mesoamerica. The impact of Olmec culture in Chiapas, Guatemala, and other parts of Mesoamerica was accomplished by the spread of their religious beliefs portrayed in a distinctive art style. The central theme of Olmec art is the were-jaguar, a jaguar combined with human baby features. Also, colossal human heads, altars, figures, stelae, and the like were all carved in a unique manner. It is possible that the Olmec contributed the symbol for zero or completion, since they also used bars and dots in place numeration, but there is no definite evidence that they had glyphs in the Preclassic period.

Formative remains are distributed over a wide area of Mesoamerica, including Chiapas, the Caribbean and Pacific coastal slopes of Guatemala, the Guatemalan highlands, and, to a lesser degree, the southern and northern lowlands. Some important centers during the Preclassic era were La Victoria on the Pacific coast of Guatemala; Izapa in southern Chiapas; Kaminaljuyú in the Guatemalan highlands; Dzibilchaltún in Yucatan; and Uaxactún and Tikal in the Petén. Each contributed culturally to the Classic period that was to emerge several centuries later.

La Victoria, dating back to 1400 B.C., had houses built on low platforms of earth, fine quality pottery, maize cultivated on the alluvial flats, and a rich supply of fish and shell foods from the coastal estuaries. Izapa, in Chiapas, was a large center of activity in late Preclassic times and boasted of eighty temple pyramids arranged around courts and plazas (Weaver, 1972). Among its most outstanding remains are stelae, altars, and gigantic stones covered with elaborate carved composition recording mythological episodes. The influence of Izapa is reflected in Pacific coast sites as well as at locations in the highlands of Guatemala. The most extraordinary advances during the Preclassic period were made at Kaminaljuyú, which was the scene of great activity throughout Preclassic and Classic times (Kidder, Jennings, and Shook, 1946). During the period 600 B.C. to A.D. 300, religious architecture flourished. Temple pyramids, which in some instances served also as burial mounds, were arranged along both sides of a long rectangular plaza. Multiple staircases led to hutlike temples atop sixty-foot-high pyramids. The pyramidal mounds were not built to their maximum height in one construction stage, but, following a common practice of Mesoamerican builders, were enlarged periodically. One pyramidal mound contained seven previous structures (Shook and Kidder, 1952). The glory and luxury evident from the architecture, stone sculpture, stelae, and ceramics signify a high degree of social stratification with power and prestige in the hands of an elite few. About 600 B.C. remains of Mamom ceramics (Preclassic) are present at both Uaxactún and Tikal in the jungle rainforest of northeastern Petén. At Tikal's North Acropolis, a large platform of early Classic temples conceals structures dating from 200 B.C., and pottery at the bedrock level dates the first inhabitants at around 600 B.C. It is in this southern lowland area that the distinctive traits of the Mayan Classic civilization began to emerge. The corbeled vault makes its appearance as well as ceremonial centers, polychrome pottery, and stone monuments bearing hieroglyphic inscriptions and calendrical dates. All demonstrate a gradual evolution toward a distinctive Classic Mayan culture. Though certain roots may well stem from Olmec-Izapa–Kaminaljuyú traditions, the Maya in the Petén experienced vigorous development on their own as exemplified by such early centers as Uaxactún and Tikal.

The Classic Period

The general blending of elements that formed the Classic Mayan culture crystallized around the third century A.D. into a high civilization that was marked by a distinctive art style, the corbeled vault, mathematical concepts including the zero, and an accurate calendrical system. An advanced writing method was also a part of the cultural heritage of these early people. As a developmental stage, the Classic period is characterized by the spectacular growth of monumental architecture, consisting of pyramids, temples, ball courts, and ritual chambers grouped in planned complexes around plazas.

The major early Classic cities were in the Petén lowlands and along the Usumacinta River. Urban/ceremonial centers developed and flourished at Tikal, Uaxactún, Palenque, Piedras Negras, and numerous smaller settlements. At Tikal, the largest of all Mayan cities, intensive construction actually was initiated in the late Preclassic period. The earliest known dated monument of the southern lowland Maya, Stela 29, was found there in an ancient refuse dump. It bears a date equated to A.D. 292. This Classic city which lasted for approximately six hundred years covered an area of about twenty to twenty-five square miles, and some three thousand separate constructions lie within the six-square-mile heart of the ruins.

At one time these monumental cities of the Petén were referred to as the "Old Kingdom," and archaeologists did not believe that the Maya moved into the northern regions of the Yucatan Peninsula until a later date. It is now clear, however, that Mayan-speaking people had settled in Yucatan as early as the Preclassic period. Dzibilchaltún, situated about ten miles north of Mérida, was one of the largest cities in Yucatan and probably also the oldest. Occupied as early as 800 B.C., it was contemporaneous with many of the Preclassic and Classic centers of the southern lowland area. The archaeological zone covers more than fifteen square miles and includes remains of several hundred temple and dwelling sites. The earlier Preclassic remains there consist of distinctive ceramics that show little similarity to that of other lowland sites and would appear to represent a local development. The people built mud-walled houses, but nothing at that time was distinctly Mayan in appearance (Andrews, 1960, 1965). During the Classic period, there appeared at Dzibilchaltún a unique structure of the northern Mayan area, the Temple of the Seven Dolls, named for a cache of clay figurines discovered in the floor of the temple. Its design is unusual: it is the only structure in the northern Mayan area that has windows. Another unusual feature of this building is its crowning tower. Although roof crests are a common feature of Mayan architecture, a superstructure in the form of a tower is rare. Excavations indicate that there was continuous occupation of the city from Preclassic times down to the arrival of the Spanish (Andrews, 1960, 1965). Although there are indications of other early settlements in Yucatan in addition to Dzibilchaltún, most of the ceremonial centers of that region were Late Classic and Postclassic, dating between A.D. 900 and 1500.

Izamal, situated about fifty miles east of Dzibilchaltún, emerged during the Classic period as a rich center because of the excellent salt beds on the nearby coast. With one of the largest pyramids in Yucatan, Kinich-Kakmó, Izamal was well known as a religious center. It had a shrine honoring the sky god Itzamná, to which large numbers came to be cured of disease (Weaver, 1972). The settlement prospered from Classic times until the fall of Mayapán in the fifteenth century A.D. At about the same time as the founding of Izamal, a number of important

Panoramic view of Uxmal, with the Nunnery on the upper left and the Pyramid of the Magician on the upper right. The House of the Turtles is in the center, and to the far right is a corner of the Governor's Palace. (Photo by Andy Dees)

Temple of the Seven Dolls at Dzibilchaltún. (Photo by Edward Moseley)

Pyramid at Izamal, one of the largest in Mexico, site of a shrine honoring the sky god Itzamná. The city of Izamal later became one of the most important Roman Catholic religious centers and home of the Virgin of Izamal. (Aerial photo courtesy of Edward Kurjack)

Detail of the ornamental stonework which forms the façade of the Nunnery at Uxmal. (Photo by Joel Whitman)

The Caracol or Observatory at Chichén Itzá. (Photo by Edward Terry)

cities were being constructed in the Puuc range to the south, a region of low hills covered with ridges of limestone and scrub vegetation. Two of these important centers were Sayil and Kabah, both of which had elaborately decorated structures.

The most imposing city in the Puuc region is Uxmal, a late Classic site situated approximately fifty miles south of Mérida. The well-preserved buildings, in the so-called Puuc architectural style, are among the most striking of Yucatan. A late Classic settlement, Uxmal is not only the most compact and uniform of Mayan cities, but it is also the most beautiful. The eight groups of buildings that have been restored cover an area of about ten acres. At what appears to be the administrative center of the city is the Palace of the Governor. This structure, 320 feet long, 40 feet wide, and 26 feet high, rests on an artificially constructed mound 50 feet high, having stone steps that lead to the summit. The entire structure is covered with a veneer of ornamented stone. The stones were carved first in a series of set patterns and then laid in different ways to form a variety of designs, giving the effect of an intricate mosaic. The exact function of the palace is not known, but it probably served some religious purpose; it seems unlikely that it ever housed a governor.

North of the palace is the ball court, spaced between the walls of two low platform structures. A stone ring was set into the wall on each side of the court. The object of the game was to pass a small rubber ball through one of the rings. Just beyond the ball court is the Nunnery, an irregular-shaped quadrangle enclosed by a low range of buildings, each with a different motif. One building is multistoried and has an intricate geometrical ornamentation; another is embellished with the long snout of Chac, the rain god; a third has as its decorative motif the simple house of the common people—rectangular in shape and identical in its features to the pole, lime, and thatch houses of the present-day Maya.

Chichén Itzá, which rose to greatness in Postclassic times, was occupied in the late Classic period. A section of the site, referred to popularly as "Old Chichén," contains several structures that have definite affiliations with those of the Puuc style found at Uxmal and other cities to the south. In this sector was discovered the only long count date known for the northern region of Yucatan, equated to A.D. 879. One unusual and important structure is the Caracol, a tenth-century round tower, thought to have been an astronomical observatory. It has a central core of masonry in which there is a spiral stairway winding up to a small observation chamber near the top of the tower. The Caracol was one of the last truly Mayan buildings erected, for central Mexican influences were to emerge in the following period.

Postclassic Developments

Beginning in the ninth century A.D. and lasting for approximately one hundred and fifty years, the Classic Mayan centers of the southern lowlands began to be abandoned. The causes for this mass exodus remain a mystery although various explanations have been offered (Morley, 1956; Thompson, 1966; Willey, 1971). Among these are sudden and violent natural catastrophes, droughts, crop failures, increased population that placed a burden on the productive capacities of land and man, rebellion against exploitation of the lower classes, and related social and cultural factors. None of these explanations is fully satisfactory; there were probably multiple reasons for the decline. With the abandonment of the Petén cities between A.D. 900 and 1050, the northern portions of the Yucatan Peninsula greatly increased in importance as a cultural region.

The Putún Maya occupied the southern part of the present-day state of Campeche, the east coast of the peninsula, and Cozumel (Thompson, 1966). Around A.D. 920 a branch of the Putún, called Itzá, established their hegemony at Chichén Itzá. They were no doubt attracted to that location because of the two large cenotes there, especially the "sacred" cenote. The name of the site prior to the arrival of the Itzá is not surely known, but Thompson suggests that it may have been Uncyabnal. The invaders, of course, gave their name to Chichén Itzá, a term meaning "at the well of the Itzá" (Thompson, 1966). This huge sinkhole measures about two hundred feet in diameter and is seventy feet deep. Around it had evolved a cult that had already given the site renown throughout Yucatan. Offerings were thrown into its waters; most often these were objects of material or ceremonial value, but evidently there were also some human sacrifices. This religious practice was probably in full swing prior to the Itzá, but received fresh impetus after their arrival. The sacred cenote continued to draw pilgrims until the Spaniards succeeded in suppressing the cult around A.D. 1560. These Itzá settlers, though of Mayan origin, are credited with the introduction of many elements of pre-Toltec Mexican influences into Yucatan, such as the representations of the rain god Tláloc at Uxmal and carvings of *atlatls* (weapons associated with central Mexico) on the door jambs of Kabah (Weaver, 1972; Barrera Vásquez and Rendón, 1969).

A second group of Putún Itzá, accompanied by Kukulcán and his band of Toltec warriors, migrated to Chichén Itzá in A.D. 987 (Thompson, 1970; Weaver, 1972). The arrival of this second wave resulted in a building surge. A whole new section was added to the city in the image of Tula, the Toltecs' original homeland in what is now the state of Hidalgo, Mexico. The buildings erected at Chichén Itzá after this invasion are predominantly Toltec in design but executed in traditional Mayan technique. Earlier ceremonial structures were built with thick walls and narrow doorways, but the Toltecs introduced a new concept in architecture that reflected religious influences. Buildings and courts were widely dispersed and more open for effective mass communication among the populace, the priests, and the gods.

At the center of Toltec-Chichén is the temple-pyramid of Kukulcán, usually called the Castillo. It is an impressive monument—nearly square at the base, with broad and steep stairways leading up from all four sides. The summit provides a commanding view of the entire city. A blend of Toltec and Mayan features is seen in the temple—corbeled vaulting combined with bas-relief carvings of Toltec warriors. Within the pyramid, a temple attributed to the earlier

Itzá, is a stone throne in the form of a red jaguar, with eyes of jade and fangs of shell (Weaver, 1972). From the summit of the Castillo one has a clear view of the Temple of the Warriors and can readily see that its architectural plan resembles that of the Temple of Quetzalcóatl at Tula. Erected on a low platform mound, this magnificent structure was dedicated to Kukulcán (Morley, 1956). At the top of the wide staircase is a Chacmool, a life-size Toltec stone figure in reclining position, legs flexed, hands holding a receptacle on the abdomen, and head turned to one side. Inside the building is an earlier structure, called the Temple of Chacmool, with bench murals depicting militaristic scenes. In a great open plaza adjacent to the Temple of the Warriors is the Group of the Thousand Columns, with each pillar carved on all four sides depicting warrior figures in Toltec style. In fact, the Toltec influences at Chichén Itzá are evident in a variety of forms but with distinctive Mayan traits. These include temple structures with interior columns, long colonnaded courts, processions of warriors, Chacmools, jaguars, eagles, skulls, human hearts, and murals depicting militaristic scenes (Weaver, 1972). One of the most striking features of the complex is the Temple of the Jaguars and the adjoining ball court, which is the most magnificent in Mesoamerica.

There seems to be little doubt that once established at Chichén Itzá the Mexicans soon managed to dominate the entire northern part of Yucatan. Their impact was felt as far south as the Puuc area, where Uxmal and neighboring sites were abandoned. Although the Mayan aristocracy seems to have maintained its identity during the Toltec period, it was subsequently lost. By the time of the arrival of the Spanish in the sixteenth century, all of the upper class claimed Mexican descent (Weaver, 1972). Between the eleventh and thirteenth centuries A.D., however, the Mexican elements at Chichén Itzá seem to have been completely absorbed into the traditional Mayan way of life, and the inhabitants of the city came to be referred to merely as the Itzás.

Around the year A.D. 987, a number of virtually autonomous cities in the northern region formed a loose political relationship or confederation called the League of Mayapán. Consisting of Uxmal, Izamal, Chichén Itzá, and, of course, Mayapán, it tended to dominate political affairs for some two hundred years, down to 1204 (Barrera Vásquez and Rendón, 1969). Out of this alliance emerged another family of Itzá lineage, the Cocoms, who became very influential. This group, utilizing Mayapán as its base of operations, forced the Itzás to abandon Chichén around A.D. 1224. The exact sequence of events is unknown, but it was in some way related to the famous legend of Hunac Ceel, a Tabascan mercenary imported by the Cocoms. He became a hero by surviving a sacrificial plunge into the cenote of Chichén Itzá and bringing to his people the prophecy of the rain god Chac that crops would be abundant in the coming year. Soon after this dramatic experience, Hunac Ceel became ruler of Mayapán and through trickery pitted the leaders of Chichén Itzá and Izamal against each other. The resulting struggle bought about the downfall of both cities. The once powerful rulers of Chichén were forced to migrate south into the Petén, where they settled on the small islands of Lakes Petén and Ekixil (Thompson, 1966).

The Castillo or Temple of Kukulcán. Note the head of the feathered serpent in the right foreground which is a part of the Temple of the Warriors. (Photo by Edward Terry)

The Chacmool at the entrance to the Temple of the Warriors at Chichén Itzá. (Photo by Joel Whitman)

The Cocoms continued to rule northern Yucatan down to the middle of the fifteenth century. Aided by warlike Mexicans from Tabasco, they dominated the region both in political and religious matters. The rulers kept a tight control over their empire by the simple expedient of forcing the head chiefs of the various city states to reside in Mayapán. Presumably, states dared not revolt with their leaders held as permanent hostages. How many Mayan states were controlled by Mayapán is not certain; Thompson (1966) believes the number was about one dozen. Mayapán eventually covered an area of about two square miles and had a population of some eight to ten thousand inhabitants. A high wall that had but two entrances surrounded the entire town. Its primary purpose was for defense, but it also provided the Cocoms a tight control over the inhabitants of the sprawling city. Cultural manifestations degenerated greatly from those that had been evident at Chichén Itzá. The religious buildings were small and poorly constructed with crudely assembled columns, and there appears to have been no ball court. In fact, the city seems to have grown without any discernible master plan (Weaver, 1972).

Meanwhile, another Mexican group known as the Xiu had wandered about the peninsula and settled in the region of the abandoned city of Uxmal between A.D. 987 and 1007 (Barrera Vásquez and Rendón, 1969). They formed alliances with neighboring towns and with their cooperation began to assert themselves in political affairs. Later, establishing their administrative center in the town of Maní, the Xiu became second in power only to the Cocoms. It was very natural that an intense rivalry and hostility developed between the two groups. This animosity continued for some 250 years, down to 1441. In that year, goaded beyond further endurance by Cocom tyranny, the other Mayan cities united under the leadership of the Xiu rulers of Maní, sacked Mayapán, and slew the Cocom ruler and his sons. After this successful uprising, the victorious chieftains withdrew to their respective provinces and towns.

With the downfall of Mayapán, all centralized government in Yucatan came to an end, and the once great Cocom empire dissolved into its component parts. Political disorganization and decay followed; all the great ceremonial centers were abandoned save Dzibilchaltún, which managed to maintain itself, though with little distinction. Yucatan fell apart, resulting in some eighteen or nineteen petty provinces. These included Sotuta, where the descendants of the Cocoms continued to rule, Maní, and T-Hoo (present-day Mérida). The city-states, urged on by ancient feuds and jealousies, waged incessant warfare against one another. These conflicts, plus such diverse calamities as famines, hurricanes, and a smallpox epidemic in 1514, reduced the country to political chaos and eased the way for final conquest by the Spanish (Sotelo Regil, 1963; Weaver, 1972).

Cultural Achievements of the Maya

In appraising the civilization of any people, the true measure is not simply the sum total of their achievements but their accomplishments in terms of their technological level—in other words, what they did with what they had. In many ways, the Maya were a Stone Age people. Though they had agriculture and learned how to make and preserve fire, they had no metal tools, no beasts of burden, no wheeled vehicles, no true arch, and no potter's wheel. Yet the Maya built monumental civil and religious structures and were supreme masters of sculpture, painting, the lapidary art, and ceramics. When we consider their abstract mental achievements, such as writing, astronomy, mathematics, the development of a calendar and chronology, and the recording of historical events, the Maya had no equals anywhere in ancient America.

It cannot be overemphasized that much that the Maya accomplished was due primarily to Indian corn. Their primitive religion was built about its cultivation and the deities who controlled its growth—the rain gods, and wind gods, the corn gods, and later the abstract gods of time and the heavenly bodies. The need for a place of worship, an appropriate sanctuary to shelter the first deities of nature and agriculture, undoubtedly gave rise to architecture. Monuments were erected at fixed intervals to mark the passage of time, and the embellishment of these monuments gave rise to Mayan sculpture. Thus, the origin of many of the higher manifestations of the civilization may be traced directly back to the complex of ideas that grew up around maize.

The pre-Columbian Maya saw themselves as insignificant beings at the mercy of a capricious universe (Morley, 1956). Attempts to reduce the mysteries of nature to understandable and predictable terms led to the creation of a priesthood whose function was to interpret the will of the gods to the mass of people. As society became more complex, the need arose for more formal religious sanctuaries such as temples. The religious philosophy, devised by the professional priesthood, was built around the increasing importance of astronomical manifestations and the development of the calendar, chronology, and associated deities. Interpreted and served by this closely organized priesthood composed of astronomers, mathematicians, prophets, ritualists, and skilled administrators, the religion was highly esoteric in nature but was shared by the common people.

The Maya had a large number of gods in their polytheistic world, and each god had clearly defined characteristics and functions (Morley, 1956). The most powerful and the most frequently invoked were: (1) *Itzamná* (or *Zamná*), lord of the heavens and lord of the day and night, who was always benevolent and was called upon especially in times of calamities; (2) *Chac*, the god of rain, deity of first importance and, by association with rain, god of the wind, thunder, lightning, fertility, and, by extension, agriculture; (3) *Ah Mun*, the corn god or god of agriculture, always represented as a youth and sometimes with an ear of corn as his headdress; (4) *Ah Puch*, the god of death (Morley, 1956), a malevolent deity, who presided over the ninth and lowest of the Mayan underworlds or hells, whose name-glyph was frequently associated with the god of war; and (5) *Ek Chuah*, the god of war, human sacrifice, and violent death. In addition, there were patron gods, thirteen of the upper world and nine of the lower world, thirteen gods of the *katunes* or twenty-year periods, and gods of each of the twenty different day names of the calendar. Other deities appeared or disappeared from the pantheon, particularly in religious art, or simply moved up and down in rank as characteristics of culture and society changed with time. Among the most significant of these in the Postclassic period were Kukulcán and Chacmool. The system became so bewildering that only the priests, whose function it was, could keep track of them all. Most of these matters were beyond the comprehension of the common people. For the average Mayan, whose paramount interest in life was his house and his cornfield, the rain god was the all-important deity. His intervention was sought by the common man more frequently than that of all the other gods combined. By Chac's goodwill he lived, and by Chac's wrath he was undone.

The Mayan calendar system was a blend of astrology and astronomy intimately woven into the fabric of religion and ritual. It defined the endless motion of the universe by means of two basic cycles—one a sacred calendar consisting of thirteen months of twenty days each and the other an approximate solar year of 365 days consisting of eighteen months of twenty days each and a separate period of five unnamed days. A permutation of these two cycles formed a still longer period of 18,980 days—the calendar round or 52-year cycle.

The long count, widely used by the lowland Mayan priests of the Classic period, was the most elaborate method of recording a particular day within this system of recurring cycles. It did so by stating the number of days that had elapsed since the first day of the Mayan calendar, usually equated to 3113 B.C. The time span of the Classic period is defined by the earliest and latest known monuments bearing long count dates A.D. 292 through approximately A.D. 900 (Weaver, 1972; Thompson, 1970).

Calendars had many functions in the rigid hierarchical society. The ruling groups, nobles and magician-priests, were able to exercise great social control over the masses, in part because of their knowledge of natural and astronomical cycles. The accuracy of the observations attests to their astronomical expertise despite the fact that their equipment was crude. The priests were consulted to determine what days the gods would view with favor for planting crops, holding ceremonials and rituals, marriages, beginning war, and many other matters. In some areas, a man took as his name or patron deity his birthdate in the *tzolkín* or sacred calendar.

By Preclassic times, the Maya had developed a numerical system that allowed for ease in performing mathematical computations. Two separate notations were utilized to signify numerals. One made use of different types of human heads to represent numbers one to thirteen, inclusive, and zero. These head-variant numerals were used for mathematical calculations and were an integral element of the sacred calendar of 260 days. In the second notation, only three symbols were needed for all operations: a dot had a numerical value of one, a bar ▬ stood for five, and a shell ⬭ or human head ⬭ represented zero or completion. By combinations of the first two symbols, the numbers one through nineteen were written. It was at this point that the symbol for zero was utilized, thus establishing a vigesimal system in contrast to the decimal method of Arabic numbers. In noting numerals above nineteen, the Maya employed a vertical system in which the values of the positions, from bottom to top, increased by twenties. Thus, the first or lowest position showed units of one, the second units of twenties, the third units of four hundred, the fourth position units of eight thousand, and so on. For the purpose of approximating the solar year in the civil or secular calendar, however, an adjustment was made in the system whereby in the third position the value was 360 rather than 400. The Mayan use of zero was one of only three inventions of that symbol. In the Old World, only the Hindus and the Babylonians used zero, and although its date of origin in the New World cannot be definitely established, its development might have been the earliest of all. It was invented by the forerunners of the Maya, probably the Olmecs of the Gulf Coast, who also seemed to have passed along an extensive accumulation of astronomical observations (Morley, 1956).

Knowledge of writing, though confined to a small segment of the population (priests and administrators), sets Middle America apart from all other cultural areas of pre-Columbian America. The writing systems generally employed symbols that stood either for sounds or for abstract ideas. No true alphabet was ever developed; therefore, no easy key to decipherment exists for present-day scholars. Mayan writing, the most complex in Middle America, deals largely with calendrical matters. Some texts, carved on monuments, record dates of accession to power and other events in the lives of Classic period rulers. Many of them include glyphs for deities, personal names, and probably the names of places. These texts vary in form and complexity, according to time, language, and culture. Hieroglyphs have been found on stone monuments, mural paintings, lintels, pottery, and jade ornaments. Some are also in "books" or codices of folded bark paper. Only three of these codices survived the Spanish Conquest but have provided valuable information for the anthropologist and historian of Mayan culture.

Under the skilled hands of the Yucatan potter, who worked without a potter's wheel, ceramics became a major art as well as a commodity of trade throughout Yucatan. Pottery was fabricated by coiling, modeling, and molding, and it took many forms: bowls, tripod dishes, bottle-necked vessels, cylindrical vases with or without spouts, incense burners, effigy vessels, and a large variety of figurines. Surface decorations included incised and stamped designs, high relief appliqué, and painted motifs. The use of hieroglyphics as a pattern element on ceremonial ware is distinctively Mayan.

Lapidaries, workers in semiprecious stones, were many and highly skilled. Jade was carved into statuettes, gorgets, and personal ornaments. This art reached its peak of excellence during the Classic period. That of Postclassic times was crude by comparison. Metalworking was unknown in Preclassic and Classic periods, and few samples survive from the Postclassic era. The majority of objects found to date come from the dredging of the sacred cenote of Chichén Itzá. Metals were not native to the Mayan area; copper and gold and the techniques of metalworking came from Panama and Costa Rica. Blanks of these two metals were imported and mainly channeled into the production of bells, cups, plaques, and articles of personal adornment. Some of the objects from the sacred cenote were apparently fashioned locally, for the embossed designs on some gold disks depict the Itzá defeating the Yucatec Maya.

No cultural facet of Mayan civilization was more impressive than that found in architecture. The hallmark of the ancient Mayan style was the widespread use of platforms and flat-topped, stepped pyramids that formed the elevated bases for the great temples and important civic structures so evident at Uxmal, Chichén Itzá, and hundreds of other sites. Sculpture and intricate designs were a fundamental part of this monumental architecture. In almost every pre-Columbian structure in Yucatan one sees carved friezes, headmasks, symbolic figures of Chac, feathered serpents, and mythological figures. Commonly associated with these are subsidiary abstract forms that include the scroll and the stepped-fret motif. Most of the art was purposeful and functional; it was dictated by the priesthood and reflected religion and social factors. The great cities of the Classic and Postclassic era remain as impressive monuments to the Mayan civilization. Yet, in many ways, the most significant reflections of the ancient Mayan culture and art are those simple and pervasive elements of domestic architecture that persist. Yucatan remains deeply influenced by its Mayan heritage.

REFERENCES

Anderson, W. French
    1971   Arithmetic in Maya Numerals. *American Antiquity* 36:54–63.
Andrews, E. Wyllys
    1960   Excavations at Dzibilchaltún, Northwestern Yucatan. *American Philosophical Society Proceedings* 104, No. 3.
    1965   Archaeology and Prehistory in the Northern Maya Lowlands, *Handbook of Middle American Indians,* Robert Wauchope, editor. Austin: University of Texas Press.
Ball, Joseph W.
    1974   A Coordinate Approach to Northern Maya Prehistory: A.D. 700–1200. *American Antiquity* 39:85–93.
Barrera Vásquez, Alfredo, and Silvia Rendón
    1969   El Libro de los Libros de Chilam Balam. 4a Ed. Colección Popular. México: Fondo de Cultura Económica.
Bernal, Ignacio, ed.
    1968   The Mexican National Museum of Anthropology, trans. by Carolyn B. Czitrom. London: Thames and Hudson.
Flannery, Kent F., ed.
    1976   The Early Mesoamerican Village. New York: Academic Press.
Goff, Charles W.
    1948   Anthropometry of a Mam-Speaking Group of Indians from Guatemala. Reprinted in Richard B. Woodbury and Aubrey S. Trik, *The Ruins of Zaculeu,* pp. 288–294. Richmond, Virginia: William Byrd Press, 1953.

Hammond, Norman, ed.
  1974   Mesoamerican Archaeology: New Approaches. Austin: University of Texas Press.
Heizer, Robert F., and Sherburne F. Cook
  1959   New Evidence of Antiquity of Tepexpan and Other Human Remains from the Valley of Mexico. *Southwestern Journal of Anthropology* 15:32–42.
Kidder, Alfred V., Jesse D. Jennings, and Edwin M. Shook
  1946   Excavations at Kaminaljuyú, Guatemala. *Carnegie Institution of Washington*. Publication 561.
Landa, Diego de
  1938   Relación de las Cosas de Yucatán. Mérida, Yucatán.
Morley, Sylvanus G.
  1946   The Ancient Maya. Stanford: Stanford University Press.
  1956   The Ancient Maya. 3d ed. Stanford: Stanford University Press.
Potter, David F.
  1976   Prehispanic Architecture and Sculpture in Central Yucatan. *American Antiquity* 41:430–448.
Rathje, William L.
  1971   The Origin and Development of Lowland Classic Maya Civilization. *American Antiquity* 36:275–285.
Roys, Ralph L.
  1966   Native Empires in Yucatan. *Revista Mexicana de Estudios Anthropológicos* 20:153–175.
Sanchez, George L.
  1961   Arithmetic in Maya. *American Anthropologist* 64:1104.
Sanders, William, and Betty J. Price
  1968   Mesoamerica: The Evolution of a Civilization. New York: Random House.
Shook, Edwin M., and Alfred V. Kidder
  1952   Mound E-III-3, Kaminaljuyú, Guatemala. *Carnegie Institution of Washington. Contribution No. 53.*
Sotelo Regil, Luis F.
  1963   *Campeche en la Historia: Tomo I, Del Descubrimiento a los Albores de su Segregación de Yucatán.* México, D. F.: Imprenta Manuel León Sánchez.
Stewart, Thomas D.
  1953   Skeletal Remains from Zaculeu, Guatemala. In Richard B. Woodbury and Aubrey S. Trik, *The Ruins of Zaculeu*, pp. 295–311. Richmond, Virginia: William Byrd Press.
Thompson, J. Eric
  1966   The Rise and Fall of Maya Civilization. Norman: University of Oklahoma Press.
  1970   Maya History and Religion. Norman: University of Oklahoma Press.
Weaver, Muriel P.
  1972   The Aztecs, Maya and Their Predecessors. New York: Seminar Press, Inc.
Willey, Gordon R.
  1971   An Archaeological Frame of Reference for Maya Culture History. In *Desarrollo Cultural de los Mayas,* Evon Z. Vogt and Alberto Ruz L., eds., pp. 137–186. México: Universidad Nacional Autónoma de México.

CHAPTER III

PEOPLES AND MONUMENTS: A SPECULATIVE ACCOUNT OF THE ORGANIZING ROLE PLAYED BY MAYAN MONUMENT BUILDING

Richard A. Krause

George W. Brainerd often spoke of the "Maya enigma," by which he meant that despite the simplicity of their technology and agriculture the ancient Maya developed a sophisticated art, a technically precise calendar, and an elaborate monumental architecture (Bell, 1956, 424). Indeed, these achievements have long been regarded with an awe and amazement that inhibits a balanced attempt to understand them. For example, Mayan art, calendrics, and architecture have often been interpreted as nonfunctional elements of culture, developed and elaborated by an economically unimportant priestly elite (Webb, 1964, 420–422). Scholars adopting this point of view have been quick to see religious significance in Mayan remains to the neglect of the evidence for civil authority these same materials contain. This particular bias is well exemplified by Betty Bell (1956, 430):

> One of the unknown factors in Maya Civilization is the type of authority that governed it during its almost 600 years of existence. Religion was of central importance to the Maya; there is little doubt that it was uniform throughout the area, and that the priests of the various centers must have co-operated closely on religious matters. The remarkable homogeneity of classic stage civilization would seem to indicate some kind of hegemony over the area, either civil or religious. Priestly control may [have] sufficed to maintain order, or there may have been some centralized political authority which has so far not been detected.

Recent scholars have been more sanguine in their attempts to understand ancient Mayan social and political life. William A. Haviland (1968) has argued for patrilateral succession to rulership at Tikal. Tatiana Proskouriakoff (1960) has suggested hereditary rule by dynastic succession at Piedras Negras. Edward B. Kurjack (1974) has posited an increase in the centralization of wealth, power, and authority from Formative to Late Classic times at Dzibilchaltún. Richard E. W. Adams (1977, 158) has characterized Classic period Mayan centers as city states, and Joyce Marcus (1973) has argued for an overarching hierarchy of political relations among Classic period Mayan centers in the central lowlands. An exhaustive discussion of these studies is beyond the scope of this chapter. Nevertheless, some of the information they contain will be used, together with other data, to provide a scientific model of the functional fit between ancient Mayan architectural accomplishments and the persistence of a kinship-based social, political, and economic order. A few prefatory comments about scientific models will serve as an introduction.

A scientific model is herein construed as a set of empirical statements that (1) describe the entities of import and (2) detail the relationships among the entities described. A statement is considered empirical if it can be tested through experiment or directed observation. Testability, however, must be understood as including testable in principle. This latter caveat simply means that it is possible to state precisely which experiential findings, if obtained, would count as evidence for disconfirmation (Krause, 1972, 106). Further, an entity simply means any set or class that is unambiguous or reproducible (Harré, 1961). The entities central to the model will be (1) the set of all Mayan population aggregates that were also communities, (2) the set of all Mayan works of monumental architecture, and (3) the set of all kinship-based social statuses that were entailed by monument building. The interentity relations posited by the model will emerge as the discussion progresses.

Ancient Mayan Communities

A community will be characterized as any group of people who normally reside in such proximity that day-to-day, face-to-face interaction is commonplace (Murdock, 1949, 79). This description certainly implies a population composed of two sexes and at least three biological generations with a division of labor by both sex and age. It excludes special-purpose or unisex occupation and residence groups such as mining and logging camps or military garrisons. In the Mayan case, it would be reasonable to view the community as an aggregate of consanguineally related households capable of satisfying basic social and material needs. The archaeological evidence for such consists of clusters of low, raised platforms that presumably served as foundations for thatched-roofed, timber, and mud plaster houses (M. Coe, 1966, 42–45). The per cluster number of house mounds would, of course, vary with the exigencies of locally available natural and/or social resources. But each cluster should be accompanied by evidence for its own civil and religious buildings, burial accommodations, storage facilities, and means of production and distribution. Multicommunity settlements, some of considerable size and complexity, are not excluded.

Although the data are far from clear on this point, most of the households in ancient Mayan communities seem to have been basic units of production and consumption. Evidently garden plots (milpas) were assigned by the community authorities on the basis of perceived need. Each household was responsible for clearing, planting, harvesting, storing, and preparing its own food as well as producing and maintaining the basic tools and implements needed for day-to-day domestic tasks (Morley, 1956, 175–178). Luxury goods of various kinds and in various quantities may have found their way to the humblest of homes, but these by no means constituted basic tools and implements. The most common intra-household division of labor probably followed lines of age and sex. Men's work tended to require mobility and/or spurts of intense physical exertion (hunting, fighting, long distance trading, and perhaps monument building). Women's work was probably long, tedious, and time consuming (house maintenance, pottery making, weaving, sewing, the preparation of food and clothes, and the care, early training, and nurture of children) (Morley, 1956, 175–178). The consanguineally related households must have been the socially stable units in the fabric of community life. It was to and from these stable units that goods, personnel, and services must have flowed in a richly networked suprahousehold web of rights, duties, privileges, and responsibilities. This network served to mute the potentially divisive pull of separate domestic group interests and focused attention upon broader community (in some cases multicommunity) and settlementwide concerns (Rathje, 1970, 359). If the archaeological remains are any indication, monumental architecture was one of these broader concerns.

Mayan Monumental Architecture

Ancient Mayan architecture has piqued the imagination of scholars and laymen for over a century (Catherwood, 1844; Gann, 1927; Morley, 1947; Thompson, 1954; Potter, 1976). From the rubble of ruined cities and ceremonial centers the fertile minds of travelers, traders, and explorers created temples, monasteries, nunneries, council chambers, administrative suites, military barracks, and astronomical observatories (Catherwood, 1844; Gann, 1927; Gordon, 1896; Holmes, 1895–97; Stephens, 1843). Mayan ruins are certainly impressive, and some of the speculation they have engendered may have great merit. Nevertheless, the hold Mayan architecture has upon the European imagination cannot reside in the scope and technical excellence of ancient Mayan building practices.

Mayan architectural assemblages, like others in Mesoamerica, grew by accretion as later buildings were built over earlier ones. The final product, after centuries perhaps, might appear massive indeed. But the largest Mayan building is little over fifty thousand cubic meters in volume, one-twentieth the size of the Pyramid of the Sun at Teotihuacán (Morley, 1956, 265).* Nor can Mayan architecture be considered technically complex. Mayan stone buildings are essentially great mounds of rubble faced with a cut stone and plaster veneer. There was no grasp of the principle of laying courses of stone. Mayan craftsmen did not properly overlap courses to break a joint. Mayan builders depended upon mortar, inertia, and stucco to hold façades together. This indicates a deficiency in the

*Recent measurements of the pyramid at Izamal indicate that it may be the largest Mayan monument, equal to or exceeding in size the Pyramid of the Moon at Teotihuacán.

Illustration shows the lack of knowledge regarding the use of key corner blocks and proper bonding technique. The Nunnery at Uxmal. (Photo by Joel Whitman)

Corbeled arch on the south side of the Nunnery at Uxmal. Note the representation of the Mayan hut in the façade over the small doorway. (Photo by Joel Whitman)

knowledge of the use of key in corner blocks and proper bonding techniques. Ignorance of the true arch limited the method of roofing and the interior width of rooms and also made the construction of multistoried edifices wasteful of material and space (Holmes, 1895-97, 28). Finally, the Mayan craftsman never achieved symmetry; right angles invariably lacked or added a few degrees so that only the visual effect was regular (Kubler, 1912, 125). Thus, from the standpoint of size, design, and technique of construction, professional engineers or skilled tradesmen need not have been employed.

The foregoing considerations do not apply to the outstanding feature of Mayan architecture—emphasis upon skillful and elaborate decoration (Morley, 1956, 265). The beautifully carved mosaic façades of Uxmal and the reticulated roofcombs of Tikal both show a preoccupation with aesthetically pleasing ornamental embellishment. Then, too, regional specialities are discernible. Within the central lowlands different Mayan centers had their own special emphasis in sculpture. Yaxchilán was a center for lintel carving. The artisans at Copán did the most innovating in three-dimensional relief. Palenque's craftsmen excelled in stucco relief work (Hewett, 1936, 188). Artisans at Copán and Quiriguá shared an interest in stone decoration in the upper portion of façades. This emphasis was lacking elsewhere. The craftsmen at Quiriguá placed a special value on sculpted wall decorations and carved interior stair risers (Morley, 1956, 321-324).

The whole northern region can be set off from the central portion of Mayaland and subdivided into Río Bec-Chennes and Puuc subareas on the basis of differences in building decoration. In the Río Bec-Chennes subarea of central Campeche and Quintana Roo, façades are the most elaborately sculpted and most ornate in the whole of the Mayan country. In the Puuc region of Yucatan, there seems to have been a great emphasis upon the individual elements of mosaics that were very skillfully carved and fitted. Multiple step and fret designs, latticework mosaics, and building corners studded with columns of long-nose god masks are found at most Puuc sites (Morley, 1956, 324).

The larger, more impressive Mayan centers exhibit a considerable variability of form in standing stone architecture. These forms include temple pyramids (the most ancient form of monument if its dirt and clay plaster predecessors are considered), multichambered buildings usually called palaces, long rectangular structures with rows of corbel vaulted rooms, ball courts, and sweat baths. It has often been noted that the so-called palaces would have been dark and damp quarters for noble or priestly residents. According to Alfred V. Kidder (1947, 11), these structures "are all alike. There are no specialized apartments, no fittings for domesticity. They are the most un-homelike quarters and . . . they contain unquestionable ceremonial features such as shrines, and altars and stelae." Furthermore, the fresco in structure BXIII at Uaxactún suggests that important persons sometimes resided in wooden structures (M. Coe, 1956, 388). Perhaps the multiroomed stone buildings were used by traditional authorities and others of importance on occasions of state. That is, elaborately decorated stone buildings may have provided the setting in which public policy decisions were solemnized, judicial pronouncements were rendered, and succession to public office was legitimized. The murals at Bonampak, for example, show prisoners of war being judged on the steps of a palacelike structure (Morley, 1956, 388). But there is an additional consideration of some importance.

The incessant rebuilding that produced the larger Mayan architectural assemblages has already been noted. If the sole purpose of temples and palaces was to provide the setting for civil and religious ceremonies, why were they so rapidly covered over? Alfred M. Tozzer (1941, 151) suggested that rebuilding marked the end of socially and religiously important time periods. Michael Coe (1956, 392–393) challenged this claim by convincingly showing that some Mayan buildings "were initially erected to house a deceased person of some importance" and that "the covering of older funerary structures with new constructions was evidently always accompanied by interments." If Coe is correct, we have every reason to believe that some of the larger Mayan buildings contained multiple tombs. We may also expect a correlation between the sequence of burials within these buildings and the sequence of rebuildings that marked the developmental history of each. In sum, Mayan monumental architecture may be viewed as an organized and presumably managed investment of community resources that emphasized the legitimacy of traditional forms of authority. It is only reasonable to look to a kinship-based web of rights and duties when seeking to identify the social basis for these traditional forms of authority.

Kinship-Based Social Status

As previously noted, there can be little doubt that ancient Mayan communities were aggregates of consanguineal kinsmen. That is, each community contained a network of interlocking parent-child and sibling ties that served as the social charter for distributing rights and duties, privileges and obligations. Of the two kinds of social bonds, parent-child links must be considered primary and sibling links secondary. This is because siblings are offspring with at least one parent in common. Thus, the recognition of a sibling tie requires the prior existence of a parent-offspring link. In any case, the existence of a parent-child or sibling tie implies an assumed biological relationship between persons. The assumed relationship, or bond of descent, may be traced through a single parent (patrilateral if male, matrilateral if female) or through both parents (bilaterally). Although some historic Mayan communities have been characterized as bilateral, it will be assumed that a unilateral principle of descent was typical of ancient communities (whether patrilateral or matrilateral is unimportant) (Haviland, 1977, 63; Kelley, 1962; Proskouriakoff, 1960, 1961, 1963–64). It should be noted, however, that a complementary social bond between offspring and nondescent-related parent may have been important in special circumstances.

The archaeological evidence at hand seems to indicate that not all parent-child and sibling bonds were of equal social value. At death, some Maya were interred in temple mounds and other public monuments and were accompanied by sumptuous grave goods (fine pottery, carved jade objects, obsidian eccentrics, baskets, and textiles) (Smith, 1950). These elaborate burials almost certainly represent venerated ancestral dead. The less important individuals were buried beneath their houses and were accompanied by a far more modest supply of grave goods (M. Coe, 1966, 45). The differential treatment accorded the dead has traditionally been interpreted as good presumptive evidence for inequalities of rank among the living (Peebles, 1974). Hence, some of the households in early Mayan communities may have constituted an aristocracy set apart from the more common families by virtue of their position in the web of parent-child and sibling links around which community life was organized.

The basis for inequalities of rank in ancient Mayan communities needs further consideration. It will be assumed that social ranking was a product of genealogical position. In other words, the number of parent-offspring and sibling links to a high-ranking ancestor or ancestress could be used to calculate one's position in the social order. The fewer the links, the higher the rank. Lineal links should, however, be distinguished from collateral links. The former are to be construed as any concatenation of parent-child ties. The latter are sibling ties in any biological generation other than one's own. Thus, two lineal links connect any individual to his father's father. One lineal link and one collateral link connect any

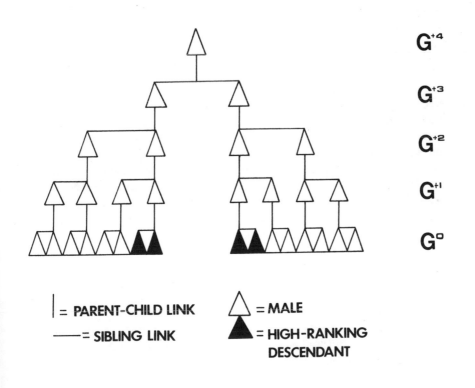

person to his father's brother. If we can assume primogeniture in calculating the genealogical links from ego to an ancestor, any chain of kin ties that includes a collateral link will be longer than one that includes only lineal links. This means that "lineal kinsmen" will always be of higher rank than "collaterals."

In kin groups of the kind being considered, there will always be far fewer "lineals" than "collaterals." As a given population grows, the number of people who must count a collateral link to claim descent from a common ancestor or ancestress will increase far faster than the number able to trace the relationship through lineal links alone. For example, let us assume patrilateral descent and a common ancestor who fathers two sons, each of whom fathers two sons, and so on. After four generations, four males will be able to count only lineal links, twelve must include collateral ties (see chart). After eight generations still only four males will be able to count lineal links alone, whereas 252 must include collateral ties. If status and prestige were spread over the genealogical net by calculating parent-child and sibling ties in the manner just described, community rewards might be characterized as flowing downward from ancestor to descendants and outward from high-ranking lineal to lower-ranking collateral kinsmen.

Interentity Relationships

The three major model components (communities, kin status, and monumental architecture) are now well enough described to begin a sketch of their mutual interdependence. Monumental architecture apparently had a dual role. On the one hand, Mayan buildings were tangible representations of the right to legitimate exercise of power and authority by a select few. On the other, they represented the community's wealth, glory, and capability. From this perspective, some Mayan buildings can be interpreted as both public and private monuments, as community shrines (perhaps dedicated to gods), and as markers of a cardinal social principle (symbols of ranking). Then, too, Mayan buildings required massed manpower to construct—manpower thus committed to the authority the monuments represented. At the same time, working together toward a common goal would have promoted worker solidarity if suitable rewards were forthcoming. In the case at hand, the rewards took the tangible form of a monument and the intangible form of civic pride and a community fund of prestige in which all might have shared, albeit differentially. Obviously, there were limits to the rewards that could be adequately distributed and the authority that could be maintained through monument building.

It has been noted that lineals could claim the greatest share of a monument's prestige yield, near collaterals could claim less, distant collaterals still less. Yet even the most distant collaterals must have provided construction labor. The disparity between labor owed and rewards received would, of course, have grown as group size increased and the kin and social gulf between lineals and collaterals widened. Thus, there would have come a time in the group's growth when the vast majority of members were only distantly related to its leaders.

They could therefore claim but little of the glory and power these authorities represented. When this happened, resentments would have resulted, and dissatisfied portions of the population might have begun to question traditionally held assumptions about the legitimate transfer and use of power. These dissidents would have formed a potential body of followers should disputes over succession to status or title have emerged among descent group members of higher rank.

The available ethnographic evidence indicates that in unilateral descent groups, disputes over succession to status or title occur most frequently among half brothers, that is, a high-ranking man's sons by separate wives (Service, 1975, 78). Each of the sons has a claim (although some claims may be stronger than others), and each may call upon his mother's relatives for support, that is, they may use the complementary bond noted earlier. As the struggle over succession unfolds, the number and disposition of each competitor's relatives may play an important role. Nevertheless, only one son can win. Each loser, however, has identified himself as a potential leader and a potential threat to the established order. Such a man may become the focal point for other dissidents, who see in him a means for advancing their own cause. Thus, a claimant to title and high status, though unsuccessful, may attract a sufficient number of determined followers among his own kinsmen and other dissatisfied segments of the population to set himself up as an authority should he so choose.

After identifying a willing body of relatives and other followers for his support, a potential authority may consider several possible moves. If his challenge has created bitterness and suspicion, he may choose to found an independent settlement. Conditions for such a move must, however, be right. There must be suitable land available beyond the parent community's reach. Then, too, founding a totally independent settlement requires a following of sufficient size and vigor to provide for the common defense and achieve economic security. If conditions for founding an independent community are not right and there is suitable space available in the parent community's hinterland, the dissident authority may found a colony that retains social, ceremonial, and economic ties to its parent while establishing an independent or pseudoindependent local authority structure. Finally, if suitable hinterland space is not available, of if the military and/or economic risks of removal are prohibitive, the potential leader may choose to remain within the parent community and seek other means to promote recognition of his claims. By carefully manipulating affinal alliances and kin ties, through success in war, trade, and other economic enterprises, a shrewd potential leader might marshall the wealth and support necessary to further his own ambitions. If these ethnographic considerations can be applied to the political process in ancient Mayan communities, they might shed new light on building practices. For example, an emergent Mayan leader, whether resident, colonist, or independent immigrant, might have advanced his cause and consolidated his position by building a monument for his ancestors, his followers, his descendants, and especially for himself.

This speculative model could account for two infrequently discussed aspects of

Mayan monumental architecture. The first of these is the occurrence of numerous multimonument settlements. If monumental architecture had the social significance and solidarity-promoting effects envisioned, multiple contemporary monuments are the predictable consequence of population growth in favorably located and politically mature settlements. It should be noted that no claim is made vis-à-vis the variable morphology of Mayan architecture. The model does, however, cast this variability in a new perspective that will be considered later. Moreover, the propensity to rebuild, refurbish, and enlarge existing monuments, behavior often relegated to religious fervor (Webb, 1964, 420–422), assumes new meaning. Rebuilding and enlargement in this model reflect succession to leadership. In other words, changes of leadership that accompany the death or removal of an authority are marked by the beginning of a new construction episode. From this point of view, Mayan architecture chronicles succession to office and title in much the same way that stelae chronicle the lifelong achievements of various officials in Mayan history. The model also contains some developmental implications that can best be explored in chronological order.

Model Implications

Prior to 800 B.C., the Mayan country was occupied by unsophisticated village-dwelling farming folk (M. Coe, 1966, 42; Hammond, 1977). The early pattern of occupation was one of a few small, autonomous farming communities, each dependent upon locally available resources. The inhabitants of such communities presumably had equal access to the means of production, and the exploitative tasks performed in any one community were similar in type and scheduling to the tasks performed in every other. At any rate, the tools and strategies used for procuring and processing locally available raw materials seem to have been similar for all groups. Under such conditions, seasonal differences in intergroup surpluses must have been minimal, any trade in foodstuffs, raw materials, or indigenous manufactured goods restricted, and the economic incentives for supracommunity management of social and natural resources limited. Yet the foundations of a kinship-based authority structure must have been laid in these early communities. The earliest suprahousehold forms of authority were probably a response to the need for conflict resolution and the need to organize and schedule community labor. Whatever the case may have been, early authority structures seem to have been weakly developed and purely local. The overall picture is one of a sparse populace gathered together in small communities, each independent of the comings and goings of others, each, in effect, a nation unto itself (M. Coe, 1966, 42–46).

The Mayan population grew rapidly between 800 and 300 B.C. (M. Coe, 1966, 46; Willey et al., 1965, 561–581). In this period, the countryside was spotted with virtually hundreds of communities, but writing had not yet appeared and there was little in the way of art. Monumental architecture was restricted to the low, earth-filled, clay-plastered mound that accompanied some communities

(Adams, 1977, 118). These structures were four-sided, flat-topped, earth- or rubble-filled platforms. Each sloped inward from base to summit, and at least one side carried a ramp or staircase that provided access from ground level to platform top. These early structures probably carried at least one perishable summit-top temple. Although the available evidence is limited, we have every reason to expect one or more richly stocked burials within each mound (M. Coe, 1966, 63–66; Morley, 1956, 180). These earth-filled temple-tombs presumably indicate the emergence of ancestor worship (Holland, 1964). From the perspective previously modeled, they also signal an internally ranked network of parent-child and sibling ties that justified hereditary access to community-specific positions of power and authority. In sum, communities with authority and prestige dispersement procedures centered on monument building had appeared by 300 B.C. It was upon the limited reward and authority distribution capabilities of these procedures that further population growth worked to produce the subsequent pattern of development.

By the second century B.C., a mixed pattern of large, populous centers, smaller satellite communities, and independent frontier settlements can be discerned (Adams, 1977, 120–121; Willey et al., 1965, 561–581). This is the pattern our model leads us to expect. Population growth and conflict over succession led to community fission, an attendant population spread, and the emergence of numerous replicas of a few parent communities. Our model also points to a purely local, but critical, demographic threshold that, if passed, limited the rate of population dispersal and led to multimonument settlements. Some Mayan sites dating to this period are large enough to put them in this category. The community at Altar de Sacrificios, in Chiapas, contained a complex of three temples around a central courtyard, and the highland Guatemalan settlement at Kaminaljuyú was marked by numerous temple mounds, some containing richly appointed burials (Adams, 1977, 118; M. Coe, 1966, 63–69; Shook and Kidder, 1952).

Now, too, the beginnings of artistic and architectural diversification can be detected. A sixty-foot-high pyramid was in use at Yaxuna, and the inhabitants at Dzibilchaltún had constructed cut stone buildings. The famous temple E-VII sub, an Ixapán-style structure adorned with stucco heads of jaguars and serpents, was in use at Uaxactún. The inhabitants of Tikal were burying important dead in masonry vaults beneath platform mounds, and an early temple on Tikal's north acropolis had been painted with an elaborate procession of human figures dressed in feather headdresses and intricate costumes (Adams, 1977, 119). A growth in traditional forms of power is certainly indicated by these developments, and the rudiments of an emphasis upon artistic embellishment seems to have been established. The former was an indigenous development; the latter may have been imported. To understand better the emergence of an emphasis upon artistic embellishment we must look back in time and beyond the Mayan country.

Multicommunity states were flourishing in the lowlands of Vera Cruz and Tabasco as early as 800 B.C. The Olmec centers at La Venta (Drucker et al.,

1959), Tres Zapotes (Sterling, 1940), and San Lorenzo (Sterling, 1955) are good examples. Soon elements of Olmec culture, particularly carved jade objects and a powerful iconography featuring cleft-headed, snarling-mouthed, puffy-faced were-jaguars (Covarrubias, 1946) spread from the Olmec heartland across the isthmus of Tehauntepec to the Pacific coast, where they appeared in modified form at El Baúl and Izapa (M. Coe, 1966, 60–63). A two-pronged entry into the Mayan lowlands may be posited. One route ran from Olmec country along the lowlands through Campeche. The other route ran from Izapa and El Baúl to the great Mayan highland site of Kaminaljuyú, thence to the Mayan lowlands (M. Coe, 1966, 60–66). Regardless of the precise route taken, it is clear that an infusion of iconography and other elements of Olmec culture—writing, calendrics, and perhaps the long count (M. Coe, 1957)—were harbingers of things to come. By 100 B.C., the ideological and intellectual prerequisites had been introduced. In the next five centuries or so, Mayaland's rapidly growing farming communities were drawn by yet other forces into multicommunity sociopolitical aggregates of some size, power, and opulence. Tikal and its satellite communities will be used as an example.

By the fourth century A.D., Tikal was surrounded by a three-level hierarchy of settlements. The lowest level consisted of numerous small communities (from thirty-five to seventy or so inhabitants), each with its own local shrine. The second level consisted of minor centers composed of a plaza surrounded by public buildings and temple pyramids. These "minor" centers presumably served the ceremonial and perhaps some of the marketing needs of the ten to fifteen small communities around them. The third level consisted of "major" centers containing several plazas, each surrounded by temple pyramids and public buildings and each connected with the others by causeways. These also contained stelae, ball courts, and sweat baths. Each "major" center served the ceremonial, political, and commercial needs of the ten or so minor centers in a one hundred-square-kilometer area (Bullard, 1960, 355–372). The three-level hierarchy of small communities, minor centers, and major centers may have been a wholly indigenous development. It is certainly a predictable outcome of continued population growth acting upon the previous pattern of populous centers, satellite communities, and frontier settlements. There is, however, a fourth level of settlement represented by the supercenter at Tikal—a development that cannot be totally accounted for by reference to purely indigenous forces. To understand this development, we must again look beyond Mayaland, this time to the emergence of an interregional trade network whose organizing force lay far to the north.

The Valley of Mexico spawned the Middle Formative market center of Tlatilco (Piña Chan, 1958), and by the first century A.D. had become the home of the greatest of all pre-Columbian commercial centers, Teotihuacán (Linné, 1934; Wolf, 1959; M. Coe, 1966). It was a true city, an unequivocal example of urbanism. At its height, Teotihuacán contained twenty square kilometers of temples, plazas, workshops, palaces, slums, drainage systems, waterways, and reservoirs organized about a grid system of avenues and streets (Millon, 1970). Teotihuacán was also the presumed center of a vast commercial empire that serviced populations in Vera Cruz, Tabasco, Oaxaca, and the Mayan country (M. Coe, 1962, 115). The *teotihuacano* presence is detectable at Kaminaljuyú, Tikal, Uaxactún, and Becán, four Classic period Mayan sites of great opulence (Shook and Kidder, 1952; M. Coe, 1956; Smith, 1950; Adams, 1977). There was certainly enough in the way of a resource difference between the Valley of Mexico and the Mayan country to make long-distance trade profitable. But the overland route of trade and travel was a long and arduous one. There were no wheeled vehicles or pack animals for the transport of heavy loads (McBride, 1945, 73). Commerce must have been primarily in high-value, easily portable objects. The Maya probably supplied quetzal feathers, jaguar pelts, cacao, and chicle. The *teotihuacanos* returned obsidian tools, elaborately decorated and finely made ceramics, utilitarian pottery, and other manufactured goods. Although the volume of such trade must have been small by modern standards, it seemingly had far-reaching effects on the pattern of social development in Mayaland.

By the fourth century A.D., some Mayan settlements, notably Tikal, Kaminaljuyú, Becán, and perhaps Uxmal had become parts of the *teotihuacano*-dominated network of interregional exchange (Adams, 1977, 161–162; W. Coe, 1965; Smith, 1950). They certainly became supercenters within their own regions, the foci of local exchange networks that influenced the distribution of people, communities, and institutions in their respective hinterlands (Leone, 1968, 127–128). When an interregional exchange net became focused upon Tikal, it was converted to a major market town. Several local transformations followed. First, the populous center attracted yet more people, for it could support persons with special talents or skills (Pfeiffer, 1977, 361). Artisans, craftsmen, scribes, and merchants apparently could make a better living at Tikal than they could in the hinterland. Second, residents of some hinterland communities began to specialize in the production of commodities with the intent of exchanging them for locally unavailable manufactured goods and luxury items (Adams, 1977, 147). The first of these transformations added substantially to the natural growth rate of the emergent supercenter, making it increasingly dependent upon the importation of food. The second created a local exchange net that, once established, developed a momentum of its own.

The authorities in each supercenter apparently managed the flow of textiles, flint and obsidian tools, featherwork, pottery, food, salt, drink, artifacts of wood, and other materials in the center's hinterland (Adams, 1977, 147). In his Palenque study, Robert L. Rands (1973) found that a substantial volume of locally made items circulated in a supercenter-specific network of exchange, but local craft products were rarely exchanged between supercenters. The Palenque study also indicated that some communities specialized in the manufacture of certain items to the exclusion of others—a pattern that still persists in the highlands of Chiapas and in parts of Yucatan. Marcus's (1973) study of Classic period glyphs strengthens the picture of a local exchange system dominated by a supercenter. Among ceremonial center emblem glyphs she discovered a hierarchy of specific cross-references. Those major centers in a given service zone contained emblem glyph references to their supercenter but to no others. Supercenter emblem glyphs, however, referred to the largest community in other service zones, not to the major or minor centers in their own hinterland.

If both imports and locally manufactured goods were being organized and distributed through a network of ceremonial and market towns (Rathje, 1970), then certain transformations in the previously modeled relationships between communities, kin class status, and monumental architecture may be expected. Even if the flow of goods and services was directed by traditional authorities, anyone, by virtue of talent, personal initiative, industry, or diligence, might have shared in the benefits of the wealth thus made available. An ambitious man might have bettered his material and social standing while still being excluded from traditional positions of real power. Classic period Mayan society was, for instance, affluent enough to support craftsmen of impressive skill (Adams, 1977, 154-155; M. Coe, 1966). High-status Maya of the period are shown adorned in elaborately carved wooden headdresses replete with splendid plumage and stone or shell encrustations. Fine-quality textiles (open weave, patterned, and tailored items) were available, as were long robes of animal skin, elaborate leather or cloth sandals, and a wide range of skillfully crafted jade jewelry. Personal and domestic servants, musicians, and entertainers are depicted in murals and other works of art (Morley, 1956, 388). Scribes are shown in modeled stucco relief (Adams, 1977, 156-157). In short, new forms of wealth may have lessened the impact of prestige distribution limits embedded in older, more traditional forms of status seeking and created a nouveau riche composed of artisans, merchants, and other entrepreneurs with talent or products to exchange. Nevertheless, if the stela interpretations are correct, there was still a tendency for the best items to accumulate in the hands of a traditional elite. In fact, the benefits conferred by trade may have strengthened the hand of aristocratic elements by superseding older limits on the number and kinds of followers they could count upon for goods, labor, and loyalty. If the new sources of wealth and the labor of a larger, controllable following were invested in traditional symbols of power and prestige (such as monumental architecture both public and private), a diversity of architectural form and intensified construction efforts would be major components of the Late Classic pattern of development.

The Late Classic may in fact be characterized as a period of architectural megalomania. The labor of thousands was invested in funerary monuments and memorial temples. The five great temples at Tikal (W. Coe, 1965), the temple of the magician at Uxmal, and the relatively large structure of Mirador (Adams, 1977, 163) were built in Late Classic times. There were five discernible Late Classic architectural styles. The greater Petén style typified by Tikal was the most widespread. It was characterized by multiplex combinations of a few basic design elements, the extensive use of polychrome, modeled stucco decoration, and uniformity in room size and construction. The Río Bec-Chennes style to the north was typified by Becán. It emphasized low façades decorated with earth monster motifs, entranceways through the gaping mouths of large monster masks, and nonfunctional towers topped with masonry dummy temples. The northernmost, or Puuc, style was the most florid. Puuc structures were decorated with multiple rain god masks, earth monster façades, and the alternation of carved mosaic latticework and step and fret motifs with zones of stark, unadorned cut stone. The large Puuc center at Uxmal was prototypical. To the southeast and the southwest of the Petén there were separate frontier styles that apparently developed very late in the Classic period. Palenque with its delicate stucco work, mansard-style roofs, and multiple inner shrines exemplified the southwestern frontier style. Copán, with its remarkable emphasis upon three-dimensional sculpted forms, was the prototype for the southeastern frontier style (Morley, 1956, 321–324).

By A.D. 650, the *teotihuacano* trade network had disintegrated (Adams, 1977, 191). Imports were no longer available to Mayan elites in the central lowlands. They were now forced to depend upon the management of locally produced and exchanged products to buttress their power and authority. Population growth continued unabated (Turner, 1974), as did the construction of larger, more elaborate palaces, temples, ball courts, reservoirs, roads, and fortifications (Morley, 1956, 269). With the collapse of foreign trade, as modest as it must have been, the Mayan communities in the central lowlands seem to have turned inward upon themselves. The earlier tendency for separation of aristocrat from commoner continued, but now in the face of the growing pressure of population upon available natural resources. To be sure, craft specialization and the entrepreneurial efforts it made possible had broadened the prestige distribution base. But lacking outside sources of wealth, there were limits to the economic growth that Mayan technology could sustain. By A.D. 800, Classic period Mayan culture and the social order it had produced began to show signs of stress. Military competition between supercenters intensified (Adams, 1977, 223). Esoteric cults and ideologies proliferated (Thompson, 1966). Ecological abuse, mismanagement, overpopulation, and bad weather were a fatal mix for many Mayan polities (Adams, 1977, 222–225). In the ninth century, Mayan culture in the central lowlands collapsed (Morley, 1956).

The populous Mayan centers of the Puuc area, however, survived the central lowland catastrophe (Andrews, 1965). They flourished for an additional century before succumbing to Mexican invaders (Ball, 1974; Pollock, 1965; Potter, 1973). The persistence of Classic Mayan culture in Yucatan may have been a consequence of more durable ties to outside sources of wealth. Mayan centers in the central lowlands were tied to overland trade, presumably conducted in easily portable, high-value items. Those in Yucatan, however, were within easy reach of the sea. Seaborne trade between Yucatan and other parts of Mexico seems a distinct probability. Furthermore, such trade could have been conducted in higher-volume, lower-value items—a trade that might well have survived the collapse of *teotihuacano* hegemony. The largest salt fields in Mesoamerica were located in the northwest corner of Yucatan (Adams, 1977, 236) near the very large Classic period site of Chunchucmil. Ceramic evidence and hints from the Mayan chronicles suggest that the Itzá, who later conquered Yucatan and established their capital at Chichén Itzá, were Chontal from lowland Tabasco (Tozzer, 1957, 33). It is tantalizing to see them as former middlemen in trade relationships between Yucatan and Mexico. As such, they would have been familiar with the peninsula's exploitable wealth, and the salt fields were certainly a prize worth the risk of military intervention. Hence the peninsula's salt and other commercially valuable resources may, on the one hand, have abetted the persistence of Classic Mayan culture in the region. On the other hand, they may have provided economic incentives for the Itzá conquest.

Itzá domination of the Yucatec Maya lasted for about two centuries (A.D. 987 to A.D. 1187) and was exercised from their colonial capital at Chichén Itzá (Morley, 1956, 80–99). The Itzá were a Toltec people, who, at least in part, imposed their will by military force. Battle scenes, in which the contending forces were clearly Maya and Toltec, were commonly represented in Chichén's graphic art. The most famous, of course, is the sea battle portrayed on gold disc C from Chichén's sacred cenote (Morley, 1956, 419).

The Toltec chronicles claim that Quetzalcóatl himself led the way to Yucatan. The largest temple in the Toltec sector of Chichén (the Castillo) is indeed dedicated to Kukulcán, the Mayan name for Quetzalcóatl. A fusion of Toltec with Mayan architectural styles marked this epoch. The Temple of the Warriors, for example, showed Mayan Chac masks at the corners, Toltec feathered serpent columns flanking the doorway, and Toltec sculptures in wall inserts. The Toltec, presumably using Mayan craftsmen, also built Mesoamerica's largest ball court at Chichén Itzá. It was over three hundred feet long, with vertical walls and small stone rings through which a solid rubber ball had to pass. Toltec sculpture showing scenes of sacrifice and war covered the ball court walls (Morley, 1956, 80–99).

The new military order at Chichén Itzá was apparently strong enough to monopolize seaborne trade. Plumbate and Silho fine orange potteries have been found at Chichén but not at late Puuc sites. These trade wares are commonly construed as markers of extralocal commerce. Their absence from late Puuc centers has thus been construed as an indicator of an increase in Yucatec Mayan economic isolation. The previously introduced model, of course, predicts that once external trade was disrupted, Mayan centers would experience a slowdown, then a decline in rate of economic growth. Intercenter military conflict and the collapse of public works and monument-building programs would follow. Indeed, the last vestiges of Classic period Mayan grandeur, the building programs at late Puuc centers, were discontinued during the first half of the Itzá reign (Adams, 1977, 240).

Throughout its two-century existence, Toltec Chichén can be viewed as a Mexican outpost with firm commercial and political ties to the Toltec capital of

Temple of the Warriors at Chichén Itzá, including a view of the thousand columns. (Photo by Edward Moseley)

Detail of Kukulkán (the Feathered Serpent) at the entrance to The Temple of the Warriors. (Photo by Joel Whitman)

Bas relief on the ball court at Chichén Itzá showing marching warriors. (Photo by Joel Whitman)

Tula in Hildago. Tula, however, fell about A.D. 1156, presumably as a consequence of internal dissention and external military pressure. As a consequence, Chichén Itzá was set adrift. Without the Mexican economic and political support it once enjoyed, Chichén became increasingly vulnerable to Yucatec Mayan hostility. In A.D. 1187, the Itzá capital was sacked by Hunac Ceel, head of the ruling Mayan lineage at Mayapán (Morley, 1956, 80–99). With Itzá power broken, Hunac Ceel proceeded to unify other Yucatec Mayan ruling lineages under the Cocom family. About A.D. 1200, he established the town of Mayapán, near Maní, as the capital of a unified Mayan state (Roys, 1962).

By Mesoamerican standards, Mayapán was not a large city (estimated maximum population of twelve thousand), nor did it represent a resurgence of Classic period Mayan grandeur (Adams, 1977, 213). The architecture was shoddy. It represented an incomplete fusion of Toltec with Mayan elements, a weak reflection perhaps of the grander works at Chichén Itzá. According to the chronicles, Mayapán was held together by force. Provincial lords were held captive in the city. Dissention was rife. Mercenary troops from Tabasco were imported to hold the lid on, but in A.D. 1446, the festering discontent exploded. The Cocom family was systematically slaughtered, their property confiscated, and their houses burned. The city was abandoned and had become a ruin by the time of the Spanish Conquest about a century later. Roys (1957) suggests that the

Detail on the platform of the Eagles and the Jaguars at Chichén Itzá. Note the human hearts held by each of the figures. (Photo by Joel Whitman)

sixteen independent Mayan states encountered by the Spaniards were the former provinces of Mayapán. The correspondence could not, however, have been exact. Some provinces must surely have expanded at the expense of others in the ninety years between Mayapán's destruction and the Spanish Conquest.

Summary

In this chapter a speculative model of the complex relationships among Mayan architectural practices and the maintenance of a kin-based social, political, and economic order was used as a springboard for examining detectable patterning in the archaeological record. The essential pattern inferences drawn from this inquiry will be summarized in rough chronological order.

Prior to 800 B.C., Mayan farming communities were egalitarian kin-based social, economic, and political units. Sometime after 800 B.C., the emergence of an ancestor cult (or the intensification of a preexisting ancestor cult) transformed basically egalitarian kin relations into internally ranked networks of parent-child and sibling links. This transformation may have proceeded unevenly (here faster, there slower), but by 300 B.C. it had engendered communities with authority and prestige distribution practices centered on the construction and maintenance of earthen funerary monuments.

Between 300 B.C. and A.D. 400, the authority and prestige-distribution limits inherent in monument building worked together with population growth to produce a dispersed pattern of populous centers, satellite communities, and frontier settlements. But population growth continued unabated. Larger populations and an infusion of Olmec knowledge and iconography strengthened traditional forms of power and authority that were now glorified in an emergent emphasis on artistic embellishment.

By A.D. 400, the most populous Mayan centers had been incorporated into a land-based *teotihuacano*-dominated trade network. Participation in the main currents of the Classic period trade in low-volume, high-value commodities brought a new prosperity to Mayaland and promoted a preexisting tendency toward craft specialization and other forms of entrepreneurship. Prosperity in turn broadened the base provided by traditional forms of prestige distribution and allowed entrenched authorities to control a larger following. The resulting increased labor force was, however, invested in traditional symbols of power and prestige, that is, elaborately embellished monuments and public works programs that extolled the virtues of those in command.

The collapse of the *teotihuacano*-dominated trade net circa A.D. 650 forced the central lowlands Maya to depend upon the management of locally available resources and limited the economic growth their technology could sustain. Unabated population growth combined with limited economic potentials and ecological mismanagement to produce severe strains in the fabric of Mayan life. In the ninth century, monument building and public works programs were discontinued in the central lowlands. We presume that the organizing social and political force behind them had collapsed. In Yucatan, however, programs of public works and monument building persisted for another century. It is tantalizing to speculate that a seaborne exchange in high-volume, low-value commodities continued after the *teotihuacano* collapse. If so, then it might have been important to the continued economic well-being of Mayan populations in Yucatan and could have provided an incentive for the Mexican conquest that ultimately brought Mayan hegemony in the peninsula to an end.

REFERENCES

Adams, Richard E. W.
  1977   *Prehistoric Mesoamerica.* Little Brown and Co. Boston.
Andrews, E. Wyllys, IV
  1965   Archaeology and Prehistory in the Northern Maya Lowlands. *Handbook of Middle American Indians.* Vol. 2:288–330. University of Texas Press. Austin.
Ball, Joseph W.
  1974   A Coordinate Approach to Northern Maya Prehistory. *American Antiquity.* Vol. 39:85–93.
Bell, Betty
  1956   An Appraisal of the Maya Civilization. *The Ancient Maya.* George Brainerd, ed. Stanford University Press. Stanford.
Bernal, Ignacio
  1958   Monte Albán and the Zapotecs. *Boletín de Estudios Oaxaqueños.* No. 1. Oaxaca.
Bullard, William R., Jr.
  1960   The Maya Settlement Pattern in Northeastern Petén, Guatemala. *American Antiquity.* Vol. 25:355–372.
Catherwood, Frederick
  1844   *Views of Ancient Monuments in Central America, Chiapas and Yucatan.* New York.
Coe, Michael
  1956   The Funerary Temple among the Classic Maya. *Southwestern Journal of Anthropology.* Vol. 12:387–493.
  1957   Cycle 7 Monuments in Middle America: A Reconsideration. *American Anthropologist.* Vol. 59, No. 4.
  1961   Social Typology and the Tropical Forest Civilizations. *Comparative Studies in Society and History.* Vol. 4:65–85.
  1962   *Mexico.* Frederick A. Praeger. New York.
  1966   *The Maya.* Frederick A. Praeger. New York.
Coe, William
  1965   Tikal: Ten Years of Study of a Maya Ruin in the Lowlands of Guatemala. *Expedition.* Vol. 8, No. 1.
Covarrubias, Miguel
  1946   El Arte Olmeca: O de La Venta. *Cuadernos Americanos.* Vol. 5:153–179.
Drucker, Philip, Robert F. Heizer, and Robert J. Squier
  1959   Excavations at La Venta, Tabasco, 1955. *Bureau of American Ethnology, Bulletin* 170. Washington, D.C.

Fried, Morton
    1967   *The Evolution of Political Society: An Essay in Political Anthropology.* Random House. New York.
Gann, Thomas W. F.
    1927   *Maya Cities: A Record of Exploration and Adventure in Middle America.* London.
Gordon, George B.
    1896   Prehistoric Ruins of Copán, Honduras. A Preliminary Report of the Explorations by the Museum, 1891–95. *Memoirs of the Peabody Museum of American Archaeology and Ethnology.* Harvard University. Vol. 1, No. 1. Cambridge, Mass.
Hammond, Norman
    1977   The Earliest Maya. *Scientific American.* Vol. 236:116–123.
Harré, R.
    1961   *Theories and Things.* Sheed and Ward. London and New York.
Haviland, William A.
    1968   Ancient Lowland Maya Social Organization. *Middle American Research Institute, Tulane University of Louisiana.* Vol. 26. New Orleans.
    1977   Dynastic Genealogies from Tikal, Guatemala: Implications for Descent and Political Organization. *American Antiquity,* Vol. 42:61–67.
Hewett, Edgar Lee
    1936   *Ancient Life in Mexico and Central America.* Bobbs-Merrill. New York.
Holland, William R.
    1964   Contemporary Totzil Cosmological Concepts as a Basis for Interpreting Prehistoric Maya Civilization. *American Antiquity.* Vol. 29:301–306.
Holmes, William H.
    1895–   Archaeological Studies among the Ancient Cities of Mexico. *Anthropological*
    1897   *Series.* Vol. 1. Field Columbian Museum, Chicago.
Kelley, David H.
    1962   Glyphic Evidence for a Dynastic Sequence at Quirigua, Guatemala. *American Antiquity.* Vol. 27:323–335.
Kidder, Alfred V.
    1947   The Artifacts of Uaxactún, Guatemala. *Carnegie Institution of Washington.* Publication 576. Washington, D.C.
Krause, Richard A.
    1972   The Leavenworth Site: Archaeology of an Historic Arikara Community. *University of Kansas Publications in Anthropology.* No. 3. Lawrence.
Kubler, George
    1912   *The Art and Architecture of Ancient America.* Penguin Books. Baltimore.
Kurjack, Edward B.
    1974   Prehistoric Lowland Maya Community and Social Organization. *Tulane University, Middle American Research Institute.* Publication 38. New Orleans.
Leone, Mark
    1968   Economic Autonomy and Social Distance: Archaeological Evidence. Dissertation. Department of Anthropology, University of Arizona.
Linné, Sigrald
    1934   *Archaeological Researches at Teotihuacán, Mexico.* Ethnographical Museum of Sweden. Stockholm.

McBride, Felix W.
1945   Cultural and Historical Geography of Southwest Guatemala. *Smithsonian Institution, Institute of Social Anthropology*. Publication 4. Washington, D.C.

Marcus, Joyce
1973   Territorial Organization of the Lowland Classic Maya. *Science*. Vol. 180:4098

Millon, René
1970   Teotihuacán: Completion of Map of Giant Ancient City in the Valley of Mexico. *Science*. Vol. 170:1077–1082.

Morley, Sylvanus G.
1947   *The Ancient Maya*. 2d ed. Stanford University Press. Stanford.
1956   *The Ancient Maya*. 3d ed. Stanford University Press. Stanford.

Murdock, George
1949   *Social Structure*. MacMillan. New York.

Peebles, Christopher
1974   Moundville: The Organization of a Prehistoric Community and Culture. Dissertation. Department of Anthropology, University of California, Santa Barbara.

Pfeiffer, John E.
1977   *The Emergence of Society: A Prehistory of the Establishment*. McGraw-Hill. New York.

Piña Chan, Román
1958   *Tlatilco*. 2 vols. Instituto Nacional de Antropología e Historia. Mexico.

Pollock, Harry E. D.
1965   Architecture of the Maya Lowlands. *Handbook of Middle American Indians*. Vol. 3:379–440. University of Texas Press. Austin.

Potter, David F.
1973   Maya Architectural Style in Central Yucatan. Dissertation. Department of Anthropology, Tulane University.
1976   Prehispanic Architecture and Sculpture in Central Yucatan. *American Antiquity*. Vol. 41:430–448.

Proskouriakoff, Tatiana
1960   Historical Implications of a Pattern of Dates at Piedras Negras, Guatemala. *American Antiquity*. Vol. 25:454–475.
1961   The Lords of the Maya Realm. *Expedition*. Vol. 4:14–21.
1963– Historical Data in the Inscriptions of Yaxchilán. *Estudios de Cultura Maya*.
1964   Vols. 3 and 4.

Rands, Robert L.
1973   The Classic Maya Collapse: Usumacinta Zone and the Northwestern Periphery. T. P. Culbert, ed., *The Classic Maya Collapse*. University of New Mexico Press. Albuquerque.

Rathje, William L.
1970   Socio-Political Implications of Lowland Maya Burials: Methodology and Tentative Hypotheses. *World Archaeology*. Vol. 1:359–368.

Roys, Ralph L.
1957   The Political Geography of the Yucatan Maya. *Carnegie Institution of Washington*. Publication 613. Washington, D.C.

1962   Literary Sources for the History of Mayapán. Harry E. D. Pollock et. al.,
       Mayapán, Yucatan, Mexico. *Carnegie Institution of Washington*. Publication
       619. Washington, D.C.

Service, Elman R.
1975   *The Origins of the State and Civilization*. W. W. Norton. New York.

Shook, Edwin M., and Alfred V. Kidder
1952   Mound E III-3, Kaminaljuyú, Guatemala. Carnegie Institution of
       Washington. *Contributions to American Anthropology and History*. Publica-
       tion 53. Washington, D.C.

Smith, S. Ledyard
1950   Uaxactún, Guatemala: Excavations from 1931–7. *Carnegie Institution of
       Washington*. Publication 588. Washington, D.C.

Stephens, John L.
1843   *Incidents of Travel in Yucatan*. First edition published by Harper and
       Brothers. Reprint. Dover. New York, 1963.

Sterling, Matthew W.
1940   An Initial Series from Tres Zapotes, Vera Cruz, Mexico. National Geographic
       Society. *Contributed Technical Papers,* i, No. 1. Washington, D.C.
1955   Stone Monuments of the Rio Chiquito, Vera Cruz, Mexico. *Bureau of
       American Ethnology*. Bulletin 157:1–28. Washington, D.C.

Thompson, John Eric Sydney
1954   *The Rise and Fall of Maya Civilization*. University of Oklahoma Press.
       Norman.
1966   *The Rise and Fall of Maya Civilization*. 2d ed. University of Oklahoma Press.
       Norman.

Tozzer, Alfred M.
1941   Landa's Relación de las cosas de Yucatán. *Papers of the Peabody Museum of
       American Archaeology and Ethnology*. Harvard University. Vol. 28. Cam-
       bridge, Mass.
1957   Chichén Itzá and Its Cenote of Sacrifice: A Comparative Study of Contem-
       poraneous Maya and Toltec. *Memoirs of the Peabody Museum of American
       Archaeology and Ethnology*. Harvard University. Vols. 11 and 12. Cam-
       bridge, Mass.

Turner, Blake L., II
1974   Prehistoric Intensive Agriculture in the Maya Lowlands. *Science*. Vol.
       185:118–124.

Webb, Malcom
1964   The Post-Classic Decline of the Petén Maya: An Interpretation in the Light of
       a General Theory of State Society. Dissertation. Department of Anthropol-
       ogy, University of Michigan.

Willey, Gordon R., William R. Bullard, John B. Glass, and James C. Gifford
1965   Prehistoric Maya Settlements in the Belize Valley. *Papers of the Peabody
       Museum of American Archaeology and Ethnology*. Harvard University. Vol.
       54, No. 1. Cambridge, Mass.

Wolf, Eric R.
1959   *Sons of the Shaking Earth*. Phoenix Books. The University of Chicago Press.
       Chicago.

CHAPTER IV

FROM CONQUEST TO INDEPENDENCE: YUCATAN UNDER SPANISH RULE, 1521-1821

Edward H. Moseley

The Mexican invasion of Yucatan disrupted political, social, and religious patterns, but it did very little to alter traditional agrarian systems or Mayan folk culture. The Spanish Conquest, however, initiated radical changes: the introduction of strange plants and hungry animals upset the ecological balance, ruthless conquistadores initiated new systems of land tenure, and zealous missionaries forced the Indians to accept a new God and Christian symbols. Cities were organized on the European model, and Spanish urban life became as much a part of the peninsula as the Mayan village. Because of its harsh geography, isolation, and Mayan heritage, the peninsula became a complex variation on the colonial theme. Three centuries of Spanish rule, often overlooked because of the mystery of pre-Columbian splendor, left an indelible mark on the region and its inhabitants.[1]

Europeans probably visited Yucatan before the end of the fifteenth century, but the first recorded contact was in 1511, when a shipwreck left thirteen men stranded on the eastern coast. Only two survived: Gonzalo Guerrero, who turned his back on his Spanish heritage, and Jerónimo de Aguilar, who learned the language and customs of his captors but later joined the expedition of Hernán Cortés.[2] Other explorers began to probe the mainland from the newly established base of Cuba. Francisco Hernández de Córdoba landed on the coast of Campeche in 1517 but was fatally wounded in the attempt. The following year, Juan de Grijalva organized a second expedition, accompanied by Pedro de Alvarado, Francisco de Montejo, and a number of other individuals who were to play significant roles in the later conquest of the Maya.[3] Grijalva returned to his island base bearing tales of unseen wealth and splendor. In 1519, Hernán Cortés, defying his superior officer, sailed from Cuba to Yucatan. Assisted by Jerónimo de Aguilar, who served as his interpreter, the great conquistador went on to defeat the Aztec Empire.[4] After the fall of Tenochtitlán the explorers turned once again to the land of the Maya. Pedro de Alvarado, probably the most intrepid lieutenant of Cortés, pushed south from the Isthmus of Tehuantepec in late 1523,

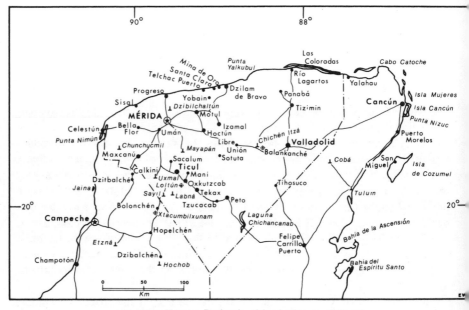

Northern Yucatan Peninsula. (Map by Eugene Wilson)

defeating the powerful Maya Quiché and establishing a basis for Spanish control in Guatemala for the next three centuries. Cristóbal de Olid, another veteran of the Aztec campaign, initiated the conquest of Honduras about the same time.[5] The stage was set for a return to Yucatan, still considered to be a huge "island" north of Guatemala. In this age of heroes, a remarkable adventurer emerged to undertake the task.

Francisco de Montejo first visited Yucatan in 1518 as a member of the Grijalva expedition. He accompanied Cortés the following year and became absorbed in the adventures of central Mexico. In 1526, having returned to Spain, Montejo was commissioned by Emperor Charles V to subdue the region of Yucatan. Based upon the medieval concept of the *adelantado* (literally "one who pushes forward"), Montejo was to recruit his own army and bear all costs of the expedition. In return he received full civil and military authority as *adelantado*, governor, and captain general. He was authorized to distribute land to loyal followers and to reserve ten square leagues as a hereditary holding for his family. Marriage to a wealthy widow, Doña Beatriz de Herrera, enabled him to purchase three ships and recruit some 250 men. Chief lieutenant for the venture was another veteran campaigner, Alonso Dávila.[6] The expedition originated in Spain, and, after a brief stop in Santo Domingo, where ships were refitted and recruits added, the small fleet reached Cozumel in early 1528. Crossing to the mainland of the peninsula and penetrating into the interior, the Spaniards were discouraged by the harsh terrain and absence of treasure. His ranks decimated by Indian attacks and diseases, Montejo sought reinforcements in Mexico City. Among the new recruits was the governor's illegitimate son, also named Francisco Montejo, called "El Hijo" (the son) in order to distinguish him from the *adelantado*, who was destined to play a key role in the heroic deeds to follow. The new force was delayed for a number of reasons, but in early 1531 crossed from Tabasco to establish a base of operations at the town of Campeche. Outstanding administrative skills were required to solve the gigantic logistical problems involved in the expedition. Having made careful preparation, the younger Montejo advanced northward, reaching the splendid ruins of Chichén Itzá in late 1532. After establishing a Spanish settlement called Ciudad Real, the commander was lulled into a false sense of security. The Maya struck swiftly, drove the invaders from the sacred city, and cut their lines of communication. Barely escaping destruction, the force finally reached the protection of Campeche, only to learn that Dávila had suffered a similar fate. Many soldiers deserted the campaign and sought a more rewarding field in Peru under the banner of Francisco Pizarro. After two years of hardship and conflict, the Spanish were confined to a narrow enclave on the west coast of the peninsula.[7]

Not until 1540 did the younger Montejo renew the campaign. A number of fresh recruits joined his ranks, including a cousin whose name was also Francisco Montejo. Known as "El Sobrino" (because he was the nephew of the elder Montejo), this young man was to play an important part in the conquest. Moving cautiously from their Campeche base, the Spanish established valuable alliances with various Mayan caciques. In Maní, just north of the Puuc hills, the Xiu chieftains gladly joined the invaders against their old enemies, the Cocomes. Following a series of victories, Montejo, the Younger, seized the Mayan city of T-Hoo on January 6, 1542, renaming it Mérida.[8] Over the next four years, other regions were brought under control, and on May 28, 1543, the town of Valladolid was founded by "El Sobrino." The northern region of the peninsula seemed to be securely in Spanish hands, and an outpost at Bacalar represented sovereignty in southern Quintana Roo.

On the night of November 8, 1546, a date representing "Death and the End" on their traditional calendar, the Maya suddenly attacked Mérida. They not only killed Spaniards and Indians who had accepted Christianity, but, as a sign of complete rejection of European culture, slaughtered horses and cattle and uprooted fruit trees and other plants brought by the invaders. Only after five months of savage fighting were the Montejos able to crush this Great Mayan Rebellion.[9]

Consolidation of Power

By March 1547, the conquest was complete, and a new society was emerging in Yucatan. At the age of sixty-seven, Francisco de Montejo was master of a vast territory stretching from the Isthmus of Tehuantepec to Guatemala. His claim was based firmly upon a royal grant and honorable conquest by arms. Assisted by members of his family and faithful veterans, the old *adelantado* set about to consolidate further his position. Dependable followers were appointed to serve in the cabildos (municipal councils) in Mérida, Campeche, and Valladolid— Spanish islands in a Mayan sea.[10] Although more than five hundred thousand Indians may have been killed during the conquest, they still greatly outnumbered the small European population and were relocated into compact villages under loyal chieftains. In Maní, the Xiu family continued to rule, becoming an integral part of the emerging power structure. The Peches of Zipatán and Chels of Yobain were rewarded with positions of continued authority for having assisted the Spanish during the Great Rebellion. Many Mayan leaders took the Spanish titles of *alcalde* (mayor) or *alguacil* (constable), although in the eastern region of the peninsula most retained the traditional designations cacique and *batab*. The Cocomes of Sotuta, who had been the most fierce opponents of the Spanish Conquest, were stripped of all political authority and relegated to common status. Within a few years, however, members of that family had accepted baptism and were allowed to return to their position of control.[11]

The political structure was closely linked to the social and economic ambitions of the conquerors. Because of an absence of precious metals and the forbidding nature of the landscape, Yucatan's major economic resource lay in the physical strength of the subjugated population. Although the cabildo of Mérida authorized forced labor after the Great Rebellion, slavery in the classic form was never widespread in the peninsula. More significant was the encomienda system that was first utilized in the Caribbean islands and then transferred to the mainland.

Indian communities were assigned to European guardians; the Maya were given protection and taught basic Christian doctrine in exchange for labor. Thus, the conquistadores were given the mission of Hispanicizing the Indians in return for service and tribute in maize and a variety of other items. When the crown threatened to eliminate encomienda privileges, the Mérida cabildo protested vigorously to the king. Although intended as a temporary assignment, at times only for a single generation, the encomiendas became footholds of power that were to continue throughout the colonial period. As might be expected, the Montejos reserved a number of tributary communities for themselves. Other important citizens such as Juan de Urrutia and Francisco Bracamonte also controlled extensive grants. By 1549, some 178 Mayan communities were administered from Mérida and Campeche, with others being controlled from Valladolid and Bacalar. The loyal Mayan nobility willingly assisted in the assignment of their subjects to the system.[12]

The question of land tenure further complicated the relationship between the Spaniards and the Maya. Prior to the conquest, the Indians had practiced communal agriculture whereby extended families were given allotments of land by caciques. The Spanish crown recognized these collective holdings and adopted laws to protect the milpas. Long after the conquest, the Maya continued to raise maize, beans, squash, and peppers—staple elements in their diet. Europeans, on the other hand, saw the ownership of land as an avenue to increased economic power and social prestige. The Maya considered the soil and its products to be sacred, whereas the Spaniard merely wanted to control the agricultural process. Thus, there was an important psychological distinction between the two groups regarding the relationship of man to land. Following the terms of his grant, Montejo set aside an entailed estate of ten square leagues. At the same time, he distributed land to his followers and relatives. Consequently, prominent families came to control ranches or estancias and identified their economic interests with the political power of the Montejos. Horses, mules, cattle, and sheep were imported from the West Indies, and, despite the rocky soil, a variety of European crops were transplanted. The first estancias were established on open lands that were represented as being worthless for agriculture. They were devoted to the production of cattle and did not need an extensive labor force. Although regulations prohibited the encomenderos from utilizing Indians on private property, such restrictions were often ignored, and many encomenderos shifted workers to their individual holdings. Over the centuries, the encomiendas and estancias evolved into haciendas. As on the medieval European manor, workers eventually came to be tied to the soil in the Yucatecan agricultural system. Indians living outside the control of the towns were called *naboríos*.[13]

The conquest was further consolidated by the actions of missionaries, determined to spread Christianity among the Maya. A Carmelite friar and two secular priests accompanied Montejo in 1528, and shortly thereafter Fray Jacobo de Testera was the first Franciscan to reach the peninsula. In 1546, six more members of that order arrived from Guatemala, the vanguard for hundreds of others who would join the missionary effort in the following decades. Learning the Mayan language, they often assisted secular authorities in negotiations with the native population. The Franciscans became a key element in the emerging power structure, basically allied with the conquistador and his supporters. Montejo, the Younger, was keenly aware of the valuable support from these dedicated and intrepid priests.[14]

By 1549, it seemed that the old *adelantado* and his family had succeeded in carving out a semiautonomous province. The governor's authority was supported by an emerging feudal nobility with a set of common interests and a religious establishment that gave a stamp of divine sanction to the new order. Despite this strong position, external pressures and internal bickering soon produced factionalism and a power struggle.

Struggles for Authority

During the age of conquest, the Spanish sovereigns granted extensive titles and privileges to ambitious and highly independent men. Following this heroic age, however, the crown hastened to replace these conquistadores with more loyal and trustworthy administrators. Christopher Columbus was sent back to Spain in chains by a royal inspector, and Hernán Cortés was pushed aside by appointed officials. In Peru, the Pizarro brothers carried out a bloody civil war against the crown in a fruitless effort to maintain their power.[15] In Yucatan, as elsewhere, the situation was complicated by petty jealousies and a series of territorial struggles.

In 1539, Governor Montejo surrendered his claims to the region south of the Gulf of Honduras, but insisted that all of the area north of that body of water was a rightful part of Yucatan. In 1547, however, Emperor Charles V granted the territory bordering the Golfo Dulce to the Dominican order. The central figure in this missionary scheme was Bartolomé de las Casas, bishop of Chiapas and defender of Indian rights. Montejo vigorously rejected these claims but was eventually forced to cede the region. When the Dominicans failed to colonize it, the resulting political vacuum was eventually filled by English logwood cutters.[16]

Meanwhile, political factionalism emerged in Mérida: Sánchez del Castillo, a resident of the city, denounced the monopoly of power exercised by the Montejo family. In a direct appeal to the crown, Sánchez charged the *adelantado* with administrative irregularities, favoritism in judicial matters, and the possession of illegal encomiendas. To complicate matters further, a jurisdictional dispute developed between the Audiencia of New Spain and that of Guatemala regarding Yucatan. Both bodies sent representatives to the region, disrupting the authority of the Montejos. To settle the question the Council of the Indies appointed Diego de Santillán as *visitador* (inspector general) to Yucatan. After conferring briefly with Viceroy Antonio de Mendoza in Mexico City, Santillán assumed his post in Mérida on June 16, 1550. One of his first actions was to deprive the Montejo family of its encomiendas. Denouncing the efforts designed to strip him of authority and privileges granted in a solemn contract, the old *adelantado* appealed directly to the crown. His trip to Spain ended in failure, and he died in 1553, never returning to the New World.[17]

In Mérida the disputes continued: citizens protested the mistreatment of their venerable patron, possibly more out of concern that they might lose their own privileges than because of a sentimental attachment to the old conquistador. The cabildo petitioned the crown for the appointment of Montejo, the Younger, to succeed his father, but this request was denied. Some of the trappings of power were retained by the family; the title of *adelantado* was given to Catalina, the legitimate daughter of the elder Montejo, and to her husband Alonso Maldonado. The son continued to occupy the Casa Montejo, symbol of the conquest and most prominent home in Mérida. When he died in 1565, however, Montejo, the Younger, was heavily in debt. His heirs retained influence in municipal affairs and prestige in social circles, but political power had shifted to the appointed officials of the crown. The era of the conquistador in Yucatan was at an end.[18]

In 1560, King Philip II appointed Dr. Diego Quijada as *alcalde mayor* of Yucatan and Tabasco, assigning that region permanently to the Audiencia of Mexico. A graduate of the University of Salamanca, the new official had previous administrative experience in Guatemala, San Salvador, and Nicaragua. Arriving in January 1562, he initiated a number of programs designed to improve the colony and to increase royal authority. He was especially interested in the construction of roads to link the principal settlements of the colony. As might have been expected, the old residents resented the newcomer and his attempts to curb their powers. When the *alcalde* revoked a municipal election in Campeche on the grounds that it was controlled by a small elite group, he alienated the most powerful families of the port. The greatest resentment, however, came over the question of control of the Indian population. Quijada took steps to end the use of Indians as *cargadores* (porters) and encouraged the importation of horses and carts for the transporting of goods. The encomenderos resented this interference in their affairs, and a group of prominent citizens demanded that road building be halted so that Indians would be available to transport their goods rather than work on those projects.[19] The growing hostility between the royal official and the older families came to be linked with a serious religious question that affected every aspect of colonial life. The *alcalde mayor* was soon overshadowed by another major figure in the history of Yucatan, Fray Diego de Landa. Virtually every aspect of life in the peninsula was dominated by the dispute centered upon the career of that missionary.

The Age of Landa: 1549–1579

By the middle of the sixteenth century, the Franciscans enjoyed a virtual monopoly in ecclesiastical affairs and exercised a strong influence in every aspect of colonial life. This power was greatest in the Mayan villages, where the brothers supervised elections, administered funds, enforced regular church atten-

Statue of Bishop Diego de Landa in Izamal. (Photo by Joel Whitman)

dance, and blocked the entrance of other Europeans. It is not surprising that the encomenderos came to view the friars as a threat to their interests and often spread rumors that the Franciscans were primarily interested in comely *mozas hermosas* with whom they engaged in lewd carnal acts.[20] It was into this setting that Diego de Landa arrived in 1549, and within a short time he became the focal point for strong emotions and petty jealousies.

Elected as the first *ministro provincial* of Yucatan in 1559, Landa boldly denounced Spanish settlers for their brutal and inhumane treatment of the Indians. At the same time, through an extensive study of the Mayan language, customs, and life-styles, he became convinced that many natives continued their pagan rites despite their participation in Christian services. The zealous missionary vowed to root out every vestige of ''heathen influence'' and to establish a truly orthodox Christianity among his charges.[21] This vow was strengthened in 1562 when rumors began to circulate throughout the peninsula that a newborn baby had been crucified by Indians in the village of Hanacti near Maní.[22] About the same time, a number of idols and human bones were discovered in a nearby cave. Landa rushed to Maní and began an intensive investigation of the surrounding villages. With authority from the Audiencia of New Spain, an inquisitional court was established. The friar and his assistants tortured a number of Indians into confessing idolatry and other forbidden practices. On June 11, 1562, the *provincial* ordered the arrest of some thirty prominent Mayan leaders, including Francisco de Montejo Xiu, governor of Maní. When these actions brought strong opposition among the natives, Landa called for assistance from secular authorities.

Diego Quijada, who had arrived in the peninsula only a few months before the inquisitorial trials, joined Landa in Maní. Escorted by an impressive force of Spanish troops, the *alcalde mayor* assisted in the establishment of a public *auto de fe,* with the initial ceremonies taking place on July 12, 1562. The bones of some twenty Indians who had practiced heathen rites were disinterred and burned in the presence of the congregated masses. Twenty-seven hieroglyphic rolls (considered to be ''works of the devil'') and five thousand idols were destroyed. Hundreds of natives confessed under torture, and on the following day Landa assigned twenty-five prominent chieftains to Quijada for imprisonment. As the investigations continued in other villages, horrible tales of pagan rites were unveiled; in the pueblo of Sotuta, witnesses testified that children had been sacrificed on the church altar and that the cacique Lorenzo Cocom had thrown three boys into the cenote of Chichén Itzá. Testimony obtained through torture was questionable, however, and many witnesses probably exaggerated in order to escape the wrath of the zealous missionaries. Some Indians committed suicide rather than submit to the grueling torment, and there were growing rumors of an impending Mayan uprising.[23]

Spanish encomenderos denounced the investigations, and the cabildo of Mérida demanded that the acts of persecution be stopped. When Landa refused to change his tactics, the municipal officials appealed to the Audiencia of Mexico,

Parish Church at Maní, built on the site of the *auto de fe* of 1562. (Photo by Edward Terry)

denouncing both Landa and the *alcalde mayor*. Before any action was taken on the appeal, a further complication developed: Francisco de Toral, first bishop of Yucatan, arrived in Mérida on August 14, 1562, only a month after the famous *auto de fe*. Finding the Spanish community still badly divided, he met with various factions and carefully sifted evidence and charges. Though a Franciscan himself, Toral concluded that Landa and his associates had been guilty of excessive zeal, and he took steps to reduce tensions. He ordered the release of many of the Indians and suggested that Landa continue investigations but without the use of torture. Landa rejected this idea, insisting that without force it would be impossible to obtain confessions from the Maya, who were guilty of abominable acts. He left Yucatan in March of 1563, determined to gain royal assistance to vindicate his honor. Landa's Franciscan supporters remained hostile to the bishop, viewing him as a traitor to their order. Toral, however, continued the investigations and corresponded directly with the Spanish crown in defense of his position. The argument was in part a clash of two strong-willed clergymen, but it also involved fundamental questions of policy and jurisdiction in the colony.

With the departure of Landa, the encomenderos continued their assault against Quijada and the Franciscans, finding a strong ally in the newly arrived bishop. Toral at one point actually excommunicated the *alcalde mayor* and appealed for the assistance of the younger Montejo, but with no lasting result.[24] There is no doubt that the hatreds against Quijada went even deeper than those against Landa; encomenderos felt that their privileges to control Indians were threatened by his policies. In 1564, the cabildo of Mérida sent a petition to the crown accusing the *alcalde mayor* of making irreligious statements and ordering Indians to do his personal will. He was also charged with having seduced the wife of an old conquistador, Garci Hernández. Throughout this struggle, however, it was clear that their principal concern was the charge that he discriminated against the original settlers in the distribution of encomiendas. The colonists, supported by the bishop, seemed to win a victory when the *alcalde mayor* was dismissed by order of the king two years before the completion of his term of office.[25] Luis de Céspedes, newly appointed governor of Yucatan, presided in a *residencia* (inquiry) on November 22, 1565, in which Quijada was found guilty on seventy-seven charges. Though the charges were dropped after an appeal to Madrid, Quijada never returned to Yucatan.[26] Thus, encomenderos working at the municipal level with the support of the local bishop triumphed over an appointed royal official utilizing the cumbersome mechanism of Spanish colonial administration. The victory was only temporary, however, for later appointees would continue to exercise extensive powers over encomienda assignments and over all aspects of the lives of citizens. Nor had Yucatan seen the last of Diego de Landa.

After his departure from Mérida in early 1563 and a visit to Mexico City, Landa arrived at the Spanish court the following year. At first, his efforts to defend his actions at Maní seemed futile, but he persisted, gaining significant support from Franciscans in the mother country. After eight years of legal squabbling, the cleric was finally exonerated. The triumph seemed complete in 1572, when Philip II appointed him second bishop of Yucatan to replace his old adversary Toral. Upon his return to Mérida, Bishop Landa vowed to renew his campaign to stamp out idolatry and establish doctrinal purity. Finding clergymen ineffective and unable to speak the Mayan language, the new prelate expelled many and replaced them with thirty newly arrived Franciscans.[27] Thus, the province became almost exclusively a Franciscan territory, in contrast to many other Spanish colonies where the secular clergy played a prominent role.[28]

During the inquisitional activities in Maní, Fray Landa had enjoyed the assistance of the *alcalde mayor*. In his new position of authority, however, he did not hesitate to challenge Governor Francisco Velázquez Gijón. He charged that royal official with flagrant abuses in the assignment of encomienda grants. When Velázquez refused to employ secular power to punish Indians charged with idolatry, Landa, in a fit of rage, excommunicated the governor. In a scene reminiscent of the medieval papacy, Velázquez fell to his knees and begged the bishop for absolution.[29] The conflicts continued with the next governor, whose fondness for card games made him a target of constant ridicule. The Franciscan's criticism was only the surface reflection of a deeper struggle for power and authority. It continued until April 29, 1579, when, during a trip to Mexico City to press his case, the venerable bishop died.[30]

Possibly the most significant single individual in the history of Yucatan, Diego de Landa has remained the center of bitter controversy. His enemies stress his role in the destruction of invaluable Mayan documents and artifacts in the name of Christianity. Apologists, on the other hand, point to his magnificent volume, *Relación de las cosas de Yucatán,* undoubtedly the most important single source for information on Mayan culture and history.[31] Landa has also been charged with cruelty against the Indians accused of pagan rituals. At the same time, he was a constant defender of the natives against secular abuses inflicted by encomenderos and crown officials.[32] There is no doubt that he ignored basic human rights as interpreted by later generations, but Landa reflected the mentality and zeal of his age.

Despite their importance, the controversies that have raged regarding the destruction of documents and human torture have actually obscured an evaluation of the most important impact of Bishop Landa upon Yucatan. He represented the profound influence of the Franciscan order in the cultural evolution of the Yucatecan Maya. Although ancient concepts and customs were never fully destroyed, they were greatly altered and blended with European ideas and symbols. Political, social, and economic institutions were deeply affected by the missionary effort. By the time of Landa's death in 1579, the groundwork for a new society had been established.

Cultural Blends and Polarizations, 1580–1700

By 1580, the age of conquest had ended; during the next 120 years a complex set of political, economic, and cultural institutions was developed in Yucatan. Though isolated in many ways, the province was an integral part of the great Hapsburg Empire and must be viewed within that system. Often depicted as an era of stagnation, the seventeenth century was in Yucatan a dynamic period, a time of building and change; urban centers developed along traditional Hispanic lines while the Mayan way of life continued to prevail in the villages and countryside. The two cultures were, however, in constant association, and it was in this period that a distinctive Yucatecan society emerged.[33]

The political structure of the colonial system was based upon the concept of absolute monarchy, which had an extensive set of laws and regulations. These were, in turn, applied selectively by various interest groups and appointed officials who shared power in the peninsula. Although within the jurisdiction of the Audiencia of Mexico, for most purposes Yucatan was administered directly from Spain through the Council of the Indies. The principal executive official, with the title after 1571 of governor and captain general, was appointed directly by the crown and enjoyed extensive powers. Of the forty individuals serving in that capacity between 1580 and 1700, not a single one was a native Yucatecan. Some were capable officers who took their duties seriously, but others were interested primarily in lining their own pockets by any means possible. Many governors flouted the strict regulations against property ownership and economic activities on the part of high officials. Along with each came a host of relatives, friends, and office seekers. Those who held the top post were from prestigious Spanish families, and several were members of the upper nobility. Even for these exalted officials life was uncertain. In 1620, Governor Francisco Ramírez Briseño, an energetic and effective adminstrator, died suddenly, allegedly poisoned by a jilted mistress. In 1644, Francisco Núñez Melián, having been in office only four months, was killed when thrown from his horse during a review. Two years later, Governor Esteban de Azcárraga died of the plague, along with many other inhabitants. Then in the midst of the famine of 1652, Governor García de Valdés y Osorio, Conde de Peñalva and one of the highest ranking nobles ever to hold office in Yucatan, was stabbed to death in bed, seemingly because he had profiteered from the sale of corn. Only twelve of the forty governors during the period served as much as a complete term of four years. Other administrative officials were assigned by royal appointment, including a lieutenant governor, treasury agents, military commanders, and *corregidores* who supervised Indian towns. A number of customs officials resided in Campeche, the only authorized port of entry for the colony.

In addition to the appointed officials, there existed a second level of political power. The *ayuntamiento* or municipal council of Mérida continued to reflect the interests of the conquerors and their descendants. At the head of the council were two individuals with the title of *alcalde ordinario,* assisted by twelve *regidores* (councilmen), and a number of lesser officials in charge of routine administrative tasks. In Campeche and Valladolid similar structures were established, though with fewer members. Positions in *ayuntamientos* came to be hereditary and thus directly represented the interests of the Creole families. At times, however, the offices were sold, thus opening the way for bribery and other abuses.

The system was designed not only to bestow power upon various officials, but also to check and limit that power. Governors were subjected to *residencias* at the end of their term as well as to periodic inspections by *visitadores.* A less formal but extremely effective check on executive power grew out of conflicting interest groups and overlapping jurisdictions. In 1604, Governor Carlos de Luna y Arellano arrested a number of *regidores* who opposed his policies. These officials in turn appealed to the Audiencia of New Spain; the *visitador* sent by that body ruled against the governor. A more complex struggle developed in 1630, when the municipal council of Mérida appealed to the Audiencia against the actions of Governor Juan de Vargas. When the visitor general arrived, Vargas insisted that an emissary from Mexico had no authority over his territory; he ordered the *visitador* to leave Yucatan within fifteen days. At that point the bishop intervened, supporting the *visitador* and his Creole allies in the *ayuntamiento.* A showdown was avoided when the governor conceded defeat and departed secretly from Mérida. Until the end of the seventeenth century, the power structure retained this delicate and uncertain balance. As was the case throughout the Spanish Empire, obedience to unpopular laws was avoided through delay, twisted interpretations, or legal red tape. Distance and barriers to communication helped to foster self-reliance within the Creole population.[34]

The Roman Catholic church occupied a key role in the governing hierarchy of the colony. Bishops were appointed directly from Spain and maintained constant communication with royal authority. In fact, there was no clear division between secular and ecclesiastical power; an example can be seen in the career of Marcos de Torres, appointed bishop of Yucatan in 1646, but in the following year named viceroy of New Spain. At times, bishops supported governors, but, as seen above, would often oppose their policies and form an alliance with the *ayuntamiento*. To complicate matters further, the Franciscans occasionally clashed openly with the secular clergy, and in 1681 were even accused of the murder of Bishop Juan de Escalante Turcios de Mendoza. Despite these fraternal struggles between secular and regular clergy, the church remained a powerful political force. Controlling extensive landed estates, the clergy provided education, hospitals, and a variety of charitable services. The priesthood offered one of the few means of social mobility; many Creoles rose to positions of authority among the Franciscans and abandoned the simple ways of the early friars. The order continued to increase its strength through the seventeenth century, often prevailing over the governors and bishops. In 1605, the *ayuntamiento* of Mérida invited the Jesuits to establish a school, thus initiating the work of that important group in the colony and laying the foundation for the University of Yucatan.[35]

By 1600, Mérida gave every sign of being the political, economic, and cultural center of a Spanish province. The Spanish architect Juan Miguel de Agüero had been commissioned to prepare plans for a cathedral soon after the completion of the conquest. In the following decades, the huge structure, designed in the Mannerist style, was slowly erected. Its simplistic lines and massive stone columns reflected the influence of the Renaissance and at the same time were representative of the austere land in which it was built. Completed in 1598, the year of the death of Philip II, this cathedral has remained the primary symbol of the Catholic faith in Yucatan. Other churches were constructed in the following decades, some with the charm and beauty characteristic of the evolving age of baroque. Among them was the Jesuit church of the Third Order (1618) and the Franciscan convent La Mejorada (1640). Secular architecture flourished; in 1612, the governor's palace was remodeled, and in the following years plans were initiated to construct a wall around the city. This undertaking was never completed, but a series of imposing arches still offer evidence of the ambitious project. Domestic architecture also played an important part in the transition. The Casa Montejo continued to be the most imposing residence, reflecting Spanish dominance over the Maya in its graphic stone carvings. Other prominent families constructed homes in the vicinity of the main plaza, utilizing local materials and Indian labor. Carved doorways and shady patios reflected marked Arabic influence, and the heirs of the conquistadores added touches of comfort and luxury. The capital was an impressive reflection of Hispanic culture in an obscure corner of the empire. In 1618, King Philip III presented Mérida with a coat-of-arms, declaring it to be "muy noble y muy leal." The event was celebrated with great jubilation in the colony.[36]

The Cathedral of San Ildefonso in Mérida, on the east side of the main plaza. Designed by Juan Miguel de Agüero, it is the largest and most impressive church in the peninsula.

The monastery of La Mejorada Church, constructed in the seventeenth century by the Franciscans. It has been converted into the School of Architecture of the University of Yucatan. (Photo by Joel Whitman)

Façade of the Casa Montejo, located on the south side of the main plaza in Mérida. The family coat of arms can be seen above the entrance, and the feet of Spanish knights flanking the shield rest on the heads of Indians. (Photo by Edward Terry)

Campeche, though founded before Mérida, lagged in its development, partly because of the constant threat of piracy along the coast, at first primarily from the French but in the late sixteenth century from the English and the Dutch. In 1598, William Parck sacked Campeche and forced a number of citizens to flee their homes. On August 11, 1653, the feared Pie de Palo (Old Peg Leg) attacked the port, and twelve years later the Englishman Jacob Jackson repeated the act. One of the most daring raids was carried out in 1685 by the Flemish corsair Laurent Graff (Lorencillo), who captured Campeche and initiated a march against Mérida itself. Only after repeated efforts were the Spanish officials able to expel him. There was a growing demand for defensive measures, and some progress was made from time to time, but the cabildos of both Mérida and Valladolid objected to spending revenues on the port city. In 1688, however, important steps were taken to fortify Campeche. Governor Juan José de la Bárcona, who was appointed that year, installed a company of cavalry and one hundred infantrymen. In February of 1690, thirty pieces of artillery were mounted, and two years later a major effort was initiated on city fortifications. Despite these efforts, the threats continued and by the end of the century were linked to growing British ambition in the entire Caribbean region.[37]

Valladolid, established by Montejo "El Sobrino," was the third Spanish city of the colony. In fact, until 1639, its population of some 2,495 inhabitants exceeded that of Campeche. Descendants of the conquistadores were proud of their heritage, and the cabildo leaders did not hesitate to challenge the governor's authority when their economic interests were threatened.[38]

Other settlements in the peninsula were Indian villages centered around Franciscan missions. Some twenty communities had between five hundred and a thousand households, the most prominent including Ticul, Maní, Oxkutzcab, Motul, Izamal, and Calkiní. Collaboration of Indian leaders was very important in the establishment of the governing system in Yucatan as in other parts of the Spanish Empire. Native chieftains of the old Mayan families still exercised a central political role, and many cultural features remained firmly rooted in the villages, but with important restrictions from the Franciscans, corregidores, and encomenderos. On at least one occasion, in the village of Tekax, Indian citizens revolted against their cacique, who was saved only by the intervention of priests. The Maya constructed huts of sticks and mud with a thatch roof, in the same style as that of their preconquest ancestors. They still tended their milpas, raised the traditional crops, paid tribute to the priests and encomenderos, and supplied workers to nearby estancias. In each community massive churches and convents were constructed, their imposing bell gables rising above the flat limestone plain, thus emphasizing the Franciscan dominance of the countryside.[39]

In the eastern and southern regions of the peninsula, Spanish control was very weak. Despite Franciscan efforts, a large number of Maya rejected Christianity and continued the old religious and social practices under their traditional leaders known as h-men. From time to time Indians fled from villages and haciendas, taking refuge in the frontier wilderness. The region of present-day Quintana Roo

Four village churches reflecting the uniformity and variety found in the Franciscan style. (Photos by Edward Moseley)

was sparsely populated with only a few encomenderos in the region of Bacalar. That settlement was abandoned in 1642 because of the constant threat of Indian attacks and the pirate raids along the Caribbean coast. After this, the English increased their activities and utilized Jamaica as a base for expansion after 1655. Around the mouth of the Belize River they initiated logwood cutting operations, thus setting the stage for their foothold on the Gulf of Honduras. Efforts on the part of Yucatecan governors to dislodge them failed by the end of the seventeenth century.[40]

Far to the south, around Lake Petén, a sizable group of Maya remained completely independent under their powerful Itzá cacique Can Ek (The Black Serpent). In 1624, Captain Francisco Mirones pushed into the region with fifty men, determined to bring it under Spanish dominance. The expedition ended in disaster as the Indians seized Mirones, cut open his chest, and ripped out his heart. Other attempts in the middle of the seventeenth century also ended in failure but left important records relating to the Maya living in that region.[41] For the next forty-five years, Petén Itzá remained a refuge for escaped peons and was considered a threat to the security of Yucatan. In 1692, King Charles II gave a special order to Martín de Urzúa y Arizmendi, a Spaniard residing in Mexico City, to conquer the region between Yucatan and Guatemala, the realm of Can Ek. It is quite obvious that by this time the title of Can Ek had been passed down from one generation to the next. The Council of the Indies instructed officials in Mexico, Yucatan, and Guatemala to assist in that endeavor. In 1694, the president of the Audiencia of Guatemala dispatched three hundred men, but the governor of Yucatan vacillated and was replaced by Urzúa. Reports from the south indicated that Can Ek might submit to Spanish rule and accept baptism, but it soon became clear that the proud leader had no intention of bowing to European demands. Urzúa marched south from Campeche in early 1697, constructed boats on the shores of Lake Itzá, and struck against the Mayan stronghold. Fearing the Spanish firearms and overcome by their opponents, many Indians jumped from their canoes and were drowned. The governor returned triumphantly to Mérida, leaving a force of fifty men to guard the southern outpost. The region was never fully incorporated into the colony, however, and the Maya continued to practice their traditional customs. There was a shifting frontier between these areas, with cultural elements of the north moving from time to time into the remote regions of the south.[42]

The demographic structure of the peninsula underwent important changes between 1580 and 1700. Some 235,000 Maya had survived the conquest by 1549, but that number declined steadily over the following decades. Periodic drought, severe famine, and epidemics of typhus, smallpox, measles, and other diseases decimated their ranks. Many fled from villages or haciendas to take refuge beyond the Spanish dominion, thus further reducing the population. By 1700, the Maya numbered only 182,500, but still comprised about 98 percent of the total population. In 1580, there were approximately 2,000 inhabitants of Spanish blood and 300 Negroes and mulattoes in the colony; by the end of the seventeenth century, the non-Indian elements reached about 20,000. Creole families, though resenting the slights from appointed officials, were fiercely proud of their European blood and considered themselves a colonial nobility. In fact, they became the very foundation of the Hispanic elite that was to dominate the region following independence.[43]

At first glance, Yucatan seemed to be a dual society, with Spanish and Creole elements dominating the three principal towns, while the Maya remained sealed off in the villages under strict Franciscan supervision. Despite social polarization and Spanish racial pride, however, the seventeenth century was an age of mixture and blending. Few Spanish women came to the colony in the early years, and numerous temporary liaisons produced an important mestizo population. These offspring of Spanish fathers and Mayan mothers tended to occupy a middle position in the social and economic system, absorbing elements of culture from both parents. Some were servants to the Spanish; others learned the mechanical arts or served as common soldiers in the militia. Within this Yucatecan society there emerged a set of strict social guidelines and cultural divisions. Only individuals of Spanish descent were allowed to wear European styles. Indians and mestizos came to adopt special clothes designed by the friars; men wore white trousers and a loose-fitting blouse and went barefoot or wore sandals, whereas women wore the *huipil,* a white cotton dress with a square neck and decorated with colorful embroidery. This distinctive dress has remained a key element in Yucatecan culture down to the present day (see Chapter V for a full discussion of this topic of dress and class distinction). Indians were required to cut their hair in a prescribed manner and were prohibited from riding horses or owning firearms. Marriages, funerals, and other public ceremonies were segregated on a racial basis.[44]

The process of cultural transfer and assimilation, though impossible to measure, progressed year after year. Franciscans required Indians to accept church doctrine and perform Catholic rituals. It is doubtful, however, that many had any real understanding of the religious system to which they were being subjected. Traditional deities were syncretized into patron saints within the Christian system; the most famous was the Virgin of Izamal, which gained the reputation in the seventeenth century for many miracles and was carried through the streets of Mérida during times of disaster. It was no coincidence that this powerful Christian symbol was housed in Izamal, one of the most sacred cities of the Maya and burial place of the great Mayan god Itzamná. Despite the efforts of Landa and his fellow Franciscans, paganism continued; Mayan folk tales persisted and reflected ancient respect for the earth, various natural forces, and especially corn. The depths of Mayan culture continued to be expressed in the persistence of the ancient language. Many Indian traits also influenced the mestizos and even the Creoles, thus making the cultural transition a two-way process.[45]

By no means stagnant, the century that ended in 1700 was a period of great importance in the shaping of Yucatan. Though the Maya were still planting their milpas and engaged in practices much older than the conquest, within the cities and villages European culture was manifested in architecture, language, dress, and customs. The mixture of bloodlines resulting in the emerging mestizo race was producing a unique Yucatecan citizen who took his place along with the European and the Maya.

Yucatan in the Age of Enlightenment and Revolution, 1700–1800

The death of Charles II, last of the Spanish Hapsburg kings, in 1700 set the way for major changes in the mother country and throughout the empire. His successor, Philip V of the House of Bourbon, initiated a series of political and economic reforms, strengthening the central government and stimulating industry. French influence penetrated intellectual circles and transferred concepts of the Enlightenment to the Iberian region. Secular authority clashed with the church, culminating in 1767 with the expulsion of the Jesuits. The high point of this process came during the reign of Charles III (1759–88), when reforms were extended to the empire. Under Charles IV, who ascended the throne in 1788, Bourbon Spain was caught up in the French Revolution and broader events of the European Continent that in turn brought major changes to the colonial region.

In Yucatan a small stream of Spaniards continued to arrive throughout the century. By far the greatest change, however, came from the major increase in Creole and mestizo elements, which by 1800 accounted for over 100,000 individuals, more than 28 percent of the total population (see Table 1). Mérida and its immediate surrounding territory had almost 30,000 inhabitants by 1794 and continued to absorb European influences. New homes were constructed reflecting the emphasis upon the classical style, and churches continued to be raised. The population increased in most of the encomienda settlements and mission towns. Umán, for example, increased from 137 inhabitants in 1688 to 1,164 in 1785. In the same period, Hoctún grew from 289 to 1,276. The Indian population, which had diminished steadily since the conquest, finally began to increase after about 1740 and doubled in the last half of the century.[46]

Table 1.   Population of Yucatan, 1610–1794

Year	Indian	Non-Indian	Total Population
1610			190,000
1639	210,000	12,500	222,500
1700	182,500	20,000	202,500
1736	127,000	34,000	161,000
1794	254,000	103,000	357,000

Source: Cook and Borah, *Essays in Population.* II, 100–114.

As Mérida and other urban centers increased in population, there was a growing demand for corn and a corresponding rise in price. Some grain was imported from Veracruz, New Orleans, Baltimore, and Charleston, but Creole landowners soon took advantage of the situation and began to produce corn for the internal Yucatecan market. Indians left their villages and settled on the estancias, thus converting them into a very different type of social unit from the sparsely populated ranches of the previous centuries. Robert Patch, in his study of the Yucatecan land system, calls these developments of the eighteenth century "a great agrarian change." The term "hacienda" was applied to the holdings; workers and their families came to be tied to the land, not only by debt peonage but also through a complex set of economic and social factors. It is important to note that the process was carried out primarily in the northwestern section of the peninsula, in a fifty-mile radius of Mérida, roughly the equivalent of the henequen zone that would become important following independence. These haciendas were the foundation of wealth and the base for the dominant social class structure of Yucatan that was to last well into the twentieth century. In the east, south, and southeastern regions of the peninsula the great majority of the Indians continued to live in their traditional agrarian communities.[47] Meanwhile, the traditional power structure of the colony was undergoing major stresses.

Suspicion and hostility, which had long prevailed between the Franciscans and members of the secular clergy, erupted into open violence. When Bishop Pedro de los Reyes Ríos, a Benedictine friar of Spanish birth, attempted to secularize a number of missions, the friars rebelled: on Ash Wednesday of 1706, they assaulted the episcopal palace, clashing with the bishop's household servants. The struggle took on political and cultural overtones because many of the Franciscans were Creoles. The issue was settled for a short time but erupted once again with the appointment of Juan Gómez de Parada, a native of Guadalajara, Mexico, as bishop. With complete support from King Philip V, the bishop initiated a full-fledged investigation of every aspect of colonial life. On October 1, 1722, he ordered sweeping changes in political organization, public education, mission administration, and regulation of Indian labor. In a moving speech, the prelate denounced the evils of the colonial system, including clerical ignorance and corruption of the encomenderos. Two years later, he issued an edict that virtually abolished the Indian labor system as it had functioned for almost two centuries, allowing Mayan workers to demand payment for their services. The cabildos of Mérida, Campeche, and Valladolid sent delegations both to Mexico City and Madrid, hinting that the actions of Bishop Gómez might spark a rebellion. They were supported fully by the encomenderos and by the Franciscans, who still smarted under the increasing power of the secular church. Just as their ancestors had rejected the reforms of Las Casas, the Creoles of the eighteenth century refused to accept any effort to deprive them of Indian labor. It seemed, however, that under the enlightened Bourbon administration the reforms of Bishop Gómez might be carried out, especially because he was supported by Governor Antonio de Figueroa (1725–33), one of the most able and honest individuals to serve in the entire colonial era. Despite a severe famine that began the year after the governor's arrival, the reforms seemed destined to be adopted by the end of his term. The pressures of colonial interest groups had been effective, however, and in 1736 the king issued a cedula that allowed the reestablishment of *repartimientos* and the system of personal services over the Indians of Yucatan. Furthermore, under a succession of weak governors over the next twenty-five years, virtually all of the innovations were ignored, reflecting the power of the traditional elite.[48] This was in contrast to most other regions of the empire where *repartimientos* were abolished.

The serenity of the colony was suddenly broken in 1761 by an event that greatly alarmed the European population. During the annual religious festival in the village of Cisteil, near Sotuta, an Indian killed a white aguardiente merchant, apparently in a fit of drunken anger. In that land of once-powerful Cocomes, old grievances once again erupted into violence. Jacinto Uc de los Santos, a young Indian who had been educated by the Franciscans in Mérida, made an emotional speech, denouncing the Spaniards for their treachery and cruelty, and called upon the Maya to rebel. Crowned with relics from the local church, he took the name Can Ek in memory of the legendary cacique of the Itzá. News of the uprising spread quickly to Valladolid and other nearby towns, creating a state of alarm among the Creole and Spanish elements. On November 26, a Spanish force marched to Cisteil and struck swiftly against the Indians, who were armed for the most part only with machetes and bows. Some six hundred Maya were killed in the struggle, but the Spanish lost only forty men. Can Ek and his associates were captured and dispatched to Mérida where they underwent a brief trial. After brutal torture, the rebel leader was executed, his body burned, and the ashes scattered in the winds. Many other Indians were also tortured and executed. The humanitarian efforts of Bishop Gómez and Governor Figueroa were pushed aside, and forces supporting the traditional colonial system were given new strength and support. Tight control measures were then taken to guard against any possible retribution by the Maya.[49] This created an atmosphere of deep resentment and tension, and the resulting fears affected the relationships among classes for many years afterward.

In the period immediately following the rebellion, some important changes were made in the colony, most of them stimulated by external factors. Governor Cristóbal de Zayas (1765–71) enforced the royal decree expelling the Jesuits. On June 12, 1767, that influential and powerful group was deported, thus greatly impairing Yucatan's educational system. Zayas also enacted Bourbon commercial reforms in 1770, bringing a major increase in trade to the colony and consequently producing revenues for the Spanish government. In that same year, as if in celebration of these changes, the protective walls of Campeche were finished after almost a century of effort.[50] After four relatively inactive governors who followed Zayas, Roberto Rivas Betancour took office in 1779 at the same time Spain entered the war of the American Revolution against the British. Governor Rivas moved against the English logwood cutters in the region of the

Río Hondo on September 15, 1779. His force occupied Cayo Cocina, took a number of prisoners, and reestablished the Spanish claim to the Gulf of Honduras. In the peace treaty of 1783, however, these gains were sacrificed in exchange for the possession of Florida. Much to the disgust of Yucatecans, Spain allowed the British to retain rights in Belize, and within a few years the English subjects were once again exercising virtual sovereignty over the region. It became the base for further extension of contraband into southern Yucatan and represented a constant threat to the security of the entire peninsula. During the French Revolution, Yucatan was the launching site for an attack against the British enclave, but a near-successful attempt once again ended in frustration.[51]

Although King Charles III, the most able of the Bourbon monarchs of Spain, died in 1788, many of his reform policies were advanced by Lucas de Gálvez, who served as governor of Yucatan from 1789 to 1792. An ambitious and energetic man, Gálvez promoted agriculture and commerce and made a major effort to improve the long-neglected road network of the region. In Mérida he carried out an extensive beautification project, constructing a park and installing street lights. He also introduced the cultivation of rice and attempted to develop a fishing industry. In keeping with Bourbon ideals, the administrative structure of the colony was revamped; twelve districts were established under the intendancy system. With expanding trade, revenues were greatly increased. Gálvez, more than any other official of Yucatan, reflected the spirit of the age of Enlightenment. It was only natural that many of the traditional elements of society were bitter in their opposition to his policies. These included the *ayuntamiento* of Mérida and many Franciscans. Bishop Luis de Piña y Mazo also became a staunch opponent of the governor. The bitterness of the quarrel set the stage for a tragic end to his brilliant career. On the night of June 22, 1792, while on his way home from a pleasant *tertulia,* Gálvez was suddenly stabbed by a mysterious horseman. Toribio del Mazo, nephew of the bishop and a rival of the slain governor for the favors of a beautiful woman, was convicted and imprisoned, though eight years later another man confessed to the crime. This tragic event, however, brought an end to many of the efforts to revitalize the colony. In the years following the death of Gálvez, the Spanish Empire was caught up in the broader tragedies of the Napoleonic wars.[52] This, in turn, would set the stage for further changes in the nineteenth century.

End of the Colonial Era, 1800–1821

Benito Pérez Valdelomar took office as governor of Yucatan on October 19, 1800, and retained that post for eleven years. During that time, the pace of life quickened, and a number of new trends emerged. A growing commercial class, both in Campeche and Mérida, enjoyed the profits of expanded trade under the Bourbon reforms. Following petitions from the capital city and Valladolid, a royal decree of February 13, 1810, opened the port of Sisal, thus ending 270 years of monopoly by the commercial interests of Campeche. Resentment from those elements was focused against Mérida and would in the years after independence bring bitterness and conflict.[53] By the turn of the century, some 1,550 individuals in Mérida were classified as "middle class." Many of the sons of this emerging bourgeoisie were influenced by European intellectual thought, including economic liberalism and Cartesian philosophy. In the Seminary of San Ildefonso, Pablo Moreno was one of the most important advocates of the concepts of rationalism. Among his pupils were Andrés Quintana Roo, son of a merchant, and a brilliant young man named Lorenzo de Zavala, both of whom would play important roles following independence. Also a part of the influential elite was Father Vicente María Velázquez, chaplain of the church of San Juan Bautista. Although to some degree influenced by new philosophies, Padre Velázquez was more in tune with traditional humanistic Christianity. In 1810, he established the Society of San Juan, its members being known as *sanjuanistas*. Devoted to social reform and utilizing the concepts of Bartolomé de las Casas, Velázquez denounced both Spanish and Creoles who mistreated the Indian population.[54] His teachings produced heated debates and denunciations from the more conservative factions of society. Then dramatic events in the mother country opened the way for more radical changes.

In 1808, Napoleon sent a French army into the Iberian Peninsula, overthrowing King Ferdinand VII and establishing his brother Joseph on the throne. Spanish communities rejected the French usurper and set up local governmental juntas. Their representatives gathered in Cádiz in September 1810 to form a national assembly or *Cortes*. That body was composed of delegates from both Spain and the colonies, including Miguel González Lastiri representing Yucatan. Influenced by the liberal concepts of the day, the Cádiz assembly produced the Constitution of 1812, a document that was to have far-reaching influence. It included many provisions for liberties and representative government and recognized six separate provinces of New Spain, including Yucatan. Each was to have a separate administration controlled by a provincial assembly (*diputación provincial*). A series of officials, including several elected within the colony, were to function directly under the Spanish central government, thus bypassing the authority of the viceroy of Mexico City. Then on November 9, 1812, the Cádiz government passed a series of revolutionary decrees abolishing *mitas, repartimientos,* and other aspects of personal services by the Indians.

Yucatan, as well as other regions of the empire, was greatly affected by these European events. In August 1810, Gustavo Nordinch De Witt, a charming agent of Napoleon Bonaparte, arrived in Mérida. Though accepted socially by some of the prominent families, he was eventually arrested as a spy and executed. This action by Yucatecan officials demonstrated their continued support of the deposed Bourbon monarch. Two years later, news of the Constitution of 1812 brought spirited debates and internal divisions in the colony. Padre Velázquez and the *sanjuanistas* vigorously supported the liberal document and rang the chapel bells to celebrate its arrival. They obtained the colony's first printing press to reproduce the Constitution, and Lorenzo de Zavala became one of the most ardent spokesmen for its adoption. Governor Manuel Artazo y Barral, taking office only shortly before its arrival, at first opposed the document but finally gave in to the concerted pressures and recognized its authority. In fact, Yucatan was the first region of New Spain to establish a provincial assembly. When the reform decrees of November 9, 1812, reached Mérida they were ardently supported by the *sanjuanistas* but bitterly opposed by the conservative elements of society called *rutineros*. For the time being, however, the will of the more liberal faction tended to dominate. It is significant to note that the revolt of Padre Hidalgo that broke out in northwest Mexico in September 1810 had virtually no impact on the isolated peninsula. The colony seemed to be oriented toward the Constitution of 1812 and dominated by the reform-minded elements of the Society of San Juan. On March 15, 1813, Yucatan elected deputies to the Cádiz Cortes, with delegates representing Mérida, Campeche, Izamal, Valladolid, Tekax, Tihosuco, and Calkiní.[55]

The Constitution and other liberal measures had a significant impact upon the church. Despite opposition by Franciscan leaders, the *sanjuanistas* pushed for the abolition of clerical *obvenciones* that were levied upon the Indians. The governor, caught between the two contending elements, hesitated for awhile, but eventually gave in to the liberal demands on February 27, 1813. Many Indians abandoned their services to the church and at times even demonstrated hostility toward the priests. By the following December, Bishop Pedro Agustín Estévez y Ugarte reported greatly reduced attendance at mass. Several parishes were abandoned, and the priests moved to Mérida. The economy of the peninsula was also disrupted because Indians stopped making cotton thread and gathering various products for sale. When the governor attempted in early 1814 to impose upon the Maya taxes that had been previously levied only on the European population, there was widespread opposition. Throughout the colony, heated discussions raged. In the Seminary of San Ildefonso a quarrel between liberal professors and the more conservative rector produced several faculty resignations and a student demonstration. Tensions created during those years were to have a long-range impact on the colony in the following decades. The established authority of both the crown and the church was weakened and controls over the Maya were so greatly disrupted that they could never be completely restored.[56]

With the defeat of Napoleon in 1814, Ferdinand VII was returned to the Spanish throne and soon after rejected the Cádiz Constitution of 1812 and its liberal precepts. News of this return to absolutism reached Mérida on July 28, 1814, and the more conservative elements received it with widespread rejoicing. They marched through the streets, tearing to shreds copies of the detested Constitution. Governor Artazo quickly initiated steps to dismantle the liberal system. Following his lead, a mob seized Father Velázquez and forced him to kneel before a picture of Ferdinand VII and confess his "errors." He was then imprisoned in the convent of San Francisco. Other *sanjuanistas* were arrested, and Lorenzo de Zavala was imprisoned in San Juan de Ulúa, Veracruz, for the next three years. At the insistence of Bishop Estévez, the governor also ordered the resumption of *obvenciones* upon the Mayan population, a further rejection of the concepts of the *sanjuanistas*. Some priests took advantage of the Indians, forced them to cut their hair in the old manner, restored corporal punishment, and imposed heavy personal services upon them.[57] Between 1814 and 1820, it seemed that the wave of liberalism had ended and that the traditional elements of absolutism had turned the clock back to the prerevolutionary age. It was impossible, however, to restore all of the old ways; controls over the Maya had been interrupted and the authority of the church weakened. New factions of Creole society had tasted political power and a variety of liberties. Upon his release from prison, Lorenzo de Zavala returned to Yucatan, revived the old ideals of liberalism, and assisted in the establishment of the first Masonic order in the region.

On April 16, 1820, word arrived from Havana that a revolt in Madrid had forced Ferdinand VII to reestablish the Constitution of 1812 and the representative system of government. Zavala met with old members of the *sanjuanistas* and established secret contacts with Masonic elements in Campeche. The governor hesitated to accept their demands for a return of the Constitution but finally gave in on May 13, making Yucatan the first province in New Spain to reestablish the provincial assembly under that liberal document.[58] Factionalism bitterly divided the body; Father Velázquez and other liberals struggled to return to the ideals of the society of San Juan. The association was never reestablished, but many of its old members joined the Confederación Patriótica, which was founded by Lorenzo de Zavala. As an illustration of the extent of their power, on June 8, 1820, the provincial assembly removed the aging Captain General Castro y Araos and replaced him with Colonel Mariano Carrillo y Albornoz, an ardent liberal.

Despite these indications of sovereignty, there were deep-seated divisions within the ruling elite and especially a growing distrust between elements from Mérida and those from Campeche who were more interested in commercial advantages for the port than in broader ideals of constitutional rule. Captain General Carrillo denounced the Franciscans for plotting his overthrow, thus creating heated disputes regarding the position of the order within the newly emerging system. Conditions became so tense that on October 3, 1820, Carrillo had to call upon four soldiers to dissolve the provincial assembly, and shortly thereafter he suspended the *ayuntamiento* of Mérida. A number of prominent citizens were arrested, including Lorenzo de Zavala, thus further splitting the ranks of the liberal factions. The confusion seemed complete when the liberal government of Spain dismissed Carrillo y Albornoz, naming Juan María Echeverri governor and captain general. He took the post on January 1, 1821.[59] Meanwhile, Lorenzo de Zavala, having been released from imprisonment, traveled to Spain as one of Yucatan's representatives to the Cortes. Despite internal squabbles, it seemed by early 1821 that Yucatan would become a semi-independent province within the Spanish system. Once again, however, external actions changed the course of events.[60]

On February 23, 1821, Agustín Iturbide, a former royalist, proclaimed the independence of Mexico with the Plan of Iguala. This ambiguous pronouncement became the rallying point for a wide range of political factions throughout the former viceroyalty, and in the course of a few months independence was achieved. In Yucatan, Governor Echeverri convened a junta of notables on September 15, and on November 2, 1821, that body declared Yucatan to be a part of the newly independent nation of Mexico. In the peninsula this union was achieved without the shedding of a drop of blood. In fact, by the end of the year, the region seemed to be solidly in support of Iturbide and the union with Mexico.[61]

Independence to the Age of Henequen: The Colonial Heritage

Lorenzo de Zavala, one of Yucatan's most prominent native sons, viewed the overthrow of Spanish rule as the dawn of a bright future.[62] Within a few years after his expression of optimism, however, it became clear that independence was merely the prelude to more conflict and strife. By late 1822, the empire of Agustín Iturbide faced open rebellion, and the ambitious young Antonio López de Santa Anna proclaimed that each province should function independently until a republic could be formed. On May 29, 1823, Yucatan agreed to this plan and declared that the state would join other regions of Mexico in the formation of a federal system in which the rights of each state would be guaranteed. A government along these lines was established under the Mexican Constitution of 1824, and Yucatan accepted it readily. It is interesting to note that at this same time Guatemala and other Central American provinces chose complete separation from the old viceregal center.[63]

The Mexican experiment in federalism worked well for the first four years, but in 1828 a series of conflicts broke out. Ideological differences arose over church-state relations, and the two broad factions of conservatives and liberals emerged. The question of federalism or centralism was closely related to these divisions and served to confuse further the political scene. By 1833, the liberal elements seemed to be in control with Valentín Gómez Farías as president, but in the following year Santa Anna proclaimed himself protector of the Catholic faith and all traditional values. When he established a highly centralized government, revolts erupted in a number of states, the most spectacular being that in Texas, which culminated in the formation of a separate republic.[64] The events in Yucatan must be viewed against the broader context of Mexican politics during this time of conflict between the forces of centralism and federalism. The situation was further complicated by the internal rivalries between Mérida and Campeche.

Political and economic differences between the two principal cities of the peninsula had been held in check during colonial days by royal authority, tradition, and bureaucratic procrastination. With the removal of Spanish control, however, latent hostilities moved to the forefront. *Campechanos* demanded that trade with Cuba through the port of Sisal be ended, but this was flatly rejected by

Mérida. In November 1829, a military force in Campeche revolted and declared José Segundo Carvajal political and military chieftain of the peninsula. This movement succeeded when the garrison in Mérida accepted the plan and over-threw the constitutional state government. Carvajal transferred the seat of gov-ernment to Campeche, thus increasing municipal hostilities. During the next four years, there was a series of attacks and counterattacks between the opposing forces. On July 5, 1834, General Francisco de Paula Toro declared in Campeche that he supported the centralized government of Santa Anna. In late July, he crushed federalist elements at Calkiní and marched triumphantly into Mérida without encountering further resistance. Toro was then elected governor and retained control of Yucatan for the next two years, ruling it as an integral part of the centralized Mexican state.[65] Thus, by 1836, the forces of Mexico City seemed triumphant in the peninsula and throughout the nation. It was at that point, however, that the Texas revolt broke out, opening once again the entire question of central power and states' rights.

Between 1837 and 1839, Santa Anna worked to reconquer Texas. He insti-tuted a military draft to strengthen the army and increased taxes to provide funds to support the project. In Campeche as well as in Mérida, there was growing resentment against these burdens imposed from Mexico City. On May 29, 1839, a young Yucatecan officer, Santiago Imán, led a revolt of troops who were scheduled to be transported to the Texas front. Raising the standard of fed-eralism, Imán based his movement in Tizimín; in early 1840 he seized Vall-adolid and demanded the restoration of the Constitution of 1824. The uprising found popular support throughout the region, and on June 16, 1840, the Mexican army abandoned Campeche, thus leaving the state under federalist rule. For the next four years, the peninsula followed a virtually independent course. Links with Texas were very close, and a naval force from the Lone Star Republic supported Yucatan against threatened Mexican invasion. In December 1843, national authorities agreed to readmit the area into the union with the understand-ing that the state would retain control over all internal affairs and keep all tax revenues. Although this pact was ratified on January 14, 1844, Mexican au-thorities never honored it. On January 1, 1846, the Yucatecan assembly decreed that it no longer had an obligation to support the Mexican government and would assume complete sovereignty. When Governor Santiago Méndez refused to ac-cept this action, the legislature dismissed him and appointed Miguel Barbachano interim governor.

The prospects for peace in the peninsula were elusive. The differences be-tween Mérida and Campeche surfaced once again. There were no clear-cut ideological lines, for both factions tended to distrust the government in Mexico City. The rivalry centered upon the two principal leaders, Santiago Méndez of Campeche and Miguel Barbachano, whose principal support was in Mérida.[66] It was in the eastern region of Yucatan, however, that subsequent major events were to take place. For the first time since the Can Ek uprising of 1761, the

Mayan population took a direct and violent hand in politics, thus initiating a vicious struggle that came to be called the Caste War.

The basic social and economic structure of Yucatan changed very little with independence. Despite expressions of liberalism relating to states' rights, the system continued to reflect major inequities, and basic attitudes were virtually unaltered from colonial times. During his epic journey in the 1840s, John Lloyd Stephens found the European elements of the population living like lords in a feudal setting, treating the Maya as inferior beings. Some Creoles utilized their haciendas for the production of export crops, primarily sugar and cotton, but most concentrated on corn and other food products for internal consumption. As in the late eighteenth century, Indians settled on the haciendas around Mérida, but the vast majority of the Maya in the eastern and southern regions continued to till their milpas in the traditional system of subsistence agriculture.[67] Within the religious structure significant changes had occurred; Franciscan power was eroded in the late colonial era, and with independence the prestige of the order with the Indians had been greatly weakened. This did not mean that the influence of Catholicism had ended but that its relationship to the controlling elite had been substantially altered.[68] This entire social pattern was to be shaken in the 1840s, and the Hispanic civilization that had dominated Yucatan for three hundred years was almost to be destroyed.

During the initial stages of the revolt by Santiago Imán in 1839, Mayan soldiers were recruited for the federalist cause. Not only did Imán promise to end traditional tributes, but in violation of a long-standing policy, he armed the Indians. The promises made were quite naturally soon forgotten or disregarded. When hostilities between Campeche and Mérida were renewed in December 1846, an adventurer named Juan Vázquez raised a sizable army of Indians in Yaxcabá. After seizing Peto, he advanced northward, and on January 15, 1847, assaulted Valladolid. Residents of the outlying barrios joined the attackers against the aristocratic elements of the central city. This action resulted in the wanton destruction of property, bloody slaughter of white citizens, and even some acts of cannibalism. A wave of fear passed through the peninsula in this opening phase of the Caste War. The pent-up fury of the natives emerged as Mayan leaders such as Cecilio Chi and Jacinto Pat called for a war of extermination against the Europeans. By the end of May 1848, the Indians occupied four-fifths of the peninsula; the whites held only Mérida, Campeche, and a few other urban settlements. Governor Barbachano prepared to abandon Mérida, but suddenly the Maya broke off the struggle and returned to their milpas to plant corn at the beginning of the rainy season.[69] The complete destruction of Yucatan's Spanish heritage had been narrowly avoided. The Maya of eastern and southern Yucatan remained virtually independent down to the end of the nineteenth century and retained much of their traditional culture combined with Catholic and European forms. It is significant to note, however, that many of the Indian workers on haciendas of the northwest actually supported their Creole masters in the epic struggle.[70] Meanwhile, a major economic transformation was under way that would usher in a new era.

Henequen, a product long known in the Yucatan Peninsula, was shipped from the port of Sisal as early as 1813. Twenty years later, the first commercial plantation was established, and by 1846 the fiber was second only to sugar as the region's most important export. Sugarcane plantations, located primarily in the eastern part of the state, were destroyed during the Caste War, and many of them were never reestablished. On the other hand, henequen production quickly recovered after 1848, greatly aided by the concentration of population in the rocky area around Mérida. This process was further assisted by increased prices and an expanding world market. It was out of the cultivation of this plant that the hacienda system and peonage were to take on their classical forms in Yucatan.[71] Mayan lands were absorbed by the expanding plantations, and the economy of the state was converted into a monoculture. With the political stability of the rule of Porfirio Díaz (1876-1911), Yucatan entered its glorious age of "Green Gold." Wealth from the production of henequen supported the Creole elite in an ostentatious manner symbolized by the massive homes that lined the Paseo de Montejo in Mérida.[72] It was evident that during this period of wealth and splendor the social, political, and economic institutions of the state remained clearly based upon the three centuries of colonial rule. By that time the Spanish heritage, the Roman Catholic religion, and the mestizo population had taken on a unique and distinctive Yucatecan character.

NOTES

1. Sylvanus G. Morley gives an opposing view: "In Yucatan the Toltec conquest changed the Maya way of life considerably more than did the Spanish" (quoted in Sylvanus G. Morley, *The Ancient Maya,* 3d ed. [Stanford, Calif.: Stanford University Press, 1956], p. 80). Although an interesting thesis, this idea would be difficult to defend in light of the great cultural innovations that arrived with the Europeans; see Mariano Picón-Salas, *A Cultural History of Spanish America,* trans. Irving A. Leonard (Berkeley: University of California Press, 1966), pp. 42-69.

2. Marvin E. Butterfield, *Jerónimo de Aguilar, Conquistador,* 2d ed. (University, Alabama: The University of Alabama Press, 1969), pp. 2-18; Sherburne F. Cook and Woodrow Borah, *Essays in Population History: Mexico and the Caribbean,* 2 vols. (Berkeley: University of California Press, 1974), II, 38; Samuel Eliot Morison gives Juan Ponce de León credit for the discovery of Yucatan. See Morison, *The European Discovery of America: The Southern Voyages A.D. 1492-1616* (New York: Oxford University Press, 1974).

3. Fray Diego de Landa, *Relación de las cosas de Yucatán,* Introduction and Notes by Héctor Pérez Martínez, 7th ed. (México, D. F.: Editorial Pedro Robredo, 1938), pp. 60-64; Francisco López de Gómara, *Cortés: The Life of the Conqueror by his Secretary Francisco López de Gómara,* trans. and ed. Lesley Byrd Simpson (Berkeley: University of California Press, 1966), pp. 30-32; Robert S. Chamberlain, *The Conquest and Colonization of Yucatan: 1517-1550* (Washington, D.C.: Carnegie Institution of Washington,

1948), pp. 11–13; Bernal Díaz del Castillo, *The Conquest of New Spain*, trans. with an introduction by J. M. Cohen (Baltimore: Penguin Books, 1963), pp. 27–43.

4. Butterfield, *Jerónimo de Aguilar*, pp. 1–14. Along with Doña Marina, Aguilar became the "eyes and ears" of Cortés.

5. Francisco Fernández del Castillo, *Don Pedro de Alvarado* (México: Ediciones de la Soc. Mex. de Geografía y Estadística, 1945), pp. 49, 53–72, 89–161; Pedro de Alvarado, *An Account of the Conquest of Guatemala in 1524 by Pedro de Alvarado*, ed. Sedley J. Mackie with a facsimile of the Spanish original, 1525 (New York: The Cortés Society, 1924); López de Gómara, *Cortés*, pp. 334–371.

6. López de Gómara, *Cortés*, pp. 36–87, 193, 327; Landa, *Relación*, pp. 84–85; Chamberlain, *Conquest*, pp. 11–33, 35–65; Eligio Ancona, *Historia de Yucatán desde la Época más Remota hasta Nuestros Días*, 4 vols. (Mérida: Imprenta de M. Heredia Argüelles, 1878), I, 252–263.

7. Alfonso Villa Rojas, *The Maya of East Central Quintana Roo* (Washington, D.C.: Carnegie Institution of Washington, 1945), pp. 10–14; Chamberlain, *Conquest*, pp. 35–149, 160–167, 179–184; Fernández del Castillo, *Don Pedro de Alvarado*, pp. 116–117; Luis F. Sotelo Regil, *Campeche en la Historia: Tomo I, Del Descubrimiento a los Albores de su Segregación de Yucatán* (México, D.F.: Imprenta Manuel León Sánchez, 1963), pp. 79–82.

8. Sotelo Regil, *Campeche*, pp. 41–47; J. Eric Thompson, *The Rise and Fall of Maya Civilization*, 2d ed. (Norman: University of Oklahoma Press, 1966), pp. 148–151; Morley, *The Ancient Maya*, pp. 94–97; William Gates, ed., *Yucatan before and after the Conquest*, 2d ed. (Baltimore: The Maya Society, 1937), pp. 138–139; "Auto de Fundación de la Ciudad de Mérida," document quoted in Ancona, *Historia*, I, 396–397; "Fundadores de la Ciudad de Mérida," document quoted in ibid., pp. 398–399; Chamberlain, *Conquest*, p. 213.

9. Chamberlain, *Conquest*, pp. 232–249; Landa, *Relación*, pp. 92–96; Villa R., *The Maya*, p. 14.

10. Chamberlain, *Conquest*, pp. 214, 281–282.

11. Cook and Borah, *Essays*, II, 6, 9, 47–48, 64; Chamberlain, *Conquest*, pp. 170–171, 252; Ancona, *Historia*, II, 186; Villa R., *The Maya*, p. 14; Francisco de Montejo Xiu (governor of Maní) and other (Indian) governors, to the king, April 12, 1567, quoted in Gates, ed., *Yucatan*, pp. 115–117; France V. Scholes and Eleanor B. Adams, eds., *Don Diego Quijada: Alcalde Mayor de Yucatán: 1561–1565*, 2 vols., Biblioteca Histórica Mexicana de Obras Inéditas (México: Antigua Librería Robredo de José Porrúa e Hijos, 1938), I, xxxviii–xxxix; Oswaldo Baqueiro Anduze, *La Ciudad Heroica* (Mérida, Yucatán, México: Imprenta Oriente, 1943), pp. 33–54; Francisco de Solano y Pérez Lila, *Autoridades Municipales indígenas de Yucatán (1657–1677)* (Mérida: Ediciones de la Universidad de Yucatán).

12. Chamberlain, *Conquest*, pp. 20–23, 38–56, 150–156, 252–278; Ancona, *Historia*, II, 6–27; Juan Francisco Molina Solís, *Historia del Descubrimiento y Conquista de Yucatán con una Reseña de la Historia de los Mayas*, 2d ed., 3 vols. (México, D.F.: Ediciones Mensaje, 1943), I, 274–275; Cook and Borah, *Essays*, II, 8–9, 40–60; Baqueiro Anduze, *La Ciudad Heroica*, pp. 30–38, 177–195; Cabildo of Mérida to the crown, June 14, 1543, AGI México 364, quoted in Chamberlain, *Conquest*, p. 174. For further information relating to the attempt by the crown to abolish the encomienda system, see Lewis Hanke, *The Spanish Struggle for Justice in the Conquest of America* (Boston:

Little, Brown and Co., 1965); Manuela Cristina García Bernal, *Los Servicios Personales en Yucatán durante el Siglo XVI* (Mérida: Ediciones de la Universidad de Yucatán, 1977); Salvador Rodríguez Losa, *La Encomienda, el Indio y la Tierra en el Yucatán Colonial* (Mérida: Ediciones de la Universidad de Yucatán, 1978).

13. Thompson, *Maya Civilization*, pp. 93, 126–127; Landa, *Relación*, p. 111; Chamberlain, *Conquest*, pp. 21, 276–277, 330–341; Molina Solís, *Historia*, II, 368–370; Baqueiro Anduze, *La Ciudad Heroica*, pp. 35–37; Robert Patch, *La Formación de Estancias y Haciendas en Yucatán durante la Colonia* (Mérida: Ediciones de la Universidad de Yucatán, 1976), pp. 10–17; Rodríguez Losa, *La Encomienda*, p. 30.

14. Ancona, *Historia*, II, 39–55, 66–67; Chamberlain, *Conquest*, pp. 31–33, 275–282, 314; Landa, *Relación*, pp. 93–99.

15. C. H. Haring, *The Spanish Empire in America* (New York: Oxford University Press, 1947), pp. 12–22; Edward Gaylord Bourne, *Spain in America: 1450–1580* (New York: Barnes and Noble, Inc., 1962), pp. 228–230; Ward J. Barrett, *The Sugar Hacienda of the Marqueses del Valle* (Minneapolis: University of Minnesota Press, 1970), pp. 9–17.

16. Fernández del Castillo, *Don Pedro de Alvarado*, pp. 116–123; Chamberlain, *Conquest*, pp. 253–266, 289–291; Villa R., *The Maya*, pp. 14–15; O. Nigel Bolland, *The Formation of a Colonial Society: Belize, from Conquest to Crown Colony* (Baltimore: Johns Hopkins University Press, 1977), pp. 25–48.

17. Chamberlain, *Conquest*, pp. 277–297; Molina Solís, *Historia*, II, 271, 387–394. The struggle over jurisdiction between the two Audiencias had begun in early 1544. The request for the establishment of a separate Audiencia for Yucatan and Tabasco was denied.

18. Molina Solís, *Historia*, II, 387–396; Ancona, *Historia*, II, 56–65, 81–93; Chamberlain, *Conquest*, pp. 296–310; Joaquín de Arrigunaga Peón, *History of the Montejo House: The Oldest Private Mansion in America* (Mérida, Yucatan, 1967).

19. Chamberlain, *Conquest*, p. 310; Ancona, *Historia*, II, 81–83, 90–93; Scholes and Adams, *Don Diego Quijada*, I, vii–xc; Sotelo Regil, *Campeche*, pp. 128–129.

20. Scholes and Adams, eds., *Don Diego Quijada*, I, xii–xiii. Here Landa's arrival is given as 1549. Other sources indicate 1554: "Información Hecha por Sebastián Vázquez, Escribano de Su Majestad Sobre los Atropellos Cometidos y Tolerados por El Doctor Diego Quixada Alcalda Mayor de las Provincias de Yucatán" (Mérida, March 25, 1565, quoted in Landa, *Relación*, pp. 261–278); Ancona, *Historia*, II, 67–71, 171–180; Cook and Borah, *Essays*, II, 56–60; Chamberlain, *Conquest*, pp. 314–320; Landa, *Relación*, pp. 96–99.

21. Landa, *Relación*, pp. 92–102. "Crueldades de los Españoles con los naturales. . . . Que los indios recibían pesadamente el yugo de la servidumbre" (pp. 121–127).

22. "Fe dada por Fray Pedro de Ciudad Rodrigo, guardián de Maní, acerca de una criatura muerta que le trajeron y las señales que tenía" (Mérida, Sept. 20, 1562, Archivo General de Indias, Escribanía de Cámara 1009B, reproduced in Scholes and Adams, eds., *Don Diego Quijada*, Document XX, Vol. I, 179–181).

23. Gates, ed., *Yucatan*, pp. 115–117; France V. Scholes and Ralph L. Roys, "Fray Diego de Landa and the Problem of Idolatry in Yucatan," *Cooperation in Research* (Washington, D.C.: Carnegie Institution of Washington, Pub. No. 501, 1938), passim; "Declaraciones de algunos testigos sobre la investigación de las idolatrías de los indios hecha por Fray Diego de Landa y sus compañeros en el año de 1562" and "Residencia de Quijada," Archivo General de Indias, Justicia 245, in Scholes and Adams, eds., *Don Diego Quijada*, I, 24–68; "Procesos contra los indios idólatras de Sotuta, Kanchunup,

Mopila, Sahcaba, Yaxcabá, Usil y Tibolón. Agosto de 1562," Archivo General de las Indias, Escribanía de Cámara 1009B, quoted in ibid., I, 71–129.

24. "Pareceres de algunos españoles sobre el castigo de los indios por idolatría, dados a solicitud del Obispo Fray Francisco de Toral, Año de 1562," Archivo General de Indias, Escribanía de Cámara 1009B, quoted in Scholes and Adams, eds., *Don Diego Quijada,* I, 129–135; "Información hecha en el pueblo de Homún sobre la idolatría de los indios. Septiembre de 1562. Residencia de Quijada," Archivo General de Indias, Justicia 249, quoted in ibid., pp. 135–162; "Diligencias sobre la revocación de las sentencias de los indios condenados por Fray Diego de Landa a traer sambenitos y servir a los españoles por término de varios años en la ciudad de Mérida, Mérida, 11 de febrero de 1563," Archivo General de Indias, Escribanía de Cámara 1009B, quoted in ibid., pp. 240–248; "Carta del obispo de Yucatán, Fray Francisco de Toral, a Su Majestad, dando relación del estado de las cosas en la provincia y pidiendo remedio," Mérida, March 3, 1564, Archivo General de Indias, Patronato 184, Ramo 52, quoted in ibid., II, 68–73.

25. Diego Rodríguez Bibanco to king, March 8, 1563, quoted in Gates, ed., *Yucatan,* pp. 117–119; "Carta de Gómez de Castrillo y otros a S. M. enterándole de los agravios hechos por el Alcalde Mayor y Otros varios Asuntos," Mérida, March 15, 1563, quoted in Landa, *Relación,* pp. 279–288; "Información Hecha por Sebastián Escribano de Su Majestad Sobre los Atropellos Cometidos y Tolerados por El Doctor Diego Quixada Alcalde Mayor de las Provincias de Yucatán," Mérida, March 25, 1565, quoted in ibid., pp. 261–278; Scholes and Adams, eds., *Don Diego Quijada,* I, lxxv–lxxxii.

26. Scholes and Adams, eds., *Don Diego de Quijada,* I, lxxxix–xcix. He was eventually suspended in office for ten years but was to die in Castille in 1571 or 1572.

27. Landa, *Relación,* p. 102; Melchior Pech, governor of Samahil province, and other governors, to the king, February 12, 1567, quoted in Gates, ed., *Yucatan,* p. 115; Scholes and Roys, "Fray Diego de Landa," passim; Ancona, *Historia,* II, 101; "Carta de Don Fray Diego de Landa a los Inquisidores de Nueva España, de 22 de Marzo de 1574," quoted in Landa, *Relación,* pp. 289–290; "Carta de Don Fray Diego de Landa a los Inquisidores de Nueva España, de 20 de Diciembre de 1575," quoted in ibid., pp. 294–295; Royal cedula, August 12, 1574 (from Audiencia of New Spain), quoted in Gates, ed., *Yucatan,* p. xiii.

28. Richard E. Greenleaf, *The Mexican Inquisition of the Sixteenth Century* (Albuquerque: University of New Mexico Press, 1969), p. 121; Ancona, *Historia,* II, 101. Ancona states: "Así se conseguía el objeto de que la Orden la dominase toda"; John Leddy Phelan, *The Millennial Kingdom of the Franciscans in the New World,* 2d ed. (Berkeley and Los Angeles: University of California Press, 1970).

29. "Carta de Don Fray Diego de Landa a los Inquisidores de Nueva España, de 19 de Enero de 1578," quoted in Landa, *Relación,* pp. 291–293; Ancona, *Historia,* II, 105–109.

30. Ancona, *Historia,* II, 109–115. He was fifty-three years old at the time of his death.

31. Scholes and Roys, "Fray Diego de Landa"; Gates, ed., *Yucatan,* p. iii: "It is perhaps not too strong a statement to make, that ninety-nine percent of what we today know of the Mayas, we know as the result either of what Landa has told us . . . , or have learned in the use and study of what he told."

32. Hanke, *The Spanish Struggle for Justice,* p. 41: "Friar Diego de Landa's torture of Indians in Yucatan suspected of idolatry shows what might have happened throughout Spanish America"; Ancona, *Historia,* II, 115–116.

33. See Irving A. Leonard, *Baroque Times in Old Mexico* (Ann Arbor: University of Michigan Press, 1959).

34. Ancona, *Historia*, II, passim. The appointment was at first for six years but later reduced to four. At times it is impossible to determine the exact term of office for a given governor, since there were conflicting claims and overlapping periods of service; Chamberlain, *Conquest*, p. 310; Carlos Loret de Mola, *Yucatán en la Patria*, 2 vols. (México, D.F.: Serie, La Honda del Espíritu, 1969), I, 8–41.

35. Ancona, *Historia*, II, 180–197, 243–265, 346.

36. Ancona, *Historia*, II, 144–148, 182–238, 337–358; Leopoldo Castedo, *A History of Latin American Art and Architecture from Pre-Columbian Times to the Present*, trans. and ed. Phyllis Freeman (New York and Washington: Frederick A. Praeger, 1969), pp. 108, 148; Pál Kelemen, *Baroque and Rococo in Latin America*, 2d ed., 2 vols. (New York: Dover Publications, Inc., 1967), I, 30, 78–87; Antonio Betancourt Pérez, *Historia de Yucatán*, 2 vols. (Mérida: Ediciones del Gobierno de Yucatán, 1970), I, 226–230.

37. Ancona, *Historia*, II, 93–367; Cook and Borah, *Essays*, II, 80–81; Sotelo Regil, *Campeche*, pp. 133–156; María Angeles Eugenio Martínez, *La Defensa de Tabasco, 1600–1717* (Sevilla: Consejo Superior de Investigaciones Científicas, Escuela de Estudios Hispano-Americanos de Sevilla, 1971), pp. 27–36.

38. Ancona, *Historia*, II, 200; Cook and Borah, *Essays*, II, 80–81; Baqueiro Anduze, *La Ciudad Heroica*, pp. 37, 177–195.

39. Cook and Borah, *Essays*, II, 5–14; Ancona, *Historia*, II, 141–142, 166–313; Castedo, *A History of Latin American Art;* Kelemen, *Baroque and Rococo;* Betancourt Pérez, *Historia de Yucatán;* Nancy M. Farriss, "Nucleation versus Dispersal: Dynamics of Population Movement in Colonial Yucatan," *Hispanic American Historical Review,* 58, No. 2 (May 1978): 187–216. Solano y Pérez Lila, *Autoridades Municipales;* Patch, *La Formación,* p. 15. Some who ruled were not of the old Indian nobility but from new families.

40. Villa R., *The Maya,* pp. 15–18; *Defensa del Tratado de Límites entre Yucatán y Belize* (México: Imprenta de "El Siglo Diez y Nueve," 1894), pp. 4–5.

41. France V. Scholes and Sir Eric Thompson, "The Francisco Pérez *Probanza* of 1654–1656 and the *Matrícula of Tipu* (Belize)," in Grant D. Jones, ed., *Anthropology and History of Yucatán* (Austin: University of Texas, 1977), pp. 43–68. Other essays in this volume give insight into the complex Mayan society in the southern region of the peninsula.

42. Ancona, *Historia*, II, 98–100, 191–216, 271–313; Loret de Mola, *Yucatán,* II, 39–40; Sir Eric Thompson, "A Proposal for Constituting a Maya Subgroup, Cultural and Linguistic, in the Petén and Adjacent Regions," in Jones, ed., *Anthropology and History,* pp. 3–42.

43. Ancona, *Historia*, II, 168–181, 324–328 ("ponían todo su empeño en conservar pura en sus venas la sangre española ... eran llamadas *nobles* en la Colonia," p. 327); José María Valdés Acosta, *A Través de las Centurias: Obra Especial que contiene apuntes históricos, relatos genealógicos, reseñas biográficas, páginas literarias, antiguos documentos y retratos, etc., etc., etc.,* 3 vols. (Mérida: Talleres "Pluma y Lápiz," 1923, 1926, and 1931). For an interesting comparison see Fred Bronner, "Peruvian Encomenderos in 1630: Elite Circulation and Consolidation," *Hispanic American Historical Review,* 57, No. 4 (November 1977): 633–659. Bronner found that by 1630 the elite of Peru were a mixture of descendants of the conquistadores and early settlers who had become "thoroughly intermingled with peninsular immigrants, especially with government offi-

cials.''; Marta Espejo-Ponce Hunt, ''The Process of the Development of Yucatan, 1600–1700,'' Ida Altman and James Lockhart, eds., *Provinces of Early Mexico: Variants of Spanish American Regional Evolution* (Los Angeles: UCLA Latin American Center Publications, University of California, 1976), pp. 33–62. In this work the author gives an interesting analysis of economic and social structure in Mérida and in other settlements within the colony.

44. Cook and Borah, *Essays,* II, 9–119; Loret de Mola, *Yucatán,* II, 16–25; Nelson Reed, *The Caste War Of Yucatan* (Stanford, California: Stanford University Press, 1964), pp. 3–49. The author describes Yucatan in the nineteenth century as a continuing society with a ''Ladino'' city and Maya or *Mazehaul* countryside. Francisco de Solano y Pérez Lila, *Estudio Socioantropológico de la Población Rural no Indígena de Yucatán: 1700* (Mérida: Universidad de Yucatán, 1975).

45. Ancona, *Historia,* II, 155–159. No attempt is made to trace the rich mythology and folk tales, but they can be found in a variety of sources, including Rodolfo Ruz Menéndez, *Por los Viejos Caminos del Mayab: Ensayos Históricos y Literarios* (Mérida: Ediciones de la Universidad de Yucatán, 1973).

46. Cook and Borah, *Essays,* II, 81–119, 176–179.

47. Patch, *La Formación.* This very informative work develops a number of significant themes relating to landholding, labor supply, and the social, economic, and political factors involved in the evolution of the hacienda system of Yucatan. Patch indicates that the so-called Caste War of 1847 was a rebellion of the free Indians of the east and south against the extension of the haciendas into their territory. Many of the campesinos in the northwest supported the whites against that uprising.

48. Betancourt Pérez, *Historia,* I, 116, 172; Loret de Mola, *Yucatán,* II, 43–69; Ancona, *Historia,* II, 321, 330, 336, 382–432.

49. Ancona, *Historia,* II, 433–450; Loret de Mola, *Yucatán,* II, 69–87. See also Eduardo Enrique Ríos, ''La Rebelión de Jacinto Canek,'' *Diario de Yucatán,* 1936, as quoted in Loret de Mola, *Yucatán,* II, 69–87. It is interesting to note that in 1780 there was a similar rebellion among the Incas of Peru led by Túpac Amaru.

50. John Lynch, *Spanish Colonial Administration, 1782–1810: The Intendant System in the Viceroyalty of the Río de la Plata* (New York: Greenwood Press, 1969), pp. 19, 23; Loret de Mola, *Yucatán,* II, 89.

51. *Defensa del Tratado de Límites,* pp. 6–8; Ancona, *Historia,* II, 451–481; Loret de Mola, *Yucatán,* II, 89–92; Conwell A. Anderson, ''Anglo-Spanish Negotiations Involving Central America in 1783,'' in Eugene R. Huck and Edward H. Moseley, eds., *Militarists, Merchants, and Missionaries: United States Expansion in Middle America* (University, Alabama: University of Alabama Press, 1970), pp. 23–34. The dangers of the British stronghold would become especially acute in the 1840s during the Caste War when supplies for Indian rebels came from the British settlements. Bolland, *Formation of a Colonial Society,* pp. 25–48.

52. Loret de Mola, *Yucatán,* II, 93–98; Ancona, *Historia,* II, 482–498.

53. Loret de Mola, *Yucatán,* II, 100–101; Ancona, *Historia,* II, 499–513.

54. Cook and Borah, *Essays,* II, 178–179; Molina Solís, *Historia,* II, 369–373; Ancona, *Historia,* II, 508–511, 528–532; Sotelo Regil, *Campeche,* pp. 183–185; Loret de Mola, *Yucatán,* II, 120; Moisés González Navarro, *Raza y Tierra: La Guerra de Castas y el Henequén* (México: El Colegio de México, 1970), pp. 43–48; Rodolfo Ruz Menéndez, *Ensayos Yucatanenses* (Mérida: Ediciones Universidad de Yucatán, 1976), pp. 79–82.

55. Nettie Lee Benson, *La Diputación Provincial y el Federalismo Mexicano* (México:

El Colegio de México, 1955), pp. 11-26; Ancona, *Historia*, II, 513-523; Sotelo Regil, *Campeche*, pp. 173-191; Loret de Mola, *Yucatán*, II, 100-102, 120-122.

56. Betancourt Pérez, *Historia*, I, 237-283; González Navarro, *Raza y Tierra*, pp. 43-48.

57. Loret de Mola, *Yucatán*, II, 120-122; González Navarro, *Raza y Tierra*, p. 49; Sotelo Regil, *Campeche*, pp. 186-191; Charles A. Hale, *Mexican Liberalism in the Age of Mora, 1821-1853* (New Haven and London: Yale University Press, 1968), pp. 23-25; Ancona, *Historia*, III, 81-97.

58. Sotelo Regil, *Campeche*, pp. 203-206; Benson, *La Diputación Provincial*, pp. 44-45; Ancona, *Historia*, III, 98-163.

59. Ancona, *Historia*, III, 178-191; Sotelo Regil, *Campeche*, pp. 207-222; Benson, *La Diputación Provincial*, p. 55. One document that reveals the degree of confusion and political unrest is a letter from Mariano Carrillo to Señores Comandantes Militares de Maxcanú, Calkiní, Hecelchakán, and Tenabo, October 4, 1820, quoted in Sotelo Regil, *Campeche*, pp. 217-218.

60. Lorenzo de Zavala stopped in Havana, where he prepared a pamphlet entitled *Idea del Estado Actual de la Capital de Yucatán* in which he strongly attacked Carrillo y Albornoz as being illegally in authority.

61. William Spence Robertson, *Iturbide of Mexico* (Durham, North Carolina: Duke University Press, 1952); Sotelo Regil, *Campeche*, pp. 223-240, 251-259; Ancona, *Historia*, III, 178-208.

62. Lorenzo de Zavala, *Ensayo Histórico de las Revoluciones de Méjico, desde 1808 hasta 1830* (Paris and New York, 1831-32), I, 9, quoted in Hale, *Liberalism*, p. 23; Justo Sierra, *The Political Evolution of the Mexican People*, trans. Charles Ramsdell (Austin and London: University of Texas Press, 1969), pp. 183-187; Benson, *La Diputación Provincial*, pp. 72, 133, 155-166, 208.

63. Benson, *La Diputación Provincial*, pp. 72-133, 156-208; Ancona, *Historia*, III, 259-307; Loret de Mola, *Yucatán*, II, 112-119; Sotelo Regil, *Campeche*, pp. 259-286, 299-322; Ruz Menéndez, *Ensayos Yucatenenses*, pp. 86-89.

64. Hale, *Mexican Liberalism*, pp. 110-126; Joseph Milton Nance, *After San Jacinto: The Texas-Mexican Frontier, 1836-1841* (Austin: University of Texas Press, 1963).

65. Ancona, *Historia*, III, 308-356.

66. Ancona, *Historia*, III, 356-458. Méndez, a federalist from Campeche, was elected governor in 1840, and Barbachano, an even more ardent defender of regional rights, was chosen vice-governor at the same time. Though born in Campeche, Barbachano came to be identified more closely with the interests of Mérida and the northern region of the peninsula.

67. González Navarro, *Raza y Tierra*, pp. 55-63, 171; John L. Stephens, *Incidents of Travel in Yucatan*, 2 vols. (New York: Dover, 1963; first edition, 1843). See especially I, 137-138; Patch, *La Formación*.

68. González Navarro, *Raza y Tierra*, p. 169; Reed, *Caste War*, pp. 23-24.

69. Ancona, *Historia*, III, 442-484; Reed, *Caste War*, pp. 48-64, 98-102; González Navarro, *Raza y Tierra*, pp. 68-88.

70. D. E. Dumond, "Independent Maya of the Late Nineteenth Century: Chiefdoms and Power Politics," in Jones, ed., *Anthropology and History*, pp. 103-138; Reed, *Caste War*, pp. 240-242. Campeche succeeded in breaking from Yucatan in 1858 to form a separate state within the Mexican republic, and the eastern region of the peninsula was

established as the separate territory of Quintana Roo, eventually also to be given statehood.

71. Loret de Mola, *Yucatán,* II, 102-104; González Navarro, *Raza y Tierra,* pp. 58-60, 179-181.

72. González Navarro, *Raza y Tierra,* pp. 182-225.

CHAPTER V

CHANGE IN THE CLASS SYSTEM OF MERIDA, YUCATAN, 1875-1935

Asael T. Hansen

Robert Redfield discussed the question of class structure in Yucatan in studies based upon field work in the 1930s.[1] In these investigations he compared the class system of Mérida with the situation in three communities of the back-country. His primary concern was to describe the way Spaniards, Indians, and Mestizos had come to live together in the peninsula. He also investigated the question of how different degrees of isolation and varying proportions of the three population elements tended to modify status relationships from one community to another.

The present study deals exclusively with Mérida. It first presents a description of the class system as it had evolved by around 1875 and then attempts an analysis of change in the following sixty years. There are two specific objectives: first, to set forth the concrete facts relating to class organization and concepts and, second, to formulate some generalizations or interpretations regarding the nature of the class system in 1875 and the process by which it changed down to 1935. The term "class" is used throughout this study in a general sense to refer to any kind of prestige, rank, or category within the social structure. The old status arrangements of the nineteenth century have been called a system of "castes." In fact, some observers have described the process that took place in Mérida as an evolution from a caste system to one of a class organization. When the evolution is complete, the Mestizo subsociety will be nonexistent and the social stratification of Mérida will clearly consist of classes as defined by any sophisticated social scientist.

In 1875, Mérida had about thirty thousand inhabitants.[2] It was just beginning to·respond to a number of powerful new influences: improvements in communication, more frequent contacts with the outside world, economic development, and resulting increased wealth. But the city was still a quiet, provincial capital. The majority of the citizens were living out their lives within the familiar channels of the long-established culture. Outside influences had touched relatively few areas of their experience and had not affected them very deeply.

By 1935, Mérida had approximately ninety-seven thousand residents. Daily newspapers, motion picture theaters, radios, and mail service by sea and air connected the community with the Euro-American world and subjected it to innumerable foreign influences. Economically, it was dependent on the international market for sisal fiber, the chief export. Periods of boom and bust in this market greatly affected the entire region. The Mexican Revolution that exploded in 1910 reached Yucatan five years later and had profound influences upon the old social order. These developments and others produced great transformations in the traditional culture.

The Old Class System

In 1875, the population of Mérida was divided into two main classes.[3] The upper class wore European clothes and was spoken of as *gente de vestido* (people of European dress) or by the alternative term *catrín*—less used in the city than in the country. Members of the lower class dressed in a distinctive Yucatecan costume and were designated Mestizos. This word, which originally was applied to individuals of mixed blood, had been redefined in popular usage by the late nineteenth century to refer to the wearers of the local costumes. It is in this sense that the term Mestizo will be employed throughout this study.[4] Within this polarized system every individual utilized one or the other of these costumes and, consequently, came to be identified with the class represented by his dress. The costume of the individual was determined at birth, with exceptions so rare that they can be ignored in this summary exposition. Marriage between classes was equally rare. Children of legitimate unions simply took the costume of their parents. In the case of informal matings between upper-class males and lower-class females, the established rule was for the offspring to follow the mother in dress.

The clothes of the two classes differed obviously in so many details that the social position of an individual could be perceived by the most casual glance. The upper class followed international fashions, though with some time lag. The dress of the lower class remained almost changeless: the costume of a Mestiza was the *huipil* (spelled thus in Yucatan but pronounced *ipil*). It was a white, loose-fitting garment with short, tight-fitting sleeves, which reached from the shoulders to a little below the knees. Colored embroidery adorned the hem, the neckline, and the margin of the sleeves. Underneath the *huipil* were one or more petticoats, decorated around the hem in white, which hung from the waist to about six inches below the outer garment. A scarf or shawl was draped over the head or the shoulders. This was usually white, but by around 1880 colored scarves began to appear. The manner of arranging the hair was equally distinctive. For dress occasions, it was pulled tightly back from the face and tied securely at the back of the head. It was then formed into a large knot to which a bright-colored bow was attached. The outfit was completed by low-heeled slippers known as *chancletas* and a special kind of jewelry used only by Mestizas. The materials, the elaborateness of the decoration, and the amount of jewelry varied, depending on her income and on the occasion for which she was grooming. A dressed-up Mestizo wore white cotton or linen trousers (*pantalones*) and a close-fitting jacket (*filipina*) of the same fabric, both stiffly starched. The jacket buttons were of gold and the hat of braided palm fibers. His work outfit was made of cheaper materials, often knee-length drawers called *calzones*. Starch was omitted, and a piece of striped denim about eighteen inches wide was wrapped around his waist to form a short apron or skirt. At all times the Mestizo wore heavy leather sandals, fancy for festivities and rough for work.

There seemed to have been almost no tendency for mestizo clothes to reflect upper-class fashions.[5] The two costumes represented separate and independent systems of dressing, each with its own canons of taste. A Mestizo who was dressed in proper style could feel well groomed, even in the presence of a fashionably clothed *de vestido* person. Although many upper-class men adhered closely to international style on somewhat formal occasions, for ordinary daily wear they frequently used trousers and a loose jacket (*guayabera*). The color of both garments was white; the material cotton or linen. Although these items were not identical with those worn by Mestizos for festive events, they were similar in general appearance. There was, however, one clear and invariable distinction: a *de vestido* man wore shoes, never sandals. If he could not afford shoes, he went barefoot. When a Mestizo had on his work clothes, including his denim apron

A rural family on the ejido in Taxkukul in 1930, illustrating the typical Mestizo costumes at that time. (Photo courtesy of Gilbert Joseph)

and *calzones,* he could be distinguished easily and unmistakably from a *de vestido* male. The clothing of women, on the other hand, was more differentiated according to class than was that of men. The whole costume was different at all times.

For purposes of clarity and simplicity, I have said in effect that there were two classes and that the dress of an individual placed him in one or the other. This does not state the situation as the inhabitants of Mérida thought of it. Rather, they felt that two kinds of people existed and that the type of clothing a person wore was an appropriate sign of the kind of person he was. The difference between *de vestido* and Mestizo were conceived of as inherent and irremovable. In later times, when some Mestizos began to abandon their dress in favor of European attire, conservatives accused them of disguising themselves in European apparel, attempting to hide their true nature. One elderly Mestizo expressed this view clearly in trying to dissuade his daughter from changing her clothes. "What's wrong with you?" he asked. "If you put clothes on a monkey, it will still be a monkey won't it? You are a Mestiza, and you will still be a Mestiza in spite of your European dress."

According to generally accepted notions, there was something about the inherent nature of the *de vestido* and Mestizos that made them differ categorically in status. Consequently, it was proper for all Mestizos to respect all *de vestido* individuals and for the latter to patronize all Mestizos, not because of clothes but because they were "just naturally inferior" to the wearers of European dress. Costume merely proclaimed these "facts" of nature.

Dress was not the only criterion of status, and all persons who wore a particular costume did not enjoy equal prestige. Social position was also influenced by wealth, occupation, education, racial traits, language, and place of residence in the city. These other marks of status differed from costume in one significant respect: whereas dress tended to divide individuals into two sharply defined categories, these other criteria ranked persons by small gradations over a broad status scale. In fact, each of the costume-limited classes included such a wide range of status that some in the Mestizo category outranked some members of the *de vestido* group on the basis of these other indicators. Nevertheless, there was a correlation between dress and the other status-determining factors. Although a few Mestizos had larger incomes than some who wore European dress, most of the well-to-do were *de vestido* and the poorer people were predominantly Mestizo. Although certain occupations were shared, the professions were the exclusive province of the *de vestido* and manual labor was done only by those of traditional regional dress.[6] Residents of the very center of Mérida all wore European clothes.[7] Surrounding this center was a zone where both costumes could be found, and farther out still, the local garb was universal. White physical traits were somewhat more evident among the *de vestido;* Indian features among the Mestizos. Many persons in both categories were bilingual, but the principal language of the *de vestido* was Spanish whereas large numbers of Mestizos spoke Maya and a minority knew no Spanish at all. Facilities for secondary and higher education were almost exclusively for the *de vestido;* schooling for the Mestizo usually ended by the third or fourth grade, and a large percentage of this group was illiterate.

During the colonial period, the correspondence between dress and the other status-determining factors had been closer so that they combined to form a well-knit series.[8] Over the three centuries of Spanish dominance an ideal pattern expressive of the situation grew up and became generally accepted. Economic and political developments of the nineteenth century partially destroyed the integrity of the series. Therefore, by 1875, there was only the rough correlation described above between costume and the other criteria of status. But the old ideal pattern still dominated the thinking of the population. The symbolic value of costume was usually sufficient to induce persons who manifested status characteristics inconsistent with their type of dress to accept this popular judgment.

The class system contained many features that did not have explicit status value but greatly affected social organization and the lives of individuals. The two groups followed separate ways of life, each with its own patterns of behavior and its own socially approved goals. Contrasts existed, for example, in religious participation, in forms of entertainment, in family organization, and in general world view. In effect, two subsocieties composed the inclusive culture of Mérida.[9] An individual was born into a particular class and learned its ways. His category became his social world; he belonged to it and it to him. Here were his relatives and his friends, persons who thought and felt as he did. He was in daily contact with members of the other category and could communicate with them on many subjects. He knew, however, that if he said some things, they would not understand and would not respond the way his fellow class members would. Each person acquired, as a part of his culture, certain procedures for dealing with members of the other class. Responses on both sides followed familiar channels and were reassuringly predictable. As long as these procedures were used, the contacts could be pleasant. Thus, the individual's experiences with members of his own group and with members of the other class combined to make him identify himself with his category.

What did this mean in terms of the operation of the class system? As indicated, Mestizos ignored upper upper-class fashions in dress, maintaining their own canons of taste. They tended to do the same regarding other factors within their way of life. Most of them were not concerned with the ambitions that motivated the *de vestido*. They expected to work with their hands and to have modest incomes. If they ranked well in their class, they were satisfied.

It is of special importance to consider the actions of the few Mestizos who became economically prosperous. In most cases, such a person continued to participate in the activities of his class. Even his expenditures for the purpose of improving his status conformed to the lower-class pattern. He dressed himself and his family in costly Mestizo clothes, giving special attention to his wife and daughters. He gave elaborate, but characteristically lower-class, celebrations in honor of his household saints. Such an individual became the center of attention in the barrio or subcommunity in which he lived, especially if he sponsored a celebration in honor of the barrio patron, a task ordinarily accomplished through the pooling of resources by many persons. The wealthy Mestizo arranged the marriages of his children to the sons and daughters of other well-to-do members of his own class. All of these factors elevated such an individual within his own social world, but did very little to alter his relationship with the *de vestido*.

These behavioral patterns rested solely on the sanction of custom. Any legal restrictions that had existed during the colonial period were revoked or allowed to lapse.[10] Furthermore, there seems to have been little forceful effort "to keep Mestizos in their place." Class relations were embodied in a social order that had the force of a moral order. "Right-thinking" persons were expected to assume and maintain their correct positions, and individuals who deviated from this pattern were subjected to ridicule and ostracism.

Despite the widespread acceptance of the established patterns, by 1875, important pressures were forcing adjustments. An increasing number of Mestizos were economically more prosperous than some who wore European clothes, thus producing strains in the class relationships. Mestizos manifested a full measure of deference only toward a member of the upper class who was wealthy. They accorded a poor *de vestido* person a modicum of respect because of his European attire, but that respect was mixed with pity. On the other hand, prosperous Mestizos were under suspicion, even when they continued to live a lower-class life. Moreover, there was a tendency to depreciate the status value of their wealth. When they adorned their women in fine clothes and expensive jewelry, the females were called "gaudy Mestizas," although similar expenditures on the grooming of *de vestido* women produced "elegant ladies." Whereas an upper-class individual of property was called "a rich man," an economically successful Mestizo was spoken of as "a rich Mestizo." Such terminology implied an effort to escape an inconsistency by seeming to believe that prosperity came in two kinds—*de vestido* wealth and Mestizo wealth.

The Process of Change

By 1875, very few Mestizos were questioning the basic feature of the class system by abandoning their traditional attire and adopting European clothes. Such a step was opposed by the majority of the upper and lower class alike. Nevertheless, the climbers, if they were successful in business or one of the honored occupations, were gradually and somewhat grudgingly accorded middle- or upper-class status. Acceptance seems to have involved a process of judging them as individuals and labeling them exceptions. In this way, the line they had crossed was left intact. Would-be climbers, who were unable to support their bid for a rise in the social scale by wealth or occupational achievement, had no satisfactory social position anywhere. They were not recognized as truly *de vestido,* and the resentment they aroused by their repudiation of Mestizo status made it difficult for them to reenter that segment of society. In neither case did these costume-changers serve as effective examples to Mestizos in general. Those who succeeded were too unusual to copy; those who failed stood as a warning to their fellows. These early class-jumpers were, however, the pioneers of a movement that eventually destroyed the old status system.

During the early years of the twentieth century, the number of costume changes increased rapidly. By about 1915, Mestizos began adopting European clothes at a rate that seemed to indicate that the traditional garb would be gone from the city within a few decades. This striking change in a basic feature of the culture of Yucatan took place without any direct pressures from the national government. At the same time, however, the Mexican Revolution of 1910 did influence the process. Many revolutionary leaders considered blue denim to be an appropriate uniform for the class-conscious proletariat they were trying to create. The fabric was worn by members of the more radical labor unions, not just while they were working, but also while they participated in political celebrations. In Yucatan, however, this idea conflicted with another point of view held by the men who exercised political power during the formative stages of the revolutionary government structure. The dominant Yucatecan Socialist party occasionally sponsored dances at which they encouraged the wearing of Mestizo clothes. High-ranking officials sometimes showed their equalitarianism by attending these events dressed as Mestizos. This ambiguity reflects the dual nature of the Mexican Revolution, especially in the state of Yucatan.

Increased contacts with the outside world helped to erode the Mestizo–*de vestido* distinction. The upper class admired the advanced Euro-American countries where universal education was held to be an unquestioned social value. Between 1880 and 1900, steps were taken to provide some basic school training for the common people of the region. Increased revenues from the sisal boom were utilized to speed up the process. After 1910, the revolutionary leaders also placed great emphasis on education. The lower class accepted the belief in the desirability of schooling. In fact, some literate Mestizos had always been active in church and community affairs and had enjoyed increased prestige in their class. Thus other Mestizos were able to respond to the new opportunities for education without any drastic modification of social attitudes.

Few citizens of Yucatan seemed to believe that the expansion of educational opportunities would have any impact on the class system. In their way of thinking, with education Mestizos would be literate, but they would still be Mestizos. They simply failed to take into account the ways educational experiences would affect the lives of those individuals involved. New problems emerged: for example, should bright Mestizo children be allowed to perform on school programs, while *de vestido* children and their parents sat and listened? The very question violated two traditional conceptions. According to the accepted categoric definitions of the classes, there should not have been any bright Mestizo children. Furthermore, in public events, *de vestido* persons were supposed to play the conspicuous roles. Yet, the institutional structure of the school contained a single standard for measuring the achievement of all pupils and offered places on programs as rewards for excellence. Another situation, though seemingly trivial to the outside observer, gave rise to much difficulty. When a school function called for a special uniform or costume, always a *de vestido* costume, serious doubts arose. Should the Mestizo children be required to abandon the dress of their class for such an event; should they be excluded or "excused" from participation; or should the impressiveness of the ceremony be sacrificed in order to preserve class distinctions in clothes? Each solution was tried, but none produced satisfactory results.

On such occasions, differences in clothes caused embarrassment and diverse difficulties. Since the schools were primarily *de vestido* institutions, it was only natural that many saw the adoption of European attire as a solution to the problem. The persons most immediately concerned—the Mestizo children— were particularly disposed to think of that as the way out. After all, they were grouped with *de vestido* youngsters as pupils and associated with them as individuals. Doubtless, the influence of the class system reached into the school and produced many discriminations in favor of the *de vestido* students, but the discriminations were variable and inconsistent rather than organized and channeled. Hence, instead of reinforcing the established class attitudes, they aroused resentment among Mestizo children and gave them a desire to escape. Furthermore, school experience separated them from their parents, both in space and in mental outlook. Parental influence was, therefore, less effective in giving children a strong sense of belonging to their class.

There was no sudden revolution in dress; the class system was far too firmly fixed for that. As time passed, however, it became increasingly common for children to change from traditional clothes when they started school or during the course of their education. Conservative parents sometimes objected. When this happened, their children often refused to continue in school rather than go dressed as Mestizos. Parental objections gradually declined, and the attitude they expressed often was replaced by another point of view. Mestizo parents, who might not think seriously of changing their own costume, came to look upon school attendance as a good excuse to have their children put on European clothes. Thus, Mestizos, who at first considered education only as a means of acquiring the useful tools of literacy and of gaining prestige within the limits of their class, came to view the schools as an avenue of escape from Mestizo status.

Developments in other fields also affected costume and class; Mestizos moved into work situations where the established rules governing class relationships did not fully apply. They became isolated from their class and identified with *de vestido* persons. These experiences tended to break the ties of an individual with his class and give him a new conception of his social position. Before, he accepted his place in the lower class and was satisfied if he rated well in that category. Now, he was disposed to compare himself, not only with other Mestizos, but with *de vestido* people as well, and he resented the categoric inferiority his costume proclaimed. In a word, his view of his status was more individualistic.

As the number of Mestizos going through this process increased, the common understanding that defined and sustained the class system decayed. Even the most conservative individuals could not avoid the influences of the pressures. When they were looked down on by their former peers, by ex-Mestizos who had adopted European clothes, they could justify themselves and bolster their status only by claiming moral superiority on grounds that they still respected the old rules and kept their costumes as Mestizos were supposed to do. But they knew that many people denied the validity of their claims; the old rules were no longer generally accepted. This knowledge undermined the conservatives' sense of certainty and rendered their assumptions of moral superiority not fully convincing, even to themselves. As the class structure collapsed around them, they were left clinging to an ideal pattern that had lost its former meaning.

There is some evidence to indicate that costume-changing took place in considerable volume first among persons near the top of the Mestizo economic structure, next among those near the bottom, and last among those in between. It is quite apparent why the process should have begun with the more successful Mestizos. They were particularly exposed to the experience described above. Except for costume, their status was already equivalent to that of many persons born in the upper class, and they knew that they could maintain a style of life appropriate to European dress. In the case of those near the bottom, another factor entered. Since they had failed to attain a satisfactory position in competition with other Mestizos, the adoption of European attire seemed to offer an easy way out. By this single act, it appeared they could leap to a point where they would outrank all Mestizos. They discovered, however, that social climbing was not so simple; if they did not increase their income or improve their occupational standing, they remained about where they had been in spite of their changed garb. Nevertheless, they had little to lose by making the switch, and it gave them at least illusory benefits. It is clear that the sanctions that supported the class system had weakened greatly when the poorest Mestizos, who were obviously unable to live the kind of life a *de vestido* person was formerly expected to live, seized on European clothes as a short cut out of their lowly state. They cheapened and, in the eyes of some, defiled the costume of the old upper class. The relative conservatism of persons in the middle of the Mestizo class can be understood against this background. On one hand, pressures that bore on successful individuals in this group affected them less strongly. On the other hand, unlike the poorer elements, they had something to lose by abandoning their costume. They occupied a substantial position in their status category, a position they hesitated to leave for an uncertain place in the rapidly expanding, culturally unrecognized group of ex-Mestizos.

Men appear to have given up traditional dress earlier and in greater numbers than women.[11] Moreover, the change proceeded along somewhat different lines.

The traditional outfit of the Mestizo males tended to lose its integrity. Therefore, the transition to European clothes could be made gradually. An individual could dispense with his striped denim apron, then become careless about the color and material of his trousers and jacket. Next he might substitute a felt hat for the traditional straw and finally put on shoes instead of sandals. In fact, the male costume came to be so disorganized that by the early twentieth century sandals became the single symbol of Mestizo status. The costume of women remained stable in almost every detail. A Mestiza continued to wear the traditional costume in its complete form until, in one momentous step, she abandoned it entirely in favor of European dress.[12] The persistence of female apparel as an integrated whole is related to the role women played in the society. One of their functions was to exhibit by clothes and jewels visible evidence of their status and that of their fathers and their husbands. This role stimulated them to elaborate their costumes and to formulate standards by which correctness could be judged. Their grooming in its entirety was supported by canons of taste so organized as to constitute a kind of code. The few women who altered important items of their dress in the direction of *de vestido* fashion were criticized by other Mestizas about as much as if they had gone all the way in adopting European clothes. It is interesting to note that one of the reasons they occasionally gave for changing to European garb was that some calamity had forced them to sell their jewelry. They argued that if they could not dress in a complete Mestiza outfit, they might as well put on European apparel. Hence, the Mestizo–*de vestido* distinction was much more fully expressed in female than in male attire.

Up to this point, little has been said of the psychological and sociological impact involved in the change of costume. Usually it was an acute personal crisis—more serious for adults than for children, more serious for women than for men. Frequently it divided friends, separated godparents from godchildren, and introduced a variety of strains into family relationships—a painful experience for everyone concerned. Children often tried to avoid being seen in public with their parents and sometimes denied that their parents were Mestizos, if they were among strangers and could lie plausibly. In the process of changing his costume an individual was often isolated from the intimate, personal world in which he had been reared. A Mestiza who gave up her traditional costume was ridiculed mercilessly. She was not called *de vestido*, but *x-cuch vestido*, a half-Maya and half-Spanish expression that could be translated as "one who hangs European clothes on herself." The obvious implication was that she did not know how to dress in her new attire and that she had no right to attempt to fool people. The emotional charge of this disparaging epithet was increased when it was shortened to *x-cuch*. In anger, the initial "*x*" became a prolonged hiss, followed by an explosive "*cuch*." No other method of casting aspersions on the class-jumpers was as common or as potent as this expression. It was applied only to females.

Many Mestizos sought to soften the impact of transition to European dress. Parents often put European clothes on a baby at birth, or within a year or two, especially for those occasions when it would be seen in public. At times they would seek *de vestido* godparents for a child at baptism or confirmation and arrange to have him brought up mostly by the godparents. In this way, his European clothes were accepted with fewer questions, and he would avoid many of the difficulties he might encounter if he lived with his parents in a neighborhood where his background was well known. Compared to adults, children of known Mestizo ancestry encountered relatively mild ridicule by reason of their adopted style of dress.

Often children changed their costumes upon entering school, as indicated above. For others, middle adolescence was a common period for change. Various social activities, especially dances, subjected young people to specific pressures in favor of European dress. In Mérida, probably between 1900 and 1910, there developed among the members of the broadly defined lower class two designations for dances: *bailes populares,* open to both Mestizos and *de vestido* persons, and *bailes de calzado,* dances for those who wore shoes rather than sandals. The latter excluded Mestizos of both sexes, though it was the footgear of males that symbolized the distinction. *Bailes de calzado* was a phrase doubtless invented by nonsocially mobile ex-Mestizos to proclaim their superiority over Mestizos. Most of them had changed their type of apparel, and that was all. They seized upon their only alleged evidence of superordination in relation to Mestizos. Upper-class people wore European garb as a matter of course and did not have to bolster their status by insulting Mestizos. Nor did really socially mobile ex-Mestizos, who had absolutely no interest in *bailes de calzado*. A young man or woman who wished to participate fully in these activities, however, was forced to become *de vestido*.

Unlike schoolchildren, young people had to face the full force of social disapproval in making the transition in dress. Not many Mestizo adults were willing to admit that dances or youthful love affairs were legitimate motives for becoming *de vestido*. Adolescents were especially sensitive to criticism, but large numbers changed their costumes anyway, testifying to the strength of the pressures on them. Girls sometimes chose Mardi Gras as the occasion for taking the step. They would put on European attire for masquerade parties and continue to wear it. For months afterward they were victims of cutting bits of ridicule, being asked slyly if they had not heard that Mardi Gras was over. A mother who changed costume in order to chaperone her *de vestido* daughters at *bailes de calzado* was generally thought to be justified in her actions. This produced one of the few cases of part-time change. Often young people differing in costume fell in love, creating an urgent desire to remove the costume differences. This was especially true if the courtship ended in marriage. Almost without exception, the one who used Mestizo dress was expected to do the changing. It was as if people in Yucatecan society believed that real Mestizo status demanded continuity and felt that when an individual broke with his class, he could not completely regain his status by returning to his original costume.

The conventions that developed around the shift of dress were not clearly formulated and did not cover all situations. Moreover, they lacked universal recognition. Even persons who changed costume often retained notions derived from the old class structure. Thus, by 1935, traditional ideas of class persisted, but many members of society compromised by accepting behavior contrary to those concepts. By that time, the class system in Mérida was so complex and unstable that to give a clear description of it would be impossible.[13] It is possible, however, to construct a composite of the situation as it existed, based upon three separate classes that may be designated "upper," "middle," and "lower." At the top of the social scale were the descendants of aristocrats who had not slipped too far down the economic ladder; persons with less elevated ancestry who had good incomes or substantial positions in honored professions; and even wealthy or professionally distinguished individuals of Mestizo origin. The last mentioned were accorded upper-class status only grudgingly, but the length of time they had to wait was decreasing. The lower class was composed of all Mestizos and of those ex-Mestizos who worked with their hands and had low incomes. It would seem logical to contend that both groups occupied substantially the same position on the social scale. They shared a common set of employments, occupied the same income level, participated together in social activities, and often intermarried.

Between these two extremes lay an emerging middle class, characterized by moderate income, white-collar employment, and an approved amount of education and refinement. They were either descended from the old *de vestido* group or their Mestizo background was sufficiently distant as to be unknown or partially forgotten. This middle class came into existence largely through a process of redefinition of the old upper and lower classes rather than through a process of falling from above or rising from below. In the past many *de vestido* persons had little claim to distinction other than their costumes. When European dress declined in importance as a mark of status and when greater emphasis was put on wealth and achievement, ordinary members of the *de vestido* grouping became "middle class," even though they kept the same general position in the total status range that they had before. They did not need to move down; the new class simply took them in where they stood. A similar process went on with reference to prosperous Mestizos. Except for costume, their status was already equivalent to that of many ordinary *de vestido* individuals. When they adopted European clothes, they, too, became "middle class" as soon as the memory of their Mestizo past faded.

In a study of the social classes of Mérida conducted in 1935, it was found that most persons interviewed identified three classes, much like the model given above. They usually floundered a good deal, however, for answers and disagreed on the character and content of each group. Expressions of social location that at first glance appeared to be status judgments turned out to be moral judgments instead. In fact, perceptions regarding the class system were strongly influenced by the position on the social spectrum held by the observers. Most informants made their class judgments on the basis of income, occupation, education, and

Street scenes in Mérida in 1978, indicating the persistence of the traditional dress among women but also the changes taking place in that society. (Photos by Joel Whitman)

Street scene in Mérida in 1978. The basin on the head of the woman is filled with *masa* for the preparation of tortillas. (Photo by Joel Whitman)

"culture." Traditional concepts also continued to be used in rating people, but were questioned and partially discredited. Race was considered, referring in part to actual physical characteristics and in part to the old grouping according to costume. Observers frequently expressed the opinion that lower-class people were ignorant and had "much Indian blood."

It might be expected that the remaining Mestizos would have been one group whose social location was still certain. This was true in the sense that their lower-class rating was virtually unquestioned. But they did not constitute the whole of the lower class, and there were divergent opinions regarding their position in comparison to ex-Mestizos. It is not surprising that ex-Mestizos looked upon those who continued to wear the local folk costume as occupying the very bottom of the social scale. Persons of *de vestido* ancestry, however, often rated ex-Mestizos lower on the social scale than individuals who had retained the traditional regional garb.

Persons whose social position was high considered the upper class to be a narrow segment of the status scale, the middle class a somewhat broader element, and the lower class a very inclusive residual segment. They appeared to think of the middle class as a downward projection of the upper class and to identify it with the upper class in contradistinction to a broad lower class. In fact, many of the elite held that the middle class was composed only of the less distinguished descendants of the old *de vestido* group, though they admitted, when questioned, that some persons of Mestizo ancestry should have been included. By contrast, lower-class persons defined the upper class so broadly that it took in most or all of the middle group as it was viewed by the elite. To them, the middle class was made up mostly of ex-Mestizos who could still be recognized as such, but who exhibited marks of status that lifted them above the common run of the lower class. From this point of view, the middle class constituted an upward extension of the lower class, occupied by individuals who were on their way up. Members of the middle class were usually described in negative terms, that is, in terms of the factors that kept them out of the upper class on the one hand and out of the lower class on the other. When they reached a point where they began to participate socially with persons of *de vestido* ancestry, there was a question as to how they should be rated. Some said that they passed into the inclusive upper class, while others thought that those who accepted the climbers became middle class themselves. The conception of the class system held by people of intermediate status approached that given in the composite statement. It was common, however, for them to emphasize more the fact that the middle class was derived from both the old *de vestido* and Mestizo groupings. When viewed in this way, the middle class may even be described as composed of two distinct parts: one oriented upward, the other downward.

If we examine what people did rather than what they said, in only one area of behavior was evidence found of a break in the middle class that reflected the old *de vestido*–Mestizo distinction: this was in dancing. A number of social clubs sponsored dances for the "better people." These ranged from aristocratic organizations that were very exclusive to others that were quite open, but all were linked by overlapping participants. On the other hand, there were a number of clubs for the common people, which also varied in status and overlapping attendance. Between the two series there was a gap; no one who attended dances at any of the lower clubs was admitted to the upper-class societies. Successful former Mestizos, who gained entrance even into the least exclusive of the upper-class clubs, had to jump the gap. Once they had arrived, they cut themselves off from the lower clubs completely. [This is an interesting contrast to the system of *bailes populares* and *bailes de calzado* discussed above. Editors' note.]

Comparison and Analysis

We shall now try to state in general terms some of the differences between the class system of 1875 and the one that had evolved by 1935. In the early period, status differences were organized into two sharply defined social categories, one above the other, and were distinguished clearly by the primary status symbol—costume. A person wore either Mestizo clothes or European clothes, and there was no doubt as to which type of dress he used. The categories were substantial social realities that everyone recognized. Within the categories, individuals were ranked by small gradations on the basis of criteria other than costume. The society attempted, with considerable success, to make these two kinds of status factors consistent with each other. According to the ideal pattern of the class system, a particular costume was supposed to be associated with a limited range of variations in the quantitative measures of status so that they would combine to form an integrated series with costume functioning as a symbol for the whole. When such integration did not exist in reality, the symbolic value of costume was sufficient to induce most people to ignore or rationalize the inconsistencies and thus sustain the validity of the ideal pattern. The individual variations were somewhat wider than the categories provided for, so that only the great emphasis placed on dress kept some persons in the inferior group from being rated above some in the superior group.

By 1935, all of the indicators of status were quantitative, distributed by imperceptible gradations over the total range from the lowliest individual to the most elevated. The ideology of the traditional two-class system persisted in a situation where it no longer fit. There were no clear class lines, no real status categories. A single individual might have exhibited different criteria in differing degrees. His income might have given him one rating, his occupation another, his education

Close-up of the crowd at a bullfight in the village of Chunchucmil in 1978. The *huipil* is still the typical dress of women in many rural areas. (Photo by Joel Whitman)

Man in a Mérida cafe in 1977, illustrating the continuation of traditional dress. (Photo by Bill Moseley)

still another, and so forth. Classes were spoken of, but were conceptual abstractions that indicated vaguely defined segments of a continuous and unbroken scale. Unlike "*de vestido*" and "Mestizo," each of which had its own special meaning, the names of the modern classes designated positions that existed only with reference to other locations on the scale. Rating involved an impossible problem in social arithmetic. In terms of the criteria of status, the population of Mérida was distributed along the social scale by minute, continuous gradations. At any point on the scale, a person chose his spouse and his intimate associates from among people of about his own position. Those who were slightly superior to him could participate beyond his reach, and those who were inferior had friends that he would avoid. These tiny segments formed an overlapping series, extending without interruption from the bottom to the top of the social scale. Only the remaining Mestizos constituted a category defined by a clear line, and this line did not separate them from lower-class ex-Mestizos in any important way. Members of the lower class tended to ape the standards and conduct of members of the higher class instead of recognizing and following a way of life of their own.

In the old system, an individual had a categoric status in his society and an individual position in his category. He was born into his class, and his relationship with members of the other category were fixed and final. He viewed them as a different kind of people from himself and his peers. Nothing he, nor anyone like him, could do would remove the differences. Consequently, he tended not to compare himself to members of the other class, and his position with reference to them had little effect on his sense of personal adequacy. Members of his own category, on the other hand, were people like himself with whom he could compete. By his own efforts, he could change his individual status relative to that of other persons in his class. His rating here influenced his sense of personal success or failure; if he stood well in his own class, he was satisfied.

By 1935, an individual had no truly categoric position, and his personal status existed with reference to the whole society. There was a disposition to think that all people were of one kind, rated according to the degree to which they possessed certain characteristics. Most of these could be gained or lost, and even racial traits could be compensated for by achievement. Competition, therefore, extended over the full range of the social scale. An individual could compare his position with that of any other person. There were no fixed limits to the distance an individual could rise or fall, or at least hope to rise or fall. He was freer, but less secure.

NOTES

The material for this chapter was collected between 1931 and 1934 in the course of a larger investigation of social and cultural change in Yucatan. The study was sponsored by Carnegie Institution of Washington, D.C., and directed by Robert Redfield.
1. Robert Redfield, "Race and Class in Yucatán," *Cooperation in Research*

(Washington, D.C.: Carnegie Institution of Washington, Publication No. 501, 1938), pp. 511–532; Robert Redfield, *The Folk Culture of Yucatán* (Chicago: University of Chicago Press, 1941), Chap. III.

2. A state census made in 1881, admittedly not very accurate, gave 27,270 as the population. Later demographic studies point out the "practical" reason for underenumeration: taxes and military service were based upon the count.

3. Published material on the old class system is almost completely lacking. This description is based primarily upon recollections of elderly informants and on the testimony of conservatives of any age whose ideas regarding the way the class system "ought to be" reflected how it had been. The limitations of these sources are apparent. It is well known that old people forget many things and modify their memories as time passes and that conservatives, being on the defensive, tend to idealize the status situation they advocate. One other type of data is utilized to some extent. The relations among the remaining representatives of the old classes were observed as fully as possible. In this case, actual behavior could be seen and verbal responses to events fresh in the speaker's mind could be recorded. When there was evidence that these relations followed a well-established pattern of long standing they were used to project a reconstruction of the past. This, too, is open to some question. Nevertheless, I believe that the description is essentially correct and that more adequate information would only provide more detail without changing the general picture.

4. This analysis leaves out of account a division in the lower class between *indios,* that is, persons with Indian surnames, and other wearers of the local costume who had Spanish surnames. The distinction, earlier of much importance, had lost most of its significance at the time of the investigation. [The author chose to capitalize "Mestizo" to give emphasis to the cultural significance of the term. Editors' note.]

5. There was some rather vague information to the contrary. Some informants said that a few Mestizos put hoops in their *huipiles* after this became the *de vestido* fashion. Also, it was reported that the number of petticoats Mestizas used and the length and fullness of their *huipiles* tended to follow trends in upper-class style. On the other hand, there are accounts of *huipiles* passed down and used through three generations.

6. The chief examples of shared occupations were independent commercial enterprises, foremen in charge of Mestizo workmen, and crafts that required considerable skill and relatively little physical exertion such as goldsmithing.

7. Except for servants who lived in the homes of their masters.

8. It cannot be argued from the sketchy available data that the integration of the series was ever absolute. But, in the eighteenth century, it appears to have been nearly true that all Mestizos were poorer than any *de vestido* persons; that Mestizos engaged in one set of occupations, *de vestido* persons in another, with no overlapping between them; that more than a rudimentary formal education was the exclusive prerogative of the *de vestido;* and so forth. Moreover, some categoric distinctions existed then that had disappeared at the time of the research for this study. For instance, Mestizos could not ride in carriages, and they formed separate regiments in the militia. *Indios,* who shared the costume with Mestizos, could not bear arms at all.

9. Some details of this class differentiation were very small. For instance, when a Mestiza went to market she carried a basket. *De vestido* women used cloth or sisal bags.

10. In the colonial period there were special legal regulations for persons with Indian surnames as contrasted to persons with Spanish surnames. Mestizos and *de vestido* persons were in separate regiments in the militia both before and after independence.

11. In a sample study for 1934, it was found that only 9 percent of males under thirty years of age used Mestizo dress, whereas 22 percent of females in the same group continued to wear the traditional costume. The percentages for the over-thirty age group still wearing Mestizo dress were 68 for the males and 86 for the females.

12. This was strictly true only of the visible parts of the costume. During the twentieth century, undergarments tended to follow *de vestido* fashions. For festive occasions the shoes and hose of young Mestizas were like those of the *de vestido*. The traditional fabrics were cotton and linen. By 1935, the party clothes of Mestizas were commonly of silk, at times even of colored silk. Older Mestizas opposed all of these trends as violations of the proper standards of traditional dress.

13. New, foreign population elements, notably Syrians and Orientals, added further complications to the status situation. They have been omitted from this discussion because we are concerned primarily with what happened to the descendants of the people who composed the old status groups.

REVOLUTION FROM WITHOUT: THE MEXICAN REVOLUTION IN YUCATAN, 1910-1940

Gilbert M. Joseph

Las cosas de Yucatán,
Dejarlas como están.

(What is Yucatan's own,
Is best left alone.)

—Regional aphorism

Introduction: Revolution and Region

In past decades—certainly before the events in Cuba in 1959—the Mexican Revolution was viewed by a majority of scholars and policy makers alike as Latin America's first and only successful revolutionary experiment. Attention was riveted on such innovative contributions as the ejido—hailed as Mexico's "way out" of its agrarian dilemma—and the PRI, the official Party of the Institutional Revolution, which seemed remarkably adept at juggling—and reconciling—such potentially conflicting goals as social justice, economic development, and political stability.[1] Now, as Mexico's Revolution labors through its seventh decade, increasingly beset by disillusionment and economic difficulties, interest in the Mexican revolutionary model has taken a different form. With the remaining hopes for civilian rule and Western-style democracy flickering dimly throughout the hemisphere, observers on the right reassess Mexico's one-party system with a view to its continued possibilities for social control combined with some measure of marginal socioeconomic benefits within the context of a corporatist state. Their counterparts on the left, increasingly skeptical about the so-called Mexican "economic miracle," probe what they regard to be the limitations of state capitalism and speculate on the possibility of a second, more thoroughgoing revolution, this time waged against the "revolutionary bourgeoisie," who, they argue, assumed control but betrayed the goals of the original 1910 upheaval.[2]

Amid the growing controversy of this debate over the Revolution's past performance and future potential, relatively little notice has been taken of Yucatan. While local historians have been active,[3] scholars and popular writers outside the peninsula have sought the meaning of the Revolution elsewhere, concentrating upon the victorious caudillo-led armies of the north, the birthplace of the Revolution, and examining the popular social movements of central Mexico, most notably *zapatismo,* the agrarian movements of Michoacán and Veracruz, and the more widespread *cristero* rebellion.[4] In bypassing Yucatan, national and international historians seem to have concurred with the assessment of the regional poet Antonio Mediz Bolio that, in Yucatan, "the Revolution appeared as something strange and exotic."[5]

Any consensus regarding the uniqueness and marginal significance of the Yucatecan revolutionary experience is likely based upon the region's "offside" geographical position and its exaggerated reputation for cultural autonomy and political separatism that have become firmly rooted in the national mind. Certainly, the revolutionary history of a region Mexicans jokingly refer to as "our sister Republic" and Yucatecans themselves proudly describe as "el país que no se parece a otro" (the country that resembles no other) is not likely to be representative of the Mexican Revolution as a whole. Even if, as has often been said, there is *no* Mexico but *many* Mexicos, the Yucatecan variant is generally regarded to be more marked in its regional identity than any other entity within the Republic. This feeling of separation was manifested as recently as 1914, when *yucatecos* petitioned to become a protectorate or part of the United States, arguing plausibly that they had more in common, geographically and economically, with the North Americans than they did with the Mexican Republic.[6]

It is not surprising then, that Yucatan's traditional isolation has been extended into the academic realm as well. However, great heuristic value may lie in the study of "exceptional regions" like Yucatan. In Yucatan, and certain other regions like Veracruz, the Revolution developed with a degree of autonomy virtually unmatched elsewhere in Mexico. Furthermore, it was precisely this degree of autonomy that made such regions the kind of exceptions which bring common Revolutionary experiences into focus and enable us better to appreciate the dynamics of the Revolution as a whole.[7]

The significance of this point will be illustrated throughout this chapter, especially when Yucatan's checkered history of agrarian reform is discussed. Moreover, if scholars agree on anything in the highly charged field of revolutionary history, it is that the Revolution can no longer be viewed as a monolithic event. For too long, generalizations made on the basis of informants and documentary materials in Mexico City have clouded the essential truth regarding the origins and development of the Mexican Revolution. At least during its first two decades, the upheaval that has been called *The* Revolution was really a series of regional phenomena, some of which perhaps deserve to be called revolutions. Each was governed, to a greater or lesser extent, by a discrete set of local social, economic, political, geographical, and cultural factors. Later, in the 1930s, the central government of President Lázaro Cárdenas reincorporated the various regions into a new Mexican political system, in effect carrying out a "reconquest of Mexico."[8] This process was likewise conditioned by regional factors and circumstances that essentially determined the success or failure of revolutionary reforms, as the case of Yucatan clearly illustrates.

Accordingly, this essay is intended to add to current efforts by a growing number of Mexican and international scholars to refine further our knowledge of the disparate phenomena that have come to be known as the Revolution. Indeed, historians of the Mexican Revolution are acting increasingly upon what one of their number has called the "regionalist impulse of our times,"[9] while simultaneously contributing to what a number of their colleagues, working in widely different fields of the discipline, have come to acknowledge as a "historiographical revolution." This "revolution" has witnessed a shift in the locus of historical initiative from the institutional superstructure to the level of local regions, communities, and interest groups. In other words, there is a shift from traditional political and institutional history done in and from the perspective of the metropolis to social, economic, and political analysis done in and from the perspective of the periphery.[10] The historian of Yucatan can make a significant contribution to this process, underscoring a number of broad areas in which the conflict in the peninsula diverges from what has emerged as the conventional view of the Mexican Revolution.

A Different Revolution

Traditional historical accounts held that over one million persons died in the violence of the Mexican Revolution.[11] Although recent research refutes these estimates, it is still clear that at least several hundred thousand perished in the fighting, a sizable loss for a nation that numbered only fifteen million in 1910. Related causes—hunger, malnutrition, and the Spanish flu that swept through Mexico in 1915 and again in 1918–19—killed many times that number. On the other hand, in the state of Yucatan and in the peninsula as a whole, the population actually increased by about twenty-five thousand during the first revolutionary decade, although census data are highly inaccurate.[12] Thus, in 1915, when writer Martín Luis Guzmán described the Mexican Revolution as a "fiesta of bullets," the U.S. consul in Yucatan observed rather matter-of-factly that "peace is raging down here as usual."[13]

The essentially nonviolent nature of the Revolution in Yucatan suggests a need to recast the conventional tripartite periodization of the Mexican Revolution fashioned by the majority of historians in Mexico and the United States.[14] The first of the three revolutionary phases or progressive stages that culminate in the final stage of "economic" or "institutionalized revolutions" is the violent or "military" phase which the conventional historical wisdom dates from 1910 to 1920. In fact, this phase with its pattern of open-ended military violence by caudillo-led bands, never took shape in Yucatan. The Revolution did not even arrive until 1915, although at that time it took on a radical character virtually unmatched elsewhere in Mexico, transforming the region into a great laboratory for social change. If there was a "military phase" in Yucatan, it occurred very briefly, over the course of only a few weeks in 1915, when General Salvador Alvarado's eight thousand Constitutionalist troops quashed small reactionary bands in token skirmishes resulting in minimal casualties. Perhaps more important, Yucatan experienced some military violence over roughly a four-month period late in 1923 and early in 1924, during the De la Huerta revolt. This episode, however, occurred during the Revolution's so-called second or "socially activist" phase, which historians have dated between 1920 and 1940 and judge to have been less violent. Furthermore, the results of this revolt were counterrevolutionary: Yucatan's socialist governor, Felipe Carrillo Puerto, was executed by insurgent troops, his death warrant quite probably bought by the large henequen hacendados whom he threatened with expropriation.

We have come to associate the notion of free-ranging band violence, which a number of Hollywood movies have helped to root in our consciousness, with the Mexican revolutionary process. This kind of violence, however, which dislocated the Mexican society and economy, was mostly restricted to the north, north-central, west-central, and south-central parts of the Republic. It particularly ravaged the Bajío and states such as Morelos, Chihuahua, San Luis Potosí, and Durango. The south, southeast, and large portions of the Gulf Coast were relatively free of such violence, and except for the notorious "Decena Trágica" (Ten Tragic Days) that preceded the assassination of Francisco I. Madero in 1913, so was Mexico City. Indeed, certain regional economies, such as Veracruz's Gulf Coast oil and Yucatan's henequen industries, actually enjoyed a golden age in terms of production and earnings during the so-called decade of violence.[15]

This is not to suggest, however, that these areas were immune from violence. The popular characterization of twentieth-century Yucatan as "el país tranquilo" is clearly a myth. Extensive documentary evidence suggests that another sort of violence—as reflected in a pronounced form of *caciquismo* (bossism)—was seemingly institutionalized in the region's rural areas. As we shall see, the nature and use of violence in the Yucatecan context presents an important problem because it suggests that the Revolution often failed to alter traditional mechanisms of social control in the countryside.[16]

The Revolutionary Process in Yucatan: Methodological Considerations

Having briefly introduced the Revolution in Yucatan as late to arrive, less violent, more radical, and largely outside the boundaries of conventional periodization, let us elaborate on the process whereby thoroughgoing revolution began to develop in Yucatan but was ultimately frustrated. In order to understand the revolutionary process fully and evaluate its successes and failures, however, we must examine events and forces at several levels, weighing macro- and micro-approaches and engaging in analysis at the regional, national, and often international levels. Few, if any, precedents for such an undertaking exist. Womack's study of Emiliano Zapata in Morelos perhaps comes closest. Writing with the verve of a novel by John Steinbeck (who wrote the script of the Marlon Brando film on the same subject), Womack engages the reader in the drama of *zapatismo* and simultaneously provides a framework for historical analysis, brilliantly incorporating the history of the region into the national context. In studying Morelos, however, a state whose highly capitalized sugar industry produced almost entirely for a national market, he necessarily exempts himself from treating the external economic linkages that challenge the historian of Yucatan. Nor does Heather Fowler Salamini, in her otherwise comprehensive examination of peasant organizations in revolutionary Veracruz, explore the significant constraints that powerful foreign interests in the oil, tobacco, and sugar sectors placed upon the regional revolutionary coalition.[17]

The historians of Brazilian regionalism, though further advanced and more sophisticated than their Mexican counterparts, have thus far also failed to provide guidance for the student of modern Yucatan. Joseph Love, their principal spokesman, has done a study of Rio Grande do Sul that, like Womack's *Zapata*, represents a successful fit of regional historical development into the larger national framework.[18] Yet, the analysis is strictly political and provides little insight into the region's economic structure and its linkages with the national and international economy. Elsewhere, however, Love admits that "the external dimension of the region as a dependent area in the international [economic] complex" is of central importance to many regional studies and that "a series of qualifications and amendments for center-periphery models as they apply to Brazil and other countries" must be developed.[19]

Turning specifically to the complexities of Yucatecan regional history during the revolutionary period, one quickly perceives that an adequate conceptualization of the problem requires an analysis of a triangular set of interrelationships among a variety of individuals, groups, and governments in Yucatan, Mexico City, and the United States. How the historian approaches these intersecting regional, national, and international relationships and weighs the various factors, internal and external to Yucatan, is crucial for an understanding of the revolutionary process.

Essentially, the much-publicized agrarian revolution that came to Yucatan in the mid-1930s came from without—that is, from Mexico City—and thus far it has failed to achieve the goals of economic development and social justice it set for itself. The main thrust of the Mexican Revolution in Yucatan was epitomized by President Cárdenas's breakup of the henequen plantations and his institution of a collective ejido program, both of which, at least in the manner they were introduced, have proved unsuccessful.[20] The Revolution came from without largely because of the failure of an earlier drive for revolution from within. To explain these developments adequately, the historian must examine the various structures and forces within and without Yucatan, some of which conspired to frustrate the Revolution. By briefly characterizing the nature of Yucatecan society on the eve of the Revolution and identifying these forces that came into conflict, the process will become more clear.

The Old Regime and Its Demise: 1910–1915

It was no accident that the Revolution was delayed five years in reaching Yucatan. The peninsula's remote location, permitting regular access only by sea, had traditionally isolated it from the Mexican political mainstream. This geographical isolation made it difficult for home-grown revolutionaries to obtain news of the progress in the rest of the Republic of the movement that began with the outbreak of Francisco Madero's revolt in November 1910. More compelling, however, was the region's deep-seated reluctance to join the revolutionary tide. In fact, in 1915, the southeastern portion of Mexico—and Yucatan in particular—revealed itself to be virtually free from revolutionary activity.[21] The Porfirian system of oligarchical rule and repression of the Mayan masses had gained an extended lease on life in Yucatan because the peninsula's agro-commercial bourgeoisie had, through skillful adaptation to changing political circumstances, maintained an unshakable hold on the levers of economic and political power.[22]

On the eve of the Revolution, indeed, right up until Alvarado's arrival in 1915, Yucatan's Mayan campesinos lived under a brutal regime of debt peonage that was accurately likened to outright slavery by John Kenneth Turner and other contemporary observers.[23] The hacendados paid their workers a nominal salary that theoretically enabled them, by dint of hard work, to pay off the debts they had accumulated.[24] Once lured into debt, however, the worker found it practically impossible to regain his freedom. In fact, by the turn of the century, the amount of the individual debt was acknowledged to be irrelevant; the worker had become a commodity of which the market value was determined by fluctuations in the henequen market. Thus the "going price" for a man was $200–300 pesos in 1895; between $1,500 and $3,000 pesos after the sharp rise in price during and following the Spanish-American War; and $400 pesos after the world economic crisis of 1907.[25] This de facto slave system, though blatantly unconstitutional, existed for the purpose of enriching substantially capitalized, technologically modern henequen plantations owned by a few hundred entrepreneurial hacendados who formed the heart of Yucatan's ruling agrocommercial bourgeoisie.

The powerful grip of United States economic interests in Yucatan prior to 1915 cannot be minimized. At this point, the peninsula had a virtual world monopoly on the export of henequen fiber, and two North American corporations, working through Yucatecan agents, controlled the entire market. One of these, International Harvester Company, far outstripped its nearest rival, Plymouth Cordage, and to meet an extraordinary demand for fiber, coopted a few extremely wealthy and powerful hacendado/export merchants—most notably, Olegario Molina and Avelino Montes—who used their economic and political influence to control the

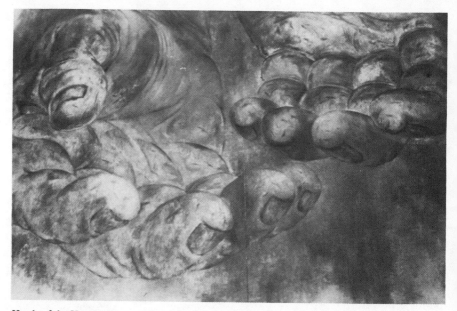

Hands of the Yucatecan campesino. Mural in the State Government Building, Mérida, by Fernando Castro Pacheco. (Photo by Joel Whitman)

local market in return for whopping commissions and kickbacks.[26] This select "collaborator" or *comprador* group, which came to be known as the "Divine Caste," functioned as a middleman, forcing down the price of fiber on the buyer's behalf, thereby often making possible a sizable profit margin for its U.S. partners, who manufactured and sold the henequen as binder twine to North American wheat farmers.[27] Although the vast majority of Yucatan's henequen producers and merchants remained outside this exclusive club and bitterly railed against it, the monopoly Yucatan enjoyed on the world market combined with incredibly low labor and production costs to permit prices high enough to ease the qualms of most irate members of the agrocommercial elite. Thus, though there existed an intraclass or intraelite fragmentation on the eve of the Revolution, the ruling group would maintain its solidarity in the face of severe threats by rival forces driving for revolution during the 1915–24 period.

Moreover, prior to the Madero revolt, Yucatan's hacendado and merchant oligarchs had constructed a multitiered repressive mechanism that commanded the respect and envy of their counterparts elsewhere in the Republic and insulated them against any immediate political threats to their power. Porfirio Díaz's defeat by Madero and the disbanding of the notorious *rurales* at the national level in 1911 had little effect on Yucatan, where the local *patrones* generally main-

tained their own police forces.[28] Nor did Victoriano Huerta's coup and subsequent defeat significantly alter the political and economic climate in Yucatan.
The local rulers had seen to it that their state won the dubious distinction of being
the first to recognize Madero's assassin in 1913. When Huerta fell a year later,
they quickly accommodated themselves to the Constitutionalists, receiving Venustiano Carranza's military governor, Major Eleuterio Avila, who was a native
son. Avila sent a momentary shock through the bourgeoisie by reading a procla-
mation abolishing forced labor on henequen plantations, but after a series of
anguished meetings among themselves and consultation with the agents of International Harvester, the hacendados found ways to bring their *paisano* to his
senses, and the decree was never enforced.[29]

By 1914, then, Yucatan's rulers had managed to keep the Revolution at arm's
length. Occasional flare-ups erupted and subsided in the countryside, and discon-
tented intellectuals continued to conjure visions of the apocalypse in the cafés
and salons of Mérida, but the objective conditions for a local revolutionary
movement plainly did not exist. Only a military stroke administered from the
outside could curb the political and repressive power of the hacendados, a fact
they appreciated only too well. But with Avila safely under control, life in the
peninsula returned to its normal rhythm, and the ruling elite believed it had
weathered the revolutionary threat.

"The First Phase": 1915–1924

At the beginning of 1915, however, when Carranza with his finance minister,
Luis Cabrera, became increasingly desperate for money to wage the Constitutionalist struggle against the *villistas* and *zapatistas,* a tighter control over
Yucatan's rich henequen receipts became more desirable. When Avila, now little
more than the hacendados' errand boy,[30] balked at Cabrera's stepped-up tax
schedule, Carranza replaced him with General Toribio de los Santos, a Mexican.
The new governor made it clear immediately that he would not be bought and
emphasized the point by pressing the new financial exactions and verbally abus-
ing the *yucatecos*. He played upon traditional regional fears by threatening to
send Yucatecan soldiers outside the peninsula and announcing his intention to
activate Avila's decree abolishing forced labor. De los Santos informed the
people that although their region "had not participated in the revolutionary
movement . . . nor felt its effects," the Revolution would *now* come to Yucatan.[31]

Stung by this first serious threat to its dominance, the oligarchy found its
champion in Colonel Abel Ortiz Argumedo, Mérida's military commander, who,
capitalizing on the discontent the governor had created at virtually every level of
regional society, united Yucatan's militia battalions and ousted De los Santos and
his *federales* from the state.[32] As the deposed leader fled, he cut the telegraph
wires linking Yucatan and Mexico City, a standard logistical tactic, but this time
infused with a special symbolic importance. Once again, Yucatan was turned in

upon itself, detached from Mexico, and, as in the past, determined to remain so. To buy time, Ortiz Argumedo—now the governor and military commander of the state—immediately pledged his loyalty to Carranza, then actively set about consolidating a separatist movement. Acting decisively, much as its predecessor had in 1849, the new government declared the sovereignty of Yucatan and sent a commission to the United States to buy arms and explore the possibility of North American protection or formal annexation.[33] Far from passively accepting the arrangement, members of the agrocommercial bourgeoisie played an active role in encouraging the break with Mexico. They contributed money to Ortiz Argumedo's war chest and enlisted their sons in his state battalion.[34]

Roughly a month later, in March 1915, it was readily apparent to Yucatan's rulers that this latest separatist gambit, which was to be their last, had failed. Not fooled, only infuriated by what he regarded to be a regional insurrection, Carranza quickly moved to bring Yucatan to bay. This time the First Chief chose as his agent of retribution Salvador Alvarado, one of his senior generals and the man who, next to Alvaro Obregón, was regarded to be his foremost strategist and administrator. As Ortiz Argumedo rounded up the remains of the state treasury and sailed for Cuba, Alvarado's powerful Army of the Southeast made short work of the *yucatecos*—essentially an amateur band of students and merchants one-tenth the federals' size—in what amounted to skirmishes with limited casualties at Halachó and Hacienda "Blanca Flor."[35]

Alvarado led an orderly "invasion" of Mérida on 19 March 1915. Over half a century later this colorful moment when the Mexican Revolution came to Yucatan was still recalled by *meridanos* with some awe:

> They came from the North . . . at dawn. They arrived singing "the Adelita," with broad brimmed hats and ammunition belts criss-crossing their chests; with muddy boots and rifles in their hands. . . .
> HUACH, HUACH squeaked the soles of their muddy boots on the newly paved streets: HUACH, HUACH, HUACH, as if to identify themselves to us as they marched through our city. . . .
> And behind them walked the women with little ones slung across their backs.[36]

> [*Huach:* a term used in Yucatan for some time to designate people from the interior of the Republic, principally soldiers in the army and manual laborers. It is not a Mayan word. Editors' note.]

After accepting control of the city, Alvarado further dispelled the *yucatecos'* doubts by declaring as his first official act that anyone caught looting or assaulting a *vecino* would be shot. Ironically, the only casualties immediately following Mérida's occupation were several criminals and two of his own soldiers, who ran afoul of this edict. Alvarado's actions reflected a basic decision that no one should be persecuted for past regional sympathies. In the weeks and months following, he refused to recognize or publicize evidence of Yucatan's recent separatism, astutely realizing that to do so might jeopardize his success in ruling the region and render the implementation of future revolutionary reforms more difficult.[37]

Antonio Mediz Bolio, who quickly became Alvarado's friend and intellectual adviser, recalls the general's dilemma at the time he took control of Yucatan:

> He found himself confronted by a land of tradition, whose internal life, sculptured drop by drop like a stalactite by the accumulation of centuries, was far removed and sheltered from the energetic reach of a Revolution which had only just touched its borders and whose impact was not appreciated because the Revolution did not yet know how to make its presence felt. . . .
>
> In spite of this, or perhaps because of it, Yucatan was one of the regions of Mexico where the Revolution was most urgently needed and would be felt most deeply. . . . But first Alvarado would have to make revolutionaries of the *yucatecos*. He would have to make the Revolution with his government, from above, for it could not issue from below. He would have to remake this society which, in many ways, still lived in the colonial period, and he would have to remake it down to its roots. . . . He would have to be not only Yucatan's revolutionary governor but also its revolutionary mentor.[38]

The invasion of Yucatan by a Mexican revolutionary army in 1915 ushered in a decade that spanned the regimes of Alvarado and his successor, Felipe Carrillo Puerto, and came to represent the "First Phase" of the Yucatecan revolutionary experience. Any historical analysis of this era must consider one essential irony: although the Revolution came from without, once arrived, a dynamic process was set in motion that, in the course of a relatively short period of time, transformed it into a characteristically Yucatecan movement.

The "First Phase" of the Revolution in Yucatan under Salvador Alvarado and Felipe Carrillo Puerto brought a number of significant reforms to the region.[39] Indeed, during the 1915–24 period, Yucatan came to be regarded by the rest of the Republic as a pace-setter, the cutting edge of the Revolution, where exciting experiments in political organization, women's rights, land, labor, and educational reform were being carried out.

Alvarado's *actuación revolucionaria* in Yucatan from 1915 to 1918 was characterized by an effective blend of bourgeois reformism in social areas and pragmatism in the political sphere. Perhaps his greatest contribution was the realization that, to be lasting, his incipient regional revolution would have to be institutionalized. Alvarado created pilot institutions like a centralized network of local revolutionary organizations (*ligas de resistencia*), which would later become constituent party units, and a state party (Partido Socialista de Yucatán), ultimately to be expanded by Carrillo into a truly regional party (the Partido Socialista del Sureste, or PSS). Under the general's aegis, Mexico's first "feminist congresses" were convened, and special feminist leagues were organized. He was also responsible for the creation of a small but powerful urban labor movement, based in Mérida and Progreso, that was successfully incorporated into the regional revolutionary coalition. In the area of education, he established a thousand new schools, the majority of these *escuelas rurales de la Revolución* in remote, previously untouched hamlets and hacienda communities.

President Carranza removed Alvarado late in 1918, thus preparing the way for Felipe Carrillo Puerto, who almost immediately pushed the Revolution to the left. Carrillo's social program represents both an extension and a radical redefinition of the theoretical precedents and reforms brought about by the more moderate Alvarado. The educational sphere provides an outstanding illustration of the different ideological orientations and revolutionary styles of these two leaders and their regimes. Alvarado, like other essentially bourgeois educators, was most concerned with raising the oppressed Yucatecan campesino from pariah to worker, transforming him from a servile *peón* into a mobile and productive *obrero*. Carrillo Puerto, on the other hand, linked the educational process with the Marxist notion of class struggle. It was not enough to transform the campesino from a social outcast into a free worker who knew his place in a bourgeois society. Rather, collectively, the workers would struggle to transform the society itself, and the revolutionary school would play an instrumental role in this process. Under the new leader, the Socialists not only continued Alvarado's school-building campaign in the countryside, but introduced the concept of the "rational school." Such a school would abolish all rewards and punishments, examinations, diplomas, and titles and would emphasize knowledge that could be acquired from manual work in the field or factory. The goal, according to the PSS, was to create a "true socialist school . . . to nourish the masses," an institution that would train "men apt for life and liberated from all dogmas." Beneath the rhetorical façade, Carrillo's Socialists envisioned a school that would transform the campesino into a class-conscious worker who would "no longer want to work for the bosses but [would] know how to profit from the price of [his] labor." Don Felipe's "rational school" provided a glimpse of the class-oriented pedagogy that would later emerge at the national level under Cárdenas, with the introduction of the *escuela socialista* during the 1933–38 period.[40]

From the above, it is apparent that Alvarado and Carrillo Puerto differed sharply on the role the Yucatecan masses would play in the revolutionary process. The general favored urban labor unions and rural resistance leagues as a means of coopting the masses and giving them a stake in the political process. But Alvarado's political mobilization, whether in the city or the countryside, always served an authority-legitimizing rather than an interest-articulating function. Alvarado was reluctant to let the masses actively participate, let alone rule, once they were brought into the political process. Carrillo, on the other hand, began his career as an agrarian agitator, politicizing the campesinos and encouraging them to accept responsibility for their own political destiny. For example, whereas Alvarado, in creating his feminist leagues, had refused to mobilize working-class women, Carrillo explicitly made rural *campesinas* the target group in the recruitment of his own *ligas feministas*.

Indeed, the basic premise of Don Felipe's more "popular" approach to revolutionary mobilization differed radically from the philosophy of his predecessor. Alvarado had cultivated the small urban proletariat as his chief civilian ally; Carrillo displayed little interest (and some hostility) toward the longshoremen, railroad workers, and electricians who comprised Yucatan's "labor aristocracy." He realized that Yucatan was overwhelmingly an agricultural region and reasoned that the campesinos and local bosses (caciques) in the agrarian sector would provide him with the base of power he needed to wage a social revolution "from above." Alvarado had been prepared to initiate only a moderate agrarian reform, and even that had been thwarted by his conservative superior Carranza. Carrillo Puerto, on the other hand, had demonstrated from his earliest days as an agrarian leader that land was the focal point of his social vision. During his leadership of the Revolution in the peninsula, the pace of agrarian reform accelerated to the point that Yucatan had distributed more land than any other state, save perhaps Zapata's Morelos. By the time of his death in 1924, Carrillo had made sure that virtually every one of the state's major pueblos had received at least a basic ejidal grant. His regime and life were snuffed out—hardly a coincidence—just at the moment he seemed ready to initiate a more sweeping agrarian reform that would have expropriated the region's henequen plantations and turned them into collective farms owned and operated by the workers who traditionally manned them.

Under Carrillo Puerto, the Mexican Revolution in Yucatan became a Yucatecan movement. His use of locally trained cadres of agrarian agitators and activist schoolteachers and his network of alliances with local power brokers (caciques)—to be discussed presently—stands in contrast to Alvarado's greater reliance on imported intellectuals and his own military commandants. The latter were, in the majority of cases, *norteños* like himself, although during the 1915–18 period, Alvarado did incorporate a number of *yucatecos* (Carrillo Puerto among them) into his administration. Carrillo, on the other hand, reinforced the regional character of his revolution in a variety of symbolic ways, most of which sought to wean the Yucatecan campesino away from the traditional attitudes and institutions of the old regime and inculcate within him a sense of ethnic pride in addition to class consciousness. The speaking of Maya and the teaching of Mayan culture and art forms were encouraged, for example, and every effort was made to recall the great tradition to which the campesinos were heir. Weekly cultural programs known as *lunes rojos* (Red Mondays) were scheduled at the headquarters of the resistance leagues. Communal work details began construction of serviceable roads to the largely inaccessible ruins of Chichén Itzá and Uxmal, both of which Carrillo was working to restore in collaboration with a team of archaeologists from the Carnegie Institution. The governor also commissioned and disseminated local editions of the *Chilam Balam* and *Popul Vuh,* the sacred books of the Yucatec and Quiché Maya, the latter of which had been relatively unknown in the peninsula. Moreover, to bind himself more directly to this usable past, Don Felipe propagated the notion among his subordinates that he was a direct descendant of Nachi Cocom, the Mayan noble, who had very

fiercely resisted Spanish conquest and was regarded as a symbol of regional pride
and autonomy. The claim was based on the fact that Felipe's ancestors had come
from Sotuta, the approximate locale of the old *cacicazgo* of the Cocomes.
Tenuous to begin with, the claim was severely undercut by his six-foot frame,
green eyes, and distinctly white appearance—hardly the best advertisements of
Mayan ancestry! Of course, he appreciated the fact that rational and factual
content need hardly be the stuff from which useful mythology is fashioned.

It is significant that the revolutionary governments of both Alvarado and
Carrillo Puerto changed the relations of production on haciendas, abolishing the
slave-peonage system, raising the consciousness and hastening the proletariani-
zation of the Yucatecan campesinos. Alvarado gave legal standing to Avila's
moribund decree "freeing the slaves," but Carrillo made sure that these changes
were carried out in practice and that the peon found himself well along the road to
becoming a unionized agricultural worker. Labor abuses on haciendas would
continue to be reported in later years, especially following Carrillo's death.
Moreover, the process whereby the rural worker was systematically mobilized
and developed a sense of class identity would fully occur only under Cárdenas in
the late 1930s and, even then, imperfectly. Yet, during the "First Phase" of the
Revolution in Yucatan, a definite beginning had been made. Alvarado established the precedent of "retroactive revolution," the realization in the minds of
campesinos and urban workers that injustices suffered years, even decades,
before might now be redressed in full. Carrillo Puerto continued and expanded
this notion, providing the rural worker with the protection and reinforcement he
had lacked under the Alvarado regime. The fact that after that time many more
Mayan campesinos took their grievances before Socialist magistrates in Mérida
and other regional centers speaks well for Don Felipe's campaign to instill ethnic
and class pride in the rural masses.

The Failure of the Revolution from Within

Why, then, was Carrillo Puerto's Yucatecan revolution defeated quickly and
relatively easily during the De la Huerta rebellion in the final weeks of 1923? A
lengthy and complex analysis would be required to answer adequately this controversial historiographical question that has become the subject of many volumes and articles in Yucatan and Mexico.[41] Traditional interpretations have
incorrectly emphasized Don Felipe's reluctance to shed the campesinos' blood in
a direct confrontation with the insurgent federals,[42] for, indeed, he *did* mobilize
the resistance leagues for combat on 12 December 1923. Some writers have put
forward the fantastic notion that Carrillo was consumed by his passion for North
American journalist Alma Reed and gave up any prospects of a fight with the
rebels in order to flee to the side of his lover.[43] Others have argued, more
plausibly, that his defeat and death were bought by the large henequen hacendados who were the targets and most bitter opponents of his agrarian reform
program.[44] Even assuming that the hacendados were implicated in Carrillo's fall,

however, it is difficult to explain the suddenness of the defeat the rebels inflicted upon the Socialists, especially in light of the fact that the PSS enjoyed the support of the much-heralded resistance leagues, which supposedly were ready to provide Carrillo with "seventy thousand strong."

Indeed, these traditional accounts of Carrillo's demise have omitted a sober analysis of the strength of the political alignment the governor had constructed to gain and maintain power within the region. The Socialists' revolutionary coalition was fragile at best. Whereas the Alvarado regime combined civilian rule with the military power of the Army of the Southeast, Carrillo's government was based solely upon civilian authority. In the absence of federal military support, it was extremely vulnerable to attack from within and without. Moreover, his coalition had suffered mass defections by the influential members of the peninsular bourgeoisie who had formerly been recruited by Alvarado but now feared and opposed Don Felipe's socialist regime. Carrillo's PSS was led by members of the petite bourgeoisie and urban working class, all of whom had become disaffected with the old regime. The party drew its support in part from the small urban labor movement (never particularly enthusiastic about Carrillo, given his preference for the *campesinado*), but mostly from the rural masses. An effective mobilization of the countryside, however, had been impeded by a poor communications network, the military opposition of Carranza's conservative central government (1919–20), and a severe economic depression (1920–22). Consequently, Carrillo had been forced to rely on existing power brokers and local rural bosses for support.

This suggests a revisionist interpretation and demystification of Felipe Carrillo Puerto, who has traditionally been viewed as a martyr, a secular saint of the proletariat, and Yucatan's Abraham Lincoln. In fact, he was a shrewd and pragmatic political leader, astute enough to realize that without sufficient guns and ammunition, and in the absence of widespread grass-roots politicization, he would have to bestow patronage upon local strongmen in order to keep his revolutionary regime in power. Carrillo's demise must also be interpreted in this revisionist light, for when push came to shove during the De la Huerta revolt, these caciques proved unreliable clients, deserting their patron in most cases. Moreover, the resistance leagues—the fabled "seventy thousand strong"—were found to be "paper tigers," organizations with highly inflated membership lists that were nominally kept behind the governor by the local bosses. Although such a political alignment was well suited to maintaining control against internal threats because it possessed a virtual monopoly of force within the region, it remained vulnerable to a swift attack from without by a powerful, well-equipped force of federal troops—precisely what occurred during the De la Huerta insurgency in December 1923.[45]

Demystifying the manner in which Carrillo Puerto consolidated and later lost power in Yucatan, however, need not suggest that he preferred to work through cacique networks rather than with the people. Carrillo was a lifelong socialist committed to bringing structural change to Yucatan. He appreciated the difficulties of waging social revolution "from above" and realized that only a mass movement that mobilized social groups and classes around a revolutionary ideology and agenda had any chance of success. The creation of a broad revolutionary base, however, would be a slow and terribly demanding process. No doubt Felipe appreciated that "as of marriage, so of revolutions: the best take years to turn out well."[46]

Unfortunately, and this must be emphasized, although the first crucial decade of the Revolution in Yucatan established institutional precedents for social change and revealed the potential of radical reform, it did not restructure society or significantly transform the region's dependent economy. The elite clique of "collaborators" was overthrown and, beginning with Alvarado, the state increasingly expanded its control over the henequen industry, establishing an exclusive government monopoly (the Comisión Reguladora del Mercado de Henequén) that bought fiber from the Yucatecan producers and sold it directly to the North American manufacturers. Yet, except perhaps for a brief period during World War I when demand was artificially high, Yucatan was unable to alter structurally the terms of its unequal relationship vis-à-vis the U.S. corporations that consumed its exports. The two early revolutionary leaders were either not inclined (Alvarado) or unable (Carrillo Puerto) to expropriate the henequen plantations on behalf of the campesinos. They were therefore unable to transform the structure of agrarian production and the nature of Yucatecan society. Despite his unpopularity with a large segment of the hacendado class, Alvarado presided over a period of great hacendado enrichment during the boom years of World War I. For all of his threats, Socialist Governor Carrillo Puerto had to contend with depressed postwar henequen prices and never had the time prior to his fall to carry out the sweeping agrarian reform he had promised. Because the core unit of the state's agrarian structure remained the henequen plantation, we must agree with Mexican historian Moisés González Navarro's assessment that Alvarado and Carrillo Puerto were merely "the two great *precursors* of the Yucatecan agrarian revolution."[47] That revolution would come later, during the Cárdenas years.

Of course, we must remember that the Mexican central government, fearful of offending the United States in the early 1920s in the wake of the Bucareli Conferences and formal recognition of the revolutionary regime, was unlikely to have sanctioned sweeping reforms had Carrillo been able to bring them about. Materials in corporate files and the United States National Archives document the North American cordage interests' powerful lobby in Washington and the U.S. government's pressure upon the Carranza and Obregón governments to avoid any actions that might have jeopardized or delayed the supply of raw henequen to the United States. Actual episodes of "gunboat diplomacy" and threats to land the marines were not uncommon because Woodrow Wilson's wartime government regarded protection of America's wheat crop—and, by extension, of its daily bread—as a matter of the highest national security.[48] In 1916, Carranza issued a flat ultimatum to General Alvarado to halt immediately his modest agrarian reform program. Obregón, also subjected to U.S. pressure in the early 1920s, might have been equally wary of Carrillo Puerto's plans to expropriate the henequen plantations. At any rate, Carrillo Puerto's assassination rendered the point moot, and we can only speculate as to what Presidents Obregón and Plutarco Elías Calles might have done had Carrillo lived and carried out more radical policies in Yucatan. It is significant, for example, that Obregón did little to save Carrillo Puerto during the De la Huerta revolt, especially when it has been argued that he could have taken action to rescue his loyal governor.[49]

Mexico City, reluctant to infuriate powerful North American economic interests, at least prior to legitimization and recognition of the revolutionary regime by the United States, was instrumental in thwarting revolutionary impulses in Yucatan. Consequently, at least for the "First Phase" of the Revolution in Yucatan (1915–24), there is much to suggest the validity of aspects of the "chain-of-colonialisms" idea. This theory, put forward by André Gunder Frank and the radical wing of the "dependency" school, posits foreign dominance of a region through intermediary control of a national metropolis.[50]

On the other hand, there were compelling domestic political reasons that might have convinced Obregón and Calles that both Carrillo and his socialist program were expendable. Don Felipe's substantial power as a regional caudillo and his growing reputation as a national figure might have begun to threaten Calles and Obregón by 1923. Following Carrillo's death, Obregón concertedly purged influential *carrillistas* from positions of power within the PSS, a fact that further substantiates this argument. Indeed, historians are now beginning to view the Obregón-Calles period as the first significant moment of consolidation and centralization in the development of Mexico's new revolutionary corporatist state.[51] This was a time when, to promote national unity and forge a modern state, the central government began systematically to undercut the power and autonomy of the regional caudillos. In certain instances, the national regime regarded these regional strongmen as too progressive or extreme. Such was the case with Adalberto Tejeda (Veracruz), Primo Tapia (Michoacán), and Carrillo Puerto, each of whom approximated, in varying degree, the radical populist style of leadership that would later emerge at the national level with Lázaro Cárdenas.[52] In other instances, such as the case of the Cedillo brothers in San Luis Potosí or that of the Figueroas in Guerrero, the federal government was critical of regional bosses for not being progressive enough, for applying a rude and anachronistic nineteenth-century political style to twentieth-century conditions.[53] In either case, whether it perceived them to be forward- or backward-looking, Mexico City found these regional chiefs out of step with *its Revolution* and therefore politically expendable.

"The Second Phase": The Years of Lázaro Cárdenas, 1934–1940

Let us return specifically to the dialectical process by which revolution, once frustrated from within, came from without, only to be frustrated again in its essential objectives.[54] Following the death of Felipe Carrillo Puerto, the 1924–34 period witnessed a reconsolidation of the power of the peninsular elite, the infiltration and weakening of Carrillo's Socialist party by that ruling group, and a sharp falloff in agrarian reform, especially within the henequen zone. Some of the governors and political leaders of these years were receptive to the bribes and blandishments of the wealthy—as traditional interpretations hold[55]—but this was certainly not true of the entire Socialist party leadership, nor was it the principal explanation for the political and economic prostration Yucatan experienced during this decade. With the exception of a brief period in the mid-1920s, the price of henequen continued to plummet on the world market, and foreign competition reduced Yucatan's former monopoly to a mere third of the market by the early 1930s. Quite clearly, money to sustain the costly reform programs of Alvarado and Carrillo Puerto had dried up. For example, the depressed economy made an expropriation of the henequen plantations temporarily unthinkable—a solution that would have required an influx of money and personnel into the region which the state could not, and the federal governments prior to Cárdenas would not, support. Nor was it acceptable to many campesinos, who were more concerned with maintaining a level of work on the plantations sufficient to sustain them and their families at the subsistence level. Predominantly an emerging proletariat, they lacked not only the desire, but also the experience and capital to operate collectively the henequen plantations on which they worked. Furthermore, many of the haciendas were no longer profitable ventures and were being gradually abandoned. To the extent that they were *agraristas,* the campesinos petitioned the Agrarian Department for small *parcelas* (plots) on which they might grow maize and beans, and perhaps henequen, to supplement the wages that were the mainstay of their existence.[56]

When the agrarian revolution did come to Yucatan, it came from without. Given the increasingly centralized nature of federal-state relations throughout the 1920–40 period, this federal hegemony was inevitable. The parameters for independent strategy and action that Alvarado, and to a lesser extent Carrillo Puerto, had enjoyed were nonexistent in the late 1920s and early 1930s. By 1934, the once proud and autonomous Partido Socialista del Sureste existed only in name; in fact, it had become the errand boy of Cárdenas's increasingly omnicompetent Partido Nacional Revolucionario (PNR). Whereas the evidence shows that Obregón and Calles had been opposed to substantial agrarian reform in the henequen zone, Cárdenas chose Yucatan precisely for the purpose of making it, along with the Laguna cotton-producing region, a showcase for his collective ejido program. The spiraling urban and rural unrest in Yucatan, which some regarded to be a bona fide *lucha de clases,* was itself fanned by *cardenista* agents and labor organizers. The struggle merely provided the federal government with a suitable pretext to attempt a restructuring of Yucatecan society.[57]

Early in August 1937, President Lázaro Cárdenas arrived in Progreso with a boatload of engineers, surveyors, and bureaucrats, and on the seventh of that month he presided over the largest single episode of agrarian reform ever carried

Scenes of rural henequen workers in their fields at Taxkukul in May 1930. (Photos courtesy of Gilbert Joseph)

out in Mexico. Henceforth all hacienda lands, whether cultivated in henequen or not, would become the property of the campesinos, with the exception of 150 hectares of henequen land and 150 hectares of woodland which the proprietor might retain as his "small property" (*pequeña propiedad*). Cárdenas further decreed that the implementation of the reform would begin immediately, with the expropriation of the largest estates first, and no proprietor would be exempt. Within only two weeks, the entourage of *técnicos* had effected the transfer of tenure, consolidating unequal segments of hundreds of haciendas into 272 collective ejidos. Cárdenas had been adamant on this issue, maintaining that since henequen production was a commercial process that demanded the collaboration of many campesinos in a common enterprise, the new ejidos should be managed and cultivated collectively.

Unfortunately, it quickly became apparent that many irregularities and contradictions were embedded in the distribution process. The planters had been promised their *cascos* (the nuclei of their haciendas, including the major buildings and machinery), but in some instances these were expropriated and distributed piecemeal to neighboring ejidos. In fact, despite presidential guidelines, some hacendados suffered total expropriation of their estates. At the other extreme, cases were reported of families that managed to preserve much more than the stipulated three hundred hectares. Typically, several members of a single family would establish legal identity and succeed in retaining a much larger block of land. By the end of 1938, it was clear that a crazy-quilt of tenure arrangements had emerged as a result of Cárdenas's reform. Once reasonably productive agro-industrial operations, many plantations were now carved up in a manner that suggested the absence of rational criteria in the planning and execution of the reform. Rarely did ejidos receive the appropriate number of henequen plants at each stage of growth which they would require to maintain continuity of production. Some received *henequenales* in full decline with few mature or young plants. Others were top-heavy in young shoots and would not realize an income for years to come. Instances were also reported in which urbanites from Mérida and Progreso had been included on the rolls of nearby ejidos while numbers of eligible campesinos in the area had been completely excluded.

Finally, although under the terms of the reform campesinos theoretically became owners of the land they cultivated, in practice the system gave them little participation in management. Many felt alienated from the operations of their new ejidos, pointing out that they had exchanged their former *patrón*—who, for all of his drawbacks, was a known quantity—for the impersonal bureaucracy of the federal government's ejidal bank. Although it provided technical assistance and doled out credit advances, the bank virtually excluded the ejidatarios from all production and marketing decisions. It is not surprising, therefore, that by 1938, the initial trickle of protest regarding the agrarian reform had broadened into a torrent, with the petitioners now including groups of ejidatarios as well as disgruntled former hacendados.[58]

The 1934–40 period, which constitutes the "Second Phase" of the Revolution in Yucatan, reveals a monocrop region caught in the throes of severe economic depression, in large part exacerbated by its external economic dependence upon the United States. Furthermore, it was forced to accept solutions dictated by a central government that, according to popular belief, did not understand Yucatan's peculiar problems. Thus, it was during the Cárdenas period that the region's condition of dependency—economic, political, and intellectual—stood out in sharp relief. Whereas local thinkers had a long-established tradition of proposing policy alternatives, during the 1930s Mexico City became the principal source for ideological solutions to local problems. Whether we consider the militantly collectivist ideology of the federal agrarian socialists, centering on the collective ejido, or the futile counterattack led by Luis Cabrera and other veteran revolutionaries on behalf of the independently owned *pequeña propiedad,* we are forced to conclude that the arguments that fueled the controversies in Yucatan surrounding Cárdenas's ejidal collectivization program were all imported from without. At the level of practice, local intellectuals had similarly been displaced. The federal schoolteachers moved into the vanguard of campesino mobilization and leadership. Consequently, Yucatecan *maestros,* once the backbone of Carrillo Puerto's resistance leagues, assumed (with some notable exceptions) a less active role.[59]

In evaluating Yucatan's condition of dependency, we should note that Gunder Frank's "chain-of-colonialisms" idea has much less validity for the Cárdenas era than it did for the "First Phase." For although Mexico City's control of the region and its henequen industry steadily increased during 1934–40, Cárdenas did *not* respond to U.S. pressure in the manner of his predecessors. Rather than acquiesce in a middleman role as they had, and impede agrarian reform impulses in the region that proved threatening to North American cordage interests, Cárdenas deliberately selected Yucatan as the proving ground for his ambitious collective ejido program that entailed the comprehensive expropriation of privately owned *henequenales.* Thus, although recent dependency literature, North American and Mexican alike, has tended to portray Cárdenas conspiratorily, as the father of a corporatist state that worked most effectively in the interests of an emerging national bourgeoisie collaborating with a foreign bourgeoisie,[60] it is difficult to fit Cárdenas's policy toward Yucatan into this neat, symmetrical framework. If Frank and other Marxian analysts are correct in their formulation of the intermediary circle of neocolonialism as consisting of a collaborator bourgeoisie in conjunction with the state, the noncollaborationist politics of Cárdenas would appear to constitute a significant exception.

Rather than overschematize, and turn Yucatan into just another regional link in the "chain-of-colonialism," we might view the problem directly from the regional level, examining Yucatan's structural dependency on a foreign-dominated market that remained even after Yucatan succeeded in industrializing its henequen and produced binder twine locally, a process that began in the 1920s and gained momentum in the 1930s and 1940s. As late as 1947, International Harvester alone still consumed almost 60 percent of Yucatan's annual yield of fiber and cordage.[61] Here, then, is a classic case where industrialization did not break the relationship of dependency and promote economic "takeoff," because industrialization issued from a monocrop economy tied to a fluctuating world market, the terms of which still favored the North American buyer over the Yucatecan seller and permitted frequent manipulation of that market in the buyer's interest. Many *yucatecos* have commented that they regarded Harvester's and the United States' "informal empire" over their region, with its legacy of economic dependence, as more enduring and damaging than the more formal domination of the old Spanish Empire or the current Mexican Republic, from which they had been able temporarily to secede on two separate occasions in the nineteenth century. Recalling a venerable central Mexican proverb, one local intellectual suggested: "To divorce one's wife is simple, to divorce one's mistress impossible."[62]

Without Revolution: Yucatan's Legacy of Frustration, 1940–1978

The regional historian who observes how sharply the fortunes of the henequen industry have declined over the past six decades finds it hard to ignore criticism emanating from every level of Yucatecan society that the Revolution that came from without in the 1930s has proved to be something less than a complete blessing. One is confronted by the stark fact that within the past half century, Yucatan fell from being Mexico's richest state to being one of its most troublesome, depressed areas. One encounters middle-class intellectuals who lament the region's loss of autonomy and cry "internal colonialism"[63] and workers who allege corruption and inefficiency in the management of the federal-state condominium (Cordemex) controlling the henequen industry.[64] Members of the former hacendado class complain bitterly that, in breaking up once-productive agroindustrial units and failing to substitute a viable and integrated economic system in place of the old plantation economy, the Revolution effectively scuttled the regional economy without conferring significant improvements upon rural workers.[65]

In leveling these charges, the Revolution's critics give little importance to the secular decline of the henequen industry, attributable, in large part, to the proliferation of international competitors and the invention of synthetic fibers. Nevertheless, the government's own statistics offer a sad commentary on the long-term effects of the revolutionary regime's henequen strategy. In 1977, the eighty thousand ejidatarios underemployed in the henequen zone received salaries ranging from U.S. $4–9 per week, in most cases less than was needed to support their families at the subsistence level. Whenever possible, ejidatarios or their family members attempt to supplement these wages with outside jobs, often in Mérida and smaller centers. According to the director of Cordemex, the zone can now adequately support only twenty-eight thousand workers. Consequently, the government must "featherbed" or subsidize the remaining ejidatarios, absorbing staggering losses in the process. During 1976–77, for example, Cordemex expected to lose substantially more than the $333.5 million pesos that it had lost in

1975–76. Production figures are even more depressing. Although the mass of campesinos is greater today than at the turn of the century, Yucatan produces substantially less fiber now, and the figures continue to decline with each passing year. An average of 140,000 tons were produced annually during the 1964–70 period. Today the yield is somewhat less than 100,000 tons, and by 1980 it is estimated that production will not even satisfy Mexico's domestic needs, let alone provide fiber for export. Only by comparing these figures with the 202,000 tons that were produced during henequen's boom period in 1916 can we get a true picture of the magnitude of the current crisis. Recently a Cordemex official estimated conservatively that it would take a federal government investment on the order of one billion pesos to improve productive capacity and put the regional fiber industry back on its feet.[66]

The agrarian reform program implemented after the 1959 Revolution in the sugar-producing areas of Cuba—like Yucatan, essentially a monocrop region—stands in sharp contrast to the policy carried out by the Cárdenas administration in the peninsula's henequen zone. Mindful, perhaps, of the neighboring Yucatecan model, under which existing plantations were broken up and new economic units were created at the cost of a significant loss in productive capacity, the revolutionary Cuban government, after expropriating the sugar plantations, opted to leave them intact, while offering substantial incentives—such as improved material conditions and worker management—to the rural proletariat manning them. It has been suggested above that Yucatan's rural workers probably would have preferred, and benefited from, a similar agrarian reform strategy. Indeed, this was precisely what Carrillo Puerto's projected reform would have done. Even Alvarado's moderate agrarian program, weighted heavily toward wage increases with little emphasis placed upon the division of existing plantations, would have had a less damaging effect on the Yucatecan economy than the 1937 reform. Unlike Cárdenas, who drew upon ideological models derived from the agrarian experience of central Mexico, both Alvarado and Carrillo geared their reform strategies to the specific characteristics of Yucatan's agrarian structure and to the relations of production that had grown out of it.[67]

Undoubtedly, few states in the Republic have experienced such a disappointing history of agrarian reform as Yucatan. Apologists for the revolutionary regime have sought—and still seek—to justify Cárdenas's massive 1937 reform, claiming that the strategy was well conceived, only poorly implemented by corrupt officials. Alternatively, government officials have claimed that the Yucatecan agrarian case is a special one, atypical of Mexican rural conditions. In doing so, they have taken great pains to preserve the central myths of the Revolution by "writing Yucatan off" as an exotic problem incapable of resolution. Leftist intellectuals and right-wing *panistas* alike have vehemently disagreed. They argue that though Yucatan's agrarian problems are unusual and the regime's failure to provide solutions is extreme, the Yucatecan case provides significant insight into the agrarian process throughout Mexico as a whole.[68]

Ironically, the viewpoints of both the "apologists" and the "critics" are not only correct, but are complementary. Yucatan's checkered history of agrarian reform and frustration is indeed idiosyncratic, yet it brings the entire process of land reform in Mexico sharply into focus. Significantly, the award-winning Argentine film, *México, la revolución congelada* (Mexico, the Frozen Revolution), chose Yucatan as its central case study in dealing with the revolutionary regime's failure to bring effective agrarian reform to Mexico. It may well be that few Mexican campesinos have experienced as many problems or disappointments as the *yucatecos*. On the other hand, virtually every problem typically encountered throughout the Mexican countryside—and in other Latin American countries that have implemented programs of agrarian reform—is to be found in contemporary Yucatan. These include overpopulation and underemployment, ejidal boundary disputes setting group against group and village against village, the illegal rental or sale of plots, caciquismo, the disenfranchisement of ejidatarios in agrarian affairs, chronic political unrest, factional violence, and assassination—to name only the more outstanding ones.[69]

The important contributions of the Mexican Revolution in Yucatan should not be minimized. For example, it ended slave-peonage and developed a political and social consciousness among the working classes. It also brought the creation of thousands of new schools and a dramatic increase in health, sanitation, and other

Mural by Fernando Castro Pacheco of Lázaro Cárdenas and Felipe Carrillo Puerto. State Government Building, Mérida. (Photo by Joel Whitman)

social welfare benefits.[70] On the other hand, an appreciation of these reforms should not blind one to the underlying truth about the Yucatecan revolutionary experience: that when one speaks of a "revolution from within" in contrast to a "revolution from without," or distinguishes the frustration of a characteristically "Yucatecan" revolution from the actual historical record of the "Mexican" Revolution *in* Yucatan, one is not merely engaging in semantical exercise. During the "First Phase" of the Revolution, from 1915 to 1924, and especially during the Socialist regime of Felipe Carrillo Puerto, forces within the region made a concerted drive for social revolution. These efforts might have succeeded had they not been undercut by external constraints compounded by significant internal weaknesses (such as low mobilization and the reliance upon traditional cacique networks). In the process, these local revolutionary forces failed to capitalize on the rich opportunities provided by World War I—most notably, soaring henequen prices—opportunities that did not repeat themselves during the 1934–40 "Second Phase." The "revolution" that came during these years was imported, and, although it conferred some important benefits upon the region, the social and economic impact registered has never approached the radical restructuring of Yucatecan society envisioned by Felipe Carrillo Puerto and the socialist revolutionaries.

ACKNOWLEDGMENTS

Research for much of this chapter was conducted in Yucatan and Mexico City with the assistance of a grant from the Social Science Research Council. I am indebted to John Womack and fellow *yucatólogos* Ramón Chacón and Allen Wells for sharing insights and data and to Julia Preston, Steve J. Stern, and Emilia Viotti da Costa, former colleagues at Yale University, for their criticisms of an earlier draft.

NOTES

Abbreviations

AC	Archivo de Carranza, CONDUMEX, Mexico City
AGE	Archivo General del Estado de Yucatán, Ramo de Gobierno, Mérida
CJD	Colección Jorge Denegre V., Mexico City
DdY	*Diario de Yucatán*
IHCA	International Harvester Company Archives, Chicago, Illinois
LAP	*Latin American Perspectives*
RUY	*Revista de la Universidad de Yucatán*
SD	U.S., Department of State, *Records of the Department of State Relating to the Internal Affairs of Mexico, 1910–1929*. Record Group 59. Microfilm Copy 274. Washington, D.C.: National Archives, 1959.

SD-CPR, *Corr.*   National Archives, U.S. Department of State Consular Post Records, *Correspondence: Progreso.* Record Group 84. Washington, D.C.

1. Eyler N. Simpson, *The Ejido: Mexico's Way Out,* Chapel Hill, N.C., 1937; Frank Brandenburg, *The Making of Modern Mexico,* Englewood Cliffs, N.J., 1964.

2. See the articles in the issue of *Latin American Perspectives* entitled "Mexico: The Limits of State Capitalism," 2, No. 2 (Summer 1975); and Adolfo Gilly, *La revolución interrumpida,* México, 1971.

3. Alvaro Gamboa Ricalde, Edmundo Bolio, Antonio Bustillos Carrillo, Roque Armando Sosa Ferreyro, Bernardino Mena Brito, Ramón Berzunza Pinto, Fidelio Quintal Martín, Renán Irigoyen, and Antonio Betancourt Pérez are most prominent among the local writers who have written extensively on the Yucatecan revolutionary experience.

4. See the regional revolutionary studies of the following authors: Michael Meyer (*orozquismo* in Chihuahua), Héctor Aguilar Camín (Sonora), Raymond Th. Buve (Tlaxcala), Heather Fowler Salamini and Romana Falcón (Veracruz), Paul Friedrich (Michoacán), Jean Meyer (the *cristero* movement), John Womack (*zapatismo* in Morelos), and Friedrich Katz (*villismo* in the north and elsewhere).

5. Antonio Mediz Bolio, "Prólogo" to Salvador Alvarado, *Actuación revolucionaria del General Salvador Alvarado,* México, 1965, p. 14; Moisés González Navarro, who devoted a portion of his study, *Raza y tierra: La guerra de castas y el henequén,* México, 1970, to the revolutionary period, and sociologists Francisco J. Paoli and Enrique Montalvo, *El socialismo olvidado de Yucatán,* México, 1977, are notable exceptions. A recent surge of interest in revolutionary Yucatan among North American scholars should also be noted. In addition to the author of this study, Ramón Chacón (California State, Humboldt), A. J. Graham Knox (University of Calgary), and Diane Roazen (University of Chicago) are also investigating various facets of the region's revolutionary experience. For the most part, it is fair to say that regional revolutionary studies have been slow to develop. For the harvest of such studies done prior to 1970 by Mexican—in most cases, local—historians, see Luis González, *Invitación a la microhistoria,* México, 1973, pp. 120–183.

6. In Yucatan, the locals often call the Mexicans "gringos." Moreover, many stubbornly refuse to refer to themselves as "mexicanos." "Somos yucatecos"—"We are Yucatecans"—they proudly tell you, revealing at the same time the high degree of uneasiness and mistrust that continue to characterize Yucatecan perceptions of, and relations with, Mexico.

7. John Womack's forthcoming study of the labor movement in revolutionary Veracruz will further underscore the importance of examining "exceptional regions."

8. Sylvia Weyl and Nathaniel Weyl, *The Reconquest of Mexico: The Years of Lázaro Cárdenas,* New York, 1939.

9. González, *Invitación,* pp. 8–72.

10. Compare similar statements on this theme by the following historians: González, *Invitación;* Eric Stokes, "Late Nineteenth Century Colonial Expansion and the Attack on the Theory of Economic Imperialism," *Historical Journal,* 12, No. 2 (1969), 286; and James Lockhart, "The Social History of Colonial Spanish America," *Latin American Research Review,* 7, No. 1 (1972), 6–45.

11. Charles C. Cumberland, *Mexico: The Struggle for Modernity,* New York, 1968, pp. 241, 245–246.

12. "El censo de 1930 comparado con los de 1895, 1900, 1910, y 1921" (official

figures from the Dpto. de la Estadística Nacional), *Diario de Yucatán*, 22 Sept. 1930, p. 5.

13. Martín Luis Guzmán, *The Eagle and the Serpent*, trans. Harriet de Onís, Garden City, N.Y., 1965, p. 163; SD-CPR, *Corr.*, *1916*, I, 125.3, Claude E. Guyant to William P. Young, 10 June.

14. The traditional periodization is articulately stated in James W. Wilkie, *The Mexican Revolution: Federal Expenditure and Social Change since 1910*, Berkeley, Calif., 1967.

15. Paul Friedrich, "A Mexican Cacicazgo," *Ethnology*, 4, No. 2 (April 1965), 190–209; Henning Siverts, "The 'Cacique' of K'ankujk'," *Estudios de cultura maya* (Mexico City), 5 (1965), 339–360; Miguel Angel Rivera, "Panixtlahuaca: Retrato de un feroz cacicazgo," *Proceso*, 27 June 1977, pp. 16–17.

16. Gilbert M. Joseph, "Caciquismo and the Revolution: Carrillo Puerto in Yucatán," in D. A. Brading, ed., *Caudillo and Peasant in the Mexican Revolution*, Cambridge, 1980. The violence that characterized Yucatecan caciquismo during the Revolution bore similarities to the backlands violence of the contemporary Brazilian "Republic of the Coronéis." See, for example, Eul-soo Pang, *Bahia in the First Brazilian Republic: Coronelismo and Oligarchies, 1889–1934*, Gainesville, Fla., 1979. The importance of caciquismo in the local revolutionary process is discussed below.

17. John Womack, *Zapata and the Mexican Revolution*, New York, 1970; Heather Fowler Salamini, *Agrarian Radicalism in Veracruz, 1920–38*, Lincoln, Nebr., 1978. Social scientists Paul Friedrich (*Agrarian Revolt in a Mexican Village*, Englewood Cliffs, N.J., 1970) and David Ronfeldt (*Atencingo: The Politics of Agrarian Struggle in a Mexican Ejido*, Stanford, Calif., 1973) have also dealt with regions producing largely for internal markets (Michoacán and the sugar-producing region of Puebla, respectively).

18. Joseph L. Love, *Rio Grande do Sul and Brazilian Regionalism, 1882–1930*, Stanford, Calif., 1971.

19. Love, "An Approach to Regionalism," in Richard Graham and Peter H. Smith, eds., *New Approaches to Latin American History*, Austin, Tex., 1974, p. 149; Love, "External Financing and Domestic Politics: The Case of São Paulo, 1889–1937," in R. E. Scott, ed., *Latin American Modernization Problems*, Urbana, Ill., 1973, pp. 236–259. Love, John Wirth and Robert Levine have recently completed a trilogy on Brazilian regionalism treating São Paulo, Minas Gerais, and Pernambuco, respectively. A preliminary statement appears in Boris Fausto, ed., *Historia geral da civilização brasileira*, 3, No. 1 (*0 Brasil Republicano: Estrutura de poder e economia, 1889–1930*), São Paulo, 1975, pp. 50–150.

20. González Navarro, *Raza y tierra*, pp. 261–283; Fernando Benítez, *Ki: El drama de un pueblo y de una planta*, México, 1962, pp. 120–235.

21. Mediz Bolio, "Prólogo," p. 14; Ramón Berzunza Pinto, "El Constitucionalismo en Yucatán," *Historia mexicana*, 12, No. 2 (Oct.–Dec. 1962), 278; Friedrich Katz, "Labor Conditions on Haciendas in Porfirian Mexico: Some Trends and Tendencies," *Hispanic American Historical Review*, 54, No. 1 (Feb. 1974), 22–23, 44–47.

22. Jorge Flores D., "La vida rural en Yucatán en 1914," *Historia mexicana*, 10, No. 3 (Jan.–March 1961), 471–483.

23. John Kenneth Turner, *Barbarous Mexico*, Chicago, 1911, pp. 9–66; Henry Baerlein, *Mexico: The Land of Unrest*, Philadelphia, 1909, pp. 143–198; Channing Arnold and Frederick J. T. Frost, *The American Egypt*, New York, 1909, pp. 321–336 and passim.

24. The Yucatecan peon's nominal salary was reasonable by Porfirian standards; however, as elsewhere in Mexico, an absolute decline in real wages made existence difficult and savings impossible. See Friedrich Katz, "El sistema de plantación y la esclavitud," *Ciencias políticas y sociales,* 8 (Jan.–March 1962), 122; Turner, *Barbarous Mexico,* p. 31.

25. Turner, *Barbarous Mexico,* p. 17; Katz, "El sistema," p. 125. That the real debt had become unimportant if the hacendado was determined to keep the peon is stressed by each of the contemporary writers mentioned above. Backed by the Porfirian political and legal establishment, the planter had the options of falsifying records, making debts hereditary, or merely declaring the indebtedness of the peon under oath.

26. See Renán Irigoyen, "El impulso a la economía de Yucatán durante el Gobierno de Alvarado," RUY, 38 (March–April 1965), 14 ff.

27. Gilbert M. Joseph, "Apuntes para una nueva historia regional: Yucatán y la Revolución Mexicana, 1915–1940," *RUY,* 109 (Jan.–Feb. 1977), 23, n. 30.

28. Katz, "Labor Conditions," pp. 44–45; González Navarro, *Raza y tierra,* p. 231.

29. It has been argued that Avila changed his mind about the decree after he received "a very fine hacienda" and "a regular sum of money" from the planters. CJD, roll 3, Toribio de los Santos to Carranza, 14 Jan. 1915; Nelson Reed, *The Caste War of Yucatan,* Stanford, Calif., 1964, p. 257; D. A. Franz, "Bullets and Bolshevists: A History of the Mexican Revolution and Reform in Yucatán, 1910–1924," Dissertation, University of New Mexico, 1973, pp. 78–79, 83, 89. Luis Amendolla, "Política regional: Yucatán," *Mañana,* 6 (19 Feb. 1944), 19–20, suggests that the eight million pesos forced loan decreed by Avila in September 1914 was actually a bribe by the *henequeneros* to ensure that emancipation remained a dead letter.

30. CJD, roll 3, De los Santos to Carranza, 14 Jan. 1915; AC, Calixto Maldonado R. to Carranza, 9 Jan. 1915; AC, Carranza to Alvarado, 16 Feb. 1915.

31. AC, Carranza to De los Santos, 20 Jan. 1915; SD, 812.00/14561; Franz, "Bullets and Bolshevists," pp. 91–93; Alvaro Gamboa Ricalde, *Yucatán desde 1910,* II, Veracruz, 1943, p. 331; Reed, *Caste War,* p. 258.

32. SD, 812.00/14554; Gamboa, *Yucatán,* II, 331; Benítez, *Ki,* p. 95.

33. SD, 812.61326/31; 812.00/14561, 14484; Santiago Pacheco Cruz, *Recuerdos de la propaganda constitucionalista en Yucatán,* Mérida, 1953, p. 52; Roberto Villaseñor, *El separatismo en Yucatán: Novel histórico-política mexicana,* México, 1916.

34. SD, 812.61326/45, 83; SD-CPR, *Corr., 1915,* II, 800, Young to Secretary of State, 23 Feb.; Florencio Avila y Castillo, *Diario Revolucionario,* Mérida, 1915, p. 163; Renán Irigoyen, *Salvador Alvarado: Extraordinario estadista de la Revolución,* Mérida, 1973, pp. 20–21.

35. Pacheco Cruz, *Recuerdos,* p. 55; Allan Moe Blein (alias Antonio Mediz Bolio), *Alvarado es el hombre,* 2ª ed., Culiacán, 1961, p. 31; Villaseñor, *El separatismo,* pp. 219–223.

36. Antonio Betancourt Pérez, "Nuestro viejo abuelo," *RUY,* 15, No. 84 (Jan.–Feb. 1973), 60–61; Eduardo Urzáiz R., "La entrada de Alvarado," *Orbe,* 41 (April 1955), 85–86; interview with José Monsreal, 24 Oct. 1975.

37. Isidro Fabela and Josefina Fabela, eds., *Documentos históricos de la Revolución Mexicana,* México, 1960–, XVII, 135, Alvarado to Carranza, 26 Sept. 1916; Avila y Castillo, *Diario,* pp. 4–5, 8; Villaseñor, *El separatismo,* pp. 226–236; Irigoyen, *Salvador Alvarado,* pp. 21–22.

38. Mediz Bolio, "Prólogo," p. 14.

39. The following analysis of the revolutionary regimes of Alvarado and Carrillo Puerto draws upon chapters 4–8 of my larger treatment, "Revolution from Without: The Mexican Revolution in Yucatán, 1915–1924," Dissertation, Yale University, 1978. This work provides extensive bibliographical references and additional archival documentation of the events described. Also see Paoli and Montalvo, *El socialismo olvidado* for a somewhat different interpretation of Carrillo's career.

40. In addition to the discussion of education in chapters 4 and 6 of "Revolution from Without," see Mary Kay Vaughan, "Education and Class in the Mexican Revolution," *LAP*, 2, No. 2 (Summer 1975), 17–33.

41. For a more complete statement of the revisionist interpretation that follows, see Joseph, "Caciquismo and the Revolution" and "Revolution from Without," chapter 8.

42. Antonio Betancourt Pérez, *El asesinato de Carrillo Puerto*, Mérida, 1974, pp. 17–28; Alma Reed, "Felipe Carrillo Puerto," *Orbe*, 3 (Dec. 1946), 20–21; J. W. F. Dulles, *Yesterday in Mexico*, Austin, Tex., 1961, p. 231.

43. R. A. Sosa Ferreyro, *El crimen del miedo*, México, 1969, pp. 42, 115; Rosa Castro, "Sobre la ruta de Carrillo Puerto, el Mesías de Motul," *Hoy*, 15 March 1952.

44. Betancourt Pérez, *El asesinato;* Jaime Orosa Díaz, *Se vende un hombre*, Mérida, 1974; Renán Irigoyen, *Felipe Carrillo Puerto, Primer gobernante socialista en México*, Mérida, 1974, p. 41.

45. Cf. the radically different assessment of Carrillo's strength in Paoli and Montalvo, *El socialismo olvidado*.

46. Womack, *Zapata*, p. 67.

47. González Navarro, *Raza y tierra*, p. 250.

48. The cordage lobby's activities and the North American government's diplomatic pressure upon Carranza and Obregón are treated in Joseph, "Revolution from Without," chapters 4 and 8.

49. Batancourt Pérez, *El asesinato*, pp. 20–21; Irigoyen, *Felipe Carrillo Puerto*, pp. 35–37.

50. See Frank's *Capitalism and Underdevelopment in Latin America*, rev. ed., New York, 1969, and the reader edited by Frank, James D. Cockcroft, and Dale Johnson, *Dependence and Underdevelopment: Latin America's Political Economy*, New York, 1972.

51. Randall G. Hansis, "Alvaro Obregón, the Mexican Revolution and the Politics of Consolidation, 1920–1924," Dissertation, University of New Mexico, 1971; also see Brading, *Caudillo and Peasant*, passim.

52. Salamini, *Agrarian Radicalism*, pp. 108–140; Friedrich, *Agrarian Revolt*, pp. 124–130.

53. Dudley Ankerson, "Caudillismo and Politics in Mexico, 1890–1940: The Case of Saturnino Cedillo," and Ian Jacobs, "Ranchero Revolt in Mexico: The Figueroas of Huitzuco and the Mexican Revolution in the State of Guerrero," in Brading, *Caudillo and Peasant*.

54. The following discussion draws heavily upon Joseph, "Revolution from Without," chapter 9.

55. The existing literature provides little insight into the demise of the Revolution in Yucatan following the assassination of Carrillo Puerto, because it concentrates almost exclusively on personalities and political groups rather than on underlying social and economic relationships. The 1925–34 decade has largely been analyzed at the level of personalities: hard-core hagiography of Carrillo Puerto gives way to invectives against the

political leaders who succeeded him, bartering his social ideals for the gold of the hacendado elite. Having proclaimed Carrillo a martyr, local historians have regarded the next decade as an empty interval, a time when the region slumbered—or drifted back into old repressive patterns—and waited for its next redeemer, Lázaro Cárdenas.

56. See the steady stream of correspondence from campesino groups protesting the implementation of an agrarian reform predicated on the breakup of existing plantations and the formation of the collective ejido, which appears in *DdY,* during the early to mid-1930s. AGE, Liga Central de Resistencia, B. García, Presidente, "Tarifa gradual para el pago de jornales en las fincas henequeneras del Estado," 12 Aug. 1933; and Siegfried Askinasy, *El problema agrario de Yucatán,* México, 1936, pp. 113–114.

57. See *DdY* for July 1936 and Fernando López Cárdenas, *Revolucionarios contra la Revolución,* México, 1938.

58. Thomas G. Sanders, "Henequen: The Structure of Agrarian Frustration," American Universities Field Staff, *Reports,* North American Series, 5, No. 3 (1977); Joseph, "Revolution from Without," chapter 9.

59. Louis Cabrera (alias Lic. Blas Urrea), "La conquista de Yucatán," *DdY,* 10 July 1936, p. 3; *Veinte años después,* México, 1937; and *Un ensayo comunista en México,* México, 1937; and see *DdY,* 26 Jan. 1936, p. 3, 9; *El Universal,* 29 and 30 July 1936, passim; and *DdY,* 7 Dec. 1936, pp. 3, 6, for rebuttals against Cabrera by leading federal *agraristas.*

60. This new literature is reviewed in James D. Cockcroft's chapter on Mexico in Ronald H. Chilcote and Joel C. Edelstein, eds., *Latin America: The Struggle with Dependency and Beyond,* New York, 1974, pp. 259–285.

61. IHCA, H. L. Boyle Files, "History of the International Harvester Company," n.d. [1947].

62. The proverb has been cited in Robin W. Winks, "On Decolonization and Informal Empire," *American Historical Review,* 81 (June 1976), 556.

63. Manuel M. Escoffié, *Yucatán en la cruz,* Mérida, 1957; Bernardino Mena Brito, *Reestructuración histórica de Yucatán,* III, México, 1969, passim.

64. *DdY,* 6 Nov. 1975, p. 1; *Novedades de Yucatán,* 11 Nov. 1974, p. 1; *Excélsior,* 22 July 1977, pp. 1, 14.

65. Gustavo Molina Font, *La tragedia de Yucatán,* México, 1941, which contains a prologue by Luis Cabrera; Manuel Zapata Casares, *Vía-Crucis del henequén,* Mérida, 1961.

66. *Excélsior,* 22 July 1977, p. 1; *Proceso,* 9 May 1977, p. 34; *Diario del Sureste,* 13 March 1975; Manuel Pasos Peniche, *Historia de la industria henequenera desde 1945,* Mérida, 1974, pp. 15–16; Malcolm K. Shuman, "The Town Where Luck Fell: The Economics of Life in a Henequen Zone Pueblo," Dissertation, Tulane University, 1974, pp. 43–44; Sanders, "Henequen," pp. 4–12.

67. Michel Gutelman, "The Socialization of the Means of Production in Cuba," in Rodolfo Stavenhagen, ed., *Agrarian Problems and Peasant Movements in Latin America,* New York, 1970, pp. 347–368, and Joseph, "Revolution from Without," chapter 9.

68. *Excélsior,* 22 July 1977, p. 1 (an official defense of the agrarian reform), and Juan José Hinojosa, "Henequén: Fracaso, espina, remordimiento," *Proceso,* 9 May 1977, p. 34.

69. A partial bibliography of negative evaluations of Yucatan's agrarian reform appears in Joseph, "Apuntes," pp. 21–22. The problems experienced by campesinos in other collective ejido regimes are described by Ronfeldt, *Atencingo* (Puebla: sugar);

Clarence Senior, *Land Reform and Democracy*, Gainesville, Fla., 1958 (La Laguna: cotton); and Rodolfo Stavenhagen, "Collective Agriculture and Capitalism in Mexico: A Way Out or a Dead End?" *LAP*, 2, No. 2 (Summer 1975), 146–163 (various regions, various crops).

70. One of the serious failings of the region's program of social security, however, is the provision that only henequen workers are entitled to receive welfare benefits.

CHAPTER VII

SOCIAL ORGANIZATION AND CHANGE IN MODERN YUCATAN

Irving L. Webber

This chapter is a study of the social organization of modern Yucatan. In sociology the term "social organization" denotes the nature of the system of relationships among the people that gives a society its distinctive form: it has to do with such fundamental matters as social stratification, racial and ethnic relationships, patterns of attitudes and values, economic and family institutions, and many others. In addition, attention is given to patterns of change in certain aspects of social organization. Social change is an ever-present phenomenon, of course, but it is of special interest when the people being studied, as in the case of Yucatan, are experiencing movement toward modernization.

Examining the social structure and functions of an entire society, with due consideration to the progressive alterations occurring in the structure and functions, is obviously an ambitious enterprise, and one can hope for and expect some degree of success only in the best of circumstances. In the case of Yucatan, however, the circumstances are by no means optimal. In such an effort as this, a writer must depend heavily upon the descriptive and analytic studies of those scholars and social scientists who have preceded him. But very few sociologists and only a handful of anthropologists have seen fit to investigate aspects of social organization of Yucatan at the societal level; for example, the excellent work of the anthropologist Robert Redfield analyzes primarily individual communities. One major source of invaluable data is the official census reports, but they in turn suffer from shortcomings. In this chapter, I shall attempt to establish a framework for understanding the social organization of Yucatan, draw together in systematic fashion the results of earlier investigations and recent observations, and offer insights based upon analysis of demographic data.

Whatever the limitations of this treatment of the topic, the genuine significance of the social-organization approach must be recognized. The society is the largest social group, made up of all others, from play groups through family units to corporations and government agencies. Every society has its own peculiar ethos, or unique combination of characteristic culture traits, which differentiates it from all other societies. These distinguishing culture traits permeate the entire system of social organization; it may be argued, therefore, that clear understanding of any people is impossible until we have learned about the pattern of social relationships and about the values, attitudes, sentiments, and beliefs which underlie that pattern. Even though Yucatan is legally and historically a part of the Republic of Mexico, it has, until recently, undergone centuries of life in isolation from the nation. As a consequence, Yucatan may be thought of—at least in large degree—as a separate society that differs in many respects from the greater Mexican society, while resembling it in other respects. To limit ourselves to looking at segments of that society, such as the history, the literature, the archeological antecedents, and the economics, would deny us the possibility of comprehending the overall social and cultural unity.

The People

Yucatan is in many respects a distinctive society. Through most of its long history, it has been insular, for there were no routes of access over land, and it was relatively isolated even from the sea (Redfield, 1941: 2). For this reason it went through a course of development somewhat apart from that of Mexico, of which it was a part during most of the more than four hundred years since the Spanish gained control in 1547. Yucatan, moreover, received little immigration of Europeans or Negroes during the colonial period and throughout most of recent history (Cook and Borah, 1974: 178–179). As compared with central Mexico, it is genetically more Indian and culturally considerably more monolithic because of the dominance of both the Mayan language and traditions (Cook and Borah, 1974: 178–179; Redfield, 1941: 2). Even the regularity of the physical environment throughout most of the peninsula sets the area apart from much of the rest of Mexico and probably has worked to minimize differences in the people and their social organization.

Even though the concern of this chapter is mainly with modern Yucatan, it may be useful to sketch its population history. In their remarkable exercise in historical demography, Cook and Borah (1974: 48) estimate that the Indian population of the peninsula in 1549 was 240,000. At that time, the conquerors and their followers, including Mexican Indians, numbered no more than a few hundred (Cook and Borah, 1974: 76–77). Cook and Borah (1974: 1) define Yucatan so that it includes not only the present-day state of that name but also Campeche and Quintana Roo. In the years that followed, the non-Indian population grew steadily. By 1639, for example, it was estimated to be 12,500; a century and a half later, in 1794, it had risen to 103,000. In the meantime, however, the native population underwent tremendous fluctuations, as these years and numbers show: 182,500 in 1700; 127,000 in 1736; and 254,000 in 1794 (Cook and Borah, 1974: 114). Since the Indians comprised the largest share of the inhabitants, these losses and gains in numbers of people are reflected in substantial falls and rises in the total population as well.

According to Cook and Borah (1974: 114–120), the enormous drop in the Indian population that occurred between the middle of the seventeenth and the middle of the eighteenth centuries—the decline from 1639 to 1736 amounted to 40 percent—resulted from various disasters and from the flight of families to lands outside direct Spanish control. During these years, droughts, famines, epidemics, and locusts afflicted the country, taking a heavy toll of life. To some extent the migration from the more populated districts of the peninsula was a reaction to the long periods of dry weather, the resulting lack of food, and the threat of disease. Faced with these contingencies, many Mayan families left the cultivated areas of Yucatan to take up residence in the largely uninhabited lands to the east, south, and west. But the Indians also withdrew into these vacant lands to escape heavy-handed Spanish administration and, at times, the depredations of French and English pirates. In any event, in the deep bush they were out of reach of tax collectors and census-takers.

The significance of deaths in the Caste War combined with the effects of the life-threatening setbacks just mentioned may be judged by the fact that Cook and Borah (1974: 124) estimate that in 1850 the total population of the entire peninsula numbered only 299,455, far less than had been present in 1794 (an estimated 357,000). Even allowing for the crudeness of the estimates, a reduction of the order of one-sixth is impressive.

Beginning in 1850, it is possible to obtain first estimates and then census figures for the state of Yucatan, which is the geographic unit dealt with primarily in this chapter. Since the middle of the nineteenth century, when the state's people were thought to number 217,223 (Cook and Borah, 1974: 124), Yucatan has grown steadily, with no setbacks for the years for which we have data: in 1900, for example, the total had climbed to 309,652; in 1950, to 516,899; and in 1970, when the most recent census count was made, to 758,355 (Cook and Borah, 1974: 124–126; Estados Unidos Mexicanos, 1972a: 3). Moreover, the growth has gone on at an increasing rate: from 1850 to 1900, the annual rate was .71 percent per year; from 1900 to 1950, 1.03 percent per year; and from 1950 to 1970, 1.94 percent.[1]

Geographic Distribution. Despite the apparent steady rise in the population of the state of Yucatan since 1850, it is by no means among the most densely populated of the Mexican states and territories. In 1970, the average density per square kilometer in the nation was 24.51 inhabitants, while in Yucatan it amounted to 19.28. Only nine of the thirty states and two territories had lower densities, although the neighboring territory of Quintana Roo, with only 1.75 inhabitants per kilometer, was lower than all but Baja California (Sanders, 1974: 14).

But the average density of population in the state is misleading because the 106 *municipios* into which the jurisdiction is divided vary enormously both in size and in population. In terms of territory, the range is from Tizimín, which encompasses about 4,132 square kilometers and is located in the northwest corner, to Suma, which embraces only about 40 kilometers and is in the north-central portion. Similar dramatic contrasts mark the distribution of population by *municipio*. Most densely settled is the *municipio* that includes the capital city of Mérida, with around 282 persons per square kilometer. At the other extreme is San Felipe, with 1.13 persons per square kilometer (Estados Unidos Mexicanos, 1972a: 3–5).

Yucatan has only one major urban center. In 1970, when the most recent census count was made, Mérida, the capital and seat of the *municipio* of the same name, had 212,097 inhabitants. It was more than eleven times as large as the next largest city, Tizimín, with 18,343 residents. Progreso (17,518), Valladolid (14,663), and Motul (12,949) were the other cities that in 1970 had 12,000 or more inhabitants (Estados Unidos Mexicanos, 1972a: 3–5). To the observer from the United States, none of these cities except Mérida deserves to be called urban; they lack the range of goods and services usually associated with an urban place, and they could more aptly be called towns.

Mérida has enjoyed for centuries its preeminence as the populated center of Yucatan. Established as the capital by Francisco de Montejo, the Younger, it immediately became entrenched as the leading city, a position that was enhanced when it became the site of a Spanish royal treasury. In 1824, when the Mexican federation came into being, Mérida was designated the capital of a state comprising the territory of the entire peninsula (Cook and Borah, 1974: 6, 120). In 1858, Campeche was made a separate state, and in 1902, Quintana Roo became a national territory. Since 1902, Mérida has been the capital of the present-day state of Yucatan (Osorio y Carvajal, 1972: 181, 266).

Within the state, Mérida is primary in a wide variety of ways. It is the legislative, political, and administrative center of Yucatan as well as the state headquarters for agencies of the national government. Culturally it occupies first place, concentrating the artistic, handicraft, educational, and musical resources of the state. In communications and transportation, the situation is the same; it is the site of the international airport and the principal railroad terminal, the apex of the network of roads and highways, and it is but a few miles from the major port of Progreso. Commerce and industry likewise are much more highly developed in this city than elsewhere in the state, and it serves as a focal point for collecting, distributing, and marketing the major agricultural products. Physicians and paramedical personnel as well as hospitals and other health-care facilities are clustered in the capital. Mérida also has the lion's share of facilities for accommodating tourists—hotels, restaurants and bars, travel agencies, entertainment centers, and shops. In addition, the city is the residence of most—if not all—of the most influential and well-to-do people of the area.

From the viewpoint of human ecology, Mérida stands by itself as the major city that, having been chosen as the capital of the peninsula centuries ago, gained and maintained a momentum propelling it toward ever greater size and importance. For the remainder of the state, on the other hand, logical man-land relationships help to explain both where the people are found and how they make their living. As Bataillon (1973: 68–69) has observed, the population tends to be located in nuclei surrounding the monasteries of the colonial epoch. In the latter

A crowded street scene in Mérida. Note the "classic" Mayan profile of the Indian woman in left foreground. (Photo by Joel Whitman)

The traditional thatched hut of the rural Maya, a style still extensively used. Note the unmortared stone walls. (Photo by Bill Moseley)

part of the sixteenth century, the Spaniards brought the Indian population together in larger towns to promote use of the encomienda system, employ natives for labor, develop haciendas, reduce the possibilities of revolt, and promote the work of Christianization by the Franciscans (Chamberlain, 1948: 283–286). To this day, these settlements persist.

Arnold Stricken stresses the role of the large agricultural estates in determining the placement of the people on the land. For about three hundred years following the conquest, the Mayan way of life underwent little change, for the rural population continued to depend upon corn as its major crop to provide food and to tend cattle. In the years before 1847, cultivation of sugarcane became a major enterprise. This new system of agriculture led to far-reaching changes in the Mayas' daily lives, for the cultivation of sugarcane altered conditions and interfered with corn production by the slash-and-burn method. Although the devastating Caste War put an end to sugar as a principal cash crop, it soon was succeeded by another field crop that required the use of broad acreage, sisal or henequen (Stricken, 1965). Thus it appears that settlement patterns imposed following the Spanish Conquest tended to persist except when displaced by those made necessary for the production of new crops whose cultivation was incompatible with corn-raising by the traditional method.

Race. We have seen that for a time after the Spanish Conquest no more than a handful of people in Yucatan were non-Indians. Estimates of the racial composition of the population in later years show a steady and rather dramatic increase in the numbers of inhabitants who were not Indian. In 1639, the Indians made up about 94 percent, in 1736, about 73 percent, and in 1794, close to 60 percent (Cook and Borah, 1974: 114). With the coming of independence three decades later, however, information about the racial character of the people became, in large part, unavailable. As Cook and Borah (1974: 121–122) point out, "Parish registers in Mexico ceased to record racial affiliation in entries for births, marriages, and deaths or to keep separate registers by race. . . . A question on race in the Mexican national census of 1921 . . . [gives] answers . . . which are probably of dubious reliability." Cook and Borah indicate that in 1810 the non-Indians (Europeans, Negroes, and some admixture of Indian) accounted for from 25 to 30 percent; and they report that Regil and Peón's data for 1845 showed that non-Indians comprised about 30 percent of the population (Cook and Borah, 1974: 128). Even allowing for the considerable margins of error that are implicit in such estimates, these figures reflect fluctuations in the relative importance of the Indian component.

Given the lack of direct evidence from censuses regarding the racial makeup, we must rely on indirect evidence. One such indication is the language spoken. In 1970, the census reported that 55.5 percent of the people aged five years and over spoke an Indian language, with Maya far and away the dominant tongue. Those who did not speak Spanish amounted to 15.8 percent (Estados Unidos Mexicanos, 1972b: 71–82). Bataillon (1973) notes, in what seems an exaggera tion, that the Mayan language, instead of losing its importance, has maintained it, even in the cities.

The relative lack of immigration of non-Indians during the colonial period and most of the nineteenth century already has been noted. At the turn of the century and for some decades afterward, Orientals in considerable number as well as some Syrians and Levantines entered the state, and later some North Americans and Germans took up residence (Redfield, 1941: 3). The 1970 census makes clear how restricted the foreign immigration has been in recent decades. In that year, only 1,005 persons of foreign birth, comprising but 5.6 percent of the state's population, were listed (Estados Unidos Mexicanos, 1972b: 71–82).

The result of the operation of these factors seems to have been the gradual development of a considerable racial mixture. In this mixture, the Indian element is of surpassing importance, for, as we have seen, relatively few Europeans and Negroes ever have been available to dilute the influence of the Mayan Indian. As Cook and Borah (1974: 179) sum up, "Relative to central Mexico, Yucatan remains more Indian in its genetic base." Ironically, the Indians who were conquered by the European invaders who arrived centuries ago have in a racial sense finally all but overcome their conquerers.

Age and Sex. In common with other underdeveloped areas, Yucatan has a very large share of its population in the younger ages. Those under fifteen years of age in 1970 amounted to 42.5 percent of the entire population. Moreover, during the preceding decade, the trend had been toward larger numbers of children in those ages, for in 1960 the corresponding percentage was 39.2. Nevertheless, the proportion of Yucatan's people under age fifteen was lower in 1970 than that in Mexico as a whole, 46.2 percent (Estados Unidos Mexicanos, 1972b: 7–10). To appreciate fully the size of this bulge in the people at the lower end of the age range, we need to recall that in the United States, taken as an example of a developed, industrialized, urbanized country, the parallel percentage for the under-fifteen population was 28.2, only two-thirds of Yucatan's proportion (U.S. Bureau of the Census, 1974: 6).

The opposite situation prevails at the other end of the array of ages, for relatively small numbers are found in the older ages in Yucatan. Thus in 1970, 4.6 percent of the state's people were aged sixty-five and over, although this figure represented some increase in that age segment since 1960, when the percentage was 3.9. Mexico in 1970 had a lower share of its people in the oldest ages—3.7 percent—than did Yucatan in that year (Estados Unidos Mexicanos, 1972b: 7–10). Again, the data for the United States are in sharp contrast: in 1970, 9.8 percent of its people were sixty-five and over, more than twice as many relatively (U.S. Bureau of the Census, 1974: 6).

The proportions of the population under age fifteen and over age sixty-four may be added together to compute the dependency ratio. The resulting figure represents in a general way the share of the total population that tends to be dependent for support in economic and other ways. Of course, in any country,

Mayan children at Maní. Note the unmortared stone walls in the background. (Photo by Edward Moseley)

not all of those less than fifteen years old are dependent (in fact, many may be in the labor force or in unpaid family work), and not everyone who attains age sixty-five retires from gainful employment. Yet, despite the fact that these qualifications may hold with special force in an underdeveloped area, the dependency ratio does have some utility as an approximate measure.

The dependency ratio of 47.1 in Yucatan as of 1970 indicates that the remaining 52.9 persons per hundred must supply the resources necessary to maintain those in the other category. In other words, each individual in the ages usually referred to as "economically active," that is, from fifteen to sixty-five, has a corresponding opposite number—or nearly one such person—who is not in those working years. Mexico's dependency ratio was even higher than that of Yucatan in the year of the most recent census, 49.9 per 100 (Estados Unidos Mexicanos, 1972b: 7–10). In comparison, the ratio for the United States in the same year was 38.1 dependents in each hundred enumerated (U.S. Bureau of Census, 1974: 6). The implication is, of course, that the lower the dependency ratio, the greater likelihood that relatively higher levels of living can be sustained, given the same levels of utilization of the classic economic factors of production.

In 1970, the sex ratio—the number of men per hundred women—in the state of Yucatan was 99.7, very close to an equal number of men and women in the population; ten years earlier it had been slightly higher, 103.0. In the most recent of the two census years, Mexico's sex ratio was almost identical with that of the state (Estados Unidos Mexicanos, 1972b: 3). This figure was considerably higher than that found in the United States the same year, 94.8 (U.S. Bureau of the Census, 1974: 26). Because so many diverse factors impinge upon the sex ratio, it is not easy to interpret these data. In the United States, for example, sex ratios have until recent years been well above 100; as late as 1940, the figure stood at 100.8. In part, the excess of men in the population arose from the effect of international immigration, for long-distance movements of people traditionally overrepresent males, especially those in the young-adult ages. In part, also, the decrease in the United States sex ratio came about because of better living conditions, including sanitary provisions, and health care. Females have a higher life expectancy than males, and to the extent that people avoid death in childhood and youth, they tend to live to the older years, when the differential in average length of life in favor of females operates. Yucatan is showing the effects of improved sanitation and the control of communicable disease in falling death rates, and the decline in the sex ratio may be a related phenomenon. It has already been pointed out that immigration from distant countries that would have brought substantial numbers of men and few if any women in fact did not occur in any great degree.

Factors in Population Growth. Earlier we saw that the population of Yucatan has grown steadily and at an increasing rate during the 120 years for which we have fairly reliable estimates and census enumerations. Some limited data permit an examination of births, deaths, and migration, the three factors that cause the growth or decline of a population. Birth rates in the state of Yucatan are relatively high, death rates fairly low, and migration of negligible importance. But the shorthand of the preceding sentence calls for further explanation to keep it from misleading the reader.

To measure births, it is convenient to use the fertility ratio. This rate shows the number of children under age five per thousand women aged from fifteen to forty-four, and it has the advantage of sidestepping the possible inadequacies of a given system of birth registration. A computation from 1970 census figures produces a fertility ratio for the state of Yucatan of 725.0 (Estados Unidos Mexicanos, 1972a: 15-26). This may be compared to the United States fertility ratio for the same year of 401.7 (U.S. Bureau of the Census, 1974: 6-7). Thus, the number of children under age five for each thousand women in the child-bearing ages of fifteen to forty-four in Yucatan was about 80 percent higher than the number found in the more modern country.

The crude death rate, that is, the number of deaths occurring per thousand people, for Yucatan in the year 1968 was 9.1. In this respect, Yucatan compared favorably with the Mexican nation as a whole, for which a rate of 9.6 was reported. Among the Mexican states and territories, the range was from 4.7 in Quintana Roo to 14.8 in Oaxaca (Sanders, 1974). The 1970 rate for the United States, on the other hand, was 9.5 deaths per thousand people (U.S. Bureau of the Census, 1974: 60). In assessing these data it must be kept in mind that death registration in the United States almost certainly is much more complete and accurate than in Mexico. Nevertheless, improvements in health conditions undoubtedly have taken place in Yucatan, and much of the difference between United States and Mexican death rates can be understood in terms of the high proportions of the population in the older ages in the former country (and thus subject to mortality caused by the so-called degenerative diseases) and the high proportions of the population in the younger ages in the latter.

The minor role played by international migration to Yucatan already has been mentioned. Movements of people from other countries to the state probably have never been of much significance numerically. As to migration into and out of Yucatan to other states and territories of Mexico, computations for the periods 1930-40, 1940-50, and 1950-60 demonstrate that there were net losses to the state in all three decades, ranging from 12,737 in the 1940s to 39,414 in the 1950s (Centro de Estudios Económicos y Demográficos, 1970: 93).

Given the high rate of reproduction and the relatively low death rate, it is not surprising that the population of the state is expected to grow rapidly in the coming years (always barring some unforeseen change in the rates of births, deaths, and/or migration). Fernando Rivera Alvarez, area coordinator of the National Population Council, reported in 1976 that the prevailing growth rate, which he said had not changed since 1940, was 2.2 percent per year. At this rate, according to Rivera Alvarez, by 1985, Yucatan would have a million inhabitants, and by the year 2000, 1,400,000 (*Diario de Yucatán,* 1976: 2). Since the state now has one of the lowest income levels in Mexico (Bataillon, 1973: 69), it is difficult to see how such an augmentation of population could fail to bring lower levels of well-being unless an economic upturn occurs. One possibility is, of course, that birth rates will decline; in 1970, Mérida, with a fertility ratio of 601.6, evidently was experiencing the phenomenon of reduced births in the metropolitan area, and its ratio was well below the state's level of 725.0 and far below that of San Felipe (853.3), the least densely populated of all the *municipios* (computed from data in Estados Unidos Mexicanos, 1972a: 15–26). But the potential effects of a drop in birth rates are limited because of the large share of the women that will be in the childbearing ages for decades to come, given that 50 percent of the population was less than twenty years of age in 1970 (*Diario de Yucatán,* 1976: 2). To illustrate, it is only necessary to point to the situation in the United States, which has a much higher median age (28.0 in 1970) and, as we have seen, a much lower fertility ratio (U.S. Bureau of the Census, 1974: 31). If fertility in the United States were to be only at the replacement level and there were no net immigration, population would increase by about forty-six million, or about 23 percent, from 1970 to 2000 (U.S. Bureau of Census, 1974: 6–7). It is, therefore, hard to find any rational basis for expecting anything short of phenomenal growth in the numbers of the people of Yucatan during the foreseeable future unless disease, famine, or war intervene.

Life in a Peasant Society

Much of the population of Yucatan may justly be called peasant. Less than 40 percent are found in centers with ten thousand or more inhabitants, and about half the population reside in places with less than five thousand inhabitants (Estados Unidos Mexicanos, 1972a: 9). Visitors to such places as Ticul, Tizimín, Progreso, and Valladolid observe that even in these relatively large "cities" Mayan huts seem to be the dwellings of a large majority of the people, who live in a way best described as rural. Mérida, the capital, is the only major exception to this rule, although a certain proportion of those in the other large population centers carry on life styles that might be characterized as townlike.

Redfield has commented that in the peasant community, "social relations are compact, congruent, and largely personal. With the growth and the spread of civilization social relations extend themselves out from the local community, lose much of their congruence (as in the development of industrial fields of activity), and develop many kinds of impersonal and formal varieties of connection. In peasant societies we see a relatively stable and very roughly typical adjustment between local and national . . . life" (Redfield, 1956: 65). Oscar Handlin stresses the sameness of peasants everywhere, characterized by "a personal bond with the land; attachment to an integrated or local community; central importance of the family; marriage a provision of economic welfare; patrilocal residence and descent in the male line; a strain between the attachment to the land and the local world and the necessity to raise money crops; and so on" (Redfield, 1956: 106).

Writing about two decades ago, Redfield identified among the peasants of modern Yucatan three closely related attitudes: what he called "an intimate and reverent attitude toward the land; the ideas that agricultural work is good and commerce not so good; and an emphasis on productive industry as a prime virtue" (Redfield, 1956: 112). In summary, he believed that he saw "a sober attitude toward work, a satisfaction in working long and hard in the fields, a disinclination to adventure or to speculate" (Redfield, 1956: 114).

Something of the nature of life in a peasant village can be gained from Redfield's description, based on his observations in 1948, of Chan Kom, located in the eastern part of the state of Yucatan not far from the monumental ruins of Chichén Itzá. In 1948, his own enumeration added up to 437 inhabitants (Redfield, 1950: 68); in 1970, according to Mary L. Elmendorf (1973: 14), the Civil Register showed 550 inhabitants.

Fewer than a third of the people of Chan Kom were living in stone houses. Even most of those who lived in houses of stone slept in the kitchens of poles and thatch. Use of the hammock for sleeping was universal; no one in Chan Kom had a bed, mosquito netting, or privy. Earlier, teachers had encouraged the construction of two shower baths, but these were abandoned. Water was obtained mainly from wells; only a few women still utilized the cenote in the plaza (Redfield, 1950: 33).

By 1948, Chan Kom had a good deal of commercial enterprise, including four stores offering a considerable variety of goods for sale. There were two bakers, preparing bread at least once a week. Masons, carpenters, and other artisans were found. Some of these skilled workers were specialized enough so that they spent little time in their milpas, or corn fields, but in general corn-raising continued to be a principal occupation of the men. Cattle- and hog-raising both were prominent sources of revenue. Although far-reaching changes had occurred since Redfield and Alfonso Villa first studied Chan Kom in the early 1930s, the village still had many of the attributes of a peasant society (Redfield, 1950: 47–66).

The people of Chan Kom continued in 1948 to identify themselves as Maya. Redfield (1950: 73) states:

In 1948, as in 1931, they think of themselves as Maya, *mazehua,* as contrasted with *dzules,* white people, people of the city. If anything, the disposition to include every enrolled citizen of the village among those who are Mayas is greater now than formerly, for the same men who in 1931 told me that certain residents at that time who had Spanish surnames were, on this evidence, not fully Maya, but "mixed Maya" or "half Maya," in 1948 insisted that the few individuals living in the village with Spanish surnames were just as Maya as the others. "They are Maya because they live just as we do. They can go into the bush, and work hard there." So even the woman from Valladolid, who wears a dress, and has a Spanish surname, is regarded as fully Maya.

Moreover, at the time of his later field work, Redfield (1950: 76) still found that no social classes existed, even though the differences in both wealth and sophistication were somewhat greater in 1948 than they had been earlier. As Redfield explains, differences in social status were not established by birth or social superiority associated with having one surname rather than another.

The foregoing brief summary provides some clues to the way people in one village lived almost three decades ago. In the 1960s, Irwin Press studied Pustunich, a peasant community in the Puuc Hills near Ticul. He reported (Press, 1977: 276):

> With few exceptions, all males make milpa in the old way, dress mestizo, speak Maya in street and home, and protect their crops with an annual round of traditional Maya ritual. The village sports a *h-men*, or Maya priest, and two well-known *curanderos*, and it still engages in large-scale communal hunts. At the same time, Technicolor movies, radios, bicycles, plastic hair curlers, enamel pans, almost universal literacy, and a top-notch traveling baseball team have been part of the village life for decades.

Pustunich had no priest for its Catholic church and had had none for as long as the inhabitants could remember. "Catholic and pagan rituals exist side by side. Neither complex has threatened the other for centuries. . . . There has been little change in either Catholic or pagan ritual since the postconquest conversion was effected" (Press, 1977: 281). In view of the persistence of traditional ways of life, it is noteworthy that for centuries Pustunich has been connected with other centers, including the capital, by good roads and has had extensive contact with outsiders (Press, 1977: 283). "Modernism has not burst upon the village with the opening of a road nor trickled to it with an itinerant backwoods merchant. For centuries, in a mainstream of social and political movement, Pustunich has had the opportunity to pick and choose what it would—or, more realistically, *could*—of 'modern' ways" (Press, 1977: 284).

Still more recently, evidently in the 1970s, James W. Ryder (1977) focused upon Pencuyut, a village in the *municipio* of Tekax, in south-central Yucatan. In this pueblo, "Today almost every household has a transistor radio. Several individuals read a newspaper regularly, although no one in the pueblo has more than a primary education. Pencuyut has four small stores, two of which have gasoline-engine maize grinders. The stores stock an extremely limited supply of goods. Many of the commercial dealings are based on the exchange of maize rather than cash" (Ryder, 1977: 198).

The ethnographic data regarding Chan Kom, Pustunich, and Pencuyut leave much to be desired as a basis for making generalizations regarding rural life in Yucatan today. The three villages represent a variety of situations, but none of them is located in the centrally important henequen-raising region. Chan Kom and Pencuyut both were and are isolated communities, neither linked by hard-surfaced road directly with the larger populated centers of the peninsula; Pustunich, on the other hand, has always been easily accessible to the outside world. Chan Kom, as Press (1977: 286–287) has pointed out, was a new village, less than forty-five years old when Redfield began his observations, that had been established by people who were dissatisfied enough to leave their previous communities. By contrast, Pustunich had a very long history and firm traditions, and Pencuyut was granted to Julián Donzel as an encomienda before 1549 (Ryder, 1977: 197).

It seems evident that rural life has changed a good deal since Redfield undertook his studies of Chan Kom. Certainly, some aspects of modern life, including television, radio, commercialism, somewhat improved transportation, and manufactured goods, have penetrated into fairly remote places. Yet the observations made by those who have visited a variety of hamlets, villages, towns, and cities in the state and the evidence from the study of Pustunich in the decade of the 1960s strongly suggest that life outside the major centers continues to be that of the peasant. Of particular interest is the fact that in Pustunich, by no means an isolated village, elements that were noted decades before in Chan Kom persisted side by side with modern elements. The milpa remains a central focus of life, livestock raising is important in some areas, henequen or fruit and vegetable culture in others. The rural costumes of a *huipil* for the girls and women and shirt and trousers for the boys and men remain surprisingly persistent. In rural areas, shoes still are relatively scarce. In such *municipios* as Kaua, Samahil, Sanahcat, and Timucuy, from 60.0 to 84.8 percent of the population aged one year and over wore huaraches or sandals or went entirely without footwear in 1970 (Estados Unidos Mexicanos, 1972a: 113–114).

Information about the extent to which utilities were accessible to the rural areas sheds further light on the rurality of much of Yucatan. In 1973, only 96 of the 1,717 populated places were served by potable water, whether or not in pipes. There were 1,519 villages and hamlets with fewer than five hundred inhabitants; only 12 of these had water service. Even among the 50 towns and cities whose population exceeded twenty-five hundred, only 22 had potable water (Servicios Coordinados de Salud Pública, 1973: Anexo 12, p. 3; Estados Unidos Mexicanos, 1972a: 9).

Sanitary sewage facilities are even more restricted. Less than 1 percent of the urban population of Mérida was served in 1973 by a sanitary sewage system; the remainder of the people in that city depended upon septic tanks (about 40 percent), open ditches, or simply utilized the outdoors. Nine in ten of the remainder of the people of Yucatan made use of ditches or the open air. Virtually all rural dwellers, then, were without sanitary facilities as the term is usually understood (Servicios Coordinados de Salud Pública, 1973: 13).

Electrical service was much more widespread, accessible to 87 percent of the population. Most of the remaining areas were considered by authorities to be so small in numbers of people and so inaccessible as to make the provision of electrical current difficult or uneconomical. In 1973, four seats of *municipios* still were without electrical service (Servicios Coordinados de Salud Pública, 1973: 16).

On balance, it seems fair to conclude that a majority of the people of Yucatan—perhaps a large majority—follow a style of life that incorporates some elements that Redfield, Handlin, and others have associated with peasants. This is not to deny that changes in the direction of a less isolated, more modern society have taken place during recent decades and are still under way. But in view of the apparent strength of modernizing influences, emanating primarily from Mérida, what is remarkable is that more sweeping alterations in the nature and quality of rural life have not taken place.

Social Stratification

The study of the system of social classes into which a society is divided is a difficult yet essential part of the sociological enterprise. There can be no doubt regarding the reality of social classes and the pervasive influence they exert in determining a people's values, attitudes, beliefs, ideas, and behavior patterns. Probably no other group characteristic is so fundamental in its significance. The difficulty lies in describing the structure of social classes in a particular society and in deciding upon the relative sizes of the several strata.

Although five- and six-class systems have been found through empirical research in American cities (Davis et al., 1941; Warner and Lunt, 1941), it is much more usual to delineate the traditional lower, middle, and upper classes, even though those with intimate knowledge of a given system may recognize that subdivisions exist within the three strata. The ubiquity of the concept of hierarchically arranged classes is suggested by the common tendency for people to refer to those who are "higher up," "on our level," or "lower than we are." Once observation and discussions with informants well acquainted with local perceptions of class matters have clarified, at least in some degree, the number and nature of the classes, the problem remains to be solved as to how large each segment is and which people (or families) correspond to each specific class.

In general, this task may be accomplished in one or more of three ways: (1) subjective classes (and their members) may be determined by asking a sample of individuals in which class they consider themselves to be; (2) reputational classes may be established by utilizing qualified informants to associate families with classes; and (3) some objective measure—income, means of earning a living, educational level, occupation—may be manipulated both to compute the size of each class and to place individuals and families into those classes. The first two methods require field surveys, which are technically demanding and expensive; in the case of Yucatan, reports of such studies, to my knowledge, are unavailable. Consequently, it is necessary to depend upon census data to reach some approximation of the social stratification by employing objective criteria.

First, it is useful to examine the distribution of the economically active population aged twelve and over in 1970 (Estados Unidos Mexicanos, 1972a: 397):

Occupation	Number	Percentage
Professional and technical workers	9,872	4.9
Public officials and officials, managers, administrators, and proprietors in the private sector	2,917	1.4
Administrative personnel	9,228	4.6
Businessmen, vendors, and those in related occupations	13,559	6.7
Personal service workers, transportation workers, and the like	15,877	7.9
Farmers, cattlemen, lumbermen, fishermen, hunters, and the like	108,231	53.7
Nonagricultural workers, machine operators, and the like	30,531	15.1
Not classified	11,415	5.7
Total	201,630	100.0

These figures make it clear that a very substantial proportion of the economically active population of Yucatan is found in what normally would be considered lower-class occupations. Personal-service workers include guards, domestics, porters, bus drivers, and soldiers, among many others; the category of farmers, cattlemen, and the like excludes proprietors of farms and cattle ranches; and the last category, nonagricultural workers, machine operators, and others, incorporates occupations falling in the labor class. Together these three classes account for more than 76.7 percent of those in the labor force. It is also likely that many of those whose data did not permit them to be placed in categories also are in this same group. It is probable that a large majority of public and private officials, managers, administrators, and proprietors are identified with the middle class. The same is true of administrative personnel, defined as persons who carry out duties required for the proper functioning of an institution or enterprise and, in general, not involving the specific objective of the organization (Estados Unidos Mexicanos, 1972a: lxxxii). Businessmen, salesmen, and the like make up a more questionable category in terms of middle-class membership, even though those who prepare and serve foods in the street are excluded; it is doubtful that many people in these occupations would normally be thought of as middle class. Combined, these three occupational classes amount to 12.7 percent of the total.

The remaining category, professional and technical workers, is difficult to interpret in the absence of more detailed information about the occupations of which it is comprised. Probably many of the physicians, engineers, architects, and lawyers so classified occupy upper-class positions; on the other hand, it is equally probable that few, if any, of the technicians, schoolteachers, clergymen, athletes, and others would have such status.

A different distribution of the labor forces aged twelve and over in 1970 (Estados Unidos Mexicanos, 1972a: 453) sheds additional light on the question of stratification:

Category	Number	Percentage
Patron, entrepreneur, or employer	9,844	4.9
Laborer or employee	57,263	28.4
Day laborer (*jornalero* or *peón*)	32,340	16.0
Self-employed	48,953	24.3
Ejidatario[2]	45,076	22.4
Unpaid family worker	8,154	4.0
Total	201,630	100.0

In general, these data provide further support for the earlier indication that a very large share of the labor force is found in categories associated with lower-class membership. Only those called *patrón,* entrepreneur, or employer, it is believed, are found predominantly in the middle and upper classes, and they make up less than one-twentieth of the economically active. The class of laborers and employees no doubt includes many white-collar workers; on the other hand, it seems unlikely that many middle-class persons are among those classified as day laborers, ejidatarios, and the self-employed, especially since the self-employed category does not include those who have any paid employees of their own.

Even though nothing precise about the size of the social classes can be concluded from an examination of the material just presented, the broad outline of the system of social stratification does emerge: a very small, even tiny, upper class; a relatively small middle class; and an enormous lower class. González Cosío (1975) estimated that in 1970 the class distribution in Mexico as a whole was:

Class	Number	Percentage
Upper class	1,073,740	2
Middle class	8,603,046	18
Lower class (*clase popular*)	38,907,925	80
Total	48,584,711	100

We have no good basis for supposing that Yucatan's situation departs from that for the nation. It is instructive to take account of the sharp contrast between such a class structure and that of the United States. In 1970, according to official census figures, white-collar workers in that country comprised 48.3 percent of employed workers aged sixteen and over (U.S. Bureau of the Census, 1974: 350). If, as is generally believed, these white-collar workers are predominantly of the middle class, then that middle stratum in the United States was more than two and a half times larger than the same stratum in Mexico. Gerhard Lenski's theory of distributive systems posits that variations in technology constitute the single most important factor in explaining differences in distributive or stratification systems, although it likewise recognizes the role of environmental differences, variations in the military participation ratio, and variations in the degree of constitutionalism, that is, the rule of right (Lenski, 1966: 59–90). Yucatan, like the nation of which it is a part, continues to have many characteristics of an agrarian society, and it is in agrarian societies that class differences are most pronounced.

The Family

As the most basic of social institutions, the family merits examination. It is regrettable, therefore, that little information except that in the census is to be found. The general opinion among scholars is that in traditional societies like that of Yucatan the family functions as a stronger and more stable unit than it does in more modern societies and that the extended family, consisting of three or more generations residing under the same roof, is more common.

Redfield (1950: 78–83) describes some aspects of the family and its organization in the village of Chan Kom in 1931 and 1948. In both years, single-family households accounted for a large majority of the arrangements. In both years, there were ten multiple-family households; these encompassed a great variety of relationships, however: two married brothers living together, a married brother and a married sister, a couple living with the man's parents and a couple living with the wife's parents, a couple living with the husband's uncle and wife, and two married friends living together. The most important of these multiple-family units in 1931 and 1948 involved a couple living with the man's parents, and Redfield notes that this reflects the traditional emphasis upon the father-son relationship. The remaining households—two in 1931 and only one in 1948—are labeled "extended domestic families"; they consist of married sons living in a single economy with their parents.

During the seventeen-year period between Redfield's two studies, some notable changes had occurred. The predominance of single-family households had increased from 73.3 percent of all households in 1931 to 84.9 percent in 1948. Multiple families and extended domestic families had declined in importance; the ten multiple-family households in 1948 accounted for only 13.7 percent of households. Redfield judged that the reduction in multiple-family households might be attributed to growth in wealth that permitted married couples who so wished to build their own houses and leave those of relatives (Redfield, 1950: 81).

The same writer comments upon the existence of the "great family," that is, large, well-established families with many members in the community. He believed that the solidarity of these great families had not lessened between 1931 and 1948; there continued to be "much visiting, borrowing, and sharing of work. A woman tends to assume the [family] loyalty of her husband; at least, it may be said that her relatives have secondary claims; if there is a conflict between her patrilineal family and his, the interests of his family prevail" (Redfield, 1950: 82). Although there were single small families in the village, he thought that a majority of the people were members of one of the great families, bearing such names as Tamay, Pat, Ceme, Ek, or Dzul. The residences of each such family tended to be grouped together, and the women washed clothes and did other work in family compounds.

Whether this evidence from one locality dating back to midcentury can be generalized to the rural Yucatan of today is, of course, open to question. If Chan Kom was somewhat representative in 1931 and still was so in 1948, then Redfield's report suggests, within broad boundaries, what would have been expected. That is, the family was seen to be a strong and highly influential force in social life, on the one hand, and it was undergoing some change in the direction of more modern organization, on the other hand. It must be granted, in any event, that the limited materials at hand do not permit any confident conclusions about many aspects of the family in rural Yucatan.

The census data provide a valuable overview to supplement our scarce monographic material. The marital status of the population of Yucatan aged 12 years and over in 1970 was as follows (Estados Unidos Mexicanos, 1972b: 33–52):

Status	Number	Percentage
Single	183,453	37.3
Married	252,218	51.2
Civil ceremony only	(35,909)	(7.3)
Religious ceremony only	(9,414)	(1.9)
Civil and religious ceremonies	(206,895)	(42.0)
Unión libre	30,726	6.2
Widowed	18,173	3.7
Divorced	2,861	.6
Separated	4,876	1.0
Total	492,307	100.0

Those who were married officially and those in *unión libre*, corresponding roughly to common-law marriage, together amounted to 57.4 percent, well over half of the population in the twelve-and-over age range. The fact that most of the married were reported to have been joined in both civil and religious rites suggests the continuing strong influence of the church. Very few married people were separated from each other, according to the official statistics, and the divorced comprised less than 1 percent. Widows, likewise, made up a small part of the people aged twelve and over.

Yucatan differed somewhat from Mexico as a whole in terms of marital status. The nation had more in the single category (40.4 percent); fewer married (45.4 percent), and more in *unión libre* (8.2 percent), and fewer in official marriages and de facto unions combined (53.6 percent); more widowed (4.2 percent); and somewhat similar proportions of divorced (.6 percent) and separated (1.3 percent). It may be misleading to reach conclusions based on comparing the Mexican nation, which is quite heterogeneous, with the state of Yucatan, but the statistics point to a somewhat more widespread prevalence of marriage, less reliance upon de facto alliances, and possibly a greater tendency for the widowed of Yucatan to remarry.

The contrasts as to marital status between Yucatan and the United States in 1970 stand out in these percentages (Estados Unidos Mexicanos, 1972b: 33–52; U.S. Bureau of the Census, 1973: 1–640):

	Yucatan (age 12+)	U.S. (age 14+)
Single	37.3	25.5
Married, living together	51.2 ⎫	61.5 ⎫
Married, separated	1.0 ⎬ 58.4	1.9 ⎬ 63.4
Unión libre	6.2 ⎭	
Widowed	3.7	7.8
Divorced	.6	3.3
Total	100.0	100.0

Being married is substantially more common in the United States and being single much less common; if the industrialized nation's figures were for those aged twelve and over, however, the differences probably would be smaller. Widowhood is more than twice as prevalent in the United States as it is in Yucatan. Probably this discrepancy results largely from the fact that relatively more men and women survive to older ages in the northern country, especially women, for whom remarriage at an advanced age is decidedly less likely than it is for elderly men. In the more secular culture of the United States, divorce is many times more common than it is in the predominantly Catholic Latin state.

Households in Yucatan tend to contain large numbers of persons. Since the Mexican definition of the family for census purposes is based upon the concept of the conjugal unit, households consisting of only one person are excluded. Only

18.3 percent of such households in 1970 were made up of two persons, though this class was more important than any other. Over 15 percent of households had eight or more members (Estados Unidos Mexicanos, 1972b: 32). In Mexico as a whole, families were larger in 1970 than those in Yucatan. Thus only 15.7 percent of households in Mexico were limited to two members, families of five or fewer persons comprised 59.2 percent in Mexico as against 63.8 percent in the state, and 20.5 percent of the households included eight or more people in Mexico, compared with 15.1 percent in Yucatan (Estados Unidos Mexicanos, 1972b: 32).

In comparison with the United States, Yucatan had in 1970 extremely large households on the average. The different definition of household in the industrialized nation, which includes one-person units, makes the analysis difficult. In the large North American country, however, 45.8 percent of households had only one or two members, while households with five or fewer members accounted for 89.3 percent of all households. Those comprised of seven or more members made up 5.1 percent in the United States but 24.1 percent—almost one-fourth of the total—in Yucatan (U.S. Bureau of the Census, 1974: 42; Estados Unidos Mexicanos, 1972b: 32).

Religion

The people of Yucatan are predominantly Roman Catholic in religious affiliation, according to the census data. In 1970, 95.3 percent of the inhabitants nominally were attached to the Catholic church; the only other entry of any significance was Protestant or Evangelical, which accounted for but 2.8 percent. Jews numbered only 276, less than one-tenth of 1 percent. Other religions together accounted for 1.6 percent of the inhabitants (Estados Unidos Mexicanos, 1972a: 117).

In the twenty-year period from 1950 to 1970, the Protestant sector increased by 75 percent, from 1.6 percent to 2.8 percent. Adherents of other religions, except the Jewish, decreased during the same period, though it should be kept in mind that the numbers are small, being only 1,585 in 1970. The sharpest rise of all was registered by those for whom "none" was reported: although these data were not reported in 1950, the proportion grew from 0.5 percent in 1960 to 1.6 percent in 1970 (Estados Unidos Mexicanos, 1953: 82; Estados Unidos Mexicanos, 1963: 311–315; Estados Unidos Mexicanos, 1972a: 117).

Such statistics as the foregoing cannot convey, of course, any genuine understanding of the nature of religious beliefs and practices in Yucatan. Direct observation suggests some comments about the social organization and practice of religion. First, Catholic churches are prominent buildings in most, if not all, populated places. Mérida has many monumental temples, and every village has its Catholic church as a major structure on the main square. Second, religious behavior surrounding Catholicism is marked by what seem to be fairly well-defined differentials. Attendance at masses is the most prevalent religious activity, although most people take part on only a limited number of special days. Except for such special occasions, many Catholics, it appears, seldom participate in religious activities. Almost universally, men are more conspicuous by their absence than by their presence in churches. Nevertheless, as we have already noticed, a large majority of all marriages include religious ceremonies. It is evident that much of the Catholicism reported in the census is no more than nominal.

In *The Folk Culture of Yucatan,* Redfield (1941) emphasizes that religion is a comparatively more important and significant part of life in the more rural districts than it is in the larger towns and especially in Mérida. He also makes quite clear another important point: that what is referred to as Catholicism is, in the rural areas, in fact an almost inextricable combination of pagan and Catholic elements. The folk themselves do not, for the most part, understand or attempt to distinguish between those aspects of their religious beliefs and behavior derived from Mayan sources and those based in Catholicism. Before Protestant Evangelical missionaries came to the village of Chan Kom, Redfield believes, the inhabitants had no clear conception of "religion" or "Catholic"; they simply did not think in such terms (Redfield, 1950: 88).

Redfield and his collaborators studied four centers in the Yucatan Peninsula during the 1930s: Mérida, the only genuine city; Dzitas, a town located on the railroad in the eastern part of the state; Chan Kom, a village in the southeastern section to which reference already has been made; and Tusik, "a tribal village of semi-independent Maya" in Quintana Roo. In the book that deals with all four of these investigations, Redfield notes that religion appears to play a more and more central part in the lives of the people as one moves from Mérida through Dzitas and Chan Kom to Tusik. What is sacred in the villages is more likely to be secular in Dzitas and much more likely to be so in Mérida (Redfield, 1950: 240–241). Within the framework of this general trend there are, however, variations.

Shaman-priests, known as *h-mens,* were found in the more rural places. They performed ceremonies in connection with agricultural processes and engaged in divination and healing of the sick. Another functionary was the *maestro cantor* (chanter), who recited Catholic prayers. As the anthropologist observes, "No priest of the church reaches Chan Kom; the prayers of the church are recited by native chanters. The chanter and the *h-men* are equally respected; each participates in the rituals led by the other; and the same congregation follows each. Each cult is as respectable, and as powerful as the other. But they are separate cults. The chanter (*maestro cantor*) has his repertory of prayers, all derived from Catholic liturgy. . . . The prayers of the *h-men,* on the other hand, are in Maya and, although they include the mention of saints, are addressed to the pagan deities" (Redfield, 1941: 106).

It must be assumed that change in the direction of the secular has occurred, to some unknown extent, since the years when Redfield and his associates did their field work. As late as the early 1930s in Mérida, pagan ceremonies were still carried on by very few of those who lived on the edges of the city (Redfield, 1941: 98), and during the intervening period the capital has continued to be the leading edge of innovation in the state. Anyone who has traveled in Yucatan, however, must be impressed with the seeming persistence of rural characteristics. The likelihood is that outside Mérida much of what was seen forty years ago remains true today, though in considerably attenuated form.

Education

Yucatecans have, on the average, low levels of education. A substantial proportion of the people are reported as unable to read and write; many have had no formal instruction whatever; and few have gone beyond the primary years of schooling. In 1970, less than three-fourths (73.8 percent) of the population aged ten and over could read and write. More than one-third (36.8 percent) of those aged six and over had never attended school. Somewhat more than half (55.3 percent) of the people in that age range had attended primary school for one or more years. Only 7.9 percent had any education at all beyond the primary grades (Estados Unidos Mexicanos, 1972b: 3).

With regard to literacy, Yucatan lagged somewhat behind Mexico as a whole, in which 76.2 percent of those aged ten and over were reported as able to read and write. The same was true of the amount of instruction received by persons aged six and over; in Mexico, 55.7 percent had had no formal education and 9.3 percent had progressed beyond the primary years of school. In both the state and the country, however, males were more likely to be literate (Estados Unidos Mexicanos, 1972b: 3).

Dropout rates of students in Yucatan are extremely high. In the year 1970, there were 116,544 children aged six and over in the primary schools of the state and 22,165 aged eleven and over in secondary and similar schools of all types. Since the primary school encompasses six years, students in the lower school averaged 19,424 per grade (a misleading average, of course, since the attrition process undoubtedly begins with the second year). Those in the three years of secondary school averaged 5,078 per grade (again an average that probably is not consonant with reality). The foregoing calculation suggests that perhaps less than four in every ten eligible to attend secondary school do so. The entire postprimary school population of Yucatan in 1970 comprised 25,595, or slightly more than one-fifth of those recorded as attending primary school during that year (Estados Unidos Mexicanos, 1972a: 208–257).

The school system of Yucatan included in 1972 a total of 803 state, federal, and private primary schools. One or more primary schools were found in all of the *municipios* except two: Chacsinkin and Tadziu, both located in the south-central area and contiguous with the *municipio* of Peto. Federal schools comprise a large majority of all primary institutions, 577 units, or 71.8 percent of the total. State schools account for most of the remainder, for only nineteen private primary schools were reported to be operating in 1972. Seventeen of the private units were in Mérida, the remaining two, in Progreso (Mexico, 1972: 33–37).

The federal primary schools in 1972 were teaching 94,357 students, 62 percent of the 152,226 in schools of all three types, while the state schools had 53,933 (35.4 percent) and the private ones only 3,936 (2.6 percent). Hence it is clear that federally operated schools play the most important role, state schools also are of much importance, and private schools have few students, with none at all outside the Mérida-Progreso area. Classes in the federal schools were largest, having an average of 42.1 students per teacher; classes in state schools were slightly smaller, 36.6 students for each teacher; and the few private institutions, which no doubt are attended mostly by upper- and upper-middle-class children, had the smallest classes of all, with a student-teacher ratio of 25.6 (Mexico, 1972: 33–37).

Secondary schools in the same year were operating in 22 of the 106 *municipios* of the state. In the official Mexican terminology, however, the category of secondary schools excludes both private schools and a public preparatory school at the secondary level, which are dealt with below. Yucatan had 40 public secondary schools in 1972, 32 (80 percent) of which were operated by the state. Since the federal schools were much larger on the average than the state schools, however, they had more than their pro rata share of the students. Thus, state units enrolled 9,236, or 64.0 percent of the secondary students, compared with 5,189 or 36.0 percent for the federal system. The average federal school had 648.6 students, compared with an average for state schools of 288.6 (Mexico, 1972: 38). Given the geographic distribution of secondary schools, it is evident that children in some parts of the state cannot readily continue their education beyond the primary level unless they commute rather long distances or take up residence in another community. Secondary schools are concentrated mainly in Mérida and the area east and south of that city. The inaccessibility of these schools is particularly marked in the eastern part of the state. In 1972, there were only four secondary schools (in Espita, Peto, Tizimín, and Valladolid) in the eastern half of the state.

Private preparatory schools are designated "escuelas preparatorias incorporadas a la Universidad de Yucatán," which is understood to indicate that such schools provide the course of study prerequisite to entry into the university. In 1972, there were 19 of these schools, mainly in Mérida. They had 2,370 students, or an average of 124.7; size varied, however, from 364 students to 44 (Mexico, 1972: 39).

In addition to the primary, public secondary, and private preparatory schools, the educational system includes several other preuniversity elements. These were in 1972 the Technological, Industrial, and Commercial School, with 925 students; the Technological Institute, 1,297 students; the School of Agricultural and Livestock Technology in the *municipio* of Tekax, 286 students; the Administration of Fine Arts, 1,107 students in music and the arts; the Administration of

Agricultural and Livestock Technological Education, with 180 students; and the Regional Literacy Administration. This last was credited with teaching 4,135 persons to read and write during the 1971–72 year (Mexico, 1972: 41–43).

Although the University of Yucatan as presently organized dates only from 1922, when it came into being by decree of Governor Felipe Carrillo Puerto, its origins can be traced to 1618. In that year, the Jesuits established themselves in the peninsula and founded the *colegios* of San Francisco Javier and San Pedro. The government took no interest in higher education until after independence, and it was not until 1867, when the Literary Institute of the State was founded, that education at the higher level divorced from the church made its appearance. Today the university encompasses a broad range of schools or faculties in the areas of biological and medical sciences, social and economic sciences, and mathematics and engineering. The divisions in existence in 1976 were Schools of Medicine, Dentistry, Veterinary Medicine, Chemistry, Nursing, Psychology, Law, Anthropology, Commerce and Administration, Economics, Engineering, Mathematics, and Architecture (established in 1975). Unlike most Latin American universities, it has no school of philosophy and letters. The university likewise operates a preparatory school (Rosado G. Cantón, 1976).

This preparatory school had 1,575 students enrolled in 1972; it thus was by far the largest school of its type, outdistancing by a great deal the enrollment of any of the private preparatory schools mentioned earlier. Students in the university proper totaled 2,271 in that year. The school with the largest enrollment was Medicine, accounting for 364 students or 15.6 percent; the School of Law was nearly as large, with 354 or 15.6 percent. The School of Anthropology, with only 24 students registered, was the smallest of the faculties in that year (Mexico, 1972: 40).

Courses of study at the university level vary in length from four to six years and lead to the title of *maestro, licenciado,* or *doctor.* According to the 1970 census, 617 persons had completed four-year courses; 2,915, five-year courses; and 406, six-year courses. The total of 3,938 constitutes one-half of 1 percent of the total population and 1.2 percent of the population aged twenty-one and over (Estados Unidos Mexicanos, 1972a: 183, 185). Although the statistic is not exactly comparable, it is interesting that in 1970 a little less than 11 percent of the United States population aged twenty-five and over had completed four years or more of college (U.S. Bureau of the Census, 1974: 119).

Higher education in Yucatan faces many problems similar to those confronting public colleges and universities in the United States, including the adequate financing of buildings and essential equipment. The University of Yucatan also wrestles with certain difficulties peculiar to its situation in a somewhat remote and isolated part of a developing country. One of these is the preparation of professors to teach in the institution. Another is coping with the rapid rise in student population, for though the university is small by standards of the developed world, it has undergone what its president has called explosive growth. Closely tied to this concern is the problem of maintaining a desirable balance between the professionals trained in the institution and the need for them in the Yucatecan society. As Alberto Rosado G. Cantón observes, "The indiscriminate production of professionals will bring about the grave problem of unemployment and underemployment which will in turn create in the youth a state of frustration which ought not to occur if we can find the formula for producing only those professionals we need in accord with the plans of both the state and federal governments" (Rosado G. Cantón, 1976: 126). The university likewise desires to expand its research activities, now at a rather low level (Rosado G. Cantón, 1976).

The state of education in Yucatan, involving as it does low average educational attainment and considerable illiteracy, high rates of attrition, relative concentration of postprimary schools in one section of the state, and very small proportions of the population with postsecondary training, must, of course, be evaluated in terms of the setting in which it exists. The territory is primarily rural and agricultural, and well over half the labor force is engaged in jobs in agriculture, livestock-raising, fishing, and hunting. Most of this production is of small scale, not what would be regarded in a modern country as commercial. The foregoing suggests that the need for an educated population is not as pressing from an economic point of view as would be the case if the economy involved large-scale enterprises in agriculture, commerce, and industry. Second, the persistence of the Mayan language, often as the first language even when Spanish is known, poses special problems for the system of education. This factor undoubtedly is coupled with the continuing strength of Mayan folkways in daily life. The results may be, though we lack empirical evidence, that parental attitudes discourage rather than encourage pursuit of more than a few years of formal schooling, at least outside the few large population centers. Still another factor is the capacity of the government to support the costs of universal education. Evidence already reviewed indicates that the schools and teacher corps would have to undergo enormous expansion in order to serve all age-eligible children, even in the primary years. This would call for a major reallocation of scarce tax revenues. At the university level, the reported preoccupation with educating people for existing and anticipated positions is a valid concern; some considerable linkage between training programs and the job market appears to be even more essential in a developing than in a developed country.

The preceding remarks do not take into account two major values of education: to prepare persons to be good citizens and leaders in a democratic society and to enable them to live fuller and richer private and public lives. In this respect, the Mexican and Yucatecan leadership must contend with an ever-present dilemma: how to allocate their limited resources for the greatest good of the greatest number in both the short run and the long run. In this process of decision, educational needs must be balanced against needs for food, housing, health, creation of employment, elements of infrastructure, maintenance of law and order, and other essentials in building a stable and modern society.

Yucatan Today and Tomorrow

The selective nature of this review of the social organization of Yucatan comes about because of two factors—limits of information at hand and limits of space. What is said in the preceding pages makes it fairly evident that the state's social organization resembles in many respects the structure of a traditional society. At the same time, it seems clear that the process of modernization has been under way for decades.

George I. Blanksten (1965) refers to modernization as "the change process by means of which a traditional non-Western system acquires characteristics usually associated with more developed or less traditional societies. These characteristics include 'a comparatively high degree of urbanization, widespread literacy, comparatively high per-capita income, extensive geographical and social mobility, a relatively high degree of commercialization and industrialization of the econ-

Street vending in Mérida near the public market, a common sight throughout the city. (Photo by Joel Whitman)

omy, an extensive and penetrative network of mass communication media, and in general . . . widespread participation and involvement by members of the society in modern social and ecomomic processes' '' (Blanksten, 1965: 225–226). What is said in this and other chapters of this volume makes it obvious that Yucatan remains for the most part in the category of traditional.

In order for the modernization process to transform a society or a part of a society, certain conditions must prevail over a considerable period of time. Other than an enlightened and capable leadership, these conditions narrow down mainly to economic resources. At present, Yucatan, as a part of the Mexican nation, lacks the necessary economic resources, and it seems unlikely that they will become available on a large scale within the next several decades. Although high hopes are held out for the gains that can be made through expanded international tourism, it is hard to see how this factor, considered in the light of the worldwide competition for the tourist's dollar, can make a significant difference. It also seems unlikely that Yucatan can benefit substantially from the production and sale of petroleum in nearby regions of Mexico. Moreover, the future modernization of the state must be thought of against the background of an alarming rise in population that promises to continue for many years whatever the success achieved by the Mexican government's enlightened population policy (Sanders, 1974).

In sum, it can be predicted with some confidence that—barring any totally unforeseen world conflagration that alters completely the present distribution of political, social, and economic power—Yucatan will proceed with modernization at a slow pace that will see it remain relatively underdeveloped well into the twenty-first century.

We should not permit ourselves to be entirely blinded by a preoccupation with the goal of making men and nations modern. As we have seen, Yucatan can also be approached as a microcosm apart, a small society with its own peculiar social organization differing somewhat from that found in other places with which it is classified. As part of the continuing Mexican social revolution, it merits close study by the serious social scientist. Whatever the shortcomings of its physical environment and the problems of well-being judged from the standpoint of the modernized countries, Yucatan remains a warm and friendly society inviting thoughtful investigation.

NOTES

1. Calculated using the formula: $P_2 = P_1 (1 + r)^t$ in which P_1 equals the population at the beginning of the period, P_2 equals the population at the end of the period, t equals the number of years included, and r equals the annual rate of increase (Davis, 1969: 140).

2. One who is legally a member of an ejido, has a parcel of land in the ejido, and derives from work in the ejido the major part of his income (Estados Unidos Mexicanos, 1972a: Indice Analítico).

REFERENCES

Bataillon, Claude
    1973   "Poblamiento y Población en la Regionalización de México." In Guillermo Bonfil Batalla et al., *Seminario sobre Regiones y Desarrollo en México*. México, D.F.: Universidad Nacional Autónoma de México, 1973. Pp. 45-70.

Blanksten, George I.
    1965   "Modernization and Revolution in Latin America." In Herbert R. Barringer et al., eds. *Social Change in Developing Areas*. Cambridge, Mass.: Schenkmen Publishing Company. Pp. 225-242.

Centro de Estudios Económicos y Demográficos
    1970   *Dinámica de la Población de México*. México, D.F.: El Colegio de México.

Chamberlain, Robert S.
    1948   *The Conquest and Colonization of Yucatan, 1517-1550*. Pub. 582. Washington, D.C.: Carnegie Institution of Washington.

Cook, Sherburne F., and Woodrow Borah
    1974   "The Population of Yucatan, 1517-1960." In Cook and Borah, *Essays in Population History: Mexico and the Carribean*. Vol. II. Berkeley: University of California Press. Pp. 1-179.

Davis, Allison, Burleigh B. Gardner, and Mary R. Gardner
    1941   *Deep South*. Chicago: University of Chicago Press.

Davis, Kingsley
    1969   *World Urbanization 1950-1970*. Volume I: *Basic Data for Cities, Countries and Regions*. Berkeley, Calif.: Institute for International Studies.

Diario de Yucatán
    1976   "La Población de Yucatán Aumenta a un Ritmo Menor que la Nacional." May 26. P. 2.

Elmendorf, Mary L.
    1973   *La Mujer Maya y el Cambio*. México, D.F.: SEP/Setentas.

Estados Unidos Mexicanos, Secretaría de Industria y Comercio, Dirección General de Estadística
    1963   *VIII Censo General de Población—1960. Estado de Yucatán*.

Estados Unidos Mexicanos, Secretaría de Economía, Dirección General de Estadística
    1953   *Séptimo Censo General de Población, 6 de Junio de 1950. Estado de Yucatán*.

Estados Unidos Mexicanos, Secretaría de Industria y Comercio, Dirección General de Estadística
    1972a *IX Censo General de Población, 1970. Estado de Yucatán*. México, D.F.: Talleres Gráficos de la Nación.
    1972b *IX Censo General de Población, 1970. Resumen General Abreviado*. México, D.F.: Talleres Gráficos de la Nación.

González Cosío, Arturo
    1975   "Conceptualización Sobre las Clases Medias en México. (D). Cuantificación y Clasificación de las Clases Medias." *El Nacional*. May 25. P. 5.

Lenski, Gerhard E.
    1966   *Power and Privilege: A Theory of Social Stratification*. New York: McGraw-Hill Book Company.

México, Gobierno del Estado de Yucatán, Dirección General de Planeación
  1972(?)*Monografía de Yucatán, 1972: Información General y Estadística*. Mérida.
Osorio y Carvajal, Ramón
  1972   *Yucatán en las Luchas Libertarias de México*. Puebla, Pue., México: Editorial José M. Cajica Jr., S.A.
Press, Irwin
  1977   "Historical Dimensions of Orientations to Change in a Yucatec Peasant Community." In Grant D. Jones, ed., *Anthropology and History in Yucatán*. Austin: University of Texas Press. Pp. 275–288.
Redfield, Robert
  1941   *The Folk Culture of Yucatan*. Chicago: University of Chicago Press.
  1950   *A Village That Chose Progress: Chan Kom Revisited*. Chicago: University of Chicago Press.
  1956   *Peasant Society and Culture*. Chicago: University of Chicago Press.
Rosado G. Cantón, Alberto
  1976   "Breve Reseña de la Problemática del Desarrollo de la Universidad de Yucatán." *Revista de la Universidad de Yucatán*, 18 (103): 123–127, Jan.–Feb.
Ryder, James W.
  1977   "Internal Migration in Yucatán: Interpretation of Historical Demography and Current Patterns." In Grant D. Jones, ed., *Anthropology and History in Yucatán*. Austin: University of Texas Press. Pp. 191–231.
Sanders, Thomas G.
  1974   *Mexico 1974: Demographic Patterns and Population Policy*. North American Series, Vol. II, No. 1. New York: American Universities Field Staff.
Servicios Coordinados de Salud Pública en el Estado de Yucatán
  1973   "I Convención Nacional de Salud. Plan Estatal de Salud Pública en el Estado de Yucatán." Typewritten.
Stricken, Arnold
  1965   "Hacienda and Plantation in Yucatan." *América Indígena*, 25: 35–63.
U.S. Bureau of the Census
  1973   *Census of Population: 1970. Detailed Characteristics, Final Report PC(1)-D1, U.S. Summary*. Washington, D.C.: U.S. Government Printing Office.
  1974   *Statistical Abstract of the United States: 1974*. Washington, D.C.: U.S. Government Printing Office.
Warner, W. Lloyd, and Paul S. Lunt
  1941   *The Social Life of a Modern Community*. New Haven, Conn.: Yale University Press.

CHAPTER VIII

THE DIVERSIFICATION QUEST: A MONOCROP EXPORT ECONOMY IN TRANSITION

Eric N. Baklanoff

The northern site of the once flourishing Mayan civilization, Yucatan, is today one of the poorest states in Mexico. For over a century the economic condition of Yucatan has been closely linked with the world market for the peninsula's major source of livelihood and foreign exchange: henequen fiber.

Yucatan—an economically backward region in a semi-industrialized nation—occupies 43,379 square kilometers, or 2.2 percent of the area of Mexico. The state had an estimated population of 758,355 in 1970, representing about 1.6 percent of the national population, but contributed only 0.5 percent of Mexico's value added by industry in that year. The state's per capita output of 5,280 pesos in 1970 was only 60 percent of the national figure of 8,685 pesos and compared most unfavorably with such relatively wealthy states as Nuevo León and México.

Beginning with the agricultural reform of 1937, the Mexican government's economic role in Yucatan has been characterized by ambivalence. On the one hand, federal intervention in the henequen sector has tended to reinforce Yucatan's traditional monocrop pattern; on the other, federal policies and investments have helped launch the state on a new and promising development path.

Events in the recent past suggest that Yucatan is in the formative stage of a diversification drive that will permit the regional economy to escape from its rigid dependence on a single export staple. These new opportunities encompass industrialization based on relatively low wage rates, introduction of non-traditional agricultural commodities, growth of livestock and fishing industries, and promotion of tourism.

This chapter analyzes the structure of Yucatan's regional economy, with special attention to agricultural and industrial diversification. Finally, the federal government's growing intrusion into the regional economy is evaluated in the perspective of the once prosperous henequen plantation system.

Occupational Structure and Entrepreneurship

The ninth general population census conveys only a rough impression of the composition of Yucatan's labor force, by sector and industry.[1] Considering that 7 percent of the labor force was classified as "unspecified," it is possible to conclude that at least 55 percent of the state's working population in 1970 was engaged in the primary sector (agriculture, forestry, and fishing), at least 24 percent was employed in the tertiary sector (commerce, transportation, and other services), and at least 14.4 percent was in the secondary sector (manufacturing, construction, mining, and electric power). Of the 29,062 workers classified in the secondary sector, 21,344 were in manufacturing, 6,385 in construction, 676 in extractive activities, and 657 in electric power.[2] Five years later, in 1975, the number of workers engaged in the secondary sector had increased to 36,902, which reflected mainly the significantly larger numbers in manufacturing (28,014) and construction (7,438).[3] Because of the rapid expansion of the total labor force between 1970 and 1975, from about 201,000 to nearly 247,000, the secondary sector's share in the latter figure increased only slightly to 14.9 percent.

With only 27 percent of the population in the labor force in 1970, Yucatan has a relatively large economically dependent population. According to the International Labor Office, on the average 100 workers had to support 142 nonworkers worldwide, and in Latin America the ratio was 100 to 220.[4] In Yucatan, 100 workers had to support 276 nonworkers in 1970, a situation that places a great burden on the productive members of the society. The state's extremely high population dependency ratio undoubtedly reflects both the large proportion of children in the population's age structure and the significant outflow of working-age groups to other parts of Mexico.

Were it not for emigration, Yucatan would have one of the highest population growth rates in the world. According to official Yucatecan statistics, the state's natural demographic rate in 1975 was over 3.5 percent.[5] In the absence of the emigration factor, Yucatan's population would therefore double about every twenty years. The actual growth rate, however, is considerably lower (2.4 percent) and reflects the substantial yearly out-migration rate, over 1.1 percent.[6] This heavy outflow of Yucatecans to other parts of Mexico appears to be a necessity if living conditions within the state are to improve. For, clearly, the dynamics of the Yucatan economy—its capacity to create new productive employment—is insufficient to accommodate its rapid natural population growth. Human fertility is particularly high in rural areas, and it is interesting to point out that 150,000 Yucatecans are scattered in more than 1,500 hamlets of less than 100 inhabitants.[7]

Economic development must be planned, organized, directed, and financed in the context of uncertainty, that is, functions associated with a very special human resource: entrepreneurship. In Yucatan the rise of the modern plantation economy was largely associated with the enterprise of the great Creole families. Their economic initiative extended beyond the agricultural estate to encompass as well the organization of railways, electric power service, ports and docks, banking, commerce, and the beginnings of industry during the final decades of the nineteenth century. Among the family names that loom importantly in the entrepreneurial landscape of that formative period are Escalante, Ancona, Cámara, Casares, Espinosa, Cantón, Gutiérrez, Molina, Peón, Bolio, Regil, Palma, and Peniche.[8] Following the uncompensated expropriation of the large estates associated with the agricultural reform of the latter 1930s, many of the old plantation families left Yucatan for Mexico City or the United States. Of those that remained in Yucatan, some continued to work their greatly diminished estate, the *pequeña propiedad,* and others diversified into such activities as industry, including the manufacture of henequen products (*cordelerías*), commerce, tourism services, and cattle raising.

Some of the largest organizations operating in contemporary Yucatan are agencies and semiautonomous enterprises of the Mexican government. The principal administrators of Cordemex, the dominant industrial firm in the peninsula, and Banco Rural, which supervises and finances the ejidos, come from other parts of Mexico and normally change every six years with new presidential administrations. Significantly, many Yucatecans, notably the campesinos, see Cordemex (like the Banco Rural) not as an organization that benefits them, "but rather as an alien institution of government, directed by outsiders who live on a distinctly more affluent level than they themselves do."[9] Nacional Financiera, the Mexican government's comprehensive development bank, through its branch office in Yucatan, has promoted and financed numerous industrial enterprises, including those located in Mérida's industrial park. Several of these recently established plants are owned and controlled by Mexicans from outside of Yucatan. Cementos Maya, S.A., the second largest industrial enterprise in Yucatan, is controlled by Monterrey interests.

As is true of many other parts of Latin America, immigrants have played a vital role in the modern development of Yucatan. Their contribution as entrepreneurs has been greatly disproportionate to their small numbers. Attracted by the henequen-based affluence of the late nineteenth century, the number of foreign-born residents in Yucatan numbered 2,500 in 1900, of which 1,479 were Spaniards and 576 were classified as "Turks," that is, persons who emigrated from Middle Eastern places under Turkish control.[10] The latter, particularly Christian Lebanese, today dominate the commerce of Mérida and the manufacture of guayabera shirts. They also operate several of the finest restaurants in the capital city and own ice-making plants and food processing firms, including Yucatan's only flour mill, Harinas del Sureste, S.A. Recently, Lebanese interests have diversified into cattle ranching in the eastern part of the state. Most of the Middle Eastern immigrants arrived in Yucatan between 1890 and 1910. Upon finding the commerce of Mérida and the other cities preempted by local and Spanish merchants, they settled in small interior towns as peddlers. After the

Mexican Revolution, their commercial interests became increasingly centered in Mérida and the other cities; the Lebanese businessmen also had an important stake in the cordage industry (the *cordelerías*), before its nationalization by the Mexican government in 1964.

Among the economically prominent Arab family names are Miguel Angel Xacur (owner of Harinas del Sureste), Alfredo Abhimerí, Asís Abraham, Juan and Aniceto Macarí, Tufic Charruf (owner of Hotel Panamericana), José Mena, Alejandro Abud, the Chapur group, and Abraham Jorge. Many of the sons and daughters of these enterprising Arab families have intermarried with the sons and daughters of the old, socially prestigious hacendado families.

Spanish immigrants initiated ice-making plants in cities and small towns; important hardware establishments that supplied the haciendas were founded by Germans, such as Ritter Bock; and, as noted in the next section, the two most advanced machine shops and foundries were established by immigrant enterprise and capital.

Yucatan's Golden Age: The Henequen Plantation Economy

Henequen, or sisal, is now cultivated throughout the tropics. Unlike jute or true hemp, henequen fiber is hard and is well suited for the manufacture of twine, cordage, and coarse fabrics. The henequen plant's life period is from fifteen to twenty years, and it needs seven to eight years to mature for the first harvest. The harvested leaves are taken to a defibration plant (or rasping machine), where the fibers are extracted before they dry. Henequen must be processed within twenty-four to twenty-eight hours after cutting, and 96 percent by bulk of the leaves is removed as waste. An efficient transport system and a processing plant nearby are therefore essential to commercial production of the fiber.[11]

Because of the considerable maturation period and long life of the henequen plant, the supply elasticity of the hard fiber is extremely low, so that the response of the quantity of henequen supplied in the market is little affected by price changes in the short run. Consequently, small changes in world demand for henequen result in disproportionally greater price changes for the primary commodity. Because of the growing world demand for sisal associated with the price rise of oil-based synthetic fibers, for example, the price of Yucatan's natural fiber increased fivefold between 1970 and 1974. Consequently, the henequen industry's contribution to Yucatan's gross product rose from 15 percent in 1970 to 40 percent in 1974.[12]

Commercial henequen production in Yucatan developed slowly but steadily from the 1830s to the latter 1870s in response to the demand for cordage associated mainly with the growth of world shipping. Yucatan exported rope, hammocks, matting, and ship rigging as well as raw henequen fiber. Operations were based on the existing agricultural unit, the hacienda, employing local initiative and local labor. This period witnessed the invention by Yucatecans of a mechanical rasping or defibration machine and after 1860 the gradual adaptation

Henequen plantation near Ticul, Yucatan. (Photo by Eugene Wilson)

Worker tending young henequen plants, Hacienda Yaxcapoíl, near Mérida. (Photo by Edward Moseley)

of steam power to henequen defibration and transportation. Among the inventors and developers of the defibration machine were the Yucatecans José Esteban Solís, José Dolores Espinosa Rendón, Manuel Prieto, and Manuel Cecilio Villamor y Armendaris. By 1890, the large haciendas had fully converted to steam engines varying in capacity from six to twenty horsepower.[13] A growing network of "Decauville" narrow-gauge rails went into the henequen fields providing efficient transportation for the tons of leaves and fiber moved from field to rasping machine, and a second network of intermediate-sized rails formed private railroads between the processing plant and major railhead.[14] The crude and dangerous "Solís machine" was gradually replaced by safer and more efficient rasping equipment.

In the period from about 1880 to 1918, Yucatan moved on an accelerated growth path based on a total commitment to henequen exports, mainly to the United States. A major innovation, the twine-binding reaper, was to create an insatiable world demand for Yucatecan sisal. The McCormick reaper, first used for wheat harvesting, was later adapted to harvesting of oats and rye as well. The new machine's success in U.S. agriculture led to its adoption in other grain-producing nations; the associated demand for binder twine in those nations opened new markets for Yucatan's premier export commodity.

This period of exceptional henequen prosperity coincided with the Díaz era in Mexico (1876–1910). Porfirio Díaz's economic advisers, who called themselves *científicos,* promoted the development of new export industries in primary commodities and the construction of railways and ports; they practiced fiscal orthodoxy and maintained law and order—two conditions deemed essential for the attraction of direct foreign investments in railways, mines, oil wells, ranches, and plantations and for the placement of Mexican government bonds in the principal capital markets abroad. Indian lands, held in common as traditional ejidos, passed by various methods into the hands of foreigners or Mexican hacendados. Debt peonage—the de facto permanent attachment of landless campesinos to the agricultural estate—characterized the socioeconomic status of the rural masses.

Yucatan's development experience in this period fitted the pattern described above with one significant difference. In the nation at large foreigners initiated, owned, and controlled most of the railways, public utilities, mines, oil wells and refineries, and numerous export-oriented agricultural enterprises. In the peninsula, on the other hand, Yucatecans initiated, owned, and maintained control over their plantations, railways, and some of their public utilities. As one local writer rhapsodized: "All the work here has been done by the sons of Yucatan, all the glory may be attached to our beloved country rather than to foreign entrepreneurs; Yucatecans were the capitalists, Yucatecans were the concessionaires, Yucatecans were the engineers and the laborers, glory to Yucatan!"[15]

With respect to public utilities, the above statement is only partially correct. U.S. interests initiated the gas works in Mérida in 1885 that for a time provided illumination for the principal streets, commercial establishments, public buildings, and private houses.[16] The gas companies eventually went into bankruptcy under the competitive pressure of electricity. The streets of Mérida were first provided with electric lights through the efforts of Miguel Espinosa Rendón, with the technical assistance of a Boston-based firm, under the direction of an American engineer, R. G. Ward. The power company passed through several Yucatecan hands, but fared poorly because its costs of operation exceeded revenues. In 1903, the utility's control and ownership passed to its principal creditor, the German firm Siemens and Halske, A.G.

U.S. engineers and technicians figured prominently in the operation and maintenance of Yucatan's public service industries: the railways, telephone and telegraph, gas and waterworks, and ports and harbors. New York bankers underwrote one-third of the working capital of the Southeastern Railway Company (Compañía de Ferrocarriles Sud-Orientales, S.A.), but the henequen elite lacked interest in this frontier project, and insufficient capital was raised to initiate construction of the line.[17]

The smaller traditional plantations of the earlier period were gradually consolidated into vast estates, with tens of thousands of acres under cultivation, run along scientific management principles geared to production of a single primary commodity for export. Initially, these "modern plantations" imported their machinery and equipment mainly from the United Kingdom and France. The large financial resources required to mechanize the defibration of henequen, as well as to bring the henequen plant to maturity for harvesting, were obtained in great measure from New York banks and U.S. brokers at commercial rates of interest. Unlike the pattern that characterized other modern plantations in Middle America and the Antilles[18]—foreign ownership and management of the enterprise—the Yucatecans maintained control over the means of production in the henequen sector.

Throughout this period, Yucatan enjoyed a monopoly in the production and export of the hard fiber. For a brief time, Manila hemp competed with henequen for the binder twine market, but ultimately the tougher sisal fiber proved its greater value for the harvesting operations. Yucatan's ability to dictate the price of henequen was not to be left unchallenged, for in 1903, J. P. Morgan, the American financier, succeeded in merging the five major American farm equipment companies into a single entity, the International Harvester Corporation. Morgan negotiated a secret contract between International Harvester and Casa Molina of Mérida, the principal buyer of fiber from the henequen plantations. This contract specified that "Molina and Company will use such efforts as should be in their power to lower the price of sisal fiber, and they shall pay only those prices which from time to time shall be dictated by I. H. Co."[19] As a result of this I. H.–Molina compact, prices of Yucatecan henequen were driven down in the years 1903 to 1912.

Exports of henequen rose from less than six million kilos in 1875 to eighty-one million in 1900—a near fourteenfold growth.[20] At the turn of the century, the hard fiber led the list of Mexico's nonmetallic export commodities. The state's

Henequen rasping machine on an hacienda south of Umán. (Photo by Joel Whitman)

Henequen fiber on drying racks. (Photo by Joel Whitman)

Packing henequen fiber. (Photo by Joel Whitman)

Making rope from henequen fiber. (Photo by Joel Whitman)

treasury depended greatly on henequen export operations, which in 1905 provided 60 percent of fiscal revenues.[21] Despite the widespread mechanization of fiber production, the labor requirements of expanded henequen cultivation were such that by the last years of the Díaz regime, substantial numbers of Yaqui Indians from Sonora and Orientals from China and Korea were brought to Yucatan as laborers.[22]

In 1910 the great majority of the 77,000 Yucatecan campesinos and 99,000 domestic servants were held in debt bondage: a peon or servant leaving the hacienda prior to clearing his debt could be apprehended by the authorities and returned to the hacienda.[23] Still, the fieldhands and servants established on the hacienda received free of charge their modest dwellings and small plots of land and were allowed to keep in their patios pigs, chickens, and sometimes cattle.[24] They also received free medical attention.

The first defibration machines were built of wood in local carpentry shops. Beginning in the mid-1860s, machine shops and foundries were organized to service the more complex steam-powered equipment. Initially these shops were set up to repair defibration equipment and to manufacture replacement parts for rasping machines, sugar mill equipment, henequen presses, and steam engines. By the turn of the century, however, several of these machine shops had developed the capability to build rasping machines and henequen presses.[25]

Among the most important of these metal-working shops and foundries were those established by two immigrants, the Armenian Carlos Pascal Caracashian and the Spaniard José Torroella. Both men found ways to improve on the old equipment and invented new, more efficient machines.[26] Whereas the earlier standard rasping machine could only handle long fibers, a new model invented by Carlos Caracashian could process both short and long fibers. Two of the machines developed by Caracashian, ''La Pascalita'' and ''La Reforma,'' were recognized for their advanced technical features and were adopted throughout the henequen zone. At the peak of its operation Caracashian's mechanical shop and foundry employed eighty individuals, worked in both bronze and steel, and contributed substantial tax revenue to the government.[27]

Carpenters and other craftsmen were increasingly engaged in the manufacture of coaches, carts, and buggies in response to the growing demand for the transportation of people and cargo within the peninsula. Other industries that made their appearance during the latter decades of the nineteenth century included ice plants, factories for the manufacture of chocolate and safety matches, pharmaceutical laboratories, and in 1899 Yucatan's only brewery, José M. Ponce y Cía.[28]

At the turn of the century, Yucatan, which had been one of Mexico's poorest provinces, became one of its wealthiest. ''Mérida blossomed,'' writes Nelson Reed. ''The streets were paved with macadam, had electricity to light them at night, were traversed by horse-drawn streetcars, and numbered in the scientific way—all of this in advance of Mexico City.''[29] The unparalleled henequen boom not only made fortunes for the hacendado families, the *gente decente*, but also

Main house of a henequen hacienda south of Umán. (Photo by Joel Whitman)

A photograph of the Caracashian machine shop-foundry and personnel in Mérida made in the early twentieth century. (Photo courtesy of the Caracashian family)

lifted the Mayan fieldhand far above the poverty found in other parts of Mexico.[30] Although the economy made only modest progress toward manufacturing industry, it offered an increasing number of skilled and semiskilled jobs to the humble but ambitious laborers. The operation of defibration machines, railways, telephone and telegraph systems, machine and carpentry shops, foundries, small factories, hardware stores, and the like demanded new talents and skills. And everywhere the construction trades "felt the influence of new money as shops, houses, and the marvelous Paseo Montejo residences"[31] were built. By 1900, the state had achieved a level of prosperity that was the envy of Mexico.

From 1903 to 1912, with the increase of henequen plantings and production in Yucatan and the slowing of world demand for henequen, fiber prices moved on a downward trend. Consequently, growers pressed for a government agency that would intervene in the market to raise prices. They were obliged with the organization in 1912 of the Regulating Commission of the Henequen Market, the forerunner of all subsequent federal interventions in the industry. The commission was to function by holding off the market sufficient henequen stocks to drive prices upward, much in the manner of the Brazilian government's "valorization" scheme for coffee. World War I broke out just as the commission started operations, and the extraordinary demand for henequen, supported by the stockpiling purchases of American buyers, sent prices soaring to a wartime peak of twenty-three cents per pound in 1918. Two years earlier, in 1916, acreage planted in henequen exceeded 212,000 hectares and fiber production reached nearly 202,000 tons—higher levels than before or since that time.[32]

Following the Armistice and the end of speculative wartime purchases of the hard fiber, prices fell precipitously. Unsold henequen accumulated in official warehouses as the commission tried unsuccessfully to reverse the declining price trend. After exhausting its financial resources in stockpiling operations, the commission became defunct in 1919.

The gravity of the postwar situation was aggravated by Yucatan's loss of its monopoly position in the world sisal market. High prices, particularly during the war, encouraged the growth of foreign sisal plantations, mainly in British East Africa and in Java. In 1908, only 2 percent of the world's hard fiber had been produced outside of Yucatan. By 1918, the share had risen to 20 percent, and five years later growers outside Mexico led in global production.[33] Furthermore, the sisal plant grown under scientific management in richer soils, using lower-paid labor, was altered to produce longer fibers and greater tensile strength. Thus Yucatan's emerging competitors held both cost and quality advantages in the international sisal trade. After World War II Yucatan's share in the world sisal market continued its protracted decline.

Agricultural Structure and Diversification

Until recently, the prevailing assessment of Yucatan's agricultural potential was pessimistic. In this view, the state was considered a semiarid region that offered extremely limited agricultural possibilities for the production of such crops as henequen that thrive on capricious seasonal rainfalls, require large quantities of unskilled labor, and grow in soils deficient in organic matter. With the rapid expansion of the highway network since the mid-1950s and more recent federal investment in irrigation, pessimism has yielded to a guarded optimism concerning the prospects for a diversified agricultural-pastoral economy. There are now over 6,000 kilometers of roads in the state, of which more than 2,000 kilometers are paved. Very few communities in any part of the state are isolated, and every region has at least one paved and generally well-maintained road that allows the population fast and efficient access to major marketing centers. Greatly improved internal transportation has provided a major stimulus to commercial livestock raising, production of vegetables, and fruit growing.

Of the 700,000 hectares under cultivation in Yucatan in 1977, only 15,500 were irrigated. This small share (2 percent of the land cultivated), however, generated nearly 6 percent of the value of agricultural production. Because there are no rivers or streams in Yucatan, newly irrigated land derives its water resources from underground wells.

The problem of agricultural development in Yucatan represents a very special challenge to farmers and agronomists. More than 95 percent of the soil is rocky; most of it is neither arable nor adaptable to large-scale mechanization. The other conditions that constrain the agricultural economy of the peninsula are the deficient and erratic rainfall and the low productivity of labor in most farm enterprises. The labor productivity problem is aggravated by the rudimentary technical capacity of most of the farm workers and a high rural population growth rate. This heavy demographic pressure and limited harvesting periods for the traditional crops result in high unemployment and underemployment rates in the rural sector.

For analytical purposes, the landmass of Yucatan is divided into five agricultural zones.[34] The sparsely populated coastal zone comprises an area of 235 square kilometers, and its predominantly sandy soils are given over to coconut plantations. Yucatan's economic life is concentrated in the henequen zone (11,482 square kilometers), located in the northwestern part of the state, where the soil is characteristically stony. A good transportation network joins cities, villages, and farms in the henequen region. Significantly, the zone contains abundant ground water at shallow depths from four to fourteen meters. Beyond the coastal and henequen zones, corn is grown by traditional slash-and-burn methods (the eastern and central corn zones, with 8,896 and 3,686 square kilometers, respectively). Of increasing importance as a source of rural income is the cattle zone (7,625 square kilometers), located in the northeast portion of the state. Finally, the fruit-growing zone (5,311 square kilometers), which includes both sides of the Sierrita Baja de Ticul, from Muna to the *municipio* of Tekax, is characterized by production of nontraditional crops, including citrus fruit, avocados, and mangoes. Isolated patches of high-quality soil are found in this part of Yucatan, and where they occur, they lend themselves to mechanical farming.

Since the 1937 agrarian reform, henequen production in Yucatan has been characterized by the coexistence of two systems: collectivized ejidos and private enterprise. The latter system includes the *pequeñas propiedades,* the residual holdings of the hacendados after expropriation of their estates, and land held in *parcelas.* The twelve thousand *parcelarios* (some of whom are also members of the collectivized ejidos) received their individual plots as a result of the agrarian legislation before 1937 or acquired title to land through purchase. During the latter 1970s, ejidos cultivated about 64 percent of the henequen land, *pequeñas propiedades* were second (27 percent), and the *parcelarios* third (9 percent).

As Roland Chardon makes clear, the new land-tenure pattern "disrupted the functional agricultural-industrial integrative unity of the henequen hacienda."[35] Productivity in the henequen ejidos since implementation of the reform has fallen dramatically. For example, annual average output per ejidatario declined from 2,633 kilos in 1938 to 1,401 kilos in 1957 to only 1,087 kilos in 1967, a near 60 percent reduction between the first and last years.[36] According to the U.N. Food and Agricultural Organization, henequen production in 1967 reached only 750 kilos per hectare on the ejidos, compared with 1,150 kilos on the *pequeñas propiedades* and 1,300 kilos by the *parcelarios.*[37] Further, the quality of fiber produced on ejidos is inferior to that grown in the private sector.

The some four hundred ejidos are given little opportunity to participate in managerial decision making. Instead, the Mexican government, through the Banco Rural, plans output and provides credit, technical advice, and a marketing outlet for ejidal production. Bank credits to the ejidos take the form of salary advances to the ejidatarios. Because of the surplus labor force in the henequen zone, each ejidatario is assigned a work quota that can be fulfilled in one or two mornings a week and for which he receives between four and nine dollars weekly. As a member of the ejido, the campesino also participates in Mexico's social security program. In the recent past, bank salary advances have greatly exceeded the sales value of henequen fiber, with the difference accruing as a debt by the ejidos to the bank. Because this debt is not expected ever to be paid, the annual losses of the bank represent in effect a massive federal subsidy to the henequen ejidos. During 1977, for example, the bank's selling price for ejido-grown fiber was 6.5 pesos per kilo, but the cost of production varied between 15.4 pesos and 22.9 pesos per kilo. The difference between the amount of salary advances or credits received by the ejidos that year (868 million pesos) and the value of production (328 million pesos) reached 540 million pesos or $24 million—the subsidy provided by the Banco Rural to the collectivized henequen sector.[38]

The Banco Rural has been characterized by gross mismanagement and corruption. Toward the end of 1977, the bank revealed that some of its officials had engaged in massive fraud involving advances to ejidatarios. A comparison of the bank's list of henequen workers and the Social Security Administration's rolls revealed a discrepancy of 30,250 names.[39] Bank officials admitted that for the years 1976–77 payments to campesinos for work not done came to 200 million pesos. After the news release regarding the "cleansing of the rolls," the Banco Rural further announced that ninety-three of its employees had been fired, including twenty officials.[40] At the beginning of 1978, the names of 51,587 campesinos remained on the bank's list compared with the highly inflated previous figure of 81,837. Even the "cleansed" list of some 52,000 names reflects overpopulation and a redundant labor force in the henequen zone.

Clearly, the henequen ejidos can no longer provide a livelihood for all of their members, and this hard reality has given impetus to the economic diversification efforts now under way in Yucatan. At the beginning of 1978, Secretary of Agriculture and Hydraulic Resources Francisco Merino Rabago announced a 7,000 million peso investment program in support of agricultural diversification for the 1979-82 period.[41] As former governor Carlos Loret de Mola aptly stated: "Yucatan produces less fiber now than at the beginning of the century and has a mass of campesinos much greater now than in 1902, than 1910, than in the 20s, and in the 30s. Our population is climbing but not our production."[42]

Table 1 shows the changes in the state's agricultural production during the decade from 1964 to 1973. For the two principal traditional crops, henequen and corn, the former shows a declining production trend over the decade, while corn increased at a moderate, if uneven pace. What is significant in this overall picture is the rapid expansion of "other products." The 78 percent production increment of these nontraditional crops should be compared with the rise of total agricultural output of only 26 percent between 1964 and 1973.

Notwithstanding considerable progress in agricultural diversification in recent years, the lion's share of Yucatan's land continues to be cultivated in henequen, corn, and beans. In 1974, about 54 percent of the agricultural area was in

Table 1.   Yucatan: Agricultural Production, 1965-1973
(1964 = 100)

Year	Henequen	Corn	Other Products	Total
1965	97	111	96	105
1966	85	58	101	80
1967	89	43	128	84
1968	83	91	161	103
1969	81	102	167	103
1970	89	109	146	111
1971	86	116	171	117
1972	86	123	164	121
1973	83	139	178	126

Source: Dirección General de Planeación, *Monografía de Yucatán 1974* (Mérida, Yucatán: Gobierno del Estado de Yucatán, 1974), no page cited.

henequen, 34 percent in corn, and just under 5 percent in beans—or a total of roughly 93 percent in the three traditional crops.[43] Fruits and other crops, mainly vegetables, occupied a little under 7 percent of the state's cropland, although their joint share in the total increased from only 5 percent in 1970. In the same period, from 1970 to 1974, the amount of acreage planted in fruit rose by 42 percent, and the acreage allocated to the other crops increased by 174 percent. Clearly, these figures indicate that the absolute amount of land cultivated in nontraditional crops is expanding rapidly, even if their share in total land use remains small.

Given the very limited opportunities for work in the henequen fields, many ejidatarios have diversified into truck gardening and the growing of fruit; others have become stone masons and stone collectors. For many campesinos, these supplementary agricultural endeavors bring substantially more income than the wages earned from the one or two mornings of work in the henequen fields. The typical truck farmer requires a small section of land, say a *mecate* (an ancient surface measure, found principally in Yucatan, used for evaluating the sowing of grains or henequen; the equivalent of twenty meters square, also a lineal measure of twenty meters), a well with an electric pump, hose pipes, and henequen bagasse for fertilizing and mulching the soil. He takes his produce—melons, cucumbers, tomatoes, cabbages, chilis, radishes, parsley—to the nearest wholesale market and collects his earnings there.

Federal authorities through the Banco Rural and its *técnicos* have tried to induce campesinos to change their production methods through such sophisticated agricultural ventures as "Plan Chac" and "Plan Tabi." These approaches usually involved expensive sprinkler irrigation systems and other capital-using methods in addition to the provision of houses, schools, and related infrastructure. Thus far, however, most of the officially planned approaches have failed while the spontaneous diversification efforts of the campesinos have succeeded.[44]

The production of fruit and other tree crops such as avocados has witnessed dynamic expansion during the past decade. As Table 2 shows, the number of orange trees increased from 241,000 in 1966 to 780,000 in 1976 (224 percent); lemon trees from 50,000 to 135,000 (169 percent); papaya trees from 36,000 to 99,000 (173 percent); and the number of avocado trees roughly doubled from 28,000 to 59,000. Income from fruit growing in Yucatan reached 164 million pesos in 1977, half of which derived from the sale of citrus fruit.

Income from cattle and beef production has come to equal that from the growing of henequen fiber. In 1977, cattle industry sales exceeded 500 million pesos, and of the estimated 90,000 head of cattle that were either sold or slaughtered, 30,000 were exported to other parts of Mexico, mainly the Federal District. Yucatan's cattle herd of 760,000 head is concentrated in the eastern part of the state, around Tizimín, but smaller concentrations are also found in the henequen zone and in the south. Large ranches dominate in the Tizimín area, and these privately owned estates are the principal source of cattle exports. Small

Table 2.   Yucatan: Trees in Production, 1966 and 1976

Tree	1966	1976	Percentage Change 1966–76
Avocado	27,780	58,749	114.8
Plum	43,609	76,359	75.1
Guayaba	23,616	40,740	72.5
Lime	15,644	26,443	69.0
Lemon	50,294	135,047	168.5
Mango	32,876	46,483	41.4
Orange	240,808	780,000	223.8
Papaya	36,297	99,070	172.9
Tamarind	6,077	28,659	371.6
Grapefruit	5,815	17,020	192.7

Source: Secretaría de Agricultura y Recursos Hidráulicos, *Yucatán en cifras: 20 años de estadísticas agropecuarias* (Mérida, 1978), n.p.

ranches typify the henequen zone, where a modest income from the sale of twenty to thirty head of cattle to the local slaughterhouse is common. Investment in the cattle industry is estimated at 2,500 million pesos, and at least ten thousand individuals are engaged in ranching.[45] The cattle industry's potential for continued growth, based on intensive grazing, is promising. Among the measures that need to be taken are introduction of new feed cultivation practices, directed herding, and improved sanitary conditions.

The poultry industry has been expanding rapidly, mainly in the vicinity of Mérida, with total sales estimated at about 380 million pesos in 1977. Growth of the industry's bird population (from 1,775,795 in 1966 to 3,126,232 in 1976) reflects both Yucatan's recent accelerated urbanization trend and the high income elasticity of demand for poultry products. The state's swine herd has fluctuated considerably in the recent past, with numbers peaking in 1966 (216,255 head), falling sharply to 146,188 in 1968, and increasing thereafter to over 190,000 head in 1976.[46] Major increments in numbers were registered in 1973–76, mainly because of the swine development program formulated specifically for ejidatarios. Income from the sale of pork came to just under 300 million pesos in 1977.

Commercial honey growing and processing provides Yucatan with a secondary, if highly variable, source of foreign exchange. There exist in the state an estimated 200,000 beehives that yielded over 13,700 tons of the syrup with a value of 206 million pesos in 1977.[47] Apiculture, which is classified as a livestock activity, offers part-time work to an estimated 15,000 persons. As a significant rural activity, apiculture enjoys a long tradition in the peninsula, dating back to the preconquest period. Most of the raw honey is processed in Yucatan for export to such customers as West Germany, the United Kingdom, Japan, and the United States. In 1973, the peninsula of Yucatan contributed 19,000 tons of total world exports of honey amounting to 125,452 tons. The peninsula ranked first among honey-exporting areas, followed in descending order of importance by Argentina (18,000 tons), China (13,900 tons), and Canada (9,864 tons). Competition among these leading exporters for the global markets is vigorous, and honey prices fluctuate greatly from year to year and over the business cycle.

Industrial Structure

Yucatan's status as a less-industrialized region is highlighted by an analysis of Mexico's ninth industrial census.[48] The actual census was taken in 1971 and is based on data obtained for the previous year. A comparison between Yucatan and Mexico reveals that the state employed 1.6 percent of the nation's industrial labor force, registered .09 percent of industrial investment, and generated only .06 percent and .05 percent of the nation's gross industrial product and value added in industry, respectively. Although the share of Yucatan's industrial labor force

Aerial view of the brewery, Cervecería Yucateca, S.A., in Mérida. (Photo courtesy of José Luis Ponce García)

corresponds to the state's share of the national population, 1.6 percent, the state's contribution to industrial investment and production is disproportionately low.

The small-scale, labor-intensive character of Yucatan's industrial structure is also borne out by the data. In 1970, for example, when the state's average industrial firm had seven employees, the national firm averaged thirteen employees, and the corresponding employment figures for the higher-income states of México and Nuevo León were twenty-five and twenty-eight, respectively.[49]

Three giant enterprises dominate the industrial landscape of Yucatan. The total net worth of all industrial establishments in the state in 1973 was estimated to exceed 542 million pesos.[50] Of this sum, the three largest enterprises—Cordemex (250 million pesos), Cementos Maya, the cement plant (125 million pesos), and the brewery Cervecería Yucateca, S.A., (45 million pesos)—accounted for a joint net worth of 420 million pesos, or 77 percent of the total.

Of the 3,595 Yucatecan establishments covered by the 1970 industrial census, 3,031 had five or fewer employees (see Table 3), with an average employment of less than two persons per establishment. The 564 larger firms—those with six or more persons—employed a total of 20,260 individuals, or an average of 36 per establishment. These larger industrial firms paid 95 percent of the wages, generated 89 percent of the value added, and represented 97 percent of the capital invested in the state's industry. The smaller establishments, with accumulated investment averaging only 14,700 pesos ($1,176) per firm, represented a negligible share of Yucatan's total industrial capital stock.

Table 4 summarizes the results of the industrial census for Yucatan: number of establishments, number of employees, wages and salaries paid, net accumulated investment, value of output, and value added. (The latter is derived by subtract-

Table 3.   Yucatan: Industrial Structure, by Size of Establishment, 1970

		5 or fewer persons	6 or more persons	Total
Number of establishments		3,031	564	3,595
Number employed		5,769	20,260	26,260
Wages and salaries	thousands	11,250	211,515	222,765
Capital invested	of	44,548	1,401,724	1,446,272
Value added	pesos	45,699	396,664	442,363

Source: Dirección General de Estadística, *IX Censo Industrial 1971,* Vol. II (México, D.F.: Secretaría de Industria y Comercio, 1973), p. 66, table 3.

Table 4. Yucatan: Industrial Output, Employment, Wages and Salaries, and Value Added, by Industry, 1970

Industry	Number of establishments	Number of employees	Wages and salaries	Net investment	Value of output	Value added
					(thousands of pesos)	
Mining	25	605	5,374	23,168	22,147	12,723
Manufacturing	3,570	25,424	217,391	1,423,104	1,207,235	429,640
Textiles	271	11,651	85,307	922,973	419,708	118,980
Food products	2,075	5,692	28,298	161,873	311,182	92,917
Apparel	427	1,521	8,871	30,637	31,282	16,462
Beverages	24	1,370	30,969	68,379	179,388	74,378
Wood products, except furniture	95	964	14,590	58,285	64,018	32,301
Nonmetallic mineral products	54	796	11,208	64,927	51,753	25,646
Shoes	149	726	5,078	13,192	18,290	9,318
Printing and publishing	70	716	11,233	26,697	37,472	17,702
Chemicals	60	448	6,823	32,015	43,866	16,482
Manuf. and repair of nonelectrical machinery	32	356	5,813	14,662	13,575	6,810
Metal products	106	303	1,615	4,613	6,607	3,591
Other manufacturing	207	881	7,586	24,851	30,094	15,053
Total	3,595	26,029	222,765	1,446,272	1,229,382	442,363

Source: Dirección General de Estadística. IX Censo Industrial 1971, Vol. I (México, D.F.: Secretaría de Industria y Comercio, 1973), pp. 43–71.

ing from the gross value of output the firm's cost of raw materials and fuels, electric power purchased, and other external outlays.) The census did not include electric power production and construction, two activities that are normally classified as components of the industrial sector. Mining, as the table indicates, plays a minor role in the state's industrial effort. Mineral production involves principally the mining of salt and quarrying.

The various branches of manufacturing have been ranked according to their levels of employment, with textiles, food products, apparel, and beverages together accounting for 75 percent of that sector's total work force. Textiles, the predominant industry, accounts for 46 percent of employment in manufacturing, 65 percent of the accumulated investment, and 28 percent of the value added in manufacturing. Yucatecan textiles (in contrast with clothing) are derived almost completely from henequen fiber, and the industry is in turn dominated by Cordemex, a multiplant establishment owned by the Mexican government.

The food products industry, which ranks second as a source of employment, is characterized by a large number of very small establishments, including 545 bakeries with 1,600 employees. Among the larger firms in this group are the eleven fish processing plants that together contribute over one-tenth of the value of production. The clothing industry ranks second in the number of establishments, third as a source of employment, but only ninth as a source of value added. Indeed, the average establishment engaged in the manufacture of apparel employs about three workers. The beverages industry, with only 24 establishments, is characterized by a relatively large average employment, investment, and value added per firm. Significantly, this industry includes the brewery and several modern bottling plants.

Data collected by the state's planning agency reveal that since the ninth industrial census there have been important advances in a number of Yucatan's manufacturing industries. Sales growth between 1970 and 1973 was particularly pronounced for the categories of cocoa, chocolate, and honey (330 percent), cement (283 percent), paper, board, and cellulose (126 percent), construction (111 percent), and repair of nonelectrical machinery (101 percent).[51] The rapid gain in sales volume of two related branches—cement and construction—is undoubtedly linked with the burgeoning tourist trade and public infrastructure investment in the peninsula.

Since the mid-1960s the federal government has been trying to reverse the high regional concentration of industry focused in the Federal District, the neighbor state of México, and the state of Nuevo León. In 1965, for example, 40 percent of the value added in manufacturing was accounted for by the Federal District, 16 percent by the state of México, and 10 percent by Nuevo León, which includes the city of Monterrey. These three places thus accounted for two-thirds of the value added in manufacturing and 55 percent of the sector's employment.[52]

The resulting official policy of industrial decentralization and regional development provided for a program of industrial cities under the direction of Nacional Financiera.[53] The first stage in the creation of an industrial city involves the acquisition of land and the creation of an infrastructure by the secretary of public works. As of December 31, 1977, the secretary had completed the initial construction of thirteen such cities, including the industrial city of Felipe Carrillo Puerto on the outskirts of Mérida.[54] This thirty-seven-hectare site is located about one mile from the international airport on the Mérida-Campeche highway. Of the industrial enterprises programmed for Carrillo Puerto, twenty-eight were in operation at the end of 1977. These firms represented a total investment of 312 million pesos and provided employment for 1,817.[55] An additional twenty-three enterprises representing a total investment of 56 million pesos were under construction or programmed.

Nacional Financiera created a Fund for Pre-Investment Studies in Yucatan under the chairmanship of former governor Carlos Loret de Mola and further deepened its involvement in the state by opening a branch in Mérida in January 1972. Since that time, Nacional Financiera has helped promote and finance numerous industrial enterprises in the state, including those located in Mérida's industrial city.

As the foregoing discussion indicates, about 85 percent of the 3,596 industrial establishments covered in the 1971 census had on average fewer than two employees. And these small firms accounted for 22 percent of Yucatan's labor force in manufacturing and mining. The value added by these household enterprises is much below factory output, but in terms of employment and as a way of life, the work of craftsmen and artisans continues to be a vital element of the Yucatecan economy.

The artisan tradition antedates the Spanish conquest of Yucatan. Thousands of individuals are still engaged in weaving, shoemaking, woodworking, sewing and embroidering, and pottery making—activities carried on by one or more members of the family in the household. Handicraft industries require little capital investment because their key resources are labor and local raw materials. They help increase income for people in rural areas, especially women and agricultural workers who are idle part of the year and who have no other employment opportunities. Craft industries, when efficiently organized, can open new external markets and generate foreign exchange earnings.

Unlike factory production, which is concentrated in the larger urban centers, household industries are scattered throughout the state in villages and small towns. The small town of Ticul, for example, specializes in pottery and women's shoes. The technology of pottery making, passed on from father to son, has changed little from pre-Hispanic times. Handmade men's shoes are produced in the village of Hunucmá, and objects of wood, such as kitchen utensils, in the village of Dzitya, near the north coast of Yucatan. This primitive woodworking industry uses locally grown trees, and all members of the family participate in elaborating the product.

In Mérida there are numerous artisans who make curiosities of henequen or cotton. Rugs, hats, hammocks, ladies' handbags, ornamental figures, and the like, using these raw materials, are frequently displayed in street markets

throughout the city. The embroideries of Yucatan are famous not only in the state
and nation, but also increasingly abroad. Home-centered embroidering is a
ubiquitous activity in the state. Indeed, it is often said that in Yucatan at least one
daughter of every family is engaged in embroidering, sewing, or weaving. Hand-
crafted products are marketed directly in open-air markets throughout the state or
are sold to middlemen. The traditional feast days and fairs offer excellent opportunities for moving large quantities of these handmade goods to the final consumer.

Yucatecan industry is thus characterized by a pronounced dualistic structure.[56]
Large-scale units, employing capital-intensive techniques, coexist with a traditional sector of small-scale household units using labor-intensive techniques.
This dualistic industrial pattern may reflect in part differential access by the
modern and traditional sectors to scarce economic resources such as credit,
public utilities, and government-sponsored technical assistance programs. To the
degree that large firms receive preferential access over the craft industries to such
resources, the allocation of the region's economic resources will be distorted.
Only by strengthening its organization and improving its efficiency will the
traditional craft sector be in a position to attract and use productively a greater
volume of financial and technical resources.

Cordemex: Nationalization of the Cordage Industry

The manufacture of henequen products in Yucatan predates the colonial
period. Mayan artisans using handicraft methods produced hammocks, fish nets,
coarse sacks, and ropes, and during the early national period Yucatan continued
to elaborate a large share of its henequen fiber into manufactured products,
mainly for export. As an example, in 1847, Yucatan exported 100,000 arrobas of
henequen in bales and about 85,000 arrobas in manufactured items.
Additionally, about 74,000 arrobas were absorbed by the national market.[57] With
the total commitment of the region's resources to a specialized henequen plantation economy after 1880, the production and export of henequen manufactures
virtually ceased.

It was not until the latter 1920s—with the convergence of propitious demand
and cost factors—that Yucatan initiated a modern cordage industry. By 1930,
local mills were absorbing 10 percent of the state's henequen fiber and producing
manufactured articles for the Mexican market. Increasingly, they were able to
compete against U.S. mills and eventually displaced U.S. production with cordage exports from Yucatan. Because of the industry's labor-intensive character,
Yucatan was able to develop a comparative advantage over the United States in
the manufacture of cordage products. Further, Yucatan's penetration of the
American market for ropes, harvest twine, and other henequen products was
reinforced by the peninsula's proximity to the United States and the absence of
U.S. tariff barriers against such products.[58] In the 1930s, the reaper was
gradually replaced by the combine harvester, which does not use binder twine,

and the demand for binder twine declined. Meanwhile, the rise in U.S. farm wage rates stimulated the introduction of automatic baling machines. With fuller utilization of American grasslands to support a growing cattle population, the use of baling machines expanded greatly, and with it, the demand for baler twine. After 1940, the demand for rope associated with U.S. naval operations could no longer be met by American mills, with the result that Yucatecan exports also satisfied an ever-growing share of the rope market. In 1944, rope made up 57 percent of the volume and 73 percent of the value of total henequen exports from Yucatan.[59] Cut off from other suppliers of hard fiber, the United States during World War II contracted to purchase Yucatan's henequen production through 1945 at prices well above the depression lows of the 1930s. On top of wartime profits, an added element served to stimulate the Yucatecan cordage industry: Henequeneros de Yucatán, the private association of mill owners, effectively subsidized the industry's expansion by selling to local mills raw fiber at less than the world market price. Given these favorable circumstances, the number of mills multiplied, and by the close of World War II, there were some ninety operating in and around Mérida.[60]

The special conditions favoring Yucatan's cordage industry during the war could not be sustained, and under the impact of lower prices, many of the smaller, less efficient mills became bankrupt or were merged with more efficient enterprises. In 1961, the federal government purchased 50 percent of the stock of the private cordage mills for 150 million pesos and retained the option to acquire the remaining shares within three years. The new semipublic entity was called Cordemex, and in 1964 the Mexican government exercised its option by purchasing remaining shares for 90 million pesos and assuming the 100-million-peso debt that the private mills had contracted with the Royal Bank of Canada.[61] Thus, with a total investment of about 340 million pesos ($27 million), the henequen manufacturing industry passed into the public sector. Significantly, the nationalization of the cordage industry was prompted by a mixture of political, social, and economic motives.[62]

With a labor force of over seventy-five hundred persons and sales of nearly 1,400 million pesos in the 1977 crop year, Cordemex has become the largest enterprise in Yucatan. The firm has sixteen manufacturing plants, eleven of which are located in the state of Yucatan. Although Cordemex has not invested in the growing of henequen directly, it has nevertheless integrated backward to the processing of henequen leaves. Thus, by 1977, the firm had invested in fourteen modern defibration plants and was building several additional plants. As a result of these investments, all of the defibration plants in Yucatan, including those of the *pequeñas propiedades* and the Banco Rural, are operating far below capacity. Cordemex's efforts to "modernize" the defibration phase of henequen production was therefore "an unwarranted spending spree leading to an over-capacity that anyone could have foreseen."[63]

On the outskirts of Mérida, Cordemex built its principal industrial complex, including luxurious air-conditioned offices, a resortlike house where important government visitors stay when they come to Yucatan, and a company town, "a middle-class enclave that contrasts to the rural simplicity of the homes of the peasants who produce the henequen."[64] Cordemex's principal administrators come from other parts of Mexico and change every six years with new presidential regimes.

By the early 1970s, Cordemex absorbed virtually all the henequen grown in Mexico, and its sales, both foreign and domestic, took shape as exclusively manufactured goods: rope, harvest twine, rough cloth, tapestries, packing materials, rugs, sacks, cushions, and the like. Benefiting from a protected national market, the company sells its products at higher prices in Mexico than abroad. Until the proliferation of independent cordage mills during the latter 1970s, the public enterprise approached the status of a monopsonist (single buyer) and monopolist (single seller) in the Mexican henequen market. In 1974, Cordemex was the nation's fifth most important export firm and ranked second in the export of manufactured products. During the 1970–76 period, Cordemex exported 63 percent of the value of its production and sold to the national market the remaining 37 percent. Of the 41,000 tons of henequen products exported in the 1976 crop year, 70 percent went to the United States, 13 percent to Canada, and 14 percent to Western Europe.[65]

Since its inception as a fully nationalized enterprise, Cordemex's operating philosophy has been marked by ambivalence: on the one hand, to rationalize the ailing cordage industry in the face of increasing international competition; on the other, to take on political-social functions. During the 1970s, at least, management has tilted in favor of the latter with predictable consequences. During the seven-year period from 1971 through 1977, Cordemex posted annual losses in all

Table 5. Cordemex: Production, Sales, and Profit or Loss, Crop Years, 1971–1977

Crop Years	Exports (tons)	Percent	Domestic (tons)	Percent	Total (tons)	Percent	Sales	Profit or loss* (millions of pesos)
71							296	(61)
72							386	(27)
73	78,617	66	40,605	34	119,222	100	487	(37)
74	82,478	65	45,071	35	127,549	100	829	132
75	63,486	66	32,254	34	95,740	100	1,235	118
76	40,819	54	34,976	46	75,786	100	826	(314)
77	73,585	64	42,205	36	115,790	100	1,385	(989)

Sources: "Cordemex, S.A. de C.V.," *El Mercado de Valores,* 35, no. 31 (August 4, 1975), 629. *Cordemex Informe Annual,* various years.
*Figures in parentheses indicate loss.

but two years, 1974 and 1975. As Table 5 shows, the firm's greatest operating loss was sustained in 1977, reaching a level of nearly one billion pesos, a magnitude equal to 70 percent of company sales that year. Part of that year's loss (308 million pesos) may be ascribed to foreign exchange losses stemming from the devaluation of the Mexican peso in tbe summer of 1976. The other components of the massive loss must be attributed to certain deep-seated operating policies of Cordemex's management. Among these are (1) maintenance of a redundant labor force and managerial-technical staff, including political favoritism in hiring practices; (2) granting excessive boosts in wages and fringe benefits; (3) paying an excessive price (well above competitive levels) for the firm's chief raw material—henequen; and (4) high interest payments, the result of a rising debt level associated with past losses.[66] It is interesting to note that Cordemex's labor force of 7,500 persons, as of March 1976, was nearly double the level six years earlier—an expansion that took place in the context of stagnation in the company's physical output. The average wage rate paid by Cordemex tripled between 1970 and 1976, and consequently the firm's wages and salaries were the highest in the Mexican textile industry.[67]

The close price relationship between henequen and synthetic fibers was again demonstrated following the OPEC cartel's successful effort in raising the price of internationally traded crude oil. The hydrocarbon-based synthetics experienced sharp increases in price reflecting the upward thrust of petroleum prices after October 1973. Consequently, the world demand for sisal, including henequen, surged as consumers substituted the lower-priced natural for the higher-priced synthetic fiber. The demand shift in favor of the natural fibers in turn forced a steep increase in their prices.

Responding to these dramatic changes in global demand, Cordemex raised its purchase price of henequen fiber, in pesos per kilo, on six occasions as shown below:

1965–June 1972	1.55
July 1972	2.00
May 1973	2.40
August 1973	2.90
January 1974	4.00
June 1974	6.00
November 1974	7.00

Beginning in July 1972, the price was raised from 1.55 pesos (the level maintained during the previous eight years) to a high of 7 pesos per kilo in November 1974—a near fivefold increase.

During the crop year ending March 31, 1975, Cordemex realized sales of 1,235 million pesos, a 49 percent gain over the previous year (see Table 5). The cost of sales reached 950 million pesos (a 74 percent jump over the previous year), reflecting both the much higher outlays for henequen fiber and a sharp 92.5 percent rise in the wages paid to Cordemex personnel.[68]

The syncronized world boom of 1973–74, which set record high prices for sisal and other raw commodities, gave way to the world recession of 1975–76. By the spring of 1976, quotations for East African sisal, for example, had fallen to one-half the levels prevailing in the fall of 1974. For Yucatan the deterioration of the world market for its Cordemex products signaled a new crisis. Would the government-controlled firm cut the price offered the henequen growers and reduce wages in its own plants in conformity with the new conditions? The answer, at least for the short run, was negative: the Mexican government would again subsidize the henequen sector.[69] During the 1976 crop year, Cordemex continued to purchase grade "A" henequen at 7 pesos per kilo at a time when the world price of the fiber had fallen substantially below that level. One company official voiced the opinion that it was "unthinkable to lower the price" to the ejidatarios and that Cordemex would absorb the loss.

The firm's physical sales volume fell markedly after the 1974 crop year (see Table 5). Total sales volume, including exports and sales in the Mexican market, declined from about 128,000 metric tons in 1974 to 96,000 tons in the following year and 76,000 tons in the 1976 crop year. The sharpest contractions took place in sales to foreign markets, which fell by more than one-half from 1974 to 1976.

Global output of sisal and henequen, the fibers most frequently used to make harvest twine, rose from 615,800 tons in 1956 to a high of 816,900 tons in 1964 and then declined to 527,000 tons in 1977.[70] This protracted decline in world demand was caused by the growing substitution of a new class of lower-cost synthetics for the natural fibers in the industrialized consuming countries. At present, synthetics compete with hard fibers in the fishing net, rope, and packing twine markets.[71] An estimated 115,000 tons of hard fiber were displaced by synthetics between 1966 and 1970. Fortunately for Yucatan, the market that was least affected by the competition from synthetic fibers was harvest twine—Cordemex's major export product.

Yucatan's position vis-à-vis other hard fiber producers has deteriorated since World War II, mainly as a consequence of the vigorous competition from the sisal-growing countries of Tanzania and Brazil and the low quality of henequen fiber. Since the latter 1950s, the other producing countries have made successful inroads into the U.S. market for harvest twine at the expense of Yucatan's share. Efforts by Cordemex to significantly penetrate European markets have proved unsuccessful because of the high tariff that protects the cordage industry in the Common Market countries and the high transportation costs. Mexico's share in world production of sisal and henequen declined from 37 percent in 1944 to 21 percent in 1976, and exports by weight accounted for only 15 percent of global hard fiber exports.[72]

Responding to a recovery in export markets, Cordemex's sales in the 1977 crop year (116,000 tons; 1,385 million pesos) expanded greatly, but as noted before, so did its operational loss. In the following year, however, production and sales volume fell, resuming what appears to be a long-term downward trend for the enterprise.

In his report to the Board of Directors, Federico Rioseco, director general of Cordemex, noted with alarm the very recent appearance of at least forty-nine private cordage mills in Mexico, fourteen of which are located in Yucatan.[73] With an estimated annual production capacity of 47,000 tons, these newly organized independent firms have absorbed fiber grown by the *pequeñas propiedades* and preempted an important share of the national market for henequen products. Significantly, in March 1978, the Yucatecan state government promulgated a new law authorizing the sale up to 30 percent of the fiber production of the *pequeñas propiedades* to the independent cordage mills. These mills, according to the director general, have caused Cordemex to operate at only 57 percent of capacity during 1977-78, and he urged the federal and state governments to "halt the proliferation of the pirate factories whose appearance is contrary to the objectives that justify the existence of Cordemex as a semiautonomous public enterprise."[74] He noted that three Cordemex plants in other parts of Mexico have had to be closed and several plants in Yucatan have had to suspend operations or reduce the number of shifts. Because of these operational adjustments, about a thousand Cordemex workers have been laid off or retired early.

Cordemex continued to lose money during the first quarter of 1978 (120 million pesos). In that period, the firm sold its products at an average price of 15 pesos per kilo (18.3 pesos in domestic markets and 13.9 pesos in export markets). Production costs, however, averaged 19.3 pesos per kilo—a loss of 4.3 pesos per kilo. As in previous years, Cordemex has continued to pay 7 pesos per kilo for class "A" fiber, which is substantially above the domestic price received by principal sisal-producing countries.

In the face of Cordemex's chronic loss record, the man on the street may well ask, "If the henequen manufacturing business is so bad, why do private mills proliferate?"[75] In a fictitious interview between a reporter and the manager of a "pirate" cordage mill (reminiscent of an Art Buchwald column), the manager pointed out that these small independent factories create employment, pay income and social security taxes, and earn a profit as well. "To what do you attribute your success?" asked the reporter. The manager responded: "We don't pay for useless ads on television; we have no air conditioning in our offices, nor luxurious quarters for visitors; and we seldom take business trips to Mexico City. In short, we know our business; we have lived with henequen since we were children."[76]

Tourism and Commercial Fishing

Tourism has become the most dynamic component of the Yucatecan economy in recent years. Next to the sale of henequen products, income from tourism services has become the most important regional export and source of foreign exchange. In 1977, an estimated 701,813 persons visited Yucatan and spent a total of 881 million pesos there. According to the secretary of tourism, these expenditures were allocated in the following ways: food, 29 percent; lodging, 25 percent; purchase of artisan products, 13.6 percent; and the remaining 32.4 percent was spent on transportation and other services.[77] The estimated 120 million pesos spent on local artisan products indicates that tourists have become an important market for Yucatan's household craft industries.

As Table 6 shows, the number of tourists visiting Yucatan increased from a negligible 32,000 in 1960 to over 700,000 in 1977. During the 1967–77 decade, the number of tourists increased three and a half fold and peso outlays seven and a half fold. From 1973 to 1977, nationals comprised 67 percent of all visitors to the state and foreigners 33 percent. Foreigners undoubtedly spent more than their numerical share would indicate; in the absence of data it is not unrealistic to assume that the foreign visitors generated at least half of Yucatan's income from tourism, or about 440 million pesos in 1977. The state's capacity to serve tourists has increased substantially, as Table 7 indicates. The number of hotels in operation expanded from 80 in 1972 to 120 in 1977, the number of quality restaurants from 62 to 138, the number of auto rental agencies more than doubled from 8 to 17, and autos for rent more than trebled from 171 to 575 during the period. Total accumulated investment in Yucatan's tourist facilities such as hotels, restaurants, auto rental agencies, taxis, and buses serving tourists exclusively was estimated at 450 million pesos ($36 million) in 1974.[78]

Table 6. Tourism in Yucatan: Number of Visitors and Their Expenditures 1960–1977

Year	Nationals	Foreigners	Total	Total Expenditures (pesos)
1960	8,422	23,361	31,783	19,069,800
1961	29,199	16,421	45,620	27,373,800
1962	76,977	20,465	97,442	58,465,200
1963	90,865	24,106	114,971	68,874,600
1964	92,347	25,548	117,895	70,137,000
1965	109,942	31,048	140,990	84,940,000
1966	130,975	41,282	172,257	103,204,200
1967	144,300	50,701	195,001	117,000,600
1968	146,429	78,847	225,276	135,165,600
1969	133,399	87,594	220,993	131,391,600
1970	159,600	125,400	285,000	171,000,000
1971	128,791	93,362	222,153	180,868,300
1972	226,377	131,693	358,070	286,306,400
1973	330,096	146,657	476,753	379,563,300
1974	382,321	172,518	554,839	442,902,700
1975	402,548	184,131	586,679	457,990,000
1976	436,664	200,724	637,388	703,176,900
1977	443,007	258,806	701,813	880,996,500

Source: Dirección General de Turismo del Gobierno del Estado, unpublished data.

Table 7.   Yucatan: Growth of Tourist Facilities, 1972–1977

Facility	1972	1973	1974	1975	1976	1977
Hotels	80	93	104	116	113	120
Rooms	2,493	2,815	3,099	3,406	3,615	3,970
Quality Restaurants	62	77	124	134	124	138
Tourist Agencies	22	30	30	34		37
Auto Rental Agencies	8	9	10	13		17
Autos for Rent	171		359	400	439	575

Source: Dirección General de Turismo del Gobierno del Estado.

Yucatan also benefits economically from the expanding tourist activity in the beach resorts of the neighboring state of Quintana Roo. The islands of Cozumel, Isla Mujeres and, most recently, Cancún attract service and construction workers from Yucatan, especially the eastern city of Valladolid. Also, to the extent that tourists bound for these beach resorts include a stop in Mérida in their travel plans, there will be a favorable impact on the city's hotels, restaurants, travel and auto rental agencies, and other facilities.

Cancún, the most ambitious tourist attraction in the region, is a fourteen-mile stretch of powdery coral beach located in the Caribbean Sea off the coast of Quintana Roo. The site possesses abundant natural resources, including broad beaches, fine white sand, clear waters, and an excellent year-round climate, as well as proximity to a number of Mayan archaeological sites. Cancún's airport can accommodate all types of aircraft and is located twelve miles southwest of the resort. Significantly, New York, Washington, and Miami are nearer by air to the island resort than they are to Puerto Rico, Jamaica, the Virgin Islands, and other Caribbean destinations, except the Bahamas.[79]

The development of Cancún was begun in 1971 under the auspices of the Mexican government's Fund for Tourism Development (FONATUR) with the help of an Inter-American Development Bank (IDB) loan for $21.5 million.[80] FONATUR's creation was part of a broader national policy to encourage regional development and to generate new sources of employment and foreign exchange. The Mexican government has invested more than $100 million, including the initial IDB loan, to turn the island into a planned beach resort that is designed to remain unspoiled and safe from overdevelopment. Private investment in Cancún exceeded $200 million in 1975, with Mexican capital accounting for 87 percent of the total.[81] In that year, the first of the resort's operation as an international tourism center, 100,000 tourists visited the site and spent a total of 130 million pesos (over $10 million).[82]

The first to benefit from the transformation of the island into a tourist center were the 130 local inhabitants, who until recently were barely making a living from small-scale fishing and subsistence farming. New jobs were created for them and for more than 23,000 new settlers, most of them from the state of Yucatan. Wages in Cancún City are high by regional standards. An estimated 40 percent of heads of households earn more than 8,000 pesos ($640) monthly, 57 percent receive incomes of between 2,000 and 8,000 pesos ($160–$640) per month, and only 4 percent receive the minimum wage.[83]

In May 1976, IDB announced the approval of a $20 million loan to help finance the second stage of Cancún's expansion.[84] Completion of Stage II of the $50 million development project will consolidate the infrastructure required to accommodate a growing tourist population up to 1980, when an estimated 4,200 hotel rooms will be available, and to provide the basic urban services for a stable population projected at 55,000 persons in 1980 who will service the hotels and live in Cancún City. Upon completion of the second stage, the resort will have a capacity to receive one million tourists annually.[85]

What explains the tremendous growth in Yucatan's "invisible" exports? To begin with, there are the monumental archaelogical sites of the Mayan civilization, the churches, plazas, and other remains of the Spanish colonial period, as well as the beach resorts. Second, tourism expenditures are highly sensitive to a rise in per capita income; hence, economic growth in the United States, Western Europe, and Mexico—the peninsula's major geographical sources of tourism receipts—has benefited Yucatan disproportionately. Also, the dramatic growth of the peninsula's tourism infrastructure, including transportation facilities, both internal and external, has contributed to the region's capacity to attract travelers. Beyond its locational advantage, Yucatan's international competitiveness has also been enhanced by the recent substantial devaluation and subsequent float of the Mexican peso. In a statistical study on the impact of devaluation and revaluation on tourism earnings, an International Monetary Fund (IMF) economist found good, if imperfect, evidence that tourist receipts are very sensitive to the price factor.[86] Following the devaluation of the peso in September 1976 (from 12.5 pesos to about 22 pesos per U.S. dollar), a vacation in Mexico suddenly became a bargain for foreign visitors. Finally, the promotional efforts by both the Mexican and state governments, as well as private tourist agencies, have helped market Yucatan's unique attractions to potential tourists.

Commercial fishing is becoming an increasingly important contributor to the Yucatecan economy, providing a livelihood directly or indirectly for an estimated 15,000 individuals, including some 4,800 fishermen.[87] Commercial fishing could hardly be considered an industry in 1950, for in that year the volume of catches barely exceeded one million kilograms with a total value of less than one million pesos. The limited catch and the absence of refrigeration and processing equipment, combined with primitive organizational and marketing know-how, precluded the possibility of exporting fish products to other parts of Mexico or abroad.

In 1977, the volume of fish catches reached 23,107,954 kilograms with a value exceeding 224 million pesos. Three species—halibut (108 million pesos), octopus (26 million pesos), and red snapper (23 million pesos)—accounted for over 70 percent of the value of fish caught in the state during that year. Of that volume, 13.6 million kilograms were landed in Progreso, 5.9 million kilograms in Celestún, the state's second largest fishing port, and the remainder were taken to such lesser ports as Dzilam Bravo, Sisal, San Felipe, and Río Lagartos.[88]

Yucatan's commercial fishing industry is organized into eighty-three private enterprises, fourteen cooperative fishing societies, two fishing ejidos, and a branch of Productos Pesqueros Mexicanos, a federal entity.[89] In 1977, 84 percent of the value of fish catches was derived from private enterprise and 16 percent from cooperatives. Yucatan's fishing fleet includes 839 boats of which 605 (72 percent) are small (one to five net tons) and therefore suitable only for coastal fishing, and the remaining 234 (28 percent) vary in size between five and sixty tons. A total of nineteen modern fish freezing plants operate in Yucatan, of which seven are located in Progreso, three each in Mérida, Celestún, and Yukalpetén, and one each in three small coastal towns. The industry is serviced by ten ice factories located at the leading fishing ports and in Mérida. There also exist twenty-one ovens for processing fish flour, twelve of which are located in Celestún and five in Progreso.

Federal investment in fishing infrastructure has been considerable in recent years. Most notably, the federal government completed the construction in 1971

The fishing dock at Puerto de Abrigo, Yukalpetén. (Photo by Joel Whitman)

of Puerto de Abrigo, Yukalpetén, a modern, sheltered harbor near Progreso. This facility has encouraged private investment in boats and additional processing equipment in the area. Capital for the construction of new vessels is mobilized in much the same way as in the United States (for example, the tuna fleets of southern California). Loans are extended by the processing plants to prospective boat owners, many of whom are captains, in exchange for extended fishing contracts for the sale of their catch.

The two largest processors in Progreso, Compañía Industrial del Golfo y Caribe and Congeladora de Progreso, market all of their fish in the United States. Three other private processors export between 40 and 50 percent of their output in frozen fillet packages, and Productos Pesqueros Mexicanos de Yucatán operates in much the same manner as its private competitors, except that it cans its fish and trucks it to Mexico City to be marketed through CONASUPO stores.[90]

The Diversification Quest: Summary and Conclusions

The "Golden Age" of Yucatan extended from about 1880 to World War I, when henequen prices, production, and exports reached historic peaks. This period of accelerated growth was based on the peninsula's total commitment to henequen exports, mainly to the United States. The supply factors that accounted for the rapid transformation of the regional economy included the growth of capital stock, major technical advances, the conversion of the traditional haciendas into modern plantations, and the expansion of the labor force. Throughout this period, Yucatan enjoyed an enviable market position—world monopoly in the export of the hard fiber. Two major demand factors—the invention of the McCormick twine-binding reaper and the rapid growth in world grain consumption—provided a continuing stimulus to the region's premier export industry. This development experience fitted the pattern that characterized other modern plantation economies in Middle America and the Antilles with one major exception: Yucatecans instead of foreigners owned and managed the agricultural estates, as well as the railways and most public utilities.

Following World War I, several factors conspired to reverse Yucatan's henequen-based prosperity. These included (1) the permanent loss of its monopoly position in hard fibers arising out of the entry of other lower-cost producers into the world sisal trade; (2) the agricultural reform of the latter 1930s, which, by radically altering the land-tenure pattern, lowered labor productivity in the henequen sector; and (3) the partial substitution of synthetic fibers for natural fibers after World War II that further reduced the world demand for sisal. Beginning with the agricultural reform of 1937, the federal government's role in Yucatan has been characterized by ambivalence. On the one hand, federal intervention in the henequen sector has reinforced the state's traditional monocrop pattern; on the other, Mexican policies and investments have helped launch the state on a new development path.

During Yucatan's golden age, the regional market was constrained by the small population, the concentration of wealth and income in the hands of the elite families, and the debt-peonage system. Toward the latter years of the nineteenth century, the export-based prosperity created "spillover" or backward linkage effects on the home market. Beginning in the mid-1860s, machine shops and foundries were organized to service the more complex steam-powered equipment. Initially, these shops were set up to repair defibration equipment and to manufacture replacement parts for rasping machines, sugar mill equipment, henequen presses, and steam engines. By the turn of the century, however, several of these machine shops had developed the capability to build rasping machines and henequen presses. Wagons, carts, and carriages were also manufactured locally, as were limited types of nondurable consumer goods. Forward linkage extending to the manufacture of henequen products was initiated in the 1920s, and today virtually all of Yucatan's henequen sales take shape as baler twine, rope, sacks, and other manufactures. The emergence of a full-blown cordage industry in Yucatan has increased significantly the value of its major export product and provided several thousands of additional industrial jobs.

The growing economic dynamism of Yucatan in the recent past is the consequence of export diversification, regional market expansion, and import-substitution, especially in nontraditional agriculture. As Table 8 shows, total agricultural sales in 1977 exceeded 2.4 billion pesos, of which crops contributed

Table 8.   Yucatan: Production of the Agricultural-Livestock Sector, 1977

	Millions of Pesos	Percent of Subtotal	Percent of Grand Total
Crops			
Henequen	510	53.2	21.0
Corn and Beans	240	25.0	9.9
Fruit	164	17.1	6.7
Vegetables	45	4.7	1.9
Subtotal	959	100.0	39.5
Livestock			
Cattle	520	35.3	21.4
Poultry and Eggs	387	26.3	15.9
Pork	287	19.5	11.8
Apiculture	220	14.9	9.0
Other	59	4.0	2.4
Subtotal	1,473	100.0	60.5
Grand Total	2,432	N/A	100.0

Sources: Gobierno del Estado de Yucatán, *Monografía de Yucatán 1978* (Mérida, 1978), and *Segundo Informe 1977-78* (Mérida, 1978).

about 40 percent and livestock production 60 percent. Significantly, gross income from henequen fiber contributed 53 percent of total crop sales but only 21 percent of the sales generated by Yucatan's combined agricultural-pastoral sector. Of total crop sales in 1977, corn and beans (two traditional crops) accounted for 25 percent, and fruit and vegetables (the nontraditional categories) contributed 22 percent. Sales by the cattle industry accounted for about 35 percent of total livestock sales and over 21 percent of the gross income of the agricultural-pastoral sector—a share that matched henequen fiber in importance. Poultry and eggs contributed over 26 percent to total livestock sales, pork, nearly 20 percent, and apiculture (beekeeping), 15 percent. Vegetables grown in Yucatan supplied less than half the requirements of the state's population in the mid-1960s; the balance had to be purchased from other parts of Mexico. Currently, the state, because of its greater agricultural production capabilities, is much less dependent upon imports of vegetables, corn, beans, and fruits.

Important, if not spectacular, changes have taken place in Yucatan since the publication of the 1956 industrial census. This census showed that in the mid-1950s henequen processing and food products constituted the major industrial branches. Other traditional industries were wood products, beer, matches, apparel, salt processing, and panama hats.[91] Yucatan's industrial profile in the mid-1970s reveals that during the past two decades growth and diversification have taken place. Coexisting with the traditional light and home-centered industries are modern, adequately capitalized firms producing nonalcoholic beverages, electronics equipment, paper and cellulose, chemicals, cement, machinery, and seafood products. The work of craftsmen and artisans continues to be a vital element of the regional economy. Household craft industries help increase income for people in rural areas, especially women and farm workers, who are idle part of the year and have no other employment opportunities. These industries require little capital investment because their key resources are labor and local raw materials.

The acceleration of industrial growth and diversification in the recent past is largely a response to regional market expansion. Among the factors that have shaped this expanded market are (1) population growth; (2) greatly improved regional infrastructure, including highways and roads, telecommunications, and electric power; (3) the emergence of an important middle class; and (4) the spectacular development of tourism during the past decade. The city of Mérida has become the commercial and industrial center for the entire peninsula, including the neighboring states of Quintana Roo and Campeche.

External markets, of course, constitute the other dynamic element in the state's economic advance. Yucatan's external sales (yielding income from abroad and other parts of Mexico) in 1977 were roughly as follows (in millions of pesos):

Cordemex (henequen products)		1,385
Foreign	752	
Domestic	633	
Tourism		881
Honey		220

Fishing	202
Cattle	173
Clothing	24
Salt	19

In sharp contrast to the situation two or three decades ago, Yucatan's current export profile reveals significant diversification among commodities and services and markets. The combined sales value of the categories other than henequen products (1,519 million pesos) exceeded the sales of Cordemex (1,385 million pesos) in 1977. In the latter 1970s, tourism income of the state—which includes expenditure by both Mexican and foreign visitors—exceeded the sales value of henequen fiber before its manufacture into products.

Thus, tourism, a new growth industry, has become, next to henequen products, the region's most important source of export-generated income. As we have noted, the state's capacity to serve tourists has increased remarkably since 1970, and the Yucatecans also benefit economically from the expanding tourist trade in the beach resorts located in Quintana Roo: Cancún, Cozumel, and Isla Mujeres. This new industry has expanded employment by generating long-term, service-intensive jobs and short-term, construction-intensive jobs. Tourist expenditures have also opened an important new market for Yucatan's traditional artisan and craft industries.

Federal intrusion in the henequen sector through the Banco Rural and Cordemex has been characterized by massive featherbedding, official corruption, and operational inefficiency. The result has been huge and growing losses to the Mexican government at every functional stage of henequen production: fiber growing, defibration, and manufacture into final products. These losses represent vast national subsidies to an industry in decline since the early 1960s. Responding perhaps to Mexico's revolutionary mystique, as well as to political expediency, the federal authorities have been "sending good money after bad." In short, the current administration of President José López Portillo will have to decide whether federal political-social objectives should continue to dominate economic-efficiency considerations in the management of Yucatan's premier export sector.

On the positive side, the Mexican government has made a major commitment to Yucatan's diversification drive as reflected both in policy initiatives and public investment projects:

Completion of the railway linkage between the state and central Mexico in 1950 and its conversion to standard gauge in 1957.

Completion of the highway linking Yucatan to other parts of the nation in 1961.

Promulgation in the mid-1960s of the federal government's policy of industrial decentralization and regional development and the resultant creation of an industrial city in Mérida.

Federal investments in the state's infrastructure, including farm-to-market roads, electric power, irrigation works, communications, and a sheltered commercial fishing port near Progreso.

Presence of Nacional Financiera, the federal government's comprehensive development bank, in Yucatan through the establishment of a regional office in Mérida in 1972.

Development of Cancún, a major international tourist resort in the neighboring state of Quintana Roo, under the auspices of the Mexican government's Fund for Tourism Development (FONATUR).

As the foregoing discussion indicates, the Mexican government has become deeply involved in the economic life of Yucatan, particularly since the mid-1960s. Per capita public investments in the state by the federal government (see Table 9) rose sharply from 1,209 pesos in 1959–64 to 3,390 pesos in 1965–70 and to a peak level of 5,440 during the five-year period 1971–75. By converting the last per capita figure into dollars ($435) and multiplying it by an estimated midpoint population of 800,000 for 1971–75 we derive a federal investment level of $348 million, or about $70 million on average per annum at the previous pegged peso-dollar exchange rate.

Over the long run, the viability of the federal government's role in the henequen sector needs to be reevaluated. Does the collectivized ejido system[92] serve the campesino's best interests? Would "privatization" of Cordemex better serve both Yucatan and the Mexican government, with the proceeds derived from its sale invested in the region's diversification programs? Can the paternalistic/dependency syndrome that has characterized the federal government's relationship with Yucatan be replaced by a mature relationship, including a more important economic role assumed by the state's political authorities?

The dynamics of the Yucatecan economy—its capacity to create new produc-

Table 9.   Per Capita Federal Public Investment in Yucatan, by Economic Category, 1959–64, 1965–70, and 1971–75 (pesos)

Category	1959–64	1965–70	1971–75
Industry	259	914	1,432
Social Infrastructure	600	565	1,325
Economic Infrastructure	219	879	1,789
Agriculture and Fishing	107	1,014	828
Administration and Defense	24	18	57
Total	1,209	3,390	5,440

Sources: Secretaría de la Presidencia, *Inversión Pública Federal, 1925–1963* (México, 1965), and *Inversión Pública Federal, 1965–1970* (México, 1970), and *Anexos a los Informes al Congreso de la Unión del Presidente de la República,* cited in Luis Miguel Ramos Boyoli and Charles Richter, "El Desarrollo Regional Mexicano: El Papel de la Inversión Pública Federal," *Comercio Exterior,* 26, No. 2 (February 1976), pp. 175–177, tables 1–3.

tive employment—is still insufficient to accommodate the state's rapid natural population growth. Clearly, both reduced human fertility and acceleration of regional output are key elements toward the achievement of a more prosperous Yucatan. To that end, serious consideration should be given to greater applied research into alternative uses of henequen and construction of a deep-water port near Progreso.[93] Further, an export-oriented industrialization strategy similar to Mexico's Border Industrialization Program might appropriately be designed to fit Yucatan's current situation. The peninsula shares with the country's nineteen-hundred-mile-long northern border zone a relatively abundant labor force and favorable location vis-à-vis the U.S. market. The success of such a labor-intensive industrialization program would hinge in part on the Mexican government's willingness to permit U.S.-based firms to invest in Yucatecan manufacturing and repair facilities and to remove the tariff on raw materials and components imported by the newly established export-oriented plants.

The 1976 decision to devalue and subsequently float the peso should strengthen Mexico's—and Yucatan's—competitive posture, providing the federal government is prepared to check domestic inflation. With the peso devaluation, Yucatan's exports—henequen and other manufactured products, processed honey, fruits and vegetables, processed fish, and tourist services—have suddenly become much less expensive in terms of dollars and other foreign currencies. Consequently, if Yucatan can make an effective supply response to this new situation, its foreign exchange earnings and regional income should be significantly stimulated.

ACKNOWLEDGMENTS

I wish to thank Ing. Manuel Mier y Terán, formerly director of planning of the State of Yucatan, and Jeffrey Brannon for their valuable observations and suggestions regarding this chapter. I am also indebted to The University of Alabama's Research Grants Committee for supporting this project.

NOTES

1. Dirección General de Estadística, *IX Censo General de Población 1970: Estado de Yucatán* (México, D.F.: Talleres Gráficos de la Nación, 1971), p. 397, table 24.

2. The large discrepancy between the 21,344 workers classified under manufacturing in the population census and the 25,424 manufacturing workers listed in the 1971 industrial census (see Table 4), probably reflects differences in classification criteria, such as the inclusion of repair workers under manufacturing in the industrial census.

3. Gobierno del Estado de Yucatán, *Monografía 1978* (Mérida, 1978), p. 102.

4. Federal Reserve Bank of Chicago, *International Letter,* No. 294 (October 1976).

5. Gobierno del Estado de Yucatán, Departamento de Industria y Comercio, *Monografía 1976* (Mérida, 1976), p. 52, table VII.

6. Loc cit.

7. "La Población de Yucatán Aumenta a un Ritmo Menor que la Nacional," *Diario de Yucatán,* May 26, 1976, p. 2.

8. Víctor M. Suárez Molina, *La Evolución Económica de Yucatán,* Vol. I (Mérida: La Universidad de Yucatán, 1977), pp. 153–54.

9. Thomas G. Sanders, *Henequen: The Structure of Agrarian Frustration,* American Universities Field Staff Report, North American Series, 5, No. 3 (Hanover, N.H., July 1977), p. 8.

10. Suárez Molina, *La Evolución Económica,* I, p. 51.

11. Roland E. Chardon, "Hacienda and Ejido in Yucatan: The Example of Santa Ana Cuca," *Annals of the Association of American Geographers,* Vol. 53, No. 2 (June 1963), p. 179, footnote 13.

12. *Cordemex Informe Anual,* March 1975.

13. Suárez Molina, *La Evolución Económica,* I, pp. 257–58.

14. Keith Hartman, "The Henequen Empire in Yucatan: 1870–1910," Dissertation, University of Iowa, 1966, pp. 45–46 and 78.

15. Quoted in ibid., p. 72.

16. Suárez Molina, *La Evolución Económica,* I, p. 357.

17. Allen Wells, "Economic Growth and Regional Disparity in Porfirian Yucatan: The Case of the Southeastern Railway Company," *South Eastern Latin Americanist,* 22, No. 2 (September 1978).

18. See Eric R. Wolf and Sidney W. Mintz, "Haciendas and Plantations in Middle America and the Antilles," *Social and Economic Studies,* 6, No. 3 (September 1957), and Arnold Strickon, "Hacienda and Plantation in Yucatan," *América Indígena,* 25 (January 1965).

19. Malcolm K. Shuman, "The Town Where Luck Fell: The Economics of Life in a Henequen Zone Pueblo," Dissertation, Tulane University, 1974, p. 25.

20. Nelson Reed, *The Caste War of Yucatan* (Stanford, Calif.: Stanford University Press, 1964), p. 231.

21. Manuel Pasos Peniche, *Historia de la Industria Henequenera desde 1945 hasta Nuestros Días* (Mérida, Yucatán: Editorial "Zamná," 1974), pp. 15–16.

22. Shuman, "The Town Where Luck Fell," p. 23.

23. David Franz, "Bullets and Bolshevists: A History of the Mexican Revolution and Reform in Yucatan, 1910–1924," Dissertation, The University of New Mexico, 1973, pp. 182–83.

24. Suárez Molina, *La Evolución Económica,* I, p. 162.

25. Ibid., p. 271.

26. "Talleres Mecánicos y de Fundación de Mérida en el Siglo XIX," *Diario de Yucatán,* March 13, 1977, p. 3.

27. Interview with Anna Rosa Caracashian, daughter of Don Carlos Caracashian, May 1977.

28. Suárez Molina, *La Evolución Económica,* I, pp. 329 and 339.

29. Reed, *Caste War,* p. 232.

30. Hartman, "The Henequen Empire," p. 119.

31. Ibid., p. 128.

32. Pasos Peniche, *Historia,* table covering the period 1901–73, pp. 53–54.

33. Shuman, "The Town Where Luck Fell," pp. 28 and 31–32.

34. Dirección de Fomento y Desarrollo, *Monografía del Estado de Yucatán 1978* (Mérida: Gobierno del Estado de Yucatán, 1978), pp. 4–5.

35. Chardon, "Hacienda and Ejido," p. 190.

36. Pasos Peniche, *Historia,* p. 66.

37. Sanders, *Henequen,* p. 7.

38. Francisco Luna Kan, *Segundo Informe* (Mérida: Ediciones del Gobierno del Estado, 1978), pp. 20–21.

39. "El Banrural Anuncia Vasta Depuración en la Zona Henequera," *Diario de Yucatán,* December 29, 1977, p. 1.

40. "La Depuración en el Banrural Peninsular," *Diario de Yucatán,* January 30, 1978, p. 1.

41. "El Ministro Merino Apoya las Medidas en la Zona Henequenera," *Diario de Yucatán,* January 12, 1978, p. 1.

42. Quoted in Shuman, "The Town Where Luck Fell," pp. 43–44.

43. Manuel Mier y Terán, "Desarrollo Agropecuario en Yucatán: Necesidad de una Planeación a Largo Plazo," *Monografía de Yucatán 1975,* Appendix 4, p. 21, table IV.

44. For an excellent discussion of the merits of the traditional campesino methods see Ignacio Argáez and Carlos Montañez, *Yucatán: Las Condiciones del Desarrollo de la Agricultura de Subsistencia* (Mérida: Escuela de Economía de la Universidad de Yucatán, 1978).

45. Franti Cardena Brito, *La Economía del Estado de Yucatán* (Mérida: Editorial del Departmento de Enseñanza de la Investigación de la Escuela de Economía de la Universidad de Yucatán, 1978).

46. Secretaría de Agricultura y Recursos Hidráulicos, *Yucatán en Cifras: 20 Años de Estadísticas Agropecuarias* (Mérida, 1978), n.p.

47. Luna Kan, *Segundo Informe,* p. 23.

48. Dirección General de Estadística, *IX Censo Industrial 1971,* Vol. II (México, D.F.: Secretaría de Industria y Comercio, 1973), pp. 65–66, table 3.

49. Ibid.

50. Dirección General de Planeación, *Monografía de Yucatán 1974* (Mérida, Yucatán: Gobierno del Estado de Yucatán, 1974), pp. 109–12.

51. Dirección General de Planeación, *Monografía de Yucatán 1975* (Mérida, Yucatán: Gobierno del Estado de Yucatán, 1975), pp. 62–63.

52. "Asemblea Anual de CONCAMIN," *El Mercado de Valores,* Vol. 27, No. 15 (April 10, 1967), pp. 315–16.

53. A total of twenty-one industrial cities and commercial parks will be established throughout the nation. See "Las Nuevas Ciudades Industriales," *El Mercado de Valores,* Vol. 35, No. 45 (November 10, 1975), pp. 917–19.

54. "Avance de las ciudades industriales," *El Mercado de Valores,* 38, No. 7 (February 13, 1978), p. 111.

55. Luna Kan, *Segundo Informe,* p. 83.

56. For an excellent discussion of "economic dualism" see Hla Myint, *Economic Theory and the Underdeveloped Countries* (London: Oxford University Press, 1971), Chapter 14, "Dualism and the Internal Integration of Underdeveloped Economies."

57. Moisés González Navarro, *Raza y Tierra: La Guerra de Castas y el Henequén* (México, D.F.: El Colegio de México, 1970), pp. 185–90.

58. Carlos Tappan de Arrigunada, "Trade, Development, and Structural Change: The Future of Mexico's Henequen Industry," Dissertation, Texas A and M University, 1971, p. 104.

59. Armour Research Foundation of Illinois Institute of Technology, *Technological Audit of Selected Mexican Industries with Industrial Research Recommendations* (Ann Arbor, Mich.: Edward Bros., 1946), p. 98.

60. Enrique Aznar Mendoza, "La Industria Henequenera desde 1919 hasta Nuestros Días," *Enciclopedia Yucatanense,* ed. Carlos A. Echanove Trujillo, Vol. 3 (México, D.F.: Edición Oficial, 1946), p. 774.

61. Antonio Rodríguez, *El Henequén: Una Planta Calumniada* (México, D.F.: Costa Amic, 1966), pp. 311-13 and 319.

62. Iván Menéndez, "El Estado y la Zona Henequera de Yucatán, 1970-1976," *Comercio Exterior,* 27, No. 12 (December 1977), p. 1511.

63. Sanders, *Henequen,* p. 9.

64. Ibid., p. 8.

65. Most of the data that support the remainder of this section are derived from the firm's annual reports, *Cordemex Informe Anual.*

66. *Cordemex Informe Anual 1977.*

67. *Cordemex Annual Report 1976.*

68. "Cordemex, S.A. de C.V.," *El Mercado de Valores,* Vol. 35, No. 31 (August 4, 1975), pp. 628-29.

69. President Echeverría indicated that the federal government would continue to support the industry as long as possible (*Diario del Sureste,* March 13, 1976, p. 1).

70. *Cordemex Annual Report 1977.*

71. Arrigunada, "Trade, Development, and Structural Change," p. 41.

72. FAO, statistics cited in Iván Menéndez, "Yucatán, la Doble Dependencia," *Comercio Exterior,* Vol. 28, No. 8 (August 1978), pp. 966 and 968, tables 5 and 6.

73. "Sesión del Consejo de Administración de Cordemex, S.A. de C.V.," *Diario de Yucatán,* May 20, 1978, p. 10.

74. Ibid.

75. Pedro R. Góngora Paz, "La Situación Económica de Cordemex," *Diario de Yucatán,* May 21, 1978, pp. 2 and 8.

76. "Defensa de la 'Piratería,'" *Diario de Yucatán,* May 22, 1978, p. 2.

77. Luna Kan, *Segundo Informe,* pp. 92-93.

78. *Monografía de Yucatán 1975,* p. 43.

79. *Christian Science Monitor,* September 16, 1975, p. 24.

80. *IDB News,* Vol. 2, No. 2 (January 1976).

81. Jerry Kirshenbaum, "No More Mañanas," *Sports Illustrated,* Vol. 42, No. 4 (January 27, 1975), p. 41.

82. *El Mercado de Valores,* Vol. 36, No. 24 (June 14, 1976), p. 459.

83. "Realizaciones del Fonatur," *El Mercado de Valores,* Vol. 36, No. 26 (June 28, 1976), p. 495.

84. Inter-American Development Bank, News Release, May 6, 1976.

85. "Desarrollo Socioeconómico del Sureste," *El Mercado de Valores,* Vol. 36, No. 14 (April 5, 1976), p. 259.

86. Andreas S. Gerakis, "Economic Man: The Tourist," *The Fund and Bank Review,* 3, No. 1 (March 1966), pp. 47-48.

87. For a good summary of the commercial fishing industry in Yucatan, including its many problems, see "La Pesca en Yucatán" and "Me Van a Cortar la Lengua," both in *Diario de Yucatán,* May 20, 1978, p. 4.

88. Luna Kan, *Segundo Informe,* Appendix.

89. Ibid.

90. CONASUPO (Compañía Nacional de Subsistencias Populares) sells basic food

products at below private retail prices to lower-income families through federally operated outlets in cities throughout Mexico.

91. Dirección General de Estadística, *Censo General de Población, 1960: Estado de Yucatán* (México, D.F.: Secretaría de Industria y Comercio, 1963), pp. viii–ix.

92. For extensive critiques of Yucatan's ejidal system see Roland P. Chardon, *Geographic Aspects of Plantation Agriculture in Yucatan* (Washington, D.C.: National Academy of Science, National Research Council, Pub. 876, 1961), and Jeff Brannon and Eric N. Baklanoff, "Mexican Regional Development: The Case of Yucatan," paper presented at the 1978 Meeting of the Southern Regional Science Association, Richmond, Va., April 13, 1978.

93. See Investigación, Formación de Empresas y Asesoría, S.C.P., *El Puerto de Altura y el Desarrollo Industrial de Yucatán* (Mérida, June 1977). This report argues that the benefits derived from a deep-water port near Mérida would greatly exceed its total cost. The current port at Progreso cannot accommodate vessels of over twelve feet draft. A deep-water port, on the other hand, would (1) open up fishing opportunities for Yucatecans in the Sound of Campeche (which is now being fished by Cubans, Russians, and Japanese) and (2) attract cruise ships with an average capacity of seven hundred passengers. Significant transportation savings could also be generated by bringing petroleum, steel, and other products and commodities to Yucatan in large vessels served by a deep-water port.

CHAPTER IX

THE RELATIONS OF
THE STATE OF YUCATAN
AND THE FEDERAL GOVERNMENT
OF MEXICO, 1823-1978

Marvin Alisky

Scholars attuned to Mexican public affairs traditionally characterize the Mexican government as a centralistic or unitary republic disguised as a federal one, run by a one-party political system.[1] A half century of economic development and social reform has urbanized and industrialized Mexico enough to force certain adjustments, prompting observers to qualify time-honored classifications, but many basic factors seem virtually unchanged.[2] From the 1820s to the 1970s, the state of Yucatan on numerous occasions has attempted to assert its politically independent posture from a strong centralized government in Mexico City. In recent years, presidential power at the apex of government has protruded into the state through the federal power to allocate funds and designate locations and conditions for carrying out national programs.

The dilemma relating to the exercise of centralized power within a system that is federal mainly in form creates a problem by no means unique to Mexico. Political scientists in recent years have brought into sharper focus the variations in federalism, such as the observations of William H. Riker: "This is an Age of Federalism. In 1964, well over half the land mass of the world was ruled by governments that with some justification, however slight, described themselves as federalisms."[3]

The current popularity of various degrees of federalism in constitutions of the newer nation-states of Asia and Africa, emerging from colonial status, reflects a search for a form of government able to accommodate diverse regions trying to mesh into a national sovereignty. North and South American federal constitutions of the last century reflect not only economic and cultural diversity but also military needs. A nation-state could confront other nation-states in trade rivalry with a larger army and more resources once a central government could rely upon its associated components for fiscal loyalty.

With the example of the United States, newly independent Mexico in 1823 tended to associate the federal form of government with individual liberty. Mexican federalists, however, failed to make the distinction that the North American colonies had been compelled to unite, whereas the Mexican provinces had been administratively centralized for three centuries. In colonial times, Mexico's chief executive was the viceroy of New Spain. The British North American colonies, by contrast, had no viceroy. At the time of independence, the thirteen North American colonies were entities in search of union.

Colonial experience had identified centralism with autocracy and despotism in the minds of many Mexican leaders.[4] The Constitution of 1824 created the Mexican republic in federal form. That of 1836 converted it to a unitary government, giving Texas its excuse to break away in the name of states' rights, and giving Yucatan further justification for its separatist tendencies. The Constitution of 1857 restored the federal form, and when it was being rewritten in 1917 in Querétaro during the Revolution, the basic ideals of federalism were once again expressed.

The Tenth Amendment to the United States Constitution proclaims, "The powers not delegated to the United States by the Constitution nor prohibited by it to the States, are reserved to the States or to the people." Although Mexico followed this model, the enumerated powers of the central government were much greater than those delegated to Congress in the United States. At Philadelphia in 1787, a bargain had to be reached that would satisfy regional pride and the needs of a new nation. In Mexico in 1824 and 1917, leaders did not have to worry about any established autonomy of individual states, for virtually none existed.

The Mexican system provides for certain variations within state legal systems. The fact that until 1971 the state of Chihuahua had a divorce law requiring no period of residence for foreigners gave the city of Ciudad Juárez a status similar to that of Reno, Nevada. Finalizing a divorce decree in Chihuahua has become more difficult, though most other Mexican states have more stringent divorce laws. In criminal law, until recently, twenty-three states did not have capital punishment whereas six did. By 1975, all of the thirty-one states had abolished or suspended the death penalty.[5] Obviously, only a modest variation in the basic laws of the Mexican states can be found. In the field of commerce, vital legal concepts ranging from labor codes to minimum wages are federal matters.

In the realm of taxation, the national government of Mexico reserves for itself the most important sources of public income. Taxing power theoretically is concurrent for the federal and state governments, but the federal Constitution gives exclusive power to the central government to tax foreign commerce, credit institutions, insurance companies, petroleum, and electric energy. Because important sources of revenue are the concern of the national rather than the state government, a system of "participation" or sharing of tax yields has developed. This often results in disguised subsidies handed back to the states on the basis of need. Of all government expenditures in Mexico in the past decade, the federal government has accounted for 80 percent, state and territorial governments, 11 percent, the Federal District surrounding Mexico City, 6 percent, and municipal governments, 3 percent of the total.[6] As economist John Evans has shown in a study of taxation, the federal government both collects and spends a large proportion of public funds.[7]

Taking into account variations in some civil and criminal laws among the states and in the apportionment of federal subsidies, we may assert that in form, the Mexican republic has "functional" federalism. In terms of the most important issues in public life, however, power is centralized in Mexico City.[8]

With regard to political parties, we also easily discern centralization. The dominant Partido Revolucionario Institucional (PRI) in recent decades has engendered widespread criticism by picking candidates for governors of the states and even mayors of major cities through the National Executive Committee of the party in Mexico City. In 1965, Carlos Madrazo, then head of the PRI, instituted a party primary in Baja California and in Chihuahua, sharply reducing discontent in those two states. He soon was ousted as party leader, and the inner circle selection of hinterland key officials grew even stronger. As a consequence, in the state of Sonora in 1967, riots broke out when the National Executive Committee of the PRI picked Faustino Félix Serna as its candidate for governor although sizable numbers of Sonorans favored Fausto Acosta Romo.[9] The conservative opposition Partido de Acción Nacional (PAN) took advantage of the engendered discontent within the ranks of the PRI to elect a *panista* mayor of Hermosillo, capital of the state of Sonora. In Baja California, too, similar discord within the PRI over the *dedazo* or finger-pointing selection from Mexico City prompted PRI members to defect and help elect one *panista* to the unicameral state legislature in 1968. From 1967 through 1969, the PAN won twenty municipal elections in the states of Chihuahua, Oaxaca, Nuevo León, Sonora, Baja California, and Michoacán. After 1970, the National Executive Committee of the PRI regained control of most municipalities and in Puebla, Guerrero, and Hidalgo defeated the organizations of regional PRI leaders who challenged Mexico City. The most spectacular example of a state publicly challenging the dominance of the federal government and its closely allied PRI, however, has been the state of Yucatan.

In the decades of this century before air travel, paved highways, and railroads, communications between Yucatan and the central region of the republic was not much improved over the flimsy links of the nineteenth century. From the Spanish conquest of the peninsula in the 1540s to the establishment of Mexican independence in the 1820s, the colonial government maintained scant communications between Mexico City and Mérida.[10] Independence from Spain engendered enough New World patriotism to motivate Yucatan to become part of the first Mexican republic, but regional pride remained strong, resulting in repeated nineteenth-century secessions. As early as 1829, the state of Yucatan launched a revolt against the central government in Mexico City, but the dissident *yucatecos* were soon pacified when the mercantile leadership in Mérida distributed bribes to obviate federal reprisals that would have followed a more prolonged struggle.

In 1836, General Antonio López de Santa Anna promulgated a centralistic Constitution in place of the federal Constitution of 1824. Mexico's resulting war with Texas caused the Mexican central government to encroach upon Yucatan's traditional fiscal status. The central government levied an *alcabala* or sales tax, increased its tariff rates, and conscripted Yucatecan men for the army fighting in Texas. The higher tariffs raised the cost of bread and basic food, and trade restrictions on maritime traffic at the port of Campeche further worsened the economy of Yucatan.[11] Resentment over these hardships prompted a revolt in May 1839 and another temporary secession. The leadership of Yucatan was divided as to policy. One faction, headed by Santiago Méndez, a prominent merchant who became governor, wished to remain out of the union until Mexico should return to federalism and restore to Yucatan its autonomy as a state instead of being merely a department within a centralistic republic. A rival group, led by Miguel Barbachano, favored complete independence.[12] Barbachano had moved from his native Campeche to Mérida in search of more local autonomy.

In May 1839, Santiago Imán, a captain in the state militia, began a revolt against the central power of Mexico City, launching his first attack at Tizimín in northeastern Yucatan. Though defeated, he regrouped his remaining rebel forces, began to arm the Indians as allies, and promised to end the special fees the church forced them to pay if they would fight under his banner. After his rebel mestizos and Indians captured Valladolid, the only important city in eastern Yucatan, thousands of Yucatecans joined their ranks. Mexican troops were driven from their last stronghold in the peninsula, the port city of Campeche, in June 1840. A little earlier, on February 8, Imán had proclaimed a provisional government for Yucatan. Until the Mexican republic returned to a federal system, the rebels proclaimed, Yucatan would remain independent.[13]

Now that the central government's troops were gone and the Yucatecans really did control their own peninsula, the rebel leadership could hold a full-scale election. Santiago Méndez, businessman and administrator, was chosen governor, and his former rival, Miguel Barbachano, was selected as vice-governor.[14] Also directly elected by the people were senators and deputies of a bicameral legislature. The few cities and large towns each elected a mayor. The state Constitution of April 6, 1825, was replaced by the new basic law of March 31, 1841. Even though the central government in Mexico City could no longer oppose such actions with troops on land, it did declare Yucatecan ships outside Mexican law and closed all mainland Mexican ports to them.

The *barbachanista* group controlled the lower house of the legislature, and on October 1, 1841, the deputies passed a resolution declaring Yucatan a republic, independent of the Mexican nation. Through the influence of Governor Méndez, however, the Senate tabled this declaration of independence.[15] Even though Yucatan retained a thin thread of legal linkage to Mexico, in everyday practice the state was conducting itself more like an independent country. Yucatan established its own trade relations with the Republic of Texas, and for a fee of $8,000 per month contracted for three Texas naval vessels to help guard the peninsula against invasion from mainland Mexico.[16]

Andrés Quintana Roo, agent of Santa Anna, came to Mérida to negotiate Yucatan's return to the national fold. The resulting treaty, signed December 28, 1841, recognized special Yucatecan rights. President Santa Anna, however, rejected the pact and sent an army to reconquer the state. Secessionist forces defeated these centralist troops in several battles and dictated a treaty of peace in December 1843. Soon the Mexican government violated the commercial provisions of this agreement—which emphasized trade relations—and again on January 1, 1846, the legislature in Mérida voted for secession.[17]

Yucatan proclaimed itself neutral in the war that erupted between Mexico and the United States in 1846. In December of that year, the Mérida government formally announced its reunion with Mexico, but then hastily explained to the commander of U.S. naval vessels blockading the western coastal waters of the peninsula that the state was still neutral in the war. The Mérida government sent José Rovira to Washington as a special envoy to gain U.S. recognition of Yucatan's neutrality. On February 1, 1847, Secretary of State James Buchanan received the emissary and promised not only to respect Yucatecan neutrality but to guarantee full trade between Campeche and U.S. ports.[18] Rovira then proposed that the United States consider the annexation of Yucatan as a state or territory. Buchanan replied that the U.S. Senate would never vote for such an annexation.[19]

Yucatan Governor Méndez next sent his son-in-law, Justo Sierra O'Reilly, to the United States to request that arms sales to the Mérida regime be permitted, for at the time the blockade prevented such shipments. On November 24, 1847, in Washington, Sierra O'Reilly sent a note to Buchanan petitioning an end to duties levied on Yucatecan vessels. On February 15, 1848, he met with the secretary of state and protested that Yucatan's neutrality was not yet being fully respected by U.S. vessels patrolling coastal waters near the peninsula.[20] Mexico's war with the United States was ending, but Mérida got its shipments of arms as a symbolic deterrent to mainland Mexico's postwar attempts to reconquer the peninsula.

During the course of their struggle against Mexican authorities, the leaders of Mérida armed the Mayan population. They also promised to reduce the burden of taxation on the Indian communities and provide other rewards and privileges. Yet once the Mexican threat had subsided, these pledges were quickly broken. In early 1847, the Maya rose against their white masters in the Caste War of Yucatan. At the height of this conflict, in the spring of 1848, Indian forces occupied most of the peninsula. The Yucatecan government could expect no assistance from Mexico in putting down the Mayan uprising, so Governor Méndez asked Secretary Buchanan for two thousand troops to subdue the Indians. On April 29, 1848, President James K. Polk asked the U.S. Congress to take measures to save the white residents of Yucatan from extinction and to prevent the peninsula "from becoming a colony of any European power."[21] Britain and Spain had each expressed an interest in the Caste War then raging between Indians and other Yucatecans. On May 17, 1848, the Senate and House committees considering bills based on President Polk's message dropped them when the press reported that a treaty had been concluded between the Indian and white leaders of Yucatan.

Within a short time, Indian attacks resumed, however, and in 1851, British agents in Belize supplied the Maya with new arms and ammunition. Exhausted after their struggle with the Indians, the Yucatecan leaders were ready to submit to the Mexican republic. They even acquiesced as the central government of Mexico City divided Campeche from Yucatan and established it as a separate state in 1858. Although the primary fighting in the Caste War ended by 1855, the rebel Mayan forces continued to hold out in the southeastern region of the peninsula for the rest of the nineteenth century, their political and religious center being the village of Chan Santa Cruz.[22]

Shortly after the defeat by the United States, central Mexico was shaken again by civil war. Supporters of the liberal Constitution of 1857 were pitted against the conservative forces of the church and the army. Benito Juárez emerged as the most outstanding leader of the Liberal party, and by the end of 1860 that faction had triumphed over the Conservatives. This, however, led to another period of foreign intervention and the establishment of an empire under Archduke Maximilian of Hapsburg, who was crowned in 1864. All of these events absorbed the energies of the central governments, both Liberal and Conservative, more than did Yucatecan affairs. Nevertheless, the peninsula was eventually drawn into the struggle. In 1863, Yucatecan militia in Campeche fought against Conservative and proempire elements. They abandoned the struggle, however, when French troops gained power in Mérida. In fact, the upper class in Mérida extended a warm and gala welcome to Empress Carlota during her visit there. The acceptance of the empire was, no doubt, related in part to the feeling of separatism by the Yucatecans.[23]

Following the withdrawal of French support, the government of Maximilian collapsed, and in 1867, Juárez had the hapless monarch executed, thus symbolizing the triumph of liberalism and Mexican nationalism. Not until the rule of Porfirio Díaz, however, beginning in 1876, did the nation find political stability and begin economic development. Díaz supporters took over all state offices in Yucatan as well as in the remainder of Mexico. Law and order were established by federal police, the *rurales,* and this enforced peace gave the peninsula superficial quiet. Based upon this political stability and the rising price of henequen, large landowners reaped huge profits in this era of "Green Gold." General Ignacio Bravo, a close friend of President Díaz, arrived in Yucatan in 1899 and in the following year initiated a campaign to crush the power of the rebel Maya. By May of 1901, he succeeded in occupying Chan Santa Cruz, at last bringing to an end the Caste War over half a century after its outbreak.[24] On November 24, 1902, President Díaz had the federal Congress officially create the Territory of Quintana Roo in the eastern portion of the peninsula, purportedly to isolate Indians in that area from the state of Yucatan. Both Congress and the president were anxious to bring about the pacification of a troubled region. In Yucatan, as well as in the rest of the nation, Díaz selected the governors, imposing a degree of nationhood from above to the age-old regionalism entwined in provincial culture. A number of Yucatecans charged that the real objective was close federal control over profits from chicle, salt, and henequen, but Díaz enjoyed the support of some of the most prominent members of the Mérida oligarchy.[25]

In February 1906, Díaz came to Mérida, the first president of Mexico to visit the peninsula. Special trains brought dozens of Mexico City officials along for the event, and gala celebrations were conducted. A brilliant torchlight procession was held, and the wealthy class took special lessons in social etiquette. A solemn mass was conducted in the cathedral in honor of the president's wife Carmen. Triumphal arches were built, and Yucatecan newspapers told of the solid loyalty of the state to the federal government, especially to the Díaz regime. But, of course, the Mexican press was then censored and guided by the dictatorship. Despite the weakened condition of the old soldier, the Mérida oligarchy seemed to accept his leadership in national affairs.[26] The Revolution that broke out in southern and central Mexico in November of 1910, however, was eventually to involve Yucatan.

In 1915, General Salvador Alvarado, acting for President Venustiano Carranza, codified a series of social reform laws for Yucatan.[27] These measures improved somewhat the working conditions of workers (peons) on plantations and haciendas throughout the state, although most of the campesinos continued to toil from sunrise to sunset on huge estates belonging to absentee landlords. Moreover, through manipulation of accounts at the hacienda store, some planters continued to charge their workers high prices for the bare necessities and thus maintained a disciplined labor force.

As late as 1957, more than 65 percent of the population of Yucatan was directly dependent on henequen and its processing and industrial by-products—ranging from rope to sacks—for its livelihood. In the 1920s, the percentage had been even higher.[28] Therefore, it came as no surprise that socialist ideals came to influence henequen workers.[29] During the Carranza administration, General Salvador Alvarado organized the Socialist party throughout Yucatan. Just as General Alvaro Obregón became president of Mexico in 1920, Yucatecan Felipe Carrillo Puerto utilized resistance leagues throughout his state to coordinate the political action for campesinos, the Socialist party, and various agrarian groups. These parties jointly persuaded the state legislature in May 1920 to select Gustavo C. Cuevas of the Liberal party as interim governor of Yucatan.[30] The former governor, Carlos Castro Morales, an agent of the federal regime in Mexico City, had resigned when he could not calm the militant workers' organizations. In the regularly scheduled popular election of 1920, Carrillo Puerto, with backing from President Obregón, easily won his campaign for governor of Yucatan.[31]

On November 14, 1923, Governor Carrillo Puerto telegraphed President Obregón pledging the support of various Yucatecan groups in the campaign of Plutarco Elías Calles for the presidency.[32] Adolfo de la Huerta, Obregón's minister of finance, let himself be persuaded to run against Calles in the 1924 election, and therefore De la Huerta had to break with Obregón, benefactor of Calles. Two trigger-happy generals who supported De la Huerta, Guadalupe Sánchez in Veracruz and Enrique Estrada in Jalisco, began insurrections against liberal reformers loyal to Obregón and Calles. It has been alleged that when aristocrats in Yucatan promised financial support to candidate De la Huerta, General Estrada promised to have an officer remove the troublesome Socialist reforming Governor Carrillo Puerto from Mérida. General Estrada's agent, Colonel Juan Ricárdez Broca, a tall and husky Tabascan with the disarming face of a child, arrested Governor Carrillo Puerto and, on the morning of January 3, 1924, killed him.[33] The basic system of land tenure remained virtually unchanged. In 1928, Calles absorbed the liberal reformers of the army, organized labor, and peasant farmers into one national political party, the Partido Nacional Revolucionario (PNR). Later to become the Partido Revolucionario Institucional (PRI), this organization has continued to dominate Mexico from its establishment until the present day. In the 1930s, the Revolutionary party eclipsed all other political groups in Yucatan as it did in the other states. During the 1934–40 administration of President Lázaro Cárdenas, aided by this organization, land reform and welfare policies again were implemented in Yucatan. Energized by the reforming zeal of the chief executive, and aided at the municipal level by committees of the party, reform policies were initiated in Mérida, Progreso, Valladolid, Tizimín, and throughout the region. Genuinely popular throughout Mexico as the institutionalizer of the Revolution, the president formulated land policies that even leaders in relatively remote localities felt obliged to support. The Socialist party, which had played such an important role during the era of Carrillo Puerto, was absorbed into the national political organization of Lázaro Cárdenas.[34]

As the Cárdenas administration went into the final third of its six-year term, federal government controls in agrarian matters became bureaucratized. During the period 1938–40, each of the ejidos in Yucatan had a commissioner, a guardian appointed by the minister of agriculture and not chosen by the peasants themselves. Unlike the ejidal officials of the 1934–37 period, these newer commissioners were not filled with missionary zeal, but rather seemed to seek the paths of least resistance. The Ejidal Credit Bank in Mérida told Yucatecan campesinos when they could bring their harvests to market and set selling prices.[35] Yucatan's longtime distrust of the central government again surfaced in political rallies, handbills, and letters to the editor of the state's newspaper.

In 1937, throughout Yucatan federal government officials had organized cooperatives for sisal workers, but by the time Mexico entered World War II as an ally of the United States against the Axis Powers, traditional aristocratic landholding families continued to play an important role in the economic system. During 1942–45, the needs of the Allies for all fiber and rope products from Yucatan brought about another economic boom in the henequen industry.[36]

During the administration of President Manuel Avila Camacho (1940–46), Minister of Internal Affairs (Gobernación) Miguel Alemán, a potential presidential candidate, took special care to see that federal officials in Yucatan did not exploit wartime exigencies under cover of the relative geographic remoteness from Mexico City. By combining appeals to patriotism with the lure of some kickbacks—controlled bribes held to the modest level of small "fees"—Alemán engendered another era of good relations between the federal government and the state of Yucatan, both during the Avila Camacho years and throughout his own term (1946–52). This mutual trust and harmony continued under President Adolfo Ruiz Cortines (1952–58). It was during this time that woman suffrage encouraged Yucatecan women to become involved in national as well as regional politics, broadening the base of public debates and campaigns in the state.

Augustín Franco Aguilar, governor of Yucatan from 1958 to 1964, indicated in his first annual report that the state's assertion of regional pride was again intensely visible.[37] Clemente López Trujillo, publisher-editor of *Diario del Sureste,* helped Secretary of State Mario Zavala Traconis and Executive Officer (Oficial Mayor) Omar Canto Catalán synthesize various grievances of producers and workers of the *economía henequenera* and transmit them in reports to the minister of agriculture in Mexico City. During the administration of President Adolfo López Mateos (1958–64), cabinet ministers were reluctant to invest substantial federal funds in Yucatan, where economically poor ejidos and small farming units could not be helped as readily as the larger farms and ranches in northern Mexico. In 1961, however, in order to further Yucatan's development, the federal government created Cordemex as an agency for buying and processing henequen fiber.

Ernesto Novelo Torres, governor of Yucatan from 1942 to 1946, had created the Yucatan Department of Economic Promotion and Agriculture.[38] A relative of his, Luis Torres Mesías, took office as governor on February 1, 1964. In his inaugural address, Torres Mesías declared that the Department of Economic Promotion helped to assure that the economy of the state would continue to parallel the national prosperity of Mexico. Yet during September 1966, before his term was half over, Governor Torres Mesías found himself in the middle of riots by henequen workers, arguments between the Ministry of Agriculture and the Banco Agrario de Yucatán (BAY),[39] and pressures between federal authorities and the economic elite of his own state. On September 19, a group of henequen workers brushed past police and walked into the office of the governor after having been told he could not see them. They wanted to know what formula was being used for distribution of subsidies and approval of loans through the BAY. Minister of Agriculture Juan Gil Preciado had provided subsidies to the cooperative association of henequen workers of the town of Maxcanú but not to similar henequen ejidos between Mérida and the coast. The governor explained that the Maxcanú fibers were of top quality and therefore came under the federal law for subsidies for fiber good enough for export, whereas some other ejidos were still producing second-grade fiber.

The delegation of protesters quietly withdrew from the governor's office, but within an hour almost two hundred campesinos had ripped up lamp posts, traffic lights, and signs on public buildings in the heart of Mérida. The commander of the 32d Military Zone of the republic, upon request of Torres Mesías, poured troops into Mérida after the local police apparently could not disperse angry henequen workers.

The next day in Mexico City, Francisco Hernández y Hernández, director of the Ejidal Credit Bank, called a press conference to assert that his bank was immediately making available to the Banco Agrario de Yucatán contingency funds so that the BAY in turn could make emergency loans to henequen ejidos.[40] The governor had weathered his worst crisis, and federal-state relations again were somewhat ameliorated. It was within this context of social and economic tension, however, that the conservative opposition felt that the Partido de Acción Nacional (PAN) could successfully challenge the PRI at the municipal level.

On November 26, 1967, the state of Yucatan held elections in each of its 105 municipalities (*municipios*).[41] PAN won the contest for mayor of Mérida, whose metropolitan population by then exceeded two hundred thousand. The *panista* candidate, Víctor Manuel Correa Rachó, received 44,354 votes to 15,446 for PRI candidate Nicolás López Rivas, who had been secretary general, second highest official in state government. Three years before, Correa had run as the PAN candidate for the same post and had received only one-third of the ballots cast. In dramatic contrast, he won the election of 1967 by defeating the PRI candidate three to one. In addition, the PAN won a seat on the Mérida Municipal

Seat of the municipal government of Mérida, west side of main plaza. (Photo by Edward Terry)

Council for Eduardo Trueba Barrera and the mayor's race in the municipality of Acanceh.

Yucatan that same November 26 also held elections for deputies for its nine-member unicameral state legislature. Two PAN candidates, Mauro León Herrera and Julio Moreno Cabrera, won seats, giving Yucatan the first two-party state legislature in Mexico in the twentieth century.[42] One of these *panistas* defeated his PRI opponent 12,374 votes to 3,610, and the second PAN candidate's margin of victory was almost as large. All thirty-one state legislatures in Mexico are unicameral bodies whose chief power is approving or changing municipal budgets. In statewide matters, the legislatures follow the lead of the governors. Yet the presence of *panistas* in the Yucatan legislature symbolized both to the governor and to the federal administration in Mexico City the intensity of Yucatan's regional spirit and longtime striving for a degree of independence from the central government. This division seemed to take on serious proportions when in January of 1968 a separatist movement known as Movimiento Autonomista Yucateco Asociado (MAYA) was organized in Yucatan.[43] Attempts by the new organization to associate with the PAN, however, were strongly rebuffed by that party's leaders both in Mérida and in Mexico City. Consequently, within a few weeks the MAYA movement began to fade. Governor Torres Mesías announced that during 1968 the federal government would invest 500 million pesos ($40 million at that time) in Yucatan to promote cattle raising, construct fishing port facilities, and grant subsidies to the henequen industry. Despite these efforts, federal-state relations continued to worsen. In February and March, henequen ejidatarios came into Mérida to protest that lower world fiber prices had reduced their wages by 10 to 15 percent.[44] Former hacendados and independent proprie-tors (*pequeños propietarios*) did not join the henequen workers' protest because beans, corn, squash, and meat production had increased in volume and value over the previous year.[45] Consequently, conflict within the state tended to focus on political debates over policies between the *priísta* governor and the *panista* mayor, and state legislators of the two parties.

In March 1968, Governor Torres Mesías told his seven-member PRI majority in the state legislature to reject a petition from Mayor Correa and the two *panista* legislators for a credit from the Financiera Peninsular Savings and Loan Com-pany. The funds would have permitted Mérida to complete seven projects, but legislative rejection of the credit request suspended these municipal public works. Federal government officials backed the position of the governor and the legisla-ture's PRI majority, further encouraging Yucatecan dissidents to continue criti-cism of the national administration.

In September 1968, *panista* Municipal Councilman Eduardo Trueba Barrera broke with Mérida Mayor Correa, accusing him of mishandling municipal funds. Correa countercharged that Trueba Barrera was now working with Governor Torres Mesías to discredit the PAN in Yucatan and, therefore, Trueba was no longer a bona fide member of the Mérida Municipal Council.[46] The state legisla-ture promptly voted that the Trueba ouster was illegal and called for his immediate reinstatement. The speaker of the Yucatan legislature, Raúl Carguera Gómez, declared on February 7, 1969, that if Mayor Correa did not permit Councilman Trueba to resume his seat by March 1, the legislature would dissolve the Mérida Municipal Council and declare the mayor's office vacant. Shortly afterward, the Federal Court of Appeals of the Seventh District in Veracruz ruled that there were no legal grounds for the ouster of Trueba.[47] This decision did not soothe the feelings of many Yucatecans who had long been suspicious of federal power. The quarrel between Correa and Trueba diminished *panista* numbers slightly, inasmuch as Trueba had some personal following which again cooperated with the PRI.

One development in January 1969, however, had encouraged optimism among all political factions in Yucatan about the state's economy. Miguel Olea Enríquez, director general of Cordemex, was elected president of the Board of Directors of the International Sisal Institute of Zurich, Switzerland, which represented the twenty-two major henequen fiber producing nations of the world. With Olea heading the Institute's board, leaders in Yucatan believed that Mexico would be able to exert direct leverage on major henequen processors to keep world prices at a level profitable to Yucatecan growers.

As the campaign for the governorship of Yucatan gained momentum in the summer of 1969, political violence erupted. On July 20, PAN and PRI supporters traded blows in the town of Tekax, and state police arrested three PAN state committeemen. The PAN demanded that the governor arrest the PRI state committeemen, who had prevented people from attending the Tekax rally by placing uprooted trees across the main road. These demands were ignored.[48]

More than 400,000 Yucatecans were registered to vote in the November 1969 election. The PAN candidate for governor was Víctor Correa, who gave up his post as mayor of Mérida to campaign. The PRI candidate was Carlos Loret de Mola, an attorney who resigned as federal senator from Yucatan to seek the office. Despite the fact that both Loret de Mola and Correa spoke to voters in almost all of the 105 municipalities of Yucatan, little more than half of the registered voters—52 percent—actually turned out at the polls on November 23. According to the official report, Loret de Mola won with 203,163 votes to 55,921 for Correa. *Panistas* immediately charged that this was a fraudulent vote count, pointing out that the official figures almost matched the preelection forecast of the National Executive Committee of PRI that its candidate would win 80 percent of the votes and the PAN challenger 20 percent. Fernando Pedraza Medina, the candidate of the Popular Socialist party (PPS), was ignored in news reports of the tabulations, his vote total being only a tiny fraction of that of the major candidates.[49]

Loret de Mola had campaigned so vigorously throughout the state that on December 12, while celebrating his victory, he collapsed from physical exhaustion and was forced to take a complete rest. Consequently, the Federal Electoral Commission announced that inasmuch as a key witness in its investigation of the election irregularity charges, Loret de Mola, was hospitalized, and inasmuch as

State Government Building in Mérida on north side of the main plaza. Constructed on the site of the Spanish colonial capitol, this structure was first occupied in 1892. (Photo by Edward Terry)

no valid evidence had been presented to the commission by the PAN, the inquiry would end.[50] *Panistas* had charged that four ballot boxes in their party's strongest neighborhoods had disappeared and that they could not obtain any police reports on these disappearances. The PAN further charged that 1,100 invalid or blank ballots were added to the PRI total and no correction was ever made even though the PRI spokesman had admitted that a clerical error existed. The persons making these charges never testified before the Federal Electoral Commission in Mexico City during its December investigation but gave statements solely to press reporters.[51] The official canvass of votes which the commission issued to the PAN had recount tabulations by state legislative districts and judicial districts rather than by individual polling stations as permitted by the electoral law of Yucatan. During the following year, *panistas* continued to condemn vote count irregularities that had occurred in the gubernatorial election.

In December 1969, Miguel Olea of Cordemex sent a message of good wishes to PRI presidential candidate Luis Echeverría in the name of henequen workers and producers. It was countersigned by the revolutionary party's National Executive Committee delegate in Yucatan. This action clearly demonstrated a close relationship in political matters among the federal government, the dominant party, and the government's chief policy maker for the henequen industry. PRI spokesmen insisted that relations between the federal government and Yucatan had never been better. Allocation of federal funds, in Yucatan as among other underfinanced states, reaffirmed presidential power. Governor Loret de Mola illustrated this clearly in his candid *Confesiones de un Gobernador,* published in 1978. He pointed out that President Echeverría devised a Promotion Committee for the Socioeconomic Development of Yucatan on May 30, 1971, and named as its coordinator Gustavo Martínez Cabañas. This administrator was to carry out the president's wishes in detail even if regional leaders had other ideas about their own needs. In fact, Martínez Cabañas knew Yucatan principally from geography book maps, never having had field experience in the state before his appointment.[52] As Echeverría's plan for the southeast unfolded, it became clear that the Development Committee in Mérida would be forced into rubberstamping decisions from Mexico City. Often political expediency outweighed economic and technical considerations.[53]

The Yucatan Legislature redistricted the state from 105 to 106 municipalities in time for the November 22, 1970, election, in which the PRI defeated the PAN for all seats in the municipal councils and the state legislature. Víctor Cervera Pacheco of the PRI won a three-year term as mayor of Mérida and in 1973 was elected deputy to the federal Congress.[54] In the November 25, 1973, municipal and state legislative elections, PRI candidates defeated all PAN candidates by the same four-to-one margin that had prevailed in 1970. The *panista* challenge to the dominant party at the polls in Yucatan seemed to end in failure.

Regional pride in standing up to the federal government in Mexico City remained strongly in evidence. Yucatecans at the National Assembly of the PRI in October 1972 helped the party adopt new rules to allow lists of tentative nominees for each state office although these measures were never put into practice.[55] In the following month, violence broke out in the town of Tizimín, reflecting peasant discontent over inflation, underemployment, and what was considered to be political cynicism on the part of the PRI. Inasmuch as a majority of these political activists were members of the PAN, that party's deputies in Congress that November aired a full debate on discontent in Yucatan. To refute the charge that national leaders were not enough concerned with Yucatecan problems, high officials of the PRI and of the federal government decided to visit Mérida on the eve of the 1973 elections for Congress. On June 20, party president Jesús Reyes Heroles and the entire National Executive Committee of the PRI met in Mérida with Governor Loret de Mola, Yucatan's two federal senators, Víctor Manzanilla Shaffer and Francisco Luna Kan, and a large cross-section of government and civic leaders, hoping to encourage state-national rapport.

On July 1, 1973, Mexican voters elected 189 PRI deputies in the republic's 194 congressional districts and only five opposition federal deputies. In Yucatan, the PRI won all federal deputy seats, the PAN drawing only 14.7 percent of the total vote, with less than one-third of the registered voters casting ballots.[56] In January of the following year, the senior cabinet official of President Echeverría, Minister of Gobernación Mario Moya Palencia, spoke in Mérida on the fiftieth anniversary of the death of Governor Carrillo Puerto. He used the occasion to plead for Yucatecan support of the federal government in return for assistance from the Echeverría administration for Yucatecan regional development.[57]

In 1975, part of the state's economic growth could be measured in terms of increased tourists. As early as June 1970, the Fund for the Promotion of Tourism Infrastructure (known in Spanish by the abbreviation Infratur) officially chose Cancún, north of Cozumel, as the site for Mexico's big resort of the future. It was estimated that by 1981 Cancún would have enough high-rise hotels and luxury-class restaurants to accommodate more visitors than Acapulco. Technically, the island is part of Quintana Roo, the recent territory that is now the thirty-first state, but many of the key operations in that resort involve Mérida. With the first group of Cancún facilities operating in 1975, the Yucatecan Tourism Department reported a 10 percent increase in volume over the previous year. The visit of Queen Elizabeth of Great Britain in February further focused worldwide attention on the peninsula as a tourist attraction. Even though the Infratur director had announced that the Cancún site was selected by feeding extensive data on all potential Mexican resort areas into a computer, the National Executive Committee of the PRI asserted periodically that the federal government chose Cancún to advance Yucatecan development.[58] Mexican officials promised a ferryboat service linking the port of Progreso with Miami, Florida, by the end of the 1970s, thereby hoping to encourage a favorable reaction among Yucatan leaders.

The PRI candidate for governor in the November 23, 1975, election was Dr. Francisco Luna Kan, an incumbent senator from Yucatan and a former federal deputy. A graduate of the National Polytechnic Institute Medical School, he was a leader of the Yucatecan League of Agrarian Communities.[59] On September 7, the state conference of the PAN had decided not to run candidates for governor, the state legislature, and municipal councils. They cited lack of guarantees from the federal government and the PRI for impartial vote tabulations and assurances that there would be no illegal obstacles during the campaign. Luna Kan was thereby assured of automatic election as governor.[60] He took office on February 1, 1976, his term to extend through January 31, 1982. Prior to the PRI victory, Yucatan electoral law had been amended so that up to three minority-party seats could be added to the state legislature should the PAN not be able to capture a regular district legislative position. But the opposition party's decision not to participate in the 1975 elections moved into the future any possibility of its gaining seats on the basis of percentages of the total vote.

On October 24, 1978, the Federal Electoral Commission promulgated new regulations giving four hours of free radio and television time per month to all political parties. Yucatecan leaders found, however, that the new opportunities for broadcast discussions were limited to national party platforms, leaving separatist state and local issues off the air as they had been since 1930.[61] Even with energetic local stations, Mérida could not exert an electronic regional critique that could challenge Mexico City ideas effectively. Thus the government of

Yucatan remained firmly under the control of the national revolutionary party. In spite of the many previous attempts to assert its regional independence,[62] the state of Yucatan in the late 1970s seems preoccupied with carrying out federal programs involving its own regional economic development.

NOTES

1. Julio A. Fernández, *Political Administration in Mexico* (Boulder: Bureau of Governmental Research and Service, University of Colorado, 1969), pp. 42–43; J. Lloyd Mecham, "Mexican Federalism—Fact or Fiction?" *Annals of the American Academy of Political and Social Science,* Vol. 208 (March 1940), pp. 23–38; William S. Stokes, *The Centralized Federal Republics of Latin America* (Claremont, Calif.: Institute for Studies in Federalism, Claremont College, 1965), pp. 94–95.

·2. James W. Wilkie, *The Mexican Revolution: Federal Expenditure and Social Change since 1910* (Berkeley: University of California Press, 1967), pp. xx–xxix, 199–203.

3. William H. Riker, *Federalism—Origin, Operation, Significance* (Boston: Little, Brown and Company, 1964), p. 1.

4. Nettie Lee Benson, *La diputación provincial y el federalismo mexicano* (México, D.F.: Colegio de México, 1955); Howard F. Cline, *Mexico: Revolution to Evolution: 1940–1960* (New York: Oxford University Press, 1963), p. 18.

5. Alfonso Quiroz Caurón, *La Pena de Muerte en México* (México, D.F.: Ediciones Botas, 1962), pp. 16–28; "Mexico: No Death Penalty," *Latin American Digest* (Arizona State University), September 1968, pp. 1–2; *El Imparcial* (newspaper in Hermosillo, Sonora), March 3, 1975.

6. Leonard Cárdenas, *The Municipality in Northern Mexico* (El Paso: Texas Western Press UTEP, 1963), Monograph 1, pp. 18–37; "Fiscal Code and Taxes," *The News* (Mexico City), November 10, 1974, p. 32; Wilkie, *Mexican Revolution,* p. 3.

7. John S. Evans, Jr., "The Evolution of the Mexican Tax System, with Special Reference to Developments since 1956," Dissertation, The University of Wisconsin, 1971, pp. 224–225. The federal government has dominated both excise taxation and sales taxation.

8. Paul L. Yates, *El Desarrollo Regional de México* (México, D.F.: Banco de México, 1961), pp. 2–27; Lucio Mendieta y Núñez, *La Administración Pública en México* (México, D.F.: Imprenta Universitaria, UNAM: 1942), pp. 7–14; Martin C. Needler, "The Political Development of Mexico," *American Political Science Review,* Vol. 55 (June 1961), pp. 308–312.

9. "Mexico: Sonora's Political Unrest," *Latin American Digest,* May 1967, pp. 1–2; *El Imparcial,* May 22 and June 11, 1967. For the 1961 pressures in selecting a governor in Sonora, see Marvin Alisky, *Governors of Mexico* (El Paso: Texas Western Press UTEP, 1965), Monograph 12, pp. 18–19.

10. Eligio Ancona, *Historia de Yucatán* (Mérida: Editorial Ancona, 1917), III, 199–206.

11. Mary W. Williams, "Secessionist Diplomacy of Yucatan," *Hispanic American Historical Review,* Vol. 9 (May 1929), pp. 132–133.

12. Justo Sierra, *The Political Evolution of the Mexican People,* Charles Ramsdell, trans. from 1st ed. 1902 (Austin: University of Texas Press, 1969), pp. 228–229.

13. John L. Stephens, *Incidents of Travel in Yucatan* (New York, 1843), I, 80–83; Albino Acereto, *Evolución Histórica de las Relaciones Políticas entre México y Yucatán* (México: Imprenta Muller, 1907), pp. 100–122.

14. Nelson Reed, *The Caste War of Yucatan* (Stanford, Calif.: Stanford University Press, 1964), pp. 27–28.

15. Ancona, *Historia,* III, 286–287.

16. George P. Garrison, ed., *Diplomatic Correspondence of the Republic of Texas* (Austin, Texas: American Historical Association, 1908), II, 37–38.

17. Sierra, *Political Evolution,* p. 230; Williams, "Secessionist Diplomacy," p. 134.

18. James Buchanan, *Works* (Philadelphia, 1890), VII, 222–224; "Secretary General of Provisional Government of Yucatan to Secretary of State of the United States, December 28, 1846," *Department of State* (Washington, D.C.), Vol. II, Report 1.

19. Trist Papers of 1847, Box 23, Manuscript Division of the Library of Congress, Washington, D.C.

20. Justo Sierra O'Reilly, *Diario de Nuestro Viaje a los Estados Unidos* (México, D.F.: José Porrúa e Hijos, 1938), reprint of *Obras de Justo Sierra O'Reilly,* pp. 96–97.

21. James D. Richardson, ed., *Messages and Papers of the Presidents* (Washington, D.C.: U.S. Government Printing Office, 1899), IV, 581–583.

22. Reed, *Caste War,* pp. 185–228; Sierra, *Political Evolution,* p. 253.

23. Eduardo Urzáiz R., *Del Imperio a la Revolución* (Mérida, 1946), pp. 32–42.

24. Reed, *Caste War,* pp. 229–292; Urzáiz, *Del Imperio,* pp. 97–153.

25. Reed, *Caste War,* p. 243; Bernardino Mena Brito, *Reestructuración Histórica de Yucatán, 1856–1913* (México, D.F.: Editores Mexicanos Unidos, 1967), II, 260–261.

26. Ernest Gruening, *Mexico and Its Heritage* (New York: Century Company, 1928), p. 664; Uráiz, *Del Imperio,* pp. 154–164.

27. Víctor Alba, *The Mexicans* (New York: Frederick A. Praeger, 1967), p. 134.

28. *Diario Oficial* (Gobernación, México, D.F.), January 30, 1957, p. 9; *Gobierno del Estado de Yucatán* (Secretario General, Mérida), January 23, 1957, p. 962.

29. Alba, *Mexicans,* p. 151; Shirley Deshon Carré, "Women's Position on a Yucatan Henequen Hacienda," Dissertation, Yale University, 1959, p. 253. See Chapter VI of this volume.

30. "Decreto del XXVI Congreso Constitucional del Estado de Yucatán," *Revista de Yucatán,* May 13, 1920, p. 1.

31. Bernardino Mena Brito, *Bolshevismo y Democracia en México* (México, D.F.: Mena Brito, 1933), p. 253; Alba, *Mexicans,* p. 152.

32. Alfonso Taracena, "La Muerte de Carrillo Puerto," *Iniciativa: Tribuna de México,* December 27, 1969, p. 4; Manuel González Ramírez, "Apéndice," en Alvaro Obregón, *Ocho Mil Kilómetros en Campaña* (México, D.F.: Fondo de Cultura Económica, 1959), pp. 521–525.

33. Associated Press dispatch from Mexico City, January 10, 1924.

34. Austin F. MacDonald, *Latin American Politics and Government,* 2d ed. (New York: Thomas Y. Crowell, 1954), p. 244; Ramón Beteta, *Pensamiento y Dinámica de la Revolución Mexicana* (México, D.F.: Editorial México Nuevo, 1950), pp. 424–425; Francisco Vázquez Pérez, *Derecho Agrario* (México, D.F.: Ediciones Botas, 1945), pp. 3–10.

35. Juan de Dios Bojórquez, *Lázaro Cárdenas* (México, D.F.: Mundial, 1934), p. 7; Ramón Fernández y Fernández, *El Problema Creado por la Reforma Agraria* (México, D.F.: Banco Nacional de Crédito Agrícola, 1941), p. 41; Alba, *Mexicans,* p. 188.

36. Howard F. Cline, "The Henequen Episode in Yucatan," *Inter-American Economic Affairs*, Vol. 2 (Autumn 1948), pp. 30–51.

37. "Informe," *Diario del Sureste*, January 31, 1959, p. 10.

38. Governor Novelo Torres had been Yucatan state treasurer, speaker of the state legislature, and senator from Yucatan in the federal Congress. See *Excélsior, Novedades,* or *El Universal*, February 17, 1968.

39. "Yucatán: Con Propósitos Inconfesables," *Hispano Americano* (in Mexico, *Tiempo*), September 26, 1966, pp. 24–25.

40. "Frentes Políticos: Yucatán," *Excélsior*, September 23, 1966.

41. A *municipio* resembles a U.S. county in geographical area, with a municipal council in its principal city or town. See Marvin Alisky, "Mexico's Municipal Civic Betterment Boards," *Public Affairs Bulletin* (ASU Institute of Public Administration), 4, No. 2 (1965), p. 1; Alisky, "Provision for Municipal Government in Latin American Constitutions," *Public Affairs Bulletin*, 7, No. 1 (1968), pp. 1–2.

42. "Mexico: Two Party State Legislature," *Latin American Digest*, March 1968, p. 1; *Excélsior*, December 3, 1967.

43. *Excélsior*, January 23, 1968.

44. *New York Times*, March 3, 1968.

45. *Christian Science Monitor*, June 7, 1968.

46. *Excélsior*, October 26, 1968.

47. "PAN and PRI Fight in Yucatan," *Latin American Digest*, March 1969, p. 2.

48. Carmen Robleda de Solís, director of women's activities for the PAN in Yucatan, charged that 140,000 ballots were locked up at the State Electoral Commission offices and never recounted; electoral officials in Mérida ignored the charge. See *Novedades*, December 1, 1969.

49. *Excélsior*, December 14, 1969.

50. Secretaría de Gobernación, *Las Juntas Computadoras de Yucatán* (México, D.F.: Registro Nacional de Electores, 1970), p. 1.

51. *Excélsior*, December 14, 1969.

52. Carlos Loret de Mola, *Confesiones de un Gobernador* (México, D.F.: Editorial Grijalbo, 1978), pp. 11–112.

53. One example of this occurred in 1972 when a huge sugar refinery was established in Quintana Roo instead of Yucatan even though economists had reported that the latter had all the potential for becoming a sugar producer.

54. "Yucatán," *Hispano Americano*, November 30, 1970, p. 45; *Excélsior*, June 26 and July 7, 1975.

55. Partido Revolucionario Institucional, *Estatutos, Declaración de Principios* (México, D.F.: Asamblea Nacional Ordinaria del PRI, 1972), pp. 69–81. The Yucatan Legislature was one of the six state legislatures that followed the direction of the PRI's National Executive Committee in increasing its unicameral body from nine to eleven members without waiting for the next official census count.

56. *Excélsior*, July 8, 1973.

57. "El Testamento de Carrillo Puerto," *Hispano Americano*, January 14, 1974, p. 36.

58. "Resort Chosen by Computer," *Latin American Digest*, May 1972, p. 1; *The News* (Mexico City), June 29, 1975.

59. *Excélsior*, August 27, 1975.

60. *Excélsior*, September 8, 1975.

61. "Reglamento de la CFE," *El Nacional,* October 25, 1978, p. 1; José Luis Fernández, *Derecho de la Radiodifusión* (México, D.F.: Editorial Olimpo, 1960), pp. 139–179; Marvin Alisky, "Radio's Role in Mexico," *Journalism Quarterly* (Winter 1954), pp. 66–72; *Ley Federal de Radio y Televisión* (México, D.F.: Secretaría de Gobernación, 1960), pp. 16, 20–24.

62. In 1978, Yucatecans were still pondering the age-old debate of centralism versus federalism as an appropriate governmental framework for Mexico, as attorney and political commentator Antonio Flores Ramírez observed in an editorial essay, "Centralismo y Federalismo: Definición Necesaria," *Diario de Yucatán,* March 3, 1978.

CHAPTER X

A PANORAMA OF LITERATURE IN YUCATAN

Edward Davis Terry

Literature may be considered primarily as the expression of the language in written form or as the art of recording human ideas with visible signs. It is principally that form of communication which contains a message that is to be stated always with the same words. Fundamentally, this is possible only with a phonetic alphabet, and it is doubtful that nonphonetic hieroglyphics and oral legends should be classified as literature. A large part of Mayan letters was initially transmitted by oral tradition or was recorded hieroglyphically. When these hieroglyphics were interpreted phonetically and a version was thus fixed, it became literature.[1] If this definition is accepted, then Mayan belles lettres is divided into two epochs: before and after the conquest. It ought not be surprising that a civilization which by A.D. 300 was using a calendar as accurate as the one we use today should have made significant advances in the liberal arts. Only three of the Mayan dialects, however, produced masterpieces composed by the Indians making use of their own traditions and style. These languages are the Quiché, Cakchiquel (both in Guatemala), and Yucatec Maya (Barrera, *Lit. Maya,* pp. 6, 9, 15, 17). The hieroglyphic material was not available to the general public but was reserved for the upper classes, especially for the priests. The Indian literature of the colonial period was recorded in the Roman alphabet that was adapted by the friars to the native languages. This new development democratized letters, for some of it then reached the common people (Barrera, *Lit. Maya,* p. 7). The outstanding indigenous literary works composed in Guatemala will be discussed here because they have influenced twentieth-century authors in the peninsula. Otherwise, this essay will treat only the most important aspects and works of the literature of Yucatan written in Maya and in Spanish from the colonial period to the present.

The *Popol Vuh,* or *El Libro del Consejo,* is considered to be the most important source of knowledge about Mayan mythology and is the point of departure for the Middle American epic.[2] It is an anonymous work, possibly recorded by several compilers who depended on their memory but were aided by pictographic documents (Barrera, *Lit. Maya,* pp. 10–11). It had been preserved through oral tradition and was written down in the Latin alphabet but in the Maya Quiché language before the middle of the sixteenth century, possibly around 1544 (Monterde, *Libro,* p. v; Recinos, p. 12). The original manuscript was discovered by Fray Francisco Ximénez in Chichicastenango-Chuilá, Guatemala, around 1700. He copied the Quiché text and translated it into the Spanish in parallel columns. When he wrote his *Historial de la Provincia de San Vicente de Chiapa y Guatemala* in 1722, he included a version of his Spanish translation of the *Popol Vuh* (Barrera, *Lit. Maya*, p. 9). Other translations were made later, but the work was known imperfectly until Georges Raynaud made an accurate one directly from the Quiché into the French in 1925. His excellent version was translated into the Spanish in 1927 by two of his students, J. M. González de Mendoza and Miguel Angel Asturias, a Nobel Prize winner in 1967. Raynaud himself supervised their rendition (Monterde, *Libro,* pp. vii–viii). The *Popol Vuh* doubtless has some Christian influence, for it is stated in the book that it was written down within the Christian society (Barrera, *Lit. Maya,* p. 11; Recinos, p. 21). Chapter One has an interesting parallel with the story of the creation as given in Genesis (Recinos, pp. 23–25). Consequently, Adrián Recinos believes that the transcribers of this late version were acquainted with the biblical text as taught by the Christian missionaries. Nevertheless, Adolph Bandelier states that the work is a collection of original traditions of the Indians of Guatemala (Recinos, p. 15).

The recorders of the *Popol Vuh* begin by saying that they will relate the beginning of the ancient history of the Quiché and that the *Popol Vuh,* where all was clear, can no longer be seen. In the translation by Recinos, the first four chapters of the first part describe the creation of the world, although the final making of man and woman, out of corn, does not take place until the initial three chapters of the third section. The second part relates the birth and adventures of the young demigods Hunahpú and Ixbalanqué and of their fathers, who had been sacrificed by evil spirits of Xibalbá, the underworld. A moral lesson is derived from the punishment of the evildoers and in the humiliation of proud Vucub-Caquix, who wanted to be the sun and the moon. The last part of the work is less literary and more historical. It gives information on the origin of the Indians of Guatemala, their emigrations, the wars, and the domination of the Quiché tribe up to a little before the Spanish Conquest. This section also lists the kings and their conquests and tells of the destruction of the small tribes that did not submit to the Quiché. Consequently, this last part of the *Popol Vuh* is of especial value in studying the pre-Columbian history of these Mayan tribes of Middle America.

The second most important work in the Maya Quiché language is the *Rabinal Achí.* A historical drama accompanied by music and dance, it was obtained by Esteban Brasseur de Bourbourg, a priest, in 1855 from a transcription made around 1850 by Bartolo Ziz, an inhabitant of Rabinal, Guatemala, who was also an actor in the play. It is the only surviving work of the pre-Hispanic theater in America.[3] Brasseur published both the Quiché text and his translation into the French in Paris in 1862 (Barrera, *Lit. Maya,* pp. 13–14). Georges Raynaud, not satisfied with Brasseur's version, made another rendition into the French. From it Luis Cardoza y Aragón made a Spanish translation that was published in *Anales de Geografía e Historia* (Guatemala) in 1929–30 (Monterde, *Rabinal,* pp. xv, xxxiii). The plot is relatively simple and consists of the capture of the Prince of the Queché by the warriors of the Prince of Rabinal. There are five principal characters who speak and two who do not. The outcome of the work is predestined, and the spectator knows what to expect. In order to survive, the Prince of the Queché must accept certain humiliations. In a formal, stylized ceremony of a ballet drama, he refuses to do this and is sacrificed at the conclusion.

The outstanding work of Cakchiquel literature is the *Anales de los Cakchiqueles,* also known as *Memorial de Técpan-Atitlán* or*Anales de los Xahil.*[4] Its ninety-six-page manuscript was discovered in 1844 by Juan Gavarrete in the archives of the Convent of San Francisco. In 1855, Brasseur de Bourbourg obtained it and made a translation into French. Later, Georges Raynaud, believing previous versions to be inaccurate, made his own rendition into the French, which was not published. Using this work, Miguel Angel Asturias and J. M. González de Mendoza made a Spanish translation that was brought out in Paris in 1928 and in Guatemala in 1936. It was published in 1946 for the third time by the National University of Mexico (Barrera, *Lit. Maya,* p. 15; Monterde, *Anales,* pp. xii–xiii).

The first section of the *Anales de los Cakchiqueles* is a document for use in legal proceedings to recover privileges lost by some Cakchiquel nobles during the colonial period. It contains the genealogy of the Xahil family, which is involved in the matter. This part has never been translated into any language nor has it been printed (Barrera, *Lit. Maya,* p. 16). The second section relates the origin of the Cakchiqueles. As in the case of the *Popol Vuh,* the names of the founding fathers of the tribe are given; the account clearly states that the group came from Tula and crossed the sea. It is interesting to note that the narrative says that they proceeded from the west, whereas the *Popol Vuh* states that the Quiché came from the east (Barrera, *Lit. Maya,* p. 16). The creation of man is related but not so artistically as in the Quiché version and with some variations in details. There is also a description of the tributes that the Cakchiqueles paid in Tula during one journey and the promises made to them by the rulers of that city. Then the return trip is related and the passage of the tribe through the sea, including the miracle of the parting of the waters so that they could pass, as in the biblical account of Moses. Later some battles are narrated in which the Cakchiqueles are defeated. At one point there is a valuable and interesting description of the confirmation of a chief and the insignia that he was given. The last section of the manuscript is an account of some personal deeds of the Xahil tribe and has not been translated, although J. Antonio Villacorta published part of it in 1943. The *Anales* is basically historical; at the beginning, however, there is a mixture of legendary tradition with fact. By the end of the work, the narrative is completely true and is contemporary with those who wrote it (Barrera, *Lit. Maya,* p. 17).

The liberal arts also flourished in Yucatan. The outstanding works of literature in that region are the *Libros de Chilam Balam,* which make up one of the most important parts of indigenous American literature.[5] They were recorded after the conquest, and therefore the script is that which the Spanish friars adapted to the phonology of Yucatecan Maya. It is not known how these books came to be called "Libros de Chilam Balam," for the name does not appear as an original title of any. Nevertheless, it is now accepted as a technical denomination to indicate this type of Yucatecan book. "Balam" is the name of the most famous of the prophets who lived shortly before the coming of the Spaniards. It is a family name, but in a figurative sense it means "jaguar" or "wizard." "Chilam" is the title that was given to the priestly class that interpreted the books and the will of the gods. The word means "he who is the mouth," that is, the mouthpiece, in this case, of the gods (Barrera, *Lit. Maya,* p. 18; Barrera and Rendón, p. 10). Chilam Balam, who lived in Maní shortly before the conquest, predicted the advent of a new religion—a prophecy that made him famous (Barrera and Rendón, p. 10).

It is supposed that the *Libros de Chilam Balam* were compiled in the following manner. The Spanish friars must have taught some native priests to read and write in their own language. Using this new knowledge, they transcribed religious and historical texts that were contained in their hieroglyphic books, including those with the predictions of Chilam Balam. Copies were made and passed on to native priests of various towns, thereby including in the title the name of the pueblo of its origin: Chumayel, Maní, and so forth. In each village additional material was added to the original base. Since these books were considered to be sacred and were read on certain occasions, the priests were interested in saving them for posterity. Consequently, the manuscripts were copied and recopied as they deteriorated. Over the years, various errors appeared in the texts. Time destroyed transcripts of the books themselves and must also have altered the understanding of them by the Mayan priests as their own culture changed. Thus the basic texts of the copies that exist today are not the original ones from the sixteenth century but are reproductions of much later copies, some from the seventeenth and others even from this century. A majority of the so-called basic texts are repeated one or more times in the *Libros,* but no versions are identical for the reasons indicated (Barrera and Rendón, pp. 10–11).

At the present time there exist more than a dozen *Libros de Chilam Balam,* but only eight are available for study: Chumayel, Tizimín, Káua, Maní, Ixil (partially), Tekax, Nah, and Tusik. The most important, best known, and most studied of these are the first five (Barrera and Rendón, pp. 10, 12; Barrera, *Lit. Maya,* p. 19). The several books contain texts that can be reconstructed by comparison with different versions and others that cannot because they are unique. Some of the latter obviously do not need to be reconstituted on account of their subject matter, simplicity, and recent compilation. Consequently, the work entitled *Libro de los Libros de Chilam Balam* is a translation of all texts of which there exist more than one version. It is based on a careful reconstruction made by collating the several books (Barrera and Rendón, p. 11). Therefore, it will remain the definitive edition until new discoveries are made.

The material contained in the *Libros* is diverse and can generally be classified as religious texts, both indigenous and Christian translated into the Maya; historical material; medical texts, sometimes with European influence; works pertaining to chronology and astrology, including explanations of the Mayan calendar and almanacs with predictions and astrology; astronomy according to the European beliefs of the fifteenth century; rituals; literary texts, Spanish novels; and unclassified miscellaneous material (Barrera and Rendón, p. 9). It is evident that the varied subject matter of the *Libros* includes all cultural stages that the Maya of Yucatan had experienced until those works were no longer compiled in the sixteenth century. There is no doubt that a large part of the historical and religious texts that are really Indian are based on the ancient hieroglyphic books, three of which survived the destructive zeal of Fray Diego de Landa and are now found in Europe (Barrera and Rendón, p. 9). These three original Mayan codices were "written" possibly three hundred years before the discovery of America, with drawings, numbers, and hieroglyphics. Known as the Codex Dresdensis, the Codex Tro-Cortesianus, and the Codex Peresianus, they may be consulted in Dresden, Madrid, and Paris, respectively.[6]

The *Songs of Dzitbalché* from Yucatan are the only collection of lyrics that has been found in the Mayan region (Barrera, *Lit. Maya,* p. 23). Unfortunately, most are incomplete. Alfredo Barrera Vásquez discovered and made an annotated translation of them, and in 1965 the Instituto Nacional de Antropología e Historia of Mexico published his version as *El Libro de los Cantares de Dzitbalché*.[7] The original manuscript is a series of sheets in bad condition that form a "book" sewn with henequen thread. There is a cover that carries in Maya the title "El Libro de las Danzas de los Hombres Antiguos que era costumbre hacer acá en los pueblos cuando aún no llegaban los blancos." Fifteen songs survive. They are doubtless the lyrics of melodies that accompanied the dances of a dramatic work. The varied topics are pre-Hispanic from the period of Toltec influence. The transcriptions that have endured, however, are probably from the late eighteenth or early nineteenth centuries. The arrangement of the lines imitates Spanish verse. These songs are of great ethnographic value, and their style is truly poetic (Barrera, *Lit. Maya,* p. 23). One example, "Canto de la Flor," Cantar 7, accompanied a purely feminine magical rite practiced in Yucatan until recently and described by Manuel Rejón García in 1905 and by Carlos Basauri in 1931. Another is a pathetic lament by a poor orphan, a dirge that is probably a text to which Diego de Landa referred in his *Relación de las Cosas de Yucatán*. A third example is Cantar 13, "Song of the Dance of the Bowman," of which forty-five lines survive, including:

> Bien aguzada has la punta de tu flecha,
> bien enastada has la cuerda
> de tu arco; puesta tienes buena
> resina de *catsim* en las plumas
> del extremo de la vara de tu flecha.[8]

This song accompanied a bloody rite of sacrifice by arrows, which was also described by Landa. Its lofty style and precise information make it a valuable

Detail of the Madrid Codex, Biblioteca Nacional, longest of the three Mayan codices that survived the zeal of Bishop Diego de Landa. (Used by permission, Museo de América, Madrid)

piece of pre-Hispanic Yucatecan literature (Barrera, *Lit. Maya,* pp. 23–28; *Dzit-balché,* p. 78).

The writings of the colonial period—religious works, dictionaries, Mayan vocabularies, and historical-religious books, produced mostly by priests—in Yucatan did not form a literary tradition. Specifically, Landa's *Relación,* in spite of its significance, was not belles lettres.[9] This paucity of noteworthy authors in the peninsula before independence ought not be surprising if we keep in mind that the very first Spanish-American novel, *El Periquillo Sarniento* by José Joaquín Fernández de Lizardi, a Mexican, was not published until 1816. More-over, no first-rate playwright appeared in Spanish America until Florencio Sán-chez, who wrote between 1900 and 1910. It does seem incredible, however, that there should have been no poet in Yucatan until the second decade of the nineteenth century, for Mexico had produced the great Sor Juana Inés de la Cruz, the "Tenth Muse," in the late seventeenth century, as well as other poets of importance.

Independence was obtained in Yucatan without bloodshed, an achievement of both Creoles and Spaniards. This total absence of fratricidal fighting created a situation unlike that in the rest of Mexico: no rancor remained towards the Spaniards on the peninsula, who were allowed to continue their normal routines. In the following section I shall discuss only the most important authors of the nineteenth and twentieth centuries with no division by literary genre, for most writers created different kinds of letters. It will become evident that the Mayan heritage of Middle America came to be an influence over the years on many authors. This is also true among even the young writers in the 1970s.

With no literary heritage when independence was attained, the intellectuals were like novices who had to start from scratch. Andrés Quintana Roo, Yuca-tan's first poet, was born in Mérida on November 30, 1787, and died in Mexico City on April 15, 1851. A product of his times, he was essentially a political writer, a fiery orator, a notable polemicist, and a great patriot. Consequently, his poetry is of a national rather than a regional character.[10] According to Marcelino Menéndez y Pelayo, Quintana Roo was "more of a magistrate and politician than poet; but even if he was not an inspired poet, his thought was elevated, his versification noble and correct, his tone serious, as suited his particular kind of talent."[11] These characteristics were a result of his classical education, for he was a Latinist influenced by Cicero and Horace. This Yucatecan was almost alone in writing patriotic verse. He, as others of his time, was influenced by the Spanish Neoclassic poet Manuel José Quintana. Quintana Roo was a revo-lutionary bard whose works, both prose and poetry, were published in periodicals and have not been collected. Few of his poems are known today (González Peña, p. 170).

Justo Sierra O'Reilly (1814–61), a politician who dedicated his life to the service of his country, is considered to be the father of the novel and, with the exception of poetry, of literature in Yucatan.[12] Before the Caste War, public attitude was not conducive to the writing of novels; such publications were

Justo Sierra O'Reilly, father of the novel in Yucatan.

considered to be frivolous and unimportant because serious political problems demanded the attention of the Yucatecans (Pren, p. 623). Consequently, Sierra O'Reilly in 1841 began his literary activity with a short narrative in which there are historical incidents as well as legends. He edited *El Museo Yucateco,* a literary journal, in Campeche from January 1, 1841, to May of 1842. This periodical may be considered the first bulwark of Yucatecan literature. In it Sierra O'Reilly published his short novels, which he called "histories" or legends: *Doña Felipa de Zanabria, Los Bandos de Valladolid,* and *El Filibustero.* He is the author of two works that are properly classified as novels: *Un Año en el Hospital de San Lázaro* (1845) and *La Hija del Judío* (1848–51). According to Luis González Obregón, the latter work is the first real historical novel written in Mexico. It relates several traditional tales of Yucatan and describes customs of the colonial period (Pren, pp. 626–27). Ermilo Abreu Gómez states that the works of Justo Sierra O'Reilly are also important in a national perspective, for he can be considered the precursor of the Mexican Romantic historical novel.[13]

Another pioneer in the novel, Gerónimo del Castillo Lenard, wrote only one novel, *Un Pacto y un Pleito* (1849), but he is considered the creator of the novel of customs in Yucatan. The work is somewhat historical, for it deals with, among other topics, the trial and execution of Emilio Gustavo N. De Witt, the French envoy, in 1810. The author wanted to write a novel with a thesis—that greed for money could bring about man's downfall. As a literary work, however, it has a lasting value as a magnificent picture of Yucatecan customs during the first two decades of the nineteenth century. Consequently, *Un Pacto* will be valuable to the sociologist or the historian who wants to study the working conditions of the Indians in Yucatan in that period. Chapter Nine is of special interest. It is called "La Hacienda del Refugio" and describes the rural customs, the branding, the planting and harvesting systems, and the organization of the Indian work under conditions equivalent to slavery and peonage (Pren, pp. 635–36).

Although born in Mexico City, Severo del Castillo (1824–72) wrote in 1869 the regional novel, *Cecilio Chi: Novela Histórica Yucateca.* Treating the Caste War, its Romantic, idyllic plot serves as a pretext for an excellent description of the local customs and the somber, military aspects of that bloody social upheaval. A second edition came out in Mérida in 1937.[14] This work is also of interest because it influences Yucatecan authors in the twentieth century.

Eligio Ancona (1835–93), the noted historian, was born in Mérida and published his first novel at the age of twenty-six. *Los Mártires del Anáhuac,* a well-known work about the conquest of Mexico, came out in 1870 (Pren, p. 638). His last and best novel, *Memorias de un Alférez,* was published in 1904 by José María Pino Suárez. Five of Ancona's novels are of a regional nature dealing with Yucatan. Each was written with the purpose of recreating chronologically an epoch in the history and life of the peninsula. The author wanted to narrate the most outstanding deeds or events in the first three centuries after the arrival of the Spaniards. A follower of Sierra O'Reilly in the field of the Romantic historical

Eligio Ancona, politician, novelist, and noted historian.

novel, Ancona wrote about the conquest in *La Cruz y la Espada* (1864). *El Filibustero* (1864) deals with the serious effects of piracy on the economic development of Yucatan, with the action set in the seventeenth century. In *El Conde de Peñalva* (1879), which takes place in the same epoch, the author describes the scarcity of food that was caused mainly by the social conditions in Yucatan: the labor systems, the exploitation of the Indians, the collection of taxes and fines from all social classes, and the private and public conduct of several captain generals. Don García Valdés y Osorio was selected by Ancona as a symbol of the vices and defects of the Spanish colonial commanders. On the other hand, in *Memorias de un Alférez* (1904) the author treats Don Lucas de Gálvez as an example of the enlightened governor, something evidently rare in Yucatan. With the action in the eighteenth century, Ancona builds his plot around the assassination of Gálvez, the causes of which are still not entirely clear and which brought about profound disturbances in the peninsula (Pren, p. 641). *La Mestiza* (1861), his first novel, was written before Ancona had developed an overall plan for his series. In technique, it is the weakest, but this work is a valuable social document about the licentious customs of a certain level of society during the nineteenth century. It deals with the *señoritos* of Mérida who believed that "the thing to do" was to seduce and to dishonor mestizas. Although he wrote six novels, Ancona evidently thought of himself as a historian, for he considered his *La Historia de Yucatán* as his most important work (Pren, p. 643).

Mexico's most outstanding Romantic dramatist, José Peón Contreras, was born in Mérida on January 12, 1843, and died in Mexico City on February 18, 1907. He came from a distinguished family and was educated at home. As precocious in science as in poetry, he received his degree in medicine at the age of nineteen. In 1863, he moved to Mexico City where he continued his medical studies, devoted himself to his profession, and represented Yucatan several times in the federal Congress, both as deputy and as senator. In 1868, Peón Contreras published his volume of *Poesías,* which show a sensitiveness of feeling. His *Romances Históricos Mexicanos* (1871) include several ballads of Indian theme, such as "Moctezuma," "El Ultimo Azteca," and "Tlahuicole." These are obviously of Aztec and not of Mayan inspiration. He also wrote two novels, *Taïde* (1885) and *La Veleidosa* (1891). His true literary field, however, was the theater. A fertile dramatic poet, he produced twenty-four plays and left three unfinished. His best play is *La Hija del Rey* (1876), a three-act drama in verse that is probably the best Mexican Romantic play. Other national writers recognized his ability and in that same year gave him a gold pen and a diploma, declaring him to be the "restorer of the theater in the homeland of Alarcón and Gorostiza." The dramatic work of Peón Contreras is of uneven quality. His best plays are those with colonial themes, while his works of contemporary setting are weak both in subject matter and technique. His plays in verse are better than those in prose, and the best of the former deal with the viceregal period. Peón Contreras was unable to revive the Romantic theater, for it was already dying

"Príncipe de las Letras Yucatecas"

José Peón Contreras, "Prince of Yucatecan Letters," was Mexico's most outstanding Romantic dramatist. (Drawing by Roldán Peniche Barrera)

when he came along. In spite of his importance in Mexican literature, his total dramatic output has never been collected in a single volume (González Peña, pp. 331–32).

Justo Sierra, one of Yucatan's most illustrious sons, was born in Campeche on January 26, 1848, and died in Madrid on September 13, 1912. The son of Justo Sierra O'Reilly, he is usually known even in Mexico without his mother's surname of Méndez. A poet, political orator, storyteller, and historian, Sierra is considered one of the great representative writers of Mexican literature of his time. According to Jesús Urueta, he had "an irresistible magic, a power of attraction and fascination that drew spirits to him naturally, as to a shelter, a place of rest, a strong tower" (González Peña, p. 271). He began his studies in Mérida and continued them in 1861 in the capital in the Colegio de San Ildefonso. Ten years later he received his law degree.

Justo Sierra's poem "Playera" (1868), inspired by the sound of the sea of his native coast, made him famous in literary circles in Mexico City. He wrote prolifically: articles, short stories, novels, and poems that were published in periodicals. After the death of his brother Santiago on April 27, 1880, of whom he was very fond, he abruptly stopped writing and went through a period of meditation and study.[15] As a result, the early Romantic became the historian, sociologist, and educator. Sierra was active in politics, serving in the Chamber of Deputies and also as a member of the Supreme Court. In all his public service, however, Justo Sierra was especially outstanding in education and was called "el maestro," which he was to two generations. He taught history in the National Preparatory School and served as undersecretary of public education. Between 1905 and 1911, he was minister of public education and fine arts. One of the most important of his cultural efforts was the reopening of the National University in 1910 (González Peña, p. 272).

Justo Sierra was a greater writer of prose than of poetry. He himself acknowledged playfully that he did not believe that he was a poet because of "a certain fundamental inability to unite idea with feeling and both with unfailing lyrical expression." Sierra does, however, have an important place in the history of Mexican poetry although his best lyrics were written when he was a young man. He was probably the first Mexican to write verses persistently after the French manner. Thus, as a precursor of *modernismo,* his influence helped bring about a complete change of direction in national poetry (González Peña, pp. 272–73). As a youth, Sierra wrote lyrical short stories that were published in periodicals. These works did not appear in book form, however, until 1896, when they came out as *Cuentos Románticos.* He called them "little poems in prose impregnated with sentimental and delirious lyricism." Three are narratives that evoke the atmosphere of his native region: "Marina," "Playera," and "La Sirena"; others are set in different countries and in diverse times. The short stories found in this collection are important in the evolution of Mexican literature in that they, together with the novels of Ignacio Altamirano, represent the point that Mexican Romanticism in fiction took on a truly literary and artistic form (González Peña,

Justo Sierra, "el maestro." Son of Justo Sierra O'Reilly, he was a poet, political orator, storyteller, and historian. Minister of Education under Porfirio Díaz, he reopened the National University of Mexico.

p. 274). The only influence of the Yucatan Peninsula in the poetry and prose of
Justo Sierra is that of the sea, which he knew as a child in Campeche. The poem
''Playera'' is an excellent sample:

> Baje a la playa la dulce niña,
> perlas hermosas le buscaré;
> deje que el agua durmiendo ciña
> con sus cristales su blanco pie . . .
>
> Cuando en Levante despunte el día
> verá las nubes de blanco tul,
> como los cisnes de la bahía,
> rizar serenos el cielo azul.
>
> Enlazaremos a las palmeras
> la suave hamaca, y en su vaivén
> las horas tristes irán ligeras,
> y sueños de oro vendrán también.[16]

The *maestro* was also a historian, but not one who delved into archives. By
teaching in the classroom and making the past come alive in speeches and books,
he molded the cultural and intellectual thought of two generations. The historian
and professor were one in him. One of Sierra's most important historical works is
Historia Política, which is found in the second part of his *México: Su Evolución
Social* (1900–1901). It is without a doubt the most profound material written on
the subject. This treatise was published separately in 1940 as *Evolución Política
del Pueblo Mexicano* (also as Volume 12 of his *Obras Completas*). Written in
magnificent prose, *Juárez: Su Obra y su Tiempo* appeared in 1905. This work is
his crowning achievement as a historian. It was finished by Carlos Pereyra
because Sierra was dedicating himself totally to his duties as minister of public
education. His speeches are considered a part of his historical works, and it has
been said that his best writings are found in his addresses (González Peña,
pp. 344–45). In discussing his prose works, mention should also be made of the
many important contributions scattered in official publications and in periodicals
of pedagogy, politics, literary criticism, and travel. *En Tierra Yankee* (1898)
falls into this last category. In this type of prose the characteristics of the poet,
historian, and public speaker blend to show a skillful writer both familiar and
picturesque, profound and very important. In addition to its intrinsic worth, the
prose work of Sierra is also significant for the study of the currents of thought
that prevailed during his time. A restless desire for learning and new ideas kept
his spirit eternally youthful, and as a historian he was always an optimist. The
Obras Completas del Maestro Justo Sierra have been published by the National
University of Mexico in fifteen volumes under the direction of Agustín Yáñez.
The excellent preliminary study to the edition, also by Yáñez, contains the best
biography of the *maestro.*[17]

A folklorist and compiler of legends, Luis Rosado Vega was born in Chemax, Yucatan, in 1873, and died in Mérida on November 1, 1958.[18] He started his literary career as a poet under the influence of the *modernistas*. A lyricist of energetic inspiration and beautiful simplicity, Rosado Vega published *Sensaciones* (1902), *Alma y Sangre* (1906), and in 1907 *Libro de Ensueño y de Dolor* (González Peña, pp. 305-6). An anthropologist with a love for the Indian and the *pueblo*, he wrote almost all of his prose with a social purpose (Pren, p. 661). Rosado Vega also developed a keen interest in the traditions of the Maya although he did not publish his first book of legends and tales of indigenous origin, *El Alma Misteriosa del Mayab*, until 1934. In the "Motivos" to this work the author states that he was undertaking a methodical compilation of Yucatecan regional folklore, for this collection was to be the first of a series that would reveal a psychological acquaintance with the ancient Mayan people.[19] His intention was to produce a popular work rather than one of literary brilliance; therefore he used the simplest expressions possible that corresponded to the atmosphere and the ideologies of the narrations. Most of the legends in this collection were unknown to the reading public because few had been published previously. His sources were the tales of the old Indians whom he got to know when he organized the Museo Histórico y Arqueológico of Mérida and was its director. Thus he personally collected these legends from them in huts, beside archaeological ruins, and in the fields (Rosado Vega, *Alma,* pp. 12-13). The symbolism of these stories reveals the high spiritual plane of the life of the Maya. They are imbued with a charming candor, beneath which is found a deep philosophical concept and a profound moral tone. Some of them are set in the early colonial period but are entirely Mayan in origin, in ideology, in forms of expression, and in all their sentiments and philosophy. Most, however, go back to the mythological past of Yucatan (Rosado Vega, *Alma,* pp. 15-16).

The tales in Rosado Vega's second book of legends, entitled *Amerindmaya,* are, in his words, "projections of the ancient land of the Maya."[20] In *El Alma* and this new collection, the author recreated more than seventy Mayan legends. An excerpt from the prologue of *Amerindmaya* makes it clear that he was unusually sensitive to social injustices perpetrated against the Indian: "Everything seems to have worked together in order to crush and destroy [the Mayan race] since it was subjected to a real calvary, to which it still is subjected."[21] Rosado Vega also wrote *Claudio Martín: Vida de un Chiclero* (México: Ediciones S. C. O. P., 1938), a novel of protest in which he showed the same social concern as in his other prose works. Dealing with one of the sensitive economic situations of Mexico, the author described the exploitation of the chicle workers in Quintana Roo. The work has been described as "an excellent portrayal of customs in that region and is a strong, cruel novel."[22]

Antonio Mediz Bolio, who was born in Mérida on October 13, 1884, initially became known in the field of literature for his Yucatecan legends, the majority of which are Mayan. His first were published in *Evocaciones* (1903): "Los Kates de Uaymil," "Kinich-Kakmó," "Nouich," "La Caverna del Tigre Negro,"

Poeta, Dramaturgo, Político y Diplomático.

Antonio Mediz Bolio, author of *La Tierra del Faisán y del Venado*. (Drawing by Roldán Peniche Barrera)

"Lágrima de Fuego," "Los Últimos Días de Chichén," "El Brindis de D. Alvar," and "Flor de Sangre." These narratives, like all the prose of the author, are characterized by their Mayan flavor and their delicate, unmistakable style abundant in Indian symbols and colorful native images (Pren, p. 659). The indigenous influence, however, is barely present in his book of poetry *En Medio del Camino* (1917), which contains one poem of Indian theme, "Canto del Mayab." Nevertheless, the Mayan element appears again in *La Tierra del Faisán y del Venado* (1922) and *Canto del Hijo de Yucatán* (1953). Mediz Bolio was known as a writer of poems, legends in prose, and plays. He was a good poet, as is evident by *En Medio del Camino*. He was outstanding in the thesis play *La Ola* (1917) and in the dramatic poem *La Flecha del Sol* (1917), which has an indigenous theme (González Peña, p. 398). The author continued to show his love for the Maya when he translated and published *El Libro de Chilam Balam de Chumayel* in 1930. He revised it at the request of the National University of Mexico, which published it in 1941. It is interesting to remember that Mediz Bolio wrote the lyrics of the haunting "El Caminante del Mayab," a song that was the theme of the motion picture *Deseada* (1950), starring Dolores del Río, and that is still popular in Yucatan today.[23]

The author is best known for his masterpiece in poetic prose, *La Tierra del Faisán y del Venado*. In writing this work he attempted to make "a stylization of the Mayan spirit, of the concept that the Indians still have—filtered through thousands of years—of their origins, of their past grandeur . . . all told with the greatest possible approximation to the genius of their language and to the state of their soul in the present. . . . I have conceived the book in Maya and have written it in Spanish."[24] The themes are taken from tradition, from the very soul of the Indian, from his current superstitions, and above all from the author's own experiences as a youth among the Maya (*Tierra*, Botas, p. 11). The contents of this work are historical and mythological accounts pertaining to the ancient cities and gods, lyrical legends of a historical nature, elegiac songs of past glories, allegorical descriptions of the Mayan dances, and examples of the character and disposition of the natives. The sources are the ancient chronicles written about the Maya—both indigenous and Spanish—and oral tradition.[25] The author has recreated the legends of the Indians, which had been influenced, at least to some degree, by European culture. The lyrical style of Mediz Bolio creates a diaphanous and melancholy tone. Book Seven, "Maní, que quiere decir que todo pasó," and the last chapter, "Después de los siete libros," are laments over the extinction of the past grandeur of the Mayan civilization. The title of the book itself is explained in the text: "The Deer was the body of Mayab [Yucatan] and the Pheasant was its spirit" (*Tierra*, Botas, p. 187).

In 1956, Mediz Bolio published *A la Sombra de mi Ceiba*.[26] He states in the preface that these accounts could be chapters of personal memoirs. Most of them had been published previously as articles in newspapers or magazines, mainly in *El Nacional* of Mexico City. At the urging of friends, he chose for publication in this volume some that he thought would interest the public. The book is divided into five sections. "De la Tierra Nativa" deals with Yucatecan subjects. One of the stories, "Mi Amigo Bel Xool," is a nostalgic account of the author's childhood playmate, a pure Mayan Indian, whom he sadly left behind on the estate his father had lost, for "Bel Xool belongs to the hacienda." It was then that Mediz Bolio first felt in the depths of his heart the injustice of men (*Sombra,* p. 43). In "Caminos del Mundo" he describes some of his experiences in Spain, Colombia, and Costa Rica. In "Testimonios y Comentarios Políticos," the author discusses events of the epoch of Porfirio Díaz and the Mexican Revolution. "La Cordial Juventud" is made up of youthful experiences. "Cerca y acerca de los Indios" deals with Mayan themes and includes happenings from ancient times to the twentieth century. One narrative, "Nuestra más Antigua Revolución," relates the destruction of Mayapán in 1441. In another article, Mediz Bolio perhaps more accurately names the Caste War "La Guerra Santa de los Mayas."

The author states that he always believed that he had learned the Mayan language before he did Spanish. He realized that subconsciously he had absorbed "the Mayan feeling for things" and that he possessed without knowing it "the genius and the mechanism of my ancestral language" (*Sombra,* p. 39). The pervading theme in his works is the intimate relationship between the Maya and their land. In all his writings on the Indians, but especially in *La Tierra del Faisán y del Venado,* we perceive the poet of indigenous Yucatan. Away from his beloved homeland, he died in Mexico City on September 15, 1957. One might truly say that the *Venado* and the *Faisán* dwelt in the spirit of Antonio Mediz Bolio.

One of the great writers of Mexico, Ermilo Abreu Gómez was born in Mérida on September 18, 1894.[27] His literary endeavors were extensive: poetry, criticism, short stories, drama, legends, and novels. A teacher of literature in the National Preparatory School in Mexico City for several years, he was visiting professor at the University of Illinois in 1947–48. Abreu Gómez became interested in the colonial period of Mexico and made important studies of Juan Ruiz de Alarcón, Carlos de Sigüenza y Góngora, and Sor Juana Inés de la Cruz. He called the attention of critics to the works of the great poetess and was considered the most devoted authority on the Mexican Tenth Muse (Sor Juana).[28] His fame as an Indianist writer and his greatest successes are derived from his short prose work *Canek* (1940), his collection of legends *Héroes Mayas* (1942), and other works of indigenous themes. The narratives of Abreu Gómez are more poems in prose than short stories, literary creations that evoke the lives of Mayan heroes.[29]

In 1951 he published the novel *Naufragio de Indios,* another indictment of the whites for their abuse of the Maya.[30] The culminating crime occurs at the end of the novel, when the ship on which a group of Indians are being transported like cattle sinks offshore from San Blas. The natives are trapped in the hold and drown. *Tata Lobo,* a picaresque novel, came out in 1952.[31] Another book of legends was published by Abreu Gómez in 1961, *Leyendas y Consejas del*

Antiguo Yucatán.[32] The author states in the preface that "Indians of my land told me some, and I read others in chronicles of different epochs." The work is divided into three parts: "Héroes Mayas" (Zamná, Nachi Cocom, and Canek), "Leyendas y Consejas," and "Las Leyendas del Popol Vuh" (only two). It is interesting to note that the legends in the last section are Maya Quiché from Guatemala, not from Yucatan. This point is a good illustration, however, of the influence of the entire Mayan tradition on Yucatecan writers.

Two representative samples of the works of Abreu Gómez are *Canek* and *Tata Lobo*. The former is based on a true incident that took place in Yucatan on December 17, 1761, an uprising of the Indians that is recorded in the archives of the Cabildo of Mérida (JLM, *Lit. Ind. Mod.*, p. 20; *Lit. Mex. XX*, p. 333). But this narrative is not just a historical legend; it is an artistic, lyrical blending of history with the sensitive spirit of the Maya. Abreu Gómez himself has related the origin of *Canek*. When the author was a child, he went with his father on trips about the peninsula. The boy would remain at the local inn, surrounded by Indians, while his father carried out his business transactions. At night the men told stories and legends of the region, one of which dealt with the life of Canek. The story and the fate of this man were engraved in the memory of young Ermilo. Later, when he read about the Mayan hero in school, he became more impressed with his legendary image. Over the years, the story of Jacinto Canek took shape in his mind until Abreu Gómez finally wrote it down. Before publishing it, he read aloud different versions to friends (*Canek*, pp. 17–18).

The first character that the author introduces is Jacinto Canek, a Mayan Indian who lives on an hacienda. Later *niño* Guy, the nephew of the owner and supposedly a retarded child, comes to the estate and Canek is told to look after him. As the story progresses, we have reasons to doubt that Guy is slow and realize that he is a sensitive child who is "different" from the other whites. On one occasion, a bucket falls into the well, and Canek has to go down to get it out. On coming up, he says that from the depths one can see the stars. The next day the bucket is lost again, and Guy says that he will descend to fetch it; "I also want to see the stars" (*Canek*, pp. 47–48). Symbolism is evident in this incident, for obviously the spirits of Canek and *niño* Guy are seeking to rise higher than those of the white hacendados, earthbound by greed. One entire section of the book, "La Doctrina," is made up of the wisdom of the Mayan race as expressed by Jacinto Canek, for each paragraph begins with "Canek dijo." For example, "Canek said: Do not become haughty from the fruits of your intelligence. . . . Intelligence is like an arrow: once it is shot from the bow, no one governs it any longer"; "Canek said: Never be afraid of your tears. No coward weeps. Only men weep. Besides, my son, tears always fall as one kneels" (*Canek*, pp. 98–99).

After many injustices, the Indians rebel, and the whites shout, "¡Se han sublevado los indios!" ("The Indians have rebelled!") (*Canek*, p. 127 ff.). This cry becomes a refrain. The uprising is finally put down, and some natives, including Canek, are executed. It is interesting to note that Abreu Gómez does

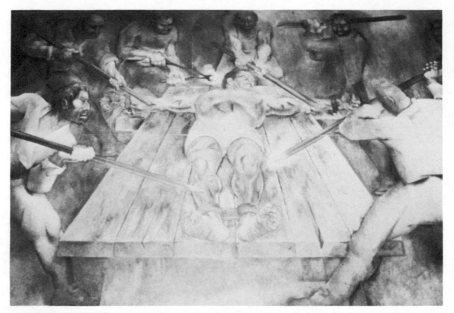

"The Torture of Jacinto Canek," mural by Fernando Castro Pacheco in the State Government Building, Mérida. (Photo by Joel Whitman)

not describe, or even imply, the horrible execution of drawing and quartering that the historical personage suffered at the hands of the Spaniards in the main plaza of Mérida. This scene is portrayed dramatically, however, by the Yucatecan artist Fernando Castro Pacheco in a mural on a wall of the state government building in the city. The author lets the reader assume that Canek is hanged from a scaffold, where even the executioner sheds tears. At the end of the work, he and the child Guy (who had died earlier) meet at a bend in the road to Cisteil and continue walking. As they reach the horizon, they begin to ascend (*Canek*, pp. 143–44).

Abreu Gómez imbues *Canek* with the spirit of the Mayan race. In the descriptions of the protagonist and other Indians, time comes to a halt and ceases to exist, for the action could have taken place at any time after the conquest. In narrating the mistreatment of Canek and other natives, there is, of course, social criticism, which is low key and is subordinated to the gentle spirit of the Maya. In my opinion, this technique makes it much more effective than if the author had preached to his readers. The literary style of the work is lyrical and the tone subdued. Nevertheless, we feel deeply Abreu Gómez's indictment not only of the abuses committed against the Indians but also those against the child. The mistreatment of Canek and Guy are really the same, for both are weak, and at times the natives seem as ingenuous as children. The sensitive Mayan spirit that the author has given to *Canek* makes his social protest very effective, while the legend itself remains an outstanding literary work of art.

Tata Lobo, contrary to Abreu Gómez's tales of indigenous themes, is not set in Yucatan but in other parts of Mexico. The author relates the story of a rogue-like character who is likable and has the redeeming quality of sincerity (p. 131). In the classic manner of the picaresque novel, Abreu Gómez describes first the family background and childhood of the protagonist, then his misadventures. Tata Lobo is preoccupied with hunger and serves several masters, or employers, in his efforts to satisfy it. This technique allows the author to give the reader a view of different aspects of Mexican society. The tricks of Tata Lobo are not cruel and/or extreme as in *Lazarillo de Tormes* (1554) or *El Periquillo Sarniento* (1816). Tata Lobo, after having suffered the slings and arrows of misfortune and having returned to San Blas where he was born, quietly dies one afternoon. Abreu Gómez succinctly implies that the protagonist has become a legend of folklore, for in later years the children of the town sing a little verse about him:

> ¡Tata Lobo!
> ¿Tata Lobo dónde está?
> Tata Lobo está en el cielo.
> Tata Lobo está en la mar.   [p. 137]

Previous literary picaresque characters are referred to in the novel by the author. Doña Inocencia, a go-between, shows an obvious point of contact with the Celestina (p. 94), a female rogue of the late fifteenth century. Pito Pérez from the state of Michoacán is in the same jail with Tata Lobo and writes to his friend José Rubén. This reference to José Rubén Romero, who wrote of the Revolution and provincial life in his native Michoacán and also a picaresque novel, *La Vida Inútil de Pito Pérez* (1938), would place the action in the time of the Mexican Revolution. In the episode in which Tata Lobo is a soldier, there are echoes of *Los de Abajo* (1915) and Demetrio Macías, its protagonist. The sentence "Donde ponía el ojo ponía la bala" (p. 115: "Where he aimed he hit the mark") is almost identical to one in the earlier novel.[33] But the time element is confused and indefinite. Towards the end of *Tata Lobo* the rebellious Indians of Tomóchic are pursued by a band of *rurales* (rural police) (p. 131). This incident might refer to the epoch of Porfirio Díaz in the late nineteenth or early twentieth century. Abreu Gómez distorts and compresses time because it is of no importance in the story: the situation of Tata Lobo is the same as that which has existed for the poor from the colonial period to the present moment.

The protagonist is a prototype of the poor and accepts the vicissitudes of life stoically, as do the Mexican people. There is no obvious social protest in this novel as there is in *Canek*. The tone is subdued, not bitter, and Abreu Gómez writes in a clear, direct style. Mild criticism of contemporary society may be inferred, nevertheless, from the injustices that are described as a part of reality. The author does not, however, comment on them. He allows the situation to speak for itself, which is the same technique previously used in *Canek*. The reader's interest is to follow the adventures of Tata Lobo and the difficulties he encounters while seeking not his fortune but the bare necessities of life. The national setting of this novel is an indication that Abreu Gómez had more than a regional scope. Another Yucatecan who had to seek opportunities elsewhere, the author died in Mexico City on July 14, 1971.

When dealing with living writers of Yucatan, one faces the dilemma of selecting authors to discuss and those to omit. Due to space limitations, I shall include here only the writers that I was privileged to interview in 1977. Related problems in this case are found in the questions, "Is there a Yucatecan literature?" and "If so, what are its characteristics?" These become especially significant because the region is no longer isolated from the rest of Mexico. Jorge Luis Borges, the great Argentine author, deals with this same problem in his essay "The Argentine Writer and Tradition" and makes points that are difficult to refute:

> The idea that Argentine poetry should abound in differential Argentine traits and Argentine local color seems to me a mistake. . . . Besides, I do not know if it is necessary to say that the idea that a literature must define itself in terms of its national traits is a relatively new concept. . . . The Argentine cult of local color is a recent European cult which the nationalists ought to reject as foreign. . . . I believe our tradition is all of Western culture, and I also believe we have a right to this tradition. . . . We should feel that our patrimony is the universe; we should essay all themes.[34]

I agree with these arguments and believe that the genius of the individual, as well as local color, helps determine regional literature. Consequently, in my judgement, Yucatecan literature consists of that written by authors born and reared in the region and also by those born elsewhere but who have settled there and continue to write, usually influenced by the environment to some degree.[35]

No discussion of literature in Yucatan can be undertaken without mentioning Alfredo Barrera Vásquez. Born in Maxcanú on November 26, 1900, he has always lived in Mérida except when his anthropological interests and duties have taken him to Spain, Bolivia, and other foreign countries.[36] He has held many important posts with Mexican institutions (for example, director of the Instituto Yucateco de Antropología e Historia) and with UNESCO. The author of numerous articles and books in anthropology and linguistics, Barrera Vásquez is also an authority on Mayan literature. In addition to translating into the Spanish and editing *El Libro de los Libros de Chilam Balam* and *El Libro de los Cantares de Dzitbalché*, among others, he compiled Mayan tales, wrote poetry, and was awarded the Eligio Ancona Prize in 1964 for his outstanding intellectual activities.[37] At the present time he is head of the Department of Philology and Linguistics of the Southeast Regional Center, Instituto Nacional de Antropología e

Historia, Mérida, and is in charge of compiling the "Great Maya-Spanish Spanish-Maya Dictionary" that is to be published in the near future.

Barrera Vásquez wrote the poem *Cruz: Poema en Cinco Puntos Cardinales* in 1937 while he was director of the Archaeological and Historical Museum of Yucatan.[38] The author was not interested in publishing his literary production but his scientific research instead. At that time, it did not seem proper to him for a man of science to write verses even though he had been an artist. Barrera Vásquez was a painter and founder of the Institute of Fine Arts in Yucatan. Things had been going badly for him as an artist then, so he changed his career radically and took up science. The poem was put away, and in Mexico City years later (1948), Fernando Castro Pacheco became acquainted with it and wanted to illustrate it. He did so with engravings from linoleum blocks. The two intended to publish the material as a book but lacked financial backing. It was stored away again with the hope that some day they could do so. In 1975, an homage to Alfredo Barrera Vásquez was held on his seventy-fifth birthday, presided over by then Governor Carlos Loret de Mola. At that time, Castro Pacheco proposed that *Cruz* be published as the "coronation" of the tribute. Consequently, Loret de Mola generously offered to help. When he went out of office shortly afterwards, he recommended to incoming Governor Francisco Luna Kan that support should be continued for the printing. Thus the work was finally published in 1976.

The poem is based on a Mayan concept of the five cardinal points, the usual four plus the center, as colors. They are divided into two groups by means of a diagonal. East and South represent red and yellow and are true colors; West and North, symbolized by black and white, respectively, are negations of color. Green, represented by the Center, is also a color and symbolizes the axis of life, the midpoint of the world. Red (East) is the color of the dawn, of blood, of fire, the origin of human activity each day. Man's most important works are done by day. Yellow (South) symbolizes the exuberance of nature, solar light, heat, fertility, the fields where agriculture can prosper and where animals multiply. Black (West) represents the dwelling of the night, the tomb of the sun. There day ends, and the terrible darkness, full of malignant spirits, begins; it is where evil lies in wait and nocturnal animals live. Even today it is said that the wind from the West is bad. White (North) is coldness, white death; harm comes from that direction, as do drizzles and the evils that winter brings. Green is man himself (life, hope), who is the center wherever he may be. The poet, incarnating the Mayan spirit, stands in the middle, the cross (roads) of the winds of the world. He becomes one with the several elements of nature (the quetzal, the serpent, the corn field) and speaks with her voice. The poet feels himself in the heart of the Mayan world, first as an individual, then as a part of the whole. He finally invokes the past tradition of the *Popol Vuh* to join him.[39] Thus *Cruz* is an interpretation of the cosmos according to indigenous beliefs. The poet, with powerful expression and imagery, has captured the genius of the native people. This is indeed one of the great poems to come out of the region.

The dust jacket of the book *Cruz: Poema en cinco puntos cardinales*, poem by Alfredo Barrera Vásquez with engravings from linoleum blocks by Fernando Castro Pacheco.

One of the mature writers of Yucatan who takes an active part in the intellectual life of its capital, Clemente López Trujillo was born in Mérida on January 2, 1905. He is a poet and bibliographer and is now director of the Division of Libraries and Archives of the state. Author of *Feria de Frutas* (1932) and *El Venado* (1941), one of the best poems written in Yucatan, he was awarded the Eligio Ancona Prize in 1971 and is also a respected writer on the national level.[40] In *Feria,* his first book of poems, López Trujillo introduced a breath of literary freshness to Yucatecan letters. In it he uses the haiku with great success:

> Mandarina
> Muchacha fácil en el tálamo,
> la desnudan los dedos sin fatiga.
> Ombligo tierno de los naranjales.

The last book of poetry published by López Trujillo is *Poesía (1932–1978),* Yucatán en las Letras (Mérida, México: Ediciones Komesa, 1979).[41]

Humberto Lara y Lara (b. October 21, 1906) almost finished the study of law before having to give it up because of financial difficulties.[42] As a young man he dedicated himself to teaching, letters, and journalism. Lara y Lara was director of the *Diario del Sureste* for fifteen years and founded and directed several newspapers and reviews, both weekly and monthly. Teaching, however, has been his first love. For many years, he was instructor of world literature in the Preparatory School of the University of Yucatan. In the School of Anthropological Sciences of the University he taught the introduction to philosophy and the history of Oriental cultures. At the present time he is professor of world literature, Spanish-American literature, and literary criticism in the Advanced Normal School and of the history of culture in the Pre-School Normal School. Lara y Lara is also manager of the publishing house Talleres Gráficos y Editorial "Zamná" in Mérida. In the field of literature he has written both prose and poetry. In prose the author has published two works of literary-historical character, *La Ermita de Santa Isabel* and *Monografía de Sisal.* He has also published short stories with Yucatecan themes that have not been collected in book form. Some are included, however, in the work "En la Montaña Chiclera," which is to come out soon. He now (1977) has in press a book of political criticism, customs, and short stories that will be entitled "Don Toribio de la Tetera." Lara y Lara's favorite prose work is "La Montaña Chiclera," a narrative in which he describes how he "lived in almost primitive jungle surroundings, with cruel exploitation of man by man" (Lara).

The author has published numerous poems in daily newspapers, reviews, and magazines. About twenty of them are lyrics for popular songs that are sung in serenades and have been recorded on phonograph records with the music of composers such as Arturo Cámara Tappan, Pastor Cervera, Manuel López Barbeito, and Candelario Lezama. He has published two books of verse, *Poema de*

Amor Perdido and *Canto a mi Raza y a su Apóstol*. The former contains fifty lyrical compositions. The title poem of the latter won first prize in the poetry contest organized to commemorate the centenary of the birth of Felipe Carrillo Puerto on November 8, 1974.[43] It consists of four poems of epic nature. The remaining three in the book, "Por el Rojo Camino Polvoriento" (1926), "Mesticita de mi Tierra," and "Estampa (Tríptico)," have regional themes. Lara y Lara indicates that he was influenced in his poetry by readings of the Romantics and the *modernistas* during his youth, from 1920 to 1940, and gives Gustavo Adolfo Bécquer and Rubén Darío among foreign poets and Luis Rosado Vega among the Yucatecans as those who possibly influenced most his lyrical production. He acknowledges that his native region and the Mayan element appear in his works. The book of his own poetry that he likes most is *Poema de Amor Perdido,* for it expresses his emotional experiences (Lara).

Now director of the Biblioteca Cepeda in Mérida, Leopoldo Peniche Vallado (b. February 23, 1908) has been a journalist since 1931 because, as he says, it is extremely difficult to live by one's writings in Mexico.[44] His literary activities have been focused mainly in three areas: journalism, theater, and critical essay. In the latter field he has preferred to write literary and artistic criticism but has also dealt with political, social, and historical topics. Some of these works were collected and published in *Teatro y Vida* in 1957.[45] Most of them, however, remain scattered in several Yucatecan, Mexican, and foreign newspapers and reviews with which he has collaborated over a period of thirty years. Peniche Vallado was awarded the Eligio Ancona Prize in 1973 for his outstanding production in the fields of literature, literary criticism, and journalism.[46] At the present time he contributes to *Cuadernos Americanos* and has done so regularly since 1964. He states that his favorite creative work is always the latest one that he has completed, which is often the case with writers who have a continual desire to surpass what they have already produced (Peniche Vallado). At the time of our interview, he was working on a historical critical essay, "Promotores e Historiadores de la Rebelión Maya de 1847 en Yucatán: Constancia Crítica," which analyzes the political actions of the former and the historiographical criterion of the latter concerning the events of that bloody episode that shook the nation.

Peniche Vallado's dramatic production is considerable. He has had seven plays produced by professional and experimental companies in the cities of Mérida, Campeche, and Jalapa, state of Veracruz. In the latter city his work *Henequén* won the only prize awarded by the judges in a nationwide contest conducted in 1960 by the National Institute of Fine Arts. Published in 1961, this play is unfortunately out of print.[47] Three other of his dramas, *La Batalla Perdida* (1962), "Comida de Almas," and *Memorias de uno de Tantos* (1974), have won prizes in local contests. Twelve of Peniche Vallado's plays have not been staged although five of these have been published. The remaining seven are still in manuscript form. The themes of the author's theatrical works are varied but are always based on reality, whether past or present, and they have a social thesis. He states that he has never produced literature simply to entertain. The dramatic structure of his plays is traditional, for Peniche Vallado says that he has not been inclined towards "surrealistic or other types of eccentricities in form and content" (Peniche Vallado).

Two plays, *La Batalla Perdida* and *Cecilio el Magno,* will provide an idea of the dramatic production of the author. The former won the prize as the best unpublished play in 1959 in the Fourth Southeast Zone Regional Dramatic Contest, sponsored jointly by the National Institute of Fine Arts and the state government, held in Mérida. It was premiered in the Theater of the University of Yucatan on November 17 that same year by the New Theater Group.[48] A drama that deals with problems of the Mexican working class, it shows the disorganized relationship among the social levels of the republic since the Revolution broke the dividing line that made the upper class impregnable (*Batalla,* p. xviii). Peniche Vallado presents in this play the case of a middle-class working family that has kept its old concepts and conduct with reference to class structure. Consequently, it goes against the notions of social progress that have prevailed since the lower middle class took over the Revolution. The ideas of the family soon clash violently with the current beliefs of their own social world. They want only the rights that they deserve as an integral part of a class they are proud to belong to. Soon they notice, however, that no one will pardon them for going against the current. Thus it becomes evident that the Revolution has not ended the attitude of previous regimes that manual labor is degrading and represents a condition of servitude. Therefore, in order to adapt to the so-called new systems of social organization, it is necessary to avoid that type of work. In this way, one can aspire to the new status where he can find an easier life and a better cultural level. Naturally, members of the family react to this situation according to their personal dispositions. The son, a worker with the same ideals as his father, struggles without compromise for the rights of his class and is not won over by flattery from the rich. Moving from one social group to another in search of personal gain is to betray his own class in his eyes. He cannot conceive of a laborer who has suffered the exploitation of the bosses wanting to become one himself and also to exploit his fellow workers. Peniche Vallado adds to this conflict the confusion that exists in the relationship among classes. These contradictions are adopted by the so-called revolutionary reality because it lacks a structure to prevent such paradoxes (*Batalla,* p. xx).

Cecilio el Magno (1968) treats Cecilio Chi, one of the most important caciques of the Caste War.[49] Nevertheless, the work is not purely historical. When the dramatic needs of an incident require it, the author has changed the facts by modifying the historical place and order even to the point of anachronism. The dates of happenings and the names of persons and places in the play are taken from the historical works of the classic Yucatecan writers Eligio Ancona, Serapio Baqueiro, and Juan Francisco Molina Solís. Peniche Vallado occasionally used fictitious material (*Cecilio,* p. 8) and also drew from the legendary versions of two works, especially *La Conjura de Xinum* by Ermilo Abreu Gómez and *Cecilio Chi* by General Severo del Castillo. In order to give realistic expressions to his work, he took a little from each—a sentence, a speech, a dramatic situation, a description, or even an occasional ideological orientation. This procedure is understandable when we consider that his purpose was not to record history but simply to dramatize a personality that, although historical, has strong epic-legendary characteristics (*Cecilio,* p. 4). The characterization of the protagonist in "Cocom" (a short tale) by Abreu Gómez influenced Peniche Vallado in his portrayal of Cecilio Chi. "'Cocom' is not only the narrative, the historical truth of the *auto* of Maní but a manner of truth that history does not seek out, and if it were to do so, would not obtain it: it is a possible truth. Therefore, one ought not be surprised that the names of the protagonists may not always be exact. If one is true, the others could be.''[50] Peniche Vallado interprets historical deeds using the same procedure. Sometimes he deforms or falsifies them, but he does not do so from a desire to distort the real truth. He is seeking an implicit or possible truth that would give ethical and aesthetic transcendence to the deed itself without taking from it the appearance of feasibility (*Cecilio,* p. 4). This technique also raises the possibility that the author was influenced, perhaps subconsciously, by the great Mexican playwright Rodolfo Usigli and his interpretation of national history in *Corona de Sombra* (1947), which deals with the tragedy of Maximilian and Carlota.[51]

Historical sources paint Cecilio Chi as a bloody, congenital criminal type without any redeeming human virtues. He is the primitive man who kills for the pleasure of killing (*Cecilio,* pp. 4–5). Nevertheless, the author deduces from the historical context of his actions certain positive qualities and even a heroic spirit when Chi's actions are directed towards the defense of his exploited race. There is, then, beneath the surface, an essence of love and sacrifice that Peniche Vallado reveals in this semihistorical interpretation in dramatic form, an explication that finds a positive function in the conventionally negative qualities of the character. The fact that the magnetic figure of Cecilio Chi had the support and sympathies of the vast majority of the Maya is not contested. He was fighting, it should be emphasized, against exploiters, not against the white race (*Cecilio,* pp. 5–6). The first immoral acts were committed by an army officer, not by an Indian; the first burning by another officer. The Mayan leader represented the legitimate and human aspirations of his people engaged in a just struggle, and he served their ideals magnanimously. The author considers these reasons sufficient to justify the heroic quality given to the character of Cecilio Chi. Peniche Vallado states that when he had to choose between his thesis and dramatic art, he sacrificed the latter. Nevertheless, he does not write "thesis for thesis' sake" and seeks a balance between the message and art (*Cecilio,* p. 8).

The Mayan and Yucatan have had a strong influence as a characteristic aspect of the theatrical work of Leopoldo Peniche Vallado, as he acknowledges. *La que Salió al Camino* (1949) is a realistic development of the legend of "La Xtabay" from the version by Antonio Mediz Bolio, with a Freudian psychoanalytical background.[52] "Venados y Hombres" is a drama of Mayan traditions and superstitions set in present-day Yucatan. The indigenous environment, however, is separated from modern civilization, and in this way the Indian ways of life and thought can be appraised without contamination. Also regional in theme, the play "Comida de Almas" is set in a small town in Yucatan during the 1930s and makes use of certain peculiar situations that have their origin in legendary ways of thinking and working (Peniche Vallado).

It is not unusual in Mexico for scientists to produce literature.[53] Carlos Urzaiz (b. December 29, 1918), a physician, has published in the field of letters *Crónicas de un Estudiante de Medicina* (1959), *Vida de Médico* (1965), *La Cucaña* (1972), and *Mi Abuelo el Diablo* (1976).[54] He has also written articles for the daily *Novedades de Yucatán* and for two local literary reviews, *Juzgue* and *Integración Sureste,* both now defunct. The themes of his works are different aspects of human conduct and social problems perceived or observed in the practice of medicine. The author is not aware of any particular influences on his literary production although he says that he has read many Spanish authors and that Cervantes has always impressed him the most. When Dr. Urzaiz first began to write, he was influenced by the style of the classic Spanish authors; now he is trying to mold his own to reflect the spoken language, that is, to be more modern. He states that the Mayan and Yucatan have indeed influenced his manner of perception although it may not be reflected greatly in what he writes (Urzaiz).

The two latest works of Carlos Urzaiz treat different aspects of human nature in today's world. *La Cucaña* is a collection of anecdotal sketches of customs, similar to that genre so popular in the nineteenth century. The author discusses different things in contemporary society, such as the clock, the horse, the bicycle, the automobile, the rest room, and barbarism. The scenes are narrated humorously and at times ironically. There is an occasional use of vocabulary that shows the influence of Spanish Golden Age writers, such as Cervantes. Moreover, allusions and choice of words point to Dr. Urzaiz's profession of medicine. At times he criticizes the weaknesses of contemporary society. In one sketch he describes various recommendations on "How to Live One Hundred Years" and then wonders who would want to live that long in the present-day world. In "La Barbarie" the author affirms that "civilization" has changed the world, then questions whether man has improved as a living being. After meditating on this point and evoking the crimes of man against man in the twentieth century, he pessimistically concludes that the cave man still survives, poorly disguised, in the frock coat.

Mi Abuelo el Diablo is a book of short stories. The title work of the collection is a humorous, fantastic tale of a wayward grandfather who disappears, then reappears in the form of a dog, only to come back still later in the shape of the devil, complete with horns and tail. "Experimento Fatal" is the story of the suicide of a female medical student who makes herself pregnant by artificial insemination. This story is the strongest condemnation by the author of a society that judges by appearances and labels as "crazy" people who are different from the "normal." In the final story, "La Muerte del Señor Acebo," there is the probable influence of Juan Rulfo, a Mexican experimental short story writer and novelist. Some of the stories have to do with medicine or death and obviously show influences of the author's profession. Two are lightly satirical of psychologists, another of surgeons and unnecessary operations. The humor of Urzaiz is often ironical. In this book there appears again his skepticism of the true progress of man and the feeling that human life is worth very little.[55]

In these two works the author dissects contemporary society and exposes some of its weaknesses and inconsistencies. His favorite technique is the use of ironical humor. The anecdotes and stories are not morbid, but the physician-writer is somewhat pessimistic about the progress of man and believes that human nature has not changed over the centuries. There is little obvious influence of Yucatan and the Mayan in his works, with only an occasional word or point of reference, such as "xtabay," showing the regional connection.

Alberto Cervera Espejo was born in Mérida on February 28, 1929. Soon after obtaining his law degree, he became a judge and served in this capacity for twenty years. He now considers himself a journalist, a profession that has interested him since he was seventeen years old, and writes for the daily *Novedades de Yucatán* and other periodicals.[56] The author has written poetry, plays, and works of a political and legal nature. Cervera Espejo is also a theatrical critic and has published in this field *Reflexiones sobre el Teatro Experimental* and *El Teatro de la Revolución en Yucatán.*[57] In 1976 he published *Historia Morrocotuda de mi Viaje a Cuba.*[58] This book consists of impressions gathered by the author in a one-week trip to that island. He says that he makes no attempt to produce a "social economic-political" study as many have done but simply to relate in a firsthand account what he saw, heard, and perceived of the Cuban phenomenon during his short visit. He wrote from hurried notes taken on a whirlwind trip and did not revise them (*Viaje,* pp. 121–22).

Cervera Espejo has published two works in the field of poetry and drama: *Poemas, Versos y otros Fantasmas* and *3 en 1 Acto* ("Graciela," "Otra vez como antes," and "El Señor Juez y Aquellos Viejos Arboles con Nidos"), both in January of 1977.[59] In *Poemas* the author has brought together verses written in 1951–53 and from 1963 to date, although the time of composition is not given for many. The work is divided into "La Ropa Interior," "Seis Odas," "Tríptico," and "La Ropa de Batalla." According to Cervera Espejo, two general themes are present: certain social problems ("La Ropa de Batalla") and some personal ones. The *fantasmas* refer to persons, memories, and realities that surrounded him (Autoprólogo, *Poemas*). He acknowledges being influenced in his poetry by Federico García Lorca, Pablo Neruda, and Nicolás Guillén (Cervera). The influence of Neruda is apparent in the "Seis Odas."

In the collection *3 en 1 Acto,* the first play, "Graciela," takes place in a small, provincial Mexican city. In a monologue of a barber to his client, the author develops the intense, personal drama of the father who is shaving the man who had "wronged" his daughter, the shame of which had resulted in her suicide, some years before. The author effectively portrays the inner struggle of the speaker, who almost kills with his razor the "villain" in the chair. This is a concise study of personal honor and justice that brings to mind the short story "Espuma y nada más" of the Colombian Hernando Téllez, a narrative of the *violencia* in Colombia. The next piece, "Otra vez como antes (Teatro en 3 Minutos)," treats the case of the unfaithful husband who is jilted by his lover, who writes him a "Dear John" of her coming marriage, thus breaking off their relationship. Turning the tables on the *macho,* the author creates a situation that, to my knowledge, has not been used before in the Spanish-American theater. The last play, "El Señor Juez y Aquellos Viejos Arboles con Nidos," is another case involving personal honor. The situation is the attempted bribery and blackmail of a judge who is soon to retire. The magistrate refuses to allow himself to be compromised even though the political consequences may be disastrous. Ironically, he had already made, but not announced, the decision desired by the would-be briber. Although the reader might expect Cervera Espejo's experience in court to have been the source of this brief drama, it is based on the Spanish translation of a short story by Ben Ames Williams (*3 en 1 Acto,* p. 66). Judging from these three one-act plays, it is obvious that the author is very interested in the ironies of fate that occur in man's everyday private life. His long years on the bench must have provided the quarry from which to draw realistic raw material.

Alberto Cervera Espejo acknowledges that Yucatan is bound to have influenced his literary production, for "all sincere works have to have influence of the environment in which they were written." Although he states that he does not deliberately seek folklore-type local color (Cervera), the regional motif is present in "Tríptico: Pozo-Choza-Ceiba" and "La Sed de la Tierra" of *Poemas.* The section "Cuando Despierten los Hombres Mayas," from the same book, carries an epigraph from the *Libro de Chilam Balam de Chumayel* and contains five poems ("El Silencio," "La Voz," "El Despertar," "La Esperanza," and "Invocación"), all of which have indigenous themes.

A professor of English and of aesthetics in the Institute of Fine Arts of Yucatan, Roldán Peniche Barrera (b. June 3, 1935) is the son of Leopoldo Peniche Vallado. He is currently head of the Department of Cultural Promotion of the state government. Profoundly interested in Mayan themes, whether from the pre-Hispanic epoch, after the conquest, or in contemporary times, he gives a social meaning to his interpretation of them.[60] The author has published two literary works, and the indigenous influence is evident in both. In *El Ultimo Sol* (1970), Peniche Barrera has combined a kind of Chilam Balamnesque language with several poetic constructions of today.[61] In the first part of *Zamná y Otras Narraciones Mayas* (1973), which deals with the greatest of the Mayan prophets, he uses a language based on biblical parables and also on some constructions of *Zarathustra* of Nietzsche.[62] The last two sections of this work have definite influences from the *Popol Vuh* and from the *Libros de Chilam Balam.* Reflecting his deep-seated feelings for the Maya, the author states that he feels a special affection for *Zamná.* Although indigenous themes are predominant in his works to date, the writings of Peniche Barrera fall in the contemporary literary current that in Mexico includes Carlos Fuentes, Juan Rulfo, and others (Peniche Barrera).

Not a native of Yucatan but certainly a part of its literary scene, Oscar Palacios was born in Yajalón, Chiapas, Mexico, in 1945. After studying medicine at the National University for three years, he moved to Mérida in 1967 to enter the Faculty of Jurisprudence of the University of Yucatan. While completing his studies, he worked as a journalist. Palacios still considers this his profession since he does not intend to make a career of law. He noted that journalism has been an important step in the lives of many excellent writers and feels that it has helped him improve his short stories and poetry.[63] The author has published three books of poetry and prose and a pamphlet of seven sonnets. Another book is in press, and he is working on a novel.[64] He is still not satisfied with his accomplishments in that he is striving to surpass what he has already written (Palacios).

Man as a universal being is the basic motif of Palacio's works. In his poetry he utilizes two aspects: common themes in life—such as love and death—and social problems, the struggle of the *pueblo* for their liberation (Palacios). It is difficult to identify the influence of other authors on Palacios, but he states that he likes poets Pablo Neruda, Nicolás Guillén, and César Vallejo, among others; in the short story he prefers Juan Rulfo, Tito Monterroso, Julio Cortázar, and several more. He does not, however, associate himself with any particular literary movement. It is obvious on reading certain of his works that Yucatan and the Mayan have influenced him profoundly. He states, nevertheless, that he has tried to penetrate the subtle psychology of the Maya but is still unsuccessful. The author is not interested in portraying the picturesque Indian of the straw huts but the man with his place on this planet who hopes for more just living conditions and struggles to defend himself through stoicism and irony (Palacios).

El Otro Tiempo (1971) consists of prose and poetry.[65] In the short commentaries he uses ironical humor to make an anecdotal analysis of various aspects of human nature, such as avarice, war, death, vanity, love, envy, and peace. In the poetry section he utilizes the universal themes of patriotism, social concern for the people, life, love, and death. The poet occasionally reveals his disillusionment with the world. In one poem he shows his antipathy for the foreign policy of the United States:

> México,
>   se nace en tí
> Para vivir en la eternidad de tu espacio,
> Aguila y Serpiente,
>   Aguila muerta
> Serpiente go home
>   Aguila levántate y anda.[66]

The poems of this collection are characterized by vibrant emotion.

The prevailing motif of *Se Solicitan Lectores* (1973), a collection of poems, is social justice, and the poet shows his admiration for personages such as Fidel Castro, Ernesto "Che" Guevara, and Martin Luther King.[67] The theme of a lost love appears in a few poems. The predominant tone of the work is ironical, which at times becomes bitter:

> Llegó la luz hace dos mil luces,
> nació y creció en la sombra de la indiferencia.
> Gloria a Dios en sus locuras
> y paz en la guerra a los hombres de buena voluntad.[68]

In *Cuentos de Insomnio* (1975), short stories, Palacios treats the motif of love in general and is also concerned with social problems.[69] The first story, "El himeneo," which takes place immediately after the wedding, is highly ironical, especially so for the Mexican; "El círculo" has the tragic realism of some tales by Horacio Quiroga, the great Uruguayan short story writer; and "Dos (Monólogo para decir a solas)" smacks of the Mexican Revolution. A few of the stories show the possible influence of the author's days as a medical student. A trace of Yucatan appears in others. *Siete Sonetos para Decir Yucatán* (1976) give the poet's interpretation of seven important epochs in the history of the region and show his love for the land and its people. Palacios is not pessimistic, but he continues to be concerned with social justice, as the opening verses of the last poem indicate:

> No todo pasó, Yucatán empieza;
> hombre maya de ayer y de mañana,
> no todo pasó en la tierra temprana
> donde lo justo aún es niebla espesa.[70]

Francisco López Cervantes, son of Clemente López Trujillo, was born in Mexico City on October 18, 1951, but his father returned with him to Mérida when the child was two years old. López Cervantes, also a poet, organized in collaboration with a small group of local writers the literary review *Platero* in 1973.[71] In the first issue the author published "Tres poemas." He finds poetry in the everyday things around him, identifies himself with the walls under contemplation (both are made of dust), and is sensitive to the works of nature (the gentle rain). In another poem, "Conquistar lo hermoso" (in No. 4), a somewhat obscure work, the poet asks us to seek the beautiful in life and to forget the ugliness of the past. Only the present exists. Man should become another who has cast aside the base and has conquered the lovely. López Cervantes has also published articles on literary criticism that show his interest in the Mayan and in contemporary movements in poetry. Judging from his writings in *Platero*, certainly an inadequate sample, he apparently has been influenced by Antonio Mediz Bolio and César Vallejo.

Many writers worthy of being included in this brief study have been omitted because of space limitations. One is José Esquivel Pren, poet, novelist, author of the monumental *Historia de la Literatura en Yucatán*, and recipient of the Eligio Ancona Prize.[72] Others are Bernardino Mena Brito, historian and novelist; Eduardo Urzaiz Rodríguez, essayist and novelist; Miguel Angel Menéndez, poet and novelist; Antonio Magaña Esquivel, critic, novelist, and playwright now living in Mexico City; Ricardo Mimenza Castillo, poet and writer of legends; Dolores Bolio, poetess and novelist; Wilberto Cantón, dramatist and poet residing in Mexico City; Carlos Moreno Medina, poet; Jesús Amaro Gamboa, novelist and short story writer; Rodolfo Ruz Menéndez, essayist and poet; and Jaime Orosa Díaz, essayist, historian, and dramatist. Some short story writers not discussed here are Carlos Villamil Castillo, Renán Escalante Mendoza, Raúl Maldonado Coello, Roger Manzanilla Cáceres, Luis Hoyos Villanueva, and Nidia Esther Rosado. Two Yucatecans who sought out greater literary opportunities in Mexico City are Juan García Ponce, short story writer and novelist, and Joaquín Bestard, novelist. Marco A. Almazán, one of the best humorists in the nation, reversed the trend and left Mexico City to live in Mérida, where he has written some ten books.[73]

On considering the panorama of literature in Yucatan, it is evident that the Mayan element is the most important motif. Not only did the Indian literature prior to the conquest produce its own masterpieces, but these works plus other local themes are still being used by writers in the twentieth century. At the present time the indigenous past and present continue to serve as an important inspiration for some authors, while others seek more universal motifs not so easily identified with the region. The vast majority of living writers in Yucatan are poets, short story writers, and essayists. There are few novelists writing today, nor have there been many during this century. In fact, when we look back at the novelistic production of Yucatan, it becomes evident that none has attained permanent literary value at the international level.[74] It seems that poetry, the short story, and the legend will continue to prosper as they have in the past. The future of literature in the state appears bright when we consider that there are many talented creative writers in the area. It is even possible that there exists a latent boom in literary production in Mérida, a new flowering of letters.[75] Yet a financial drought may nip it in the bud since there are few opportunities for these authors to publish their works. In fact, belles lettres in the region may now be in a period of crisis for this reason.

Important indicators of literary and artistic activity in a community are the organizing of literary discussion groups, usually with generational tendencies, and the periodic publication of journals that serve as outlets for their writings. The fact that there is only one literary review in which authors may publish their works locally may reveal an unhealthy state of affairs of intellectual activity. The literary supplements of the three daily newspapers, of course, offer publication opportunities. Nevertheless, only one, the *Diario del Sureste,* actively seeks the participation of young writers. The government must be the patron of the arts; yet it does little to foster the development of cultural expressions beyond giving limited subsidies to organizations charged with public education. The Eligio Ancona Prize was established by the state government in 1960, but the competition for this award has been reduced by the inability of young writers to make their works known before the prize is awarded. Actually, it has been granted only thirteen times, through 1978. Thus it may be that only a select few are able to compete for this prize although there are doubtless others worthy of it.[76] At the moment the principal sponsors of cultural activity in Yucatan are the University of Yucatan and the government of the state. In early 1978, the latter began a series of monographs through its "Fondo Editorial" that are to be published on Yucatecan subjects, past and present, in almost any discipline.[77] Thus new efforts are being made locally to afford outlets to authors for their production, but only the future will tell whether this difficulty has been surmounted. A related aspect of the economic problem is that the writer has to make his living in activities other than the literary arts, hence the amount of his production is limited, in this case by lack of time for writing. Probably the greatest danger is that he may become bogged down with the frustrations of a bureaucratic job and vegetate.[78] In the state, the problem is more acute than in Mexico City, where there exist more opportunities for the writer to receive payment for his talents (such as writing scripts for motion pictures and television).

The geographic and cultural isolation of Yucatan has been detrimental to local writers not only financially but also because it has deprived them of the opportunity to exchange ideas with other national authors as well as to make contacts with the large publishing houses—all of which are located in Mexico City. Although the writer is not so isolated as he was fifteen years ago, the problem still exists.[79] In sum, the young author who expects to prosper in the field of letters will probably find it necessary to move to the national capital, at least long enough to get to know other intellectuals and to make contacts with the big publishing houses. This is what every Yucatecan who has achieved national or international recognition has done so far.

NOTES

1. Alfredo Barrera Vásquez, *La Literatura Maya: Corta Memoria sobre el Tema* (Mérida, Yucatán, México: Ediciones de la Universidad de Yucatán, 1969), pp. 5–7. Hereafter cited as Barrera, *Lit. Maya*. This essay is also found in the *Revista de la Universidad de Yucatán,* No. 62 (1969).

Webster's New International Dictionary of the English Language, 2d ed., unabridged, defines literature as follows: "3 . . . a The total of preserved writings belonging to a given language or people. b Specif., that part of it which is notable for literary form or expression, as distinguished, on the one hand, from works merely technical or erudite, and on the other, from journalistic or other ephemeral literary writings; belles-lettres."

2. Francisco Monterde, ed., *El Libro del Consejo,* trans. Georges Raynaud, J. M. González de Mendoza, and Miguel Angel Asturias, 3d ed., Biblioteca del Estudiante Universitario, No. 1 (México: Universidad Nacional Autónoma de México, 1964), p. v; Adrián Recinos, trans., *Popol Vuh: Las Antiguas Historias del Quiché,* 4th ed., Colección Popular, No. 11 (México: Fondo de Cultura Económica, 1960), p. 15. Hereafter cited as Monterde, *Libro,* and Recinos, respectively.

3. Francisco Monterde, ed., *Teatro Indígena Prehispánico (Rabinal Achí),* Biblioteca del Estudiante Universitario, No. 71 (México: Ediciones de la Universidad Nacional Autónoma, 1955), p. viii. Hereafter cited as Monterde, *Rabinal.*

Queché, literally "numerous forests," was the name applied to a group of three large tribes (p. 96), not to be confused with the Quiché, a bigger linguistic group.

4. Barrera, *Lit. Maya,* p. 15; Francisco Monterde, ed., *Anales de los Xahil,* trans. Georges Raynaud, Miguel Angel Asturias, and J. M. González de Mendoza, Biblioteca del Estudiante Universitario, No. 61 (México: Ediciones de la Universidad Nacional Autónoma, 1946), p. v. Hereafter cited as Monterde, *Anales.*

5. Alfredo Barrera Vásquez and Silvia Rendón, *El Libro de los Libros de Chilam Balam,* Colección Popular, No. 42 (México: Fondo de Cultura Económica, 1969), p. 9; Antonio Mediz Bolio, *Libro de Chilam Balam de Chumayel,* Biblioteca del Estudiante Universitario, No. 21 (México: Ediciones de la Universidad Nacional Autónoma, 1941), p. ix. Hereafter cited as Barrera and Rendón, and Mediz Bolio, *Chilam,* respectively.

6. Albertina Saravia E., ed., *Popol Vuh: Antiguas Historias de los Indios Quichés de Guatemala,* 2d ed., Colección Sepan Cuantos, No. 36 (México: Editorial Porrúa, 1966), p. xiv. Michael Coe describes a fourth pre-Conquest Mayan manuscript, the Grolier Codex, that dates from the thirteenth century. Some archaeologists, however, doubt its authenticity. See Coe, *The Maya Scribe and His World* (New York: The Grolier Club, 1973), pp. 150–54.

7. Alfredo Barrera Vásquez, *El Libro de los Cantares de Dzitbalché,* Serie Investigaciones, 9 (México: Instituto Nacional de Antropología e Historia, 1965).

8. "You have the point of your arrow well sharpened, / well strung have you the cord / of your bow; you have put good / *catsim* resin on the feathers / at the end of the shaft of your arrow." Barrera, *Lit. Maya,* p. 27; *Dzitbalché,* pp. 77–78.

9. "Literature" as used in this essay refers to the belles lettres: poetry, drama, novel, and the like. Thus Fray Diego de Landa and other priests did not write literature but chronicles. For more on this point, see José Esquivel Pren, "Historia de la Poesía, la Novela, el Humorismo, el Costumbrismo, la Oratoria, la Crítica y el Ensayo," in *Enciclopedia Yucatanense,* V (1946), 331. Hereafter cited as Pren.

He also points out "el hecho inaudito e increíble de que desde el año 1542 en que fue fundada la actual ciudad de Mérida, hasta la segunda decena del siglo diecinueve, no haya habido en Yucatán ningún poeta, ni se haya escrito nada que sea digno de dar este nombre a su autor" (pp. 350–51).

10. "El primer yucateco poeta—no poeta yucateco en la acepción conferida" (Pren, p. 361).

11. Marcelino Menéndez y Pelayo, cited in Carlos González Peña, *History of Mexican Literature,* trans. Gusta Barfield Nance and Florene Johnson Dunstan, 3d ed. (Dallas, Texas: Southern Methodist University Press, 1968), p. 170. Hereafter cited as González Peña.

12. Pren, p. 623; John S. Brushwood and José Rojas Garcidueñas, *Breve Historia de la Novela Méxicana* (México: Ediciones de Andrea, 1959), p. 24.

13. Ermilo Abreu Gómez, *Clásicos, Románticos, Modernos* (México: Ediciones Botas, 1934), p. 99; also cited in Pren, p. 630.

14. Severo del Castillo, *Cecilio Chi: Novela Histórica Yucateca* (Mérida, Yuc.: Editorial del Sureste, de Felipe Rosas Garibaldi, 1937). Five hundred copies were printed. Pren, p. 646.

15. Agustín Yáñez, "Don Justo Sierra: Su Vida, sus Ideas y su Obra," in *Poesías,* Vol. I of *Obras Completas del Maestro Justo Sierra* (México, D.F.: Universidad Nacional Autónoma de México, 1948), pp. 79–80. This volume will be cited as *Obras.*

16. Justo Sierra, "Playera," in *Obras,* I, 235–36.

17. González Peña, p. 345; *Obras,* 15 vols., 1948–49 [1950]. Volume I lists fifteen

volumes and gives the title of Vol. XV as *"Escritos Diversos e Indices* (En prensa)." I have not seen this volume nor found it in bibliographical references.

18. The *Diccionario Porrúa de Historia, Biografía y Geografía de México,* 3d ed. (1970) and Brushwood and Rojas Garcidueñas, *Breve Historia* (p. 121), give his place of birth as Chemax and the date as 1873. González Peña (p. 305) gives his place of birth as Valladolid and the date as June 21, 1876.

19. Luis Rosado Vega, *El Alma Misteriosa del Mayab* (México: Ediciones Botas, 1934), p. 9. Hereafter cited as Rosado Vega, *Alma.*

20. Rosado Vega, *Amerindmaya* (México: Ediciones Botas, 1938), title page: "Proyecciones de la vieja Tierra del Mayab, de aquella que fue en su día tierra encantada de maravilla, de amor, de ensueño, de fe." Hereafter cited as Rosado Vega, *Amerindmaya.*

21. Rosado Vega, *Amerindmaya,* p. 8. Also cited in Pren, pp. 661–62.

22. Pren, p. 664. Brushwood and Rojas Garcidueñas, *Breve Historia,* p. 121.

23. Antonio Mediz Bolio, *Libro de Chilam Balam de Chumayel,* Biblioteca del Estudiante Universitario, No. 21 (México: Ediciones de la Universidad Nacional Autónoma, 1941).
I had the pleasure of seeing *Deseada,* filmed on an hacienda near Chichén Itzá, in Mexico City in 1951.

24. Mediz Bolio, *La Tierra del Faisán y del Venado* (Buenos Aires: Contreras y Sanz Editores, 1922), p. iv; 4th ed. (México: Ediciones Botas, 1965), p. 11. The first edition is a beautifully decorated volume but hard to find. Consequently, future page references are to *Tierra,* Botas.

25. José Luis Martínez, Introducción, *Literatura Indígena Moderna: A. Mediz Bolio, E. Abreu Gómez, A. Henestrosa* (México: Ediciones Mensaje, 1942), p. 17; *Tierra,* Botas, p. 11. Henceforth the first work will be cited as JLM, *Lit. Ind. Mod.*

26. Antonio Mediz Bolio, *A la Sombra de mi Ceiba: Relatos Fáciles* (México: Ediciones Botas, 1956). Hereafter cited as *Sombra.*

27. Henrique González Casanova, Prólogo, in Ermilo Abreu Gómez, *Canek: Historia y Leyenda de un Héroe Maya,* 20th ed., Edición Homenaje (México: Ediciones Oasis, 1969), pp. 11–12. Hereafter cited as *Canek.* His birth date is verified in Cecilia Silva de Rodríguez, *Vida y Obras de Ermilo Abreu Gómez* (México: Publicaciones del Boletín Bibliográfico de la Secretaría de Hacienda y Crédito Público, 1971), p. 7; his death date is taken from Jaime Orosa Díaz, "Vida y Obras de Ermilo Abreu Gómez," *Diario del Sureste,* May 19, 1972.

28. José Luis Martínez, *Literatura Mexicana: Siglo XX, 1910–49,* Primera Parte, Clásicos y Modernos Creación y Crítica Literaria, 3 (México: Antigua Librería Robredo, 1949), pp. 17–18. Hereafter cited as JLM, *Lit. Mex. XX.*

29. JLM, *Lit. Mex. XX,* p. 53; Luis Leal, *Breve Historia del Cuento Mexicano* (México: Ediciones de Andrea, 1956), p. 115.

30. Ermilo Abreu Gómez, *Naufragio de Indios* (México: Ediciones Botas, 1951).

31. Abreu Gómez, *Tata Lobo,* Letras Mexicanas, 5 (México: Fondo de Cultura Económica, 1952). Hereafter cited as *Tata Lobo.*

32. Abreu Gómez, *Leyendas y Consejas del Antiguo Yucatán* (México: Ediciones Botas, 1961).

33. "Donde pone el ojo pone la bala," Mariano Azuela, *Los de Abajo: Novela de la Revolución Mexicana,* Colección Popular (México: Fondo de Cultura Económica, 1965), p. 139. *The Underdogs* is considered the best of the novels of the Revolution.

34. Jorge Luis Borges, *Labyrinths: Selected Stories & Other Writings,* ed. by Donald

A. Yates and James E. Irby (New York: New Directions, 1964), pp. 180, 181, 184, and 185. Read the entire essay for Borges's cogent discussion of this matter.

35. On this same topic see the comments of Alberto Cervera Espejo, "Panorama Actual de la Literatura Yucateca," *Memoria de la Semana de Literatura en Yucatán* (Mérida: Ediciones de la Universidad de Yucatán, 1977), p. 116. Hereafter cited as Cervera, "Panorama."

36. I have obtained some information and opinions in many discussions with Dr. Barrera since 1967. He verified his birth place and date in a letter dated May 15, 1978. Additional data may also be found in a Cordemex flyer sent out in 1977 announcing the coming publication of the "Great Maya-Spanish Spanish-Maya Dictionary."

37. Alfredo Barrera Vásquez, *Recopilación de Cuentos Mayas,* Colección Lunes (México, D.F., 1947). On the title page of this brief work the author's second surname is spelled "Vázquez," which is incorrect. He writes it as given above.

This honor was first authorized in 1960 by the government of the state of Yucatan in order to recognize the merits of Yucatecan writers, artists, and scientists who have been outstanding at the local, national, or international levels as selected by an ad hoc committee of local judges. Other recipients of the award were José Esquivel Pren (essayist, poet, novelist, critic; 1960), Gustavo Río Escalante (professor, composer, singer; 1961), Gonzalo Cámara Zavala (essayist, historian; 1962), Joaquín Ancona Albertos (engineer, professor, mathematician, university president; 1963), Santiago Burgos Brito (essayist, professor, art and literary critic; 1965), Ermilo Abreu Gómez (professor, essayist, dramatist, short story writer, novelist, critic; 1970), Clemente López Trujillo (journalist, poet, essayist, bibliophile; 1971), Fernando Castro Pacheco (painter, sculptor, engraver, professor; 1972), Leopoldo Peniche Vallado (essayist, dramatist, journalist, professor; 1973), Arcadio Poveda Ricalde (professor, astronomer, nuclear physicist; 1976), Silvio Zavala Vallado (professor, historian; 1977), and Cirilo J. Montes de Oca Ramírez (professor, pioneer of radiology in Yucatan; 1978). José Castillo Torre (poet, orator, politician) could not receive his prize because he was seriously ill. This information was sent me by Roldán Peniche Barrera, Head, Department of Cultural Promotion, State of Yucatan.

38. Alfredo Barrera Vásquez, *Cruz: Poema en Cinco Puntos Cardinales* (Mérida, Yucatán, 1976) [*Cross: Poem in Five Cardinal Points*]. The poem was written in 1937 ("when I was young"), and the engravings were done by Fernando Castro Pacheco in 1948 (see colophon). The state government under Governor Carlos Loret de Mola, who wrote a brief presentation to the volume (pp. 7-9), sponsored the printing (conversation with the author in Mérida in May 1977).

39. Much of the information and some of the interpretations of the two preceding paragraphs are found in Barrera Vásquez, *Cruz,* in *El Búho, Revista Semanal,* supplement to *Diario del Sureste,* October 9, 1977, p. 2. This entire issue (eight pages) is taken up by the poem, with illustrations by Fernando Castro Pacheco taken from the original edition of 1976.

Marcel Smith, professor of English at The University of Alabama, has made an English translation of *Cruz.*

40. Jaime Orosa Díaz, *Nombres en las Letras y en la Vida* (Mérida, Yucatán: Universidad de Yucatán, 1975), p. 163.

I gathered this opinion of *El Venado* from personal interviews. Unfortunately, I was unable to obtain a copy while in Mérida.

41. Cervera, "Panorama," pp. 117-18. The haiku is an unrhymed Japanese verse form of three lines containing five, seven, and five syllables, respectively; also, a poem in this form:

Mandarin Orange
Easy girl in the marriage bed,
Tireless fingers strip her.
Tender navel of the orange groves.

The title has the double meaning of "female mandarin" or even "mandarin's wife."
Another point lost in the translation is that "ombligo" also means "center." In fact, the
entire poem has a double level of imagery, one erotic.

In June 1979, as this work was going to press, I received a copy of López Trujillo's
latest book, *Poesía (1932–1978)*, Yucatán en las Letras (Mérida, México: Ediciones
Komesa, 1979). New poetical works included are "Homenaje a Luis Rosado Vega"
(1973), "Variaciones sobre una Lágrima" (1974), "En la Ascensión de Carlos Pellicer"
(1978), "Poemánticos" (1978), and "Otros Poemánticos" (1979).

42. Señor Lara y Lara was kind enough to furnish me some biographical and other
personal information in an interview in Mérida in May of 1977. Hereafter cited as Lara.

43. Humberto Lara y Lara, *Canto a mi Raza y a su Apóstol* (Mérida, Yucatán, México:
Talleres Gráficos y Editorial "Zamná," 1974). While in Mérida, I was unable to consult a
copy of *Poema de Amor Perdido*.

44. Personal information and opinions are from an interview I had with the author in
May 1977 in Mérida. Hereafter cited as Peniche Vallado.

45. Leopoldo Peniche Vallado, *Teatro y Vida: Ensayos—Artículos* (Mérida, Yucatán,
México: Ediciones del Liceo Peninsular de Estudios Literarios, 1957).

46. *El Premio Eligio Ancona 1973* [Mérida, México], Ediciones del Departamento de
Extensión Cultural de la Universidad de Yucatán [1973], p. [12].

47. Leopoldo Peniche Vallado, *Henequén* (Mérida, México: Ediciones de la Universidad de Yucatán, 1961). I was unable to consult this work while in Mérida.

48. Peniche Vallado, *La Batalla Perdida* (Mérida, México: Ediciones de Escritores y
Artistas de Yucatán, Asociados, 1962), pp. v, vii. Hereafter cited as *Batalla*.

49. Peniche Vallado, *Cecilio el Magno* (Mérida, Yucatán, México: Ediciones de la
Universidad de Yucatán, 1968). Its subtitle, *Dramatic Exegesis of the Culminating Episodes of the Life of the Greatest Leader of the Indigenous Rebellion of Yucatan, 1847–49,*
is significant. Hereafter cited as *Cecilio*.

50. The quotation is from a criticism by Andrés Henestrosa in *Cecilio*, p. 4.

51. *Crown of Darkness*. "Antihistorical, in sum, does not mean to me to correct
history, which is made up of deeds that have happened, but to rectify the historicist and
limited interpretation of the deeds and to place them on man's level, who is the one who
creates them" (Rodolfo Usigli, Advertencia, *Corona de sombra: Pieza Antihistórica en
Tres Actos,* ed. Rex Edward Ballinger [New York: Appleton-Century-Crofts, Inc., 1961],
p. xvi). The translation is mine. This play was written in 1943 and first published in 1947.

52. Leopoldo Peniche Vallado, *La que Salió al Camino* (Mérida, México: Ediciones
de la Universidad de Yucatán, 1949). Out of print.

53. An excellent example is Mariano Azuela, the leading novelist of the Mexican
Revolution and author of *Los de Abajo (The Underdogs)*. He served as physician and
surgeon under General Julián Medina, one of Pancho Villa's followers.

54. Dr. Carlos Urzaiz was kind enough to furnish me some biographical and other
personal information in an interview in Mérida in May of 1977. He gave me copies of *La
Cucaña* [Mérida, México, 1972] and *Mi Abuelo el Diablo* (Mérida, Yucatán, México,
1976). Occasionally the year of publication for *La Cucaña* is given as 1971; the colophon

of my copy, however, reads April 20, 1972. References to the interview will be cited as Urzaiz.

55. This is an accurate portrayal of the Mexican's attitude toward the value of life. Octavio Paz analyzes this point in *The Labyrinth of Solitude: Life and Thought in Mexico,* trans. Lysander Kemp (New York: Grove Press, Inc., 1961), p. 58. Carlos Fuentes uses the line "Life is cheap, life is worth nothing . . . " as one of the epigraphs to *The Death of Artemio Cruz,* trans. Sam Hileman (New York: Farrar, Straus and Girous, 1964). It is taken from a Mexican popular song.

56. The author kindly gave me biographical and other personal information in an interview in Mérida in May 1977. Hereafter cited as Cervera.

57. Alberto Cervera Espejo, *Reflexiones sobre el Teatro Experimental* (Mérida, Yucatán, México: Ediciones de la Universidad de Yucatán, 1973); and *El Teatro de la Revolución en Yucatán* (Mérida, Yucatán, México: Ediciones del Gobierno del Estado, 1973).

58. Cervera Espejo, *Historia Morrocotuda de mi Viaje a Cuba* (Mérida, Yucatán, México: Ediciones Gotero, 1976). Hereafter cited as *Viaje.*

59. Cervera Espejo, *Poemas, Versos y Otros Fantasmas* (Mérida, México [Ediciones del Gobierno del Estado], 1977); and *3 en 1 Acto* (Mérida, México [Ediciones del Ayuntamiento de Mérida], 1977). The former will be cited as *Poemas,* the latter as *3 en 1 Acto.*

60. The author was kind enough to give me biographical information and opinions in an interview in Mérida in May of 1977. Hereafter cited as Peniche Barrera.

61. Roldán Peniche Barrera, *El Ultimo Sol: Meditaciones de la Mística Maya* (Mérida, Yucatán, 1970).

62. Peniche Barrera, *Zamná: Mística y Esencia de un Profeta y Otras Narraciones Mayas* ([Mérida, México]: Universidad de Yucatán, 1973).

63. From an interview in Tuscaloosa, Alabama, in December 1977. Hereafter cited as Palacios.

64. In a letter from Mérida dated June 1, 1978, the author informed me, "My novel continues to progress. By the end of the year I expect to send you a copy" (my translation). In June 1979, as this work was going to press, I received a copy of his novel, *Confesiones de un Virus* (Mérida, Yucatán, México: Ediciones Ahora, 1979).

65. Oscar Palacios, *El Otro Tiempo (Análisis Prosopopéyicos) . . . Poemas* (Mérida, Yucatán, México: Editorial Biblioteca Génesis, 1971).

66. Palacios, "Credo Segundo," *El Otro Tiempo,* pages unnumbered. "Mexico / one is born in thee / In order to live in the eternity of thy space, / Eagle and Serpent, / Dead Eagle / Serpent go home / Eagle arise and walk."

67. Palacios, *Se Solicitan Lectores (Algo Cercano a la Poesía)* (Mérida, Yucatán, México: Editorial Dosis Organización, S.A., 1973). Hereafter cited as *Se Solicitan.*

68. "Natividad del universo," *Se Solicitan,* p. 75. "The light arrived two thousand years ago, / He was born and grew up in the shadow of indifference. / Glory to God in his mad acts / and peace in the war on men of goodwill."

69. Oscar Palacios, *Cuentos del Insomnio* (Mérida, Yucatán, México: Editorial Dosis, 1975).

70. Palacios, *Siete Sonetos para Decir Yucatán* (Mérida, Yucatán, México: Editorial Dosis, 1976). "All is not over, Yucatan begins; / Maya of yesterday and tomorrow, / all is not over in the unfulfilled land / where justice is still a thick mist."

71. In May 1977, López Cervantes kindly gave me the following copies of *Platero:*

No. 1 (September 1973), No. 4 (October 1974), No. 5 (July 1975), and No. 6 (September 1976). The only works of the author's available to me were the few published in these four issues.

72. José Esquivel Pren, *Historia de la Literatura en Yucatán,* 15 vols. Esquivel Pren is the historian of literature in Yucatan. The first three volumes came out in 1957, 1959, and 1960. Long out of print, they have been reprinted along with the rest of the work, which is being published by the University of Yucatan. According to a letter from Oscar Palacios dated June 1, 1978, the University would not sell any volumes until the last is off the press. Consequently, I was not able to consult this work. For additional information and a listing of the table of contents, see Rodolfo Ruz Menéndez, ''La Historia de la Literatura en Yucatán, del Lic. José Esquivel Pren. Doce volúmenes. 5,624 páginas,'' *Memoria de la Semana de Literatura en Yucatán* (Mérida, Yucatán: Ediciones de la Universidad de Yucatán, 1977), pp. 203–12.

73. For these and other writers, see the previously cited articles by Alberto Cervera Espejo and Roldán Peniche Barrera in *Memoria de la Semana de Literatura en Yucatán.*

74. This opinion is supported by some writers in Yucatan. Dr. Carlos Urzaiz stated in his interview, ''On the other hand, we lack novelists. In the past there were some, but if one judges their work impartially, we have to confess that they never attained permanent literary value.'' Alberto Cervera Espejo says that ''it is a fact that the novel has fallen into decay in our times. Definitely there are almost no novelists in the Yucatan of this century, at least in the proportion in which there were in the past century'' (''Panorama,'' p. 124). The translations are mine. Carlos González Peña states, ''From a strictly literary point of view, the first novelist who appears in the history of our literature is Don Ignacio Manuel Altamirano'' (p. 331). Altamirano published his first novel, *Clemencia,* in 1869.

75. This is an opinion that Humberto Lara y Lara expressed in my interview with him. In view of the numerous young authors producing good works, I can agree with him. It was a unanimous opinion of the authors interviewed that there are talented writers in Yucatan, but that a lack of financial support prevents many from publishing their works.

76. From my interview with Leopoldo Peniche Vallado.

77. Information from a letter from Oscar Palacios dated March 27, 1978. The first in this series is *El comercio entre los mayas antiguos* by Amalia Cardos de Méndez.

78. Opinions expressed in the interviews with Carlos Urzaiz and Leopoldo Peniche Vallado.

79. Cervera Espejo vividly expressed the opinion that this is a problem common to other writers in Mexico and all of Hispanic America: ''Each one is imprisoned in the bottom of his well.'' The translation is mine.

CHAPTER XI

FOUR CENTURIES OF ARCHAEOLOGY IN YUCATAN: A BIBLIOGRAPHICAL ESSAY

Alfredo Barrera Vásquez

In 1558, Juan Díaz, in his *Itinerario de la Armada del Rey Católico a la Isla de Yucatán,*[1] described a town that he had seen on the island of Cozumel while participating in the expedition of Juan de Grijalva forty years previously. Around 1574, Bernal Díaz del Castillo also told of the first three Spanish expeditions, describing briefly the villages that he had seen on the coast of Yucatan. Yet it was Fray Diego de Landa in 1566 who gave in his *Relación de las Cosas de Yucatán* the first detailed account of Mayan archaeological sites, including sketches of the vertical projection of the Mayan pyramid of T-Hoo, upon which was built the Spanish Convent of San Francisco in Mérida. He also described the pyramid of Izamal, which was briefly explored in 1969, and that of Kukulcán in Chichén Itzá. Landa gave an eyewitness account of the ruins of a Mayan civilization whose link to the past was beginning to weaken. Certain aspects of that ancient cultural heritage, however, have endured until today. This essay is a brief summary of the major developments of archaeology in Yucatan from the early conquest to contemporary times.

Thirteen years after Landa's *Relación,* the encomenderos of Yucatan responded to a questionnaire entitled "Instrucción y Memoria de las Relaciones que han de hazer para la descripción de las Indias, que su Magestad manda hazer, para el buen gobierno y ennoblecimiento dellos."[2] In their replies some of the encomenderos made mention of the Mayan ruins. A typical example is the "Relación de Valladolid,"[3] signed by Don Diego Sarmiento Figueroa and seven other residents before a notary public, Bartolomé Martínez Espinal. This account described the pyramid, temple, and idols that existed in the plaza of what was then called *Saquiwae,* which was also the name of the principal idol that was worshiped there. The narrative also told of ceremonies and customs that had been practiced. An excerpt from the document follows:

> In the midst of this town of Valladolid at the time it was settled, there was in the plaza a very high *cu* [pyramid] of hand wrought stone. A very white stone room

[Translated from the Spanish by Dorothy Andrews de Zapata and Edward Davis Terry. This essay was given as a lecture at The University of Alabama in the spring of 1970.]

that could be seen from afar was on top of it. Inside, the Indians kept the [principal] idol . . ., and would go up to that room to worship it. This *cu,* round in shape, occupied an area of more than four hundred paces, the upper part straight but not very wide. It was called a *cu* because that was what the Indians called the gods they worshipped. Their idols were made of clay in the shape of flowerpots like those used for sweet basil, very wide mouthed, with feet. Distorted and deformed faces with ugly expressions had been made on them. The Indians would put inside this [principal] idol a resin that was called *copal,* as incense, which they would offer and burn in reverence. It gave off a very strong aroma, and with it they continually performed their rites, ceremonies, and worship. It is still there today, and one can see well where this *cu* was. [p. 19]

At one point the "Relación de Valladolid" gives a brief description of the temple of Kukulcán at Chichén Itzá. These data reflect well the Postclassic period and the influence of central Mexico. The idol-shaped incensories that it mentions were without a doubt similar to those that were recovered in Mayapán and are on exhibit in the Instituto Yucateco de Antropología e Historia in Mérida, and to those that the Lacandón Indians still use (the Lacandón Indians, members of the Yucatecan linguistic group, live in Chiapas, Mexico, and in Petén, Guatemala).

After this initial period, there was apparently little archaeological interest in Yucatan for almost three hundred years. For example, the oldest known description of Uxmal was written in 1588 but was not published until 1872 in Madrid. Supposedly made by Fray Antonio de Ciudad Real, it is found in the book *Relación Breve y Verdadera de las Cosas que Sucedieron al R. P. Fray Alonso Ponce en las Provincias de la Nueva España.*[4] The Spaniards, of course, were not very interested in the ruins as a means to seek information about the past of the people that they were conquering or had conquered. If by chance they did excavate, it was to look for things of commercial value. Landa, with respect to this, used an accurate phrase: "No andavan a desenterrar muertos sino a buscar oro entre los vivos."[5]

A revival of interest in the Mayan past occurred in the nineteenth century. The book *Antiquités Mexicaines* by Capitain Guillaume Dupaix was published in Paris in 1834. Although Dupaix's work referred principally to Mitla (Oaxaca) and to Palenque (Chiapas), it contained (Vol. 1) the first notice of Uxmal, written by Lorenzo de Zavala, that appeared in Europe. The following year, Jean Frédéric Macimilien de Waldeck, proceeding from Palenque, was in Uxmal. He was undoubtedly the one who for the first time drew details, although not very accurately, of this famous Mayan city. Inspired by the writings of Dupaix and of Waldeck (1838), a German scientist, Emmanuel Friederichstal, made a quick trip to Yucatan. In 1841, he published an account of his journey in the specialized Parisian journal *Nouvelles Annales de Voyages.* According to his critics, this work was full of inaccuracies but was well illustrated.

In 1839, the United States appointed John Lloyd Stephens as special agent to the United Provinces of Central America. His diplomatic mission failed: by the time he arrived in Guatemala the confederation was in shambles and he could find no government with which to negotiate. During the following year, the frustrated agent spent most of his time exploring the ancient Mayan sites, accompanied by a British draftsman, Frederick Catherwood. In 1841, Stephens published a volume entitled *Incidents of Travel in Central America, Chiapas and Yucatan,* with illustrations by Catherwood. Although neither man was a trained archaeologist, they were so accurate in their descriptions and drawings that they actually laid the foundations for Mayan archaeology. They made a second expedition in 1841, this time concentrating upon the upper peninsula. Two years later, a second work was published, *Incidents of Travel in Yucatan.* Both of the productions of Stephens and Catherwood contributed valuable information concerning life in Yucatan at that time, data of value in a variety of fields, including history, ethnography, medicine, economics, and biology.

Without a doubt, however, the archaeological aspect is the most valuable. Stephens had the collaboration of Fray Estanislao Carrillo in the field of archaeology and of Juan Pío Pérez in Mayan philology. The narrative and the magnificent illustrations of the archaeological ruins they visited created a growing interest throughout Europe and the United States in the civilization of the ancient Maya.

The Count de Saint Priest and the Viscount de Chateaubriand, publishers of *Antiquités Mexicaines* by Dupaix, began to take a keen interest in Mayan archaeology. The publication of such a work had aroused much interest in scientific

Drawing by Frederick Catherwood in 1843 of the Casa de las Monjas at Chichén Itzá.

circles of Europe and had started a controversy that resulted in a proposal by Chateaubriand to organize an expedition to explore the Mayan area in order to clarify whether Palenque was antediluvian. The expedition was to be made up of learned men chosen from various European nations for the purpose of studying the ruins of Palenque, as well as other ancient Mayan sites in Yucatan. This project, called the "Expedición Trans-Atlántica," was discussed in a letter from Saint Priest to the governor of Yucatan, Santiago Méndez, dated January 29, 1844. He indicated that he had solicited support for the expedition of "all the kings, of all the princes, and of all the socially, politically, and scientifically prominent people in Europe." An excerpt from the letter follows:

> Nobody is ignorant of the fact that Yucatan is an inexhaustible mine of historical and archaeological marvels, and that there are more ruins to be seen and to be studied in that country than in all the rest of America. Therefore, the exploration of Yucatan, to be carried out fully and in the most complete way, is the principal objective of the trans-Atlantic expedition. I believe then, sir, that Your Excellency will not be surprised to know that of all the states that make up the American continent, Yucatan is the one from which the Commission expects the most effective cooperation. Nevertheless, the Commission, for which I am the spokesman, fears that the glorious struggle in which the Yucatecans are now engaged will be a source of difficulties and obstacles of such nature that they will thwart the expedition or reduce the results of it. For this reason I am charged with soliciting from Your Excellency the information necessary to clear up all doubt and to calm all the uneasiness. [*Registro Yucateco,* Vol. 1, 1845, pp. 238–41]

Apparently, aid and support were general in Europe, but the authorities in America were never able to give their effective consent—which was imperative. Yucatan, the principal objective, was in a crisis on account of its efforts to repudiate the centralism that had been established in Mexico City. In fact, it had declared its independence of the Republic. During that period, there was no opportunity to attend to scientific matters and even less in 1845, when the long and terrible Caste War broke out. Consequently, the expedition was not carried out. This is perhaps the first archaeological research project that was planned for Yucatan, but unfortunately it failed. If it had been accomplished, less primitive methods might have been used afterwards in systematic investigation of the material remains of the Mayan civilization.

The first excavator in the Puuc region was Fray Estanislao Carrillo, a resident of Ticul and a very good friend of John L. Stephens. He was the discoverer of the two-headed jaguar throne that today is located on a platform facing the main façade of the "Governor's Palace" in Uxmal (*Registro Yucateco,* Vol. 2, p. 268). In his report signed with the pseudonym of "Un curioso" and dated May 25, 1845, Fray Carrillo said that he had removed the throne in 1841, "in an excavation that I ordered made at the request of the travelers Catherwood and Cabot, companions of my illustrious and learned friend Mr. Stephens." Carrillo was also the discoverer of the walled city of Chacchob.

In the second half of the nineteenth century, interest in the ancient Mayan civilization continued to grow. Arthur Morelet was another traveler who included Yucatan in his itinerary. In 1857, he published in Paris his *Voyage dans l'Amérique Centrale, le Cuba et le Yucatan*. Then Joseph Désiré Charnay made explorations in the Mayan region from 1857 to 1886. He published the results in two works: one in 1863 in Paris entitled *Cités et ruines américaines, Mitla, Palenque, Izamal, Chichén Itzá, Uxmal. Recueillies et Photographiées par . . . avec un texte par M. Eugene Viollet-le-Duc*. The second work came out in 1885: *Les anciennes Villes du Nouveau Monde: Voyages d'exploration au Mexique et dans l'Amérique Centrale*. Charnay also published several articles in the *Revue d'Ethnographie* of Paris between 1882 and 1886, in *La Nature* in 1886, in the *Bulletin de la Société d'Anthropologie* of Paris in 1887, and in the *Journal de la Société d'Américanistes* in 1904 and 1906. His long account, *Ma Dernière Expédition au Yucatan* (1886), appeared in the series *La Tour de Monde*. Charnay was one of the first travelers to make use of photography in studying archaeological ruins, although actually Catherwood had used the daguerreotype and the camera obscura as a basis for his excellent illustrations.

Augustus Le Plongeon, a contemporary of Charnay, was the originator of the name *chacmool*, as certain statues lying on their backs are known today. He discovered the first of these in Chichén Itzá. Le Plongeon, however, was a bold, disoriented person, whose only contribution to archaeological research was the misnomer that he gave to these statues of Toltec origin. Furthermore, there is evidence that he used explosives on the structure called "Las Monjas" at Chichén Itzá. Others continued to explore and to write about Yucatan. Padre Crescencio Carrillo y Ancona published several articles on anthropological and archaeological themes between 1863 and 1886: in the *Repertorio Pintoresco* (Mérida, 1863); in *El Mexicano* (Mérida, 1866); and in the *Anales del Museo Nacional de México* (1886). Abbey Charles Etienne Brasseur de Bourbourg visited Yucatan and wrote a report in 1867 entitled *Rapport sur les ruines de Mayapan et Uxmal au Yucatan (Mexique)*, which is in Volume 2 of *Archives de la Commission Scientifique du Mexique* (Paris). In the same volume he also published an *Essai historique sur le Yucatan et description des ruines de Ti-Hoo (Mérida) et d'Izamal*.

The beginning of systematic exploration, for the purpose of finding data of value and examining them, dates from the latter part of the nineteenth century. Europe and the United States vied eagerly for the opportunity to study the Mayan civilization. In 1880, Alfred Percival Maudslay made his first visit to the Mayan area, utilizing photography in his studies. He also wrote on archaeology in the monumental work *Biologia Centrali-Americana*, which was published in London from 1889 to 1902. Marshall H. Saville began in 1892 to take an interest in the Maya. The following year he published an article, "The Ruins of Labná," in *The Archaeologist* (Vol. 1, No. 12). He was principally interested in artisan techniques: goldwork, mosaics, woodcarving, and the like. But he also took an interest in the *sacbés*[6] of Yucatan and wrote of them in two articles. The first was published in 1930 in *Indian Notes* by the Museum of American Indians, the second in 1935 in *Antiquity* (Vol. 9) in Gloucester, England.

In 1895, Henry C. Mercer came to Yucatan to explore the caves of the Puuc region, although Stephens had first written about them in 1843. Mercer published in 1896 the results of this expedition in one of the classic books on speleology in Yucatan: *The Hill Caves of Yucatan*,[7] which started scientific interest in these areas unexplored before him. William H. Holmes published his book *Archaeological Studies among the Ancient Cities of Mexico* in two parts in 1895–97. The first part is entitled *Monuments of Yucatan;* the second is called *Monuments of Chiapas, Oaxaca, and the Valley of Mexico.* It was issued by the Field Columbian Museum of Chicago.

Disagreements concerning Yucatan arose occasionally among scholars. The first work of Teobert Maler, "Yukatekische Forschungen," was published in 1895 in *Globus* (Berlin). In 1902, he brought out two other reports with the same title in that journal. The Peabody Museum of Harvard University published the results of his field research in Guatemala between 1901 and 1911. Several years later, Maler attacked the arbitrary acts, plundering, and smuggling that were going on in Yucatan in a series of controversial articles in the *Revista de Yucatán* (July 21–28, 1926). According to him, these misdeeds were being perpetrated especially by Edward H. Thompson, who was then owner of Chichén Itzá. In those articles, however, Maler also referred to three other archaeologists, Leopoldo Batres, Charles P. Bowditch, and Frederick W. Putnam. Batres, an official of the Museo Nacional de México who participated in several explorations in Chichén Itzá and in Uxmal, published reports of little scientific value. In 1895, he took part in a dispute with Edward Seler during the Eleventh Meeting of the International Congress of the Americanists held in Mexico City, concerning the ancient ruins that were found in Yucatan. Bowditch was a laboratory archaeologist, who by preference devoted himself to studying the Mayan calendar system. He published, in addition to his works on chronology and epigraphy, an article, "On the Age of Maya Ruins," in the *American Anthropologist* (Vol. 3, 1901). His notes appeared in 1901 and 1903 in the *Memoirs of the Peabody Museum* (Vol. 2, Nos. 1–2). Bowditch was also the critic of Maler's work, and the latter's rancor towards him was a result of this situation.

From 1897 through 1938, Edward H. Thompson, who was the first person to drag the Sacred Cenote of Chichén Itzá, published five important works on Yucatan: "The Caves of Loltún, Yucatan," in the *Peabody Museum Memoirs* (Vol. 1, No. 2, 1897); "The Chultunes of Labná," in the same year and series (Vol. 1, No. 3); "Archaeological Researches in Yucatan," also in the *Peabody Museum Memoirs* in 1904 (Vol. 3, No. 1); "The Home of a Forgotten Race. Mysterious Chichén Itzá in Yucatan, Mexico," in 1914 in the *National Geographic Magazine* (Vol. 25); and "The High Priest's Grave, Chichén Itzá, Yucatan, Mexico," in collaboration with J. Eric Thompson, in the *Field Museum Anthropological Series* (Chicago, 1938, No. 27).

As the twentieth century dawned, scientific interest in Yucatan continued at a steady pace. In 1900, Thomas W. F. Gann published one of the first systematic reports on Mayan archaeological sites. It was entitled *Mounds in Northern Honduras* and appeared in the *Smithsonian Institution Nineteenth Annual Report* that covered the period 1897–98. Edward Seler visited Yucatan at the beginning of the century and made a rapid study of its flora and of its pre-Hispanic ruins. In 1906, he brought out an article entitled "Studien in den Ruinen von Yucatan" in the *Deutsche Gesellschaft für Anthropologie*. Seler also published others on Chichén Itzá in 1908 and on Uxmal in 1913, 1915, and 1917.

Other scientists who wrote about Yucatan during the first decade of the twentieth century were Maurice de Périgny and Adela Breton. Although his interest was concentrated more on Guatemala, Périgny explored Yucatan and published in 1908 "Yucatan Inconnu" in the *Journal de la Société des Américanistes* in Paris (Vol. 5, pp. 67–84). Also in 1908, Breton published an article entitled "Mounds at Acanceh," in *Man* (London, No. 17).

Sylvanus Griswold Morley, one of the giants of Mayan archaeology, made his first explorations of Yucatan in 1907, when he visited Acanceh, Uxmal, Xtocche, Tabi, Labná, Kabah, Zayil, Kiuic, Mayapán, and Chichén Itzá. He began publishing on the area in 1910 with his study "A Group of Related Structures at Uxmal, Mexico," in the *Journal of Archaeology* of the Archaeological Institute of America (Vol. 14, No. 1). Three years later, the Carnegie Institution issued another of his works: "Archaeological Research at the Ruins of Chichén Itzá, Yucatan." This city was studied later by a group under Morley's direction.

Raymond E. Merwin in 1913 completed his dissertation on "The Ruins in the Southern Part of the Peninsula of Yucatan with Special Reference to Their Place in the Maya Culture." To my knowledge, this study has not been published, but it is available in the Harvard University Library. Merwin's director was Alfred M. Tozzer, who unfortunately had not explored Yucatan as a field archaeologist although he had studied it profoundly as an ethnohistorian. The stratigraphic method and its application to Mayan chronology began with Merwin's work.

There also appeared in 1913 one of the classic works in Mayan research: Herbert J. Spinden's book *A Study of Maya Art: Its Subject Matter and Historical Development,* published by the Peabody Museum of Harvard University as Volume 6 of its *Memoirs*. Although a general work that does not refer particularly to Yucatan, it is, nevertheless, of great help in the identification and comparison of many aspects of the material culture of the Maya, especially because it made an effort to point out the chronological sequence of forms. In 1924, Samuel K. Lothrop published the results of his studies of Tulum (Carnegie Institution of Washington, Pub. 335). This is an excellent work in which several methods are combined: graphic, illustrative, reconstruction, comparative, cultural, chronological, and historical. It is a pioneer study in scientific exploration.

By the first quarter of the present century, it was evident that progress had been made in the science of exploration, excavation, exposition, and comparison of the material culture of the ancient Mayan civilization. Stratigraphy was done with good method and technique; comparative studies led to historical conclusions; and materials and literature accumulated. After 1925, there was increased activity in the Mayan field. Archaeological studies were complemented by investigations in several other areas, including ecology, ethnography, ethnohistory, and philology.

Several institutions contributed to this progress in scientific activity. Maudslay, who apparently was sponsored by the British Museum, made his expeditions from 1881 to 1894. The Peabody Museum of Harvard University sponsored twelve explorations between 1888 and 1915; and in 1923, the Carnegie Institution of Washington began its archaeological works in Yucatan. These expeditions lasted until 1960 and included the complete exploration of Mayapán. Other institutions followed them: Tulane University of Louisiana, the Instituto Nacional de Antropología e Historia, and finally The University of Alabama. The names of the scientists are many, and the list of their publications even longer.[8]

The Departamento de Monumentos Prehispánicos of the Instituto Nacional de Antropología e Historia, a specialized office of the Mexican government, has accomplished important works in Chichén Itzá, Uxmal, Kabah, Zayil, Labná, Xlabpak, Dzibilchaltún, Ekmul, Izamal, and Balaankanché. The following archaeologists were involved in these projects: Miguel Angel Fernández in Chichén Itzá (1925); José A. Erosa Peniche in Chichén Itzá (1946); Alberto Ruz Lhuillier in Uxmal (1951–52, 1954–55); Jorge R. Acosta in Chichén Itzá (1951), and in Uxmal (1958); Víctor Segovia in Aké (1951–53), in Ekmul (1964), and in Izamal (1968); Ponciano Salazar Ortegón in Chichén Itzá (1952); César Sáenz in Uxmal, Kabah, Xlabpak, and other places (1952–69); and Raúl Pavón Abreu in Balaankanché (1959).

The three major projects completed in Yucatan have been those at Chichén Itzá and at Mayapán, carried out by the Carnegie Institution, and at Dzibilchaltún by Tulane University in cooperation with the National Geographic Society and with the financial aid of the National Science Foundation and the American Philosophical Society. The names of persons connected with these projects are many. The project directors had as collaborators a large group of enterprising investigators at all levels, from undergraduate students to Ph.D.'s. Moreover, other institutions contributed additional research personnel specialized in different scientific and technical fields. Some of the major participants in the project at Chichén Itzá were Sylvanus G. Morley as director, Herman Beyer, George W. Brainerd, Adela C. Breton, David L. De Harport, Jean Charlot, Alfred V. Kidder, J. O. Kilmartin, P. S. Martin, A. A. Morris, E. H. Morris, John P. O'Neil, H. E. D. Pollock, Edith B. and Oliver G. Ricketson, Jr., H. B. Roberts, Lawrence Roys, Karl Ruppert, Edwin M. Shook, Robert E. Smith, Gustav Strömsvik, J. Eric S. Thompson, and George C. Vaillant. Several of those just cited also participated in the study of Mayapán, walled capital of the last Mexican epoch in Yucatan; they were H. E. D. Pollock as director, Edwin M. Shook, Robert E. Smith, Gustav Strömsvik, and J. E. S. Thompson. Other scholars who contributed to this work were Robert M. Adams, Jr., William R. Bullard, Jr., A. Chowning, M. R. Jones, Tatiana Proskouriakoff, A. L. Smith, P. E. Smith, and D. E. Thompson. The bibliography of these two projects is vast. Each person mentioned produced one or several reports and monographs that were published in special volumes, in yearbooks, in the series *Current Reports* of the Carnegie Institution, and in other places.

In the restoration at Dzibilchaltún, there were several new collaborators, including its brilliant director E. Wyllys Andrews, Willard Sloshberg, Ellen Ann Childs, Adrian Anderson, John Newberry, William J. Folan, John E. Feistel, Robert E. Funk, George E. Stuart, Gene Stuart, Eduardo Toro, William E. Moore, David Bolles, Edward B. Kurjack, John C. Scheffler, John W. Cottier, Leroy V. Joesink-Mandeville, Dolores Skaer, Willard V. Clerk, Sylvia Meluzin, J. Franklin Newsom, Gordon Ketterer, Mrs. Merle Greene, Richard E. Stewart, Luis Marden, and Bates Littlehales.

Numerous additional explorations have been completed, some superficially and others thoroughly, in various archaeological sites in Yucatan by several of the authors cited and by others. Andrews, untiring in these activities, made preliminary surveys of a number of sites in the state of Yucatan, including Tzemé, Kulubá, and Ikil. The reports on these last two were published in *Notes on Middle American Archaeology and Ethnology* of the Carnegie Institution (1941), and in Publication 31 of the Middle American Research Institute, Tulane University, in 1965. Frans Blom worked at Uxmal in 1930, and in 1935 published a note on Labná in *Maya Research* (Vol. 2). Miguel Angel Fernández explored Acanceh around 1938 and gave his report before the XXVII Congreso Internacional de Americanistas in Mexico City in 1939. Aké was investigated by the brothers Ralph and Lawrence Roys in 1949 and by the latter and Edwin M. Shook during 1951–53. Tatiana Proskouriakoff and Víctor Segovia occasionally participated in the project. The report was published in *Memoirs of the Society for American Archaeology (American Antiquity,* Vol. 31) in 1966. Shook investigated Oxkintok and published his findings in the *Revista Mexicana de Estudios Antropológicos* in 1940. Morley explored Ekbalam and published his report in the *Year Book* (Vol. 27) of the Carnegie Institution (1927–28). Ruppert and A. L. Smith published in *Current Reports* (Carnegie Institution, 1957) a study of the types of dwellings in Uxmal, Kabah, Zayil, Chichén Itzá, and Chacchob. César Lizardi Ramos, who explored in Quintana Roo but not in Yucatan, published a great many articles on Yucatecan archaeological themes. Señora Marta Foncerrada de Molina wrote books, articles, and guides on Uxmal. *La Escultura Arquitectónica de Uxmal,* published in 1965 by the Universidad Nacional Autónoma de México, is her most important work.

The possibility of obtaining archaeological data from subterranean sources has interested scientists since the nineteenth century. The classic book of Henry C. Mercer, *The Hill Caves of Yucatan,* gives information about a number of the caves in the Puuc region, including the one at X-Kukicán. These caverns, cenotes, and caves were significant sources of water and therefore of great impor-

Interior of the Loltún cavern near Oxkutzcab, Yucatan. (Photo by Andy Dees)

Ruins at the archaeological site of X-Kukicán, location of excavations conducted by The University of Alabama from 1965 to 1969. (Photo by Edward Terry)

tance in the lives of the Maya. It was for this reason that they were always used in rites honoring the water gods; however, they also served as refuge in times of trouble. In spite of their importance, the exploration of these caves has been carried out with a scientific purpose only on a very few occasions. The most important systematic explorations were those made at the caves of Loltún, not far from X-Kukicán; Balaankanché near Chichén Itzá; and Chaac. Edward H. Thompson, sponsored by Harvard University, explored the cave at Loltún in 1887 (Vol. I, *Memoirs of the Peabody Museum*). E. Wyllys Andrews and others studied the cave at Balaankanché in 1959 (Tulane University, Middle American Research Institute, Miscellaneous Series No. 11, 1961; and Publication No. 32, 1970). Andrews also explored the cave at Chaac under the auspices of a joint research program in Yucatan by the National Geographic Society and Tulane University. Tulane published the corresponding report, magnificently illustrated, as its Publication No. 31, in 1965. Various members of the Dzibilchaltún team participated in this exploration, including Dr. Andrews's son Anthony. J. E. S. Thompson in 1959 published an interesting article on the importance of the caves in the Mayan culture in *Mitteilungen aus dem Museum für Volkerkunde* (No. 25), in Hamburg. Gustav Strömsvik explored the cave of Dzab-Na in Tecoh and reported his findings in *Current Reports* (1956) of the Carnegie Institution.

In November of 1965, The University of Alabama began its efforts to develop an archaeological research project in the zone of X-Kukicán. Although this project did not have the resources that were available to those at Chichén Itzá, Mayapán, and Dzibilchaltún, it can be considered for its importance as one of the most promising. It deals with an area to the south of the hills of Ticul in the heart of the Puuc region, where no visible evidence has been found of the influence of central Mexico on the Postclassic period. This vast zone is full of surface remains and also has many caves of incalculable value for their pre-Hispanic human contents. The project was started under the direction of David L. DeJarnette. [Alfredo Barrera Vásquez was codirector. Editors' note.] Collaborators were John W. Cottier, Edward B. Kurjack, Jerry J. Nielsen, and Boyce N. Driskell. Three short and modest periods of investigation were completed between 1965 and 1969, but the work was performed with good methods and techniques. DeJarnette, unfortunately, was not able to be present during the third field session, having become seriously ill soon after he arrived in Mérida and before the actual work started. The preliminary reports have been prepared, giving the first results of the project.

The sinkholes of Yucatan, called cenotes, had attracted scientific interest even before the caves. The first attempt to explore the bottom of the cenote at Chichén Itzá for the purpose of proving the accounts of Fray Diego de Landa[9] was made by Désiré Charnay around 1882, using an apparatus called ''Toselli's automatic sounding machine.'' He failed, however, according to his own account given in his previously cited *Les anciennes villes du Nouveau Monde* (1885; English edition, London, 1887). Edward H. Thompson, who followed him, had better results in 1904. Thompson's efforts were financed by Stephen Salisbury and

Charles P. Bowditch. The dredging lasted until 1909. Although Thompson did further exploring the following year with the financial backing of Walter Austin, he was never able to complete his project. Not until 1960 was it possible to make an exploration using an apparatus called an "air lift," under the auspices of the Instituto Nacional de Antropología e Historia de México and the National Geographic Society of Washington, with the collaboration of the Club de Exploración y Deportes Acuáticos de México. Unfortunately, the results were not so successful from an archaeological point of view as had been hoped. Other projects have been proposed in order to continue the search with scientific methods, but so far none has been undertaken.

Although explorations of the cenotes have been concentrated principally on the one in Chichén Itzá because of its fame, investigation of the well in Dzibilchaltún was an important part of that project. Archaeologists recovered many valuable artifacts, some of which are on display there. In addition, amateur divers have explored others in a preliminary manner although no reports have been published of these possibly clandestine operations. Nevertheless, I know for certain that the cenotes at Yaaxcabá and Valladolid have been investigated and that some diving explorations have been carried out in the waters at Xcah, near Libre Unión on the road to Chichén Itzá.

From this brief panorama, one can get an idea of how archaeology has de-

The cenote at Dzibilchaltún. (Photo by Edward Terry)

veloped in Yucatan from the vague descriptions of the first Europeans on the peninsula to 1970. Chronologies and terminologies have been established for the cultural periods of the Maya. Today there are highly scientific techniques available for dating ceramics and other objects; these techniques include comparison, analysis, and taxonomic methods that are gradually allowing scientists to define the cultural development and the relationship of the human groups of the area as to space and time. The data that are contributed by the archaeologist, who excavates and restores, are complemented by those from other scientists who have equally efficient methods.

There is still, however, much to be done in this area. The Mayan-Christian correlation has not yet been definitively and clearly established. The hieroglyphics are yet a challenge. There is the enigma of the origin of the Mesoamerican writing, calendar, and mathematics. Are they really Olmec inventions? Even today we do not have sufficient data on how the people of the Classic period lived. It is necessary to determine precisely the function of the ceremonial centers, whose architecture was monumental, with relation to the population centers, obviously modest and utilitarian. The function of the buildings themselves must also be studied in detail. It is not yet clear why the great ceremonial centers of the central subareas were abandoned suddenly and why certain cultural traits, such as the so-called "long count" of the calendar system, ceased to be utilized.

Throughout Yucatan there are still numerous large and small sites, both on the coast and inland, with prehistoric material remains not yet touched by archaeologists. In the Puuc region, innumerable natural subterranean chambers are found. The archaeological zone of X-Kukicán, with its caves and monumental complexes, awaits the termination of the labor already begun. A great many cenotes must also contain precious data.

It is evident that there will be an increase in archaeological activity in Yucatan as additional financial support becomes available to continue existing projects and to open up new ones. The future of archaeology in Yucatan lies in the hands of those who have the academic capacity to study and to interpret the pre-Hispanic monuments in order to add to the knowledge of past human conduct.

NOTES

1. *Itinerary of the Armada of the Catholic King to the Isle of Yucatan.*
2. "Instruction and Report of the Accounts that are to be made for the Description of the Indies, which Your Majesty Ordered Compiled, for the Good Government and Ennoblement of them."
3. "Account of Valladolid."
4. *A Brief and True Account of the Things that Happened to Fray Alonso Ponce in the Provinces of New Spain,* in *Colección de Documentos Inéditos para la Historia de España* (Madrid, 1872), pp. 57–58.
5. "They did not go around digging up the dead but seeking gold among the living."
6. Sacbé is the name the ancient Maya gave to the roads that they constructed to

connect their ceremonial centers. The road surfaces were similar to macadam. They utilized crushed rock in different degrees until they achieved a fine powder on the final surface, which they packed with heavy rock rollers. The name is made up of *sac,* meaning white, false, artificial; and *be,* way or path. The meaning of *sacbé,* then, is artificial way, although it is also translated as white way, because of the double meaning of the word *sac.*

7. A reprint of this monograph appeared recently (Teaneck, N.J.: Zephyrus Press, 1975), with a new introduction by Sir J. Eric S. Thompson, as part of a series, Speleologia, under the editorship of Richard A. Watson of Washington University.

8. The author prepared an extensive bibliography, but it was necessary to omit it because of space limitations. A copy can be obtained, however, by writing to the editors at P.O. Box 1974, University, Alabama 35486. Editors' note.

9. Fray Diego de Landa, speaking of Chichén Itzá, wrote: ''Chichén Itzá is a very fine site . . . we will describe later the decoration of the principal building and will tell about the well into which they threw living men in sacrifice as well as other beautiful things,'' in Alfred Marston Tozzer, *Landa's Relación de las Cosas de Yucatán,* Papers of the Peabody Museum of American Archaeology and Ethnology, Harvard University, 18 (Cambridge, Mass.: The Museum, 1941), 19.

INDEX